Disabilities
SOURCEBOOK

Third Edition

Health Reference Series

Third Edition

Disabilities
SOURCEBOOK

Basic Consumer Health Information about Disabilities That Affect the Body, Mind, and Senses, Including Birth Defects, Sensory Disabilities, Speech Disorders, Intellectual and Cognitive Disabilities, Learning Disabilities, Psychiatric Disorders, Degenerative Diseases, and Disabilities Caused by Injury and Trauma, Such as Amputation, Spinal Cord Injury, and Traumatic Brain Injury

Along with Facts about Assistive Technology, Physical and Occupational Therapy, Living Space Modifications, Maintaining Health and Wellness, Education, and Support, Legal, Financial, Insurance Issues, a Glossary of Related Terms, and Resources for Additional Help and Information

OMNIGRAPHICS

155 W. Congress, Suite 200 Detroit, MI 48226

Bibliographic Note

Because this page cannot legibly accommodate all the copyright notices, the Bibliographic Note portion of the Preface constitutes an extension of the copyright notice.

* * *

Omnigraphics, Inc.

Editorial Services provided by Omnigraphics, Inc.,
a division of Relevant Information, Inc.

Keith Jones, *Managing Editor*

* * *

Library of Congress Cataloging-in-Publication Data

Names: Omnigraphics, Inc.

Title: Disabilities sourcebook : basic consumer health information about disabilities that affect the body, mind, and senses, including birth defects, hearing and vision loss, speech disorders, learning disabilities, psychiatric disorders, degenerative diseases, and disabilities caused by injury and trauma, such as amputation, spinal cord injury, and traumatic brain injury; along with facts about assistive technology, physical and occupational therapy, maintaining health and wellness, special education, legal, financial, education, and insurance issues, a glossary of related terms, and resources for additional help and information / Keith Jones, managing editor.

Description: Third edition. | Detroit, MI : Omnigraphics, Inc., [2016] | Series: Health reference series | Includes bibliographical references and index.

Identifiers: LCCN 2015035590 | ISBN 9780780813847 (hardcover : alk. paper) | ISBN 9780780814141 (ebook)

Subjects: LCSH: People with disabilities--United States--Handbooks, manuals, etc. | People with mental disabilities--United States--Handbooks, manuals, etc.

Classification: LCC HV1553 .D544 2016 | DDC 362.4--dc23

LC record available at http://lccn.loc.gov/2015035590

Table of Contents

Part III: Assistive Technology and Treatment Options That Help People with Disabilities

Part IV: Staying Healthy with a Disability

Part VII: Additional Help and Information

Preface

About This Book

Over 53 million—about one in five adults living in the United States—experience physical, cognitive, emotional, or sensory disabilities that impede their daily life. Since the passage of American with Disabilities Act (ADA), people with disabilities have made a lot of progress, making use of the opportunities offered to them through various channels. Yet studies have been consistently revealing the fact that people living with disabilities suffer from health ailments more than the healthy populace, and that most of the health problems faced by the disabled are preventable.

Disabilities Sourcebook, Third Edition offers people with disabilities and their caregivers information about birth defects, hearing and vision loss, speech disorders, intellectual and cognitive disabilities, learning disabilities, and other types of impairment caused by chronic illness, injury, and trauma. It discusses assistive technology, home use devices, mobility aids, and therapies. Information about the importance of nutrition, exercise, personal hygiene, health insurance and pain management is also provided. For parents of children with disabilities, the book offers information about special education, including early intervention services, individualized education programs, and financial aid and scholarships. Legal, employment, housing, and financial concerns of people with disabilities are also discussed. The book concludes with a glossary of related terms and directories of resources for additional help and information.

How to Use This Book

This book is divided into parts and chapters. Parts focus on broad areas of interest. Chapters are devoted to single topics within a part.

Part One: Introduction to Disabilities provides statistical information on the prevalence of physical, cognitive, emotional, and sensory impairments. It identifies common barriers that people with disabilities face in mainstream society, such as access to communication, social, and physical barriers, and it offers tips on communicating with and caring for people with disabilities. Abuses encountered by women, the elderly, and children with disabilities is also discussed.

Part Two: Types of Disabilities identifies the symptoms, diagnosis, and treatment of the most common forms of disabling conditions, including birth defects, sensory disabilities, speech disorders, intellectual and cognitive disabilities, learning disabilities, psychiatric disabilities, degenerative diseases, and disabilities caused by injury and trauma.

Part Three: Assistive Technology and Treatment Options That Help People with Disabilities provides information about devices, therapies, and supports that help people with disabilities attend school, engage in work, and enjoy recreational activities.Facts about home use medical devices, communication and hearing aids, and low vision devices are provided. Information on finding accessible transportation, and therapies--speech, occupational, physical, and recreational therapies--that therapists use to assist people with disabilities is also discussed.

Part Four: Staying Healthy with a Disability discusses strategies for maintaining physical health and emotional wellness in people who have disabilities. Patients and caregivers will find information on healthy eating, weight management, and physical activity, as well as tips on managing bowel and bladder problems, pressure sores, pain, depression, and anxiety. The part also discusses health insurance concerns, tips on dealing with hospitalization, considerations when choosing a long-term care setting, and family support services.

Part Five: Special Education and Support Services for Children with Disabilities identifies laws that support the education of children with disabilities, such as the Individuals with Education Act (IDEA), the No Child Left Behind Act, and Section 504 of the Rehabilitation Act. It also includes information on evaluating children for disability, individualized education programs (IEPs), and scholarships and financial aid available for disabled students at various levels.

Part Six: Legal, Employment, and Financial Support for People with Disabilities describes disability rights laws that protect people with disabilities from discrimination, such as the Americans with Disabilities Act (ADA) and the Fair Housing Amendments Act. It also discusses housing and safety issues for people with disabilities and addresses employment and workplace concerns, Social Security disability benefits, and end-of-life planning.

Part Seven: Additional Help and Information provides a glossary of important terms related to disabilities. A directory of organizations that help people with disabilities and their families is also included, along with a list of organizations for athletes with disabilities, and resources for finding financial help for assistive devices.

Bibliographic Note

This volume contains documents and excerpts from publications issued by the following U.S. government agencies: Agency for Healthcare Research and Quality (AHRQ); Bureau of Labor Statistics (BLS); Centers for Disease Control and Prevention (CDC); Centers for Medicare and Medicaid Services (CMS); Computer/Electronic Accommodation Program (CAP); Disability.gov; Eldercare Locator; Federal Communications Commission (FCC); Internal Revenue Service (IRS); Military OneSource; National Council on Disability (NCD); National Endowment for the Arts (NEA); National Eye Institute (NEI); National Heart, Lung, and Blood Institute (NHLBI), National Highway Traffic Safety Administration (NHTSA), National Institute of Arthritis and Musculoskeletal and Skin Diseases (NIAMS), National Institute Of Biomedical Imaging And Bioengineering (NIBIB); National Institute of Child Health and Human Development (NICHD); National Institute of Dental and Craniofacial Research (NIDCR); National Institute of Diabetes and Digestive and Kidney Diseases (NIDDK); National Institute of Mental Health (NIMH); National Institute of Neurological Disorders and Stroke (NINDS); National Institute on Aging (NIA); National Institute on Deafness and Other Communication Disorders (NIDCD); NIHSeniorHealth; Office on Women's Health (OWH); Ready.gov; Substance Abuse and Mental Health Services Administration (SAMHSA); Transportation Security Administration (TSA); U.S. Agency for International development (USAID); U.S. Census Bureau; U.S. Department of Education (ED); U.S. Department of Health & Human Services (HHS); U.S. Department of Justice; U.S. Department of Veterans Affairs (VA); U.S. Food and Drug Administration (FDA); U.S. Library of Congress (LOC); U.S. Social Security Administration (SSA); and WhiteHouse.gov.

About the Health Reference Series

The *Health Reference Series* is designed to provide basic medical information for patients, families, caregivers, and the general public. Each volume takes a particular topic and provides comprehensive coverage. This is especially important for people who may be dealing with a newly diagnosed disease or a chronic disorder in themselves or in a family member. People looking for preventive guidance, information about disease warning signs, medical statistics, and risk factors for health problems will also find answers to their questions in the *Health Reference Series*. The *Series*, however, is not intended to serve as a tool for diagnosing illness, in prescribing treatments, or as a substitute for the physician/patient relationship. All people concerned about medical symptoms or the possibility of disease are encouraged to seek professional care from an appropriate health care provider.

A Note about Spelling and Style

Health Reference Series editors use *Stedman's Medical Dictionary* as an authority for questions related to the spelling of medical terms and the *Chicago Manual of Style* for questions related to grammatical structures, punctuation, and other editorial concerns. Consistent adherence is not always possible, however, because the individual volumes within the *Series* include many documents from a wide variety of different producers, and the editor's primary goal is to present material from each source as accurately as is possible. This sometimes means that information in different chapters or sections may follow other guidelines and alternate spelling authorities.

Our Advisory Board

We would like to thank the following board members for providing guidance to the development of this Series:

- Dr. Lynda Baker, Associate Professor of Library and Information Science, Wayne State University, Detroit, MI

- Nancy Bulgarelli, William Beaumont Hospital Library, Royal Oak, MI

- Karen Imarisio, Bloomfield Township Public Library, Bloomfield Township, MI

- Karen Morgan, Mardigian Library, University of Michigan-Dearborn, Dearborn, MI

- Rosemary Orlando, St. Clair Shores Public Library, St. Clair Shores, MI

Health Reference Series Update Policy

The inaugural book in the *Health Reference Series* was the first edition of Cancer Sourcebook published in 1989. Since then, the Series has been enthusiastically received by librarians and in the medical community. In order to maintain the standard of providing high-quality health information for the layperson the editorial staff at Omnigraphics felt it was necessary to implement a policy of updating volumes when warranted.

Medical researchers have been making tremendous strides, and it is the purpose of the *Health Reference Series* to stay current with the most recent advances. Each decision to update a volume is made on an individual basis. Some of the considerations include how much new information is available and the feedback we receive from people who use the books. If there is a topic you would like to see added to the update list, or an area of medical concern you feel has not been adequately addressed, please write to:

Managing Editor
Health Reference Series
Omnigraphics, Inc.
155 W. Congress, Ste. 200
Detroit, MI 48226

Part One

Introduction to Disabilities

Chapter 1

What Is a Disability?

A disability is any condition of the body or mind (impairment) that makes it more difficult for the person with the condition to do certain activities (activity limitation) and interact with the world around them (participation restrictions).

There are many types of disabilities, such as those that affect a person's:

- Vision

- Movement

- Thinking

- Remembering

- Learning

- Communicating

- Hearing

- Mental health

- Social relationships

Text in this chapter is excerpted from "Disability Overview," Centers for Disease Control and Prevention (CDC), July 22, 2015.

- Although "people with disabilities" sometimes refers to a single population, this is actually a diverse group of people with a wide range of needs. Two people with the same type of disability can be affected in very different ways. Some disabilities may be hidden or not easy to see.

According to the World Health Organization (WHO), disability has three dimensions:

1. **Impairment** in a person's body structure or function, or mental functioning; examples of impairments include loss of a limb, loss of vision or memory loss.

2. **Activity limitation**, such as difficulty seeing, hearing, walking, or problem solving.

3. **Participation restrictions** in normal daily activities, such as working, engaging in social and recreational activities, and obtaining health care and preventive services.

Disability can be:

- Related to conditions that are present at birth and may affect functions later in life, including cognition (memory, learning, and understanding), mobility (moving around in the environment), vision, hearing, behavior, and other areas. These conditions may be
  - Disorders in single genes (for example, Duchenne muscular dystrophy);
  - Disorders of chromosomes (for example, Down syndrome); and
  - The result of the mother's exposure during pregnancy to infections (for example, rubella) or substances, such as alcohol or cigarettes.

- Associated with developmental conditions that become apparent during childhood (for example, autism spectrum disorder and attention-deficit/hyperactivity disorder or ADHD).

- Related to an injury (for example, traumatic brain injury or spinal cord injury).

- Associated with a longstanding condition (for example, diabetes), which can cause a disability such as vision loss, nerve damage, or limb loss.

- Progressive (for example, Alzheimer's disease), static (for example, limb loss), or intermittent (for example, some forms of multiple sclerosis).

What is impairment?

Impairment is an absence of or significant difference in a person's body structure or function or mental functioning. For example, problems in the structure of the brain can result in difficulty with mental functions, or problems with the structure of the eyes or ears can result in difficulty with the functions of vision or hearing.

- **Structural impairments** are significant problems with an internal or external component of the body. Examples of these include a type of nerve damage that can result in multiple sclerosis, or a complete loss of a body component, as when a limb has been amputated.

- **Functional impairments** include the complete or partial loss of function of a body part. Examples of these include pain that doesn't go away or joints that no longer move easily.

What is the difference between activity limitation and participation restriction?

The World Health Organization (WHO) published the International Classification of Functioning, Disability and Health (ICF) in 2001. The ICF provides a standard language for classifying body function and structure, activity, participation levels, and conditions in the world around us that influence health. This description helps to assess the health, functioning, activities, and factors in the environment that either help or create barriers for people to fully participate in society.

According to the ICF:

- **Activity** is the execution of a task or action by an individual.

- **Participation** is a person's involvement in a life situation.

The ICF acknowledges that the distinction between these two categories is somewhat unclear and combines them, although basically, activities take place at a personal level and participation involves engagement in life roles, such as employment, education, or relationships. Activity limitations and participation restrictions have to do with difficulties an individual experiences in performing tasks and engaging in social roles. Activities and participation can be made easier or more difficult as a result of environmental factors, such as technology, support and relationships, services, policies, or the beliefs of others.

The ICF includes the following in the categories of activities and participation:

- Learning and applying knowledge

- Managing tasks and demands

- Mobility (moving and maintaining body positions, handling and moving objects, moving around in the environment, moving around using transportation)

- Managing self-care tasks

- Managing domestic life

- Establishing and managing interpersonal relationships and interactions

- Engaging in major life areas (education, employment, managing money or finances)

- Engaging in community, social, and civic life

It is very important to improve the conditions in communities by providing accommodations that decrease or eliminate activity limitations and participation restrictions for people with disabilities, so they can participate in the roles and activities of everyday life.

Chapter 2

Statistics on People with Disabilities in the United States

People with Disabilities: Who are they and what do we know?

The *Morbidity and Mortality Weekly Report* (MMWR) has published a new report describing the percentage of adults with disabilities in the United States living in communities. This report is based on questions used for the first time in the 2013 Behavioral Risk Factor Surveillance System (BRFSS) that allow respondents to identify specific functional types of disability, such as mobility (serious difficulty walking or climbing stairs), cognitive (serious difficulty concentrating, remembering or making decisions), vision (serious difficulty seeing), self-care (difficulty dressing or bathing) and independent living (difficulty doing errands alone). According to this report, over 53 million adults living in communities in the United States have a disability. Highest percentages are generally found in southern states and lowest are mostly in

This chapter includes excerpts from "Key Findings: Prevalence of Disability and Disability Type among Adults, United States – 2013," Centers for Disease Control and Prevention (CDC), August 20, 2015; and text from "Americans with Disabilities: 2010," U.S. Census Bureau, February 25, 2013.

mid-western and Rocky Mountain states. Although anyone can have a disability, and a disability can occur at any point in a person's life, disability was more commonly reported by women, older people (65 or more years), and racial and ethnic minority groups. Although progress has been made since the passage of the Americans with Disabilities Act (ADA) twenty-five years ago giving people with disabilities better opportunities to achieve their potential, studies consistently show that people living with a disability have poorer health than people without a disability, and that many of the health issues related to this poor health are preventable. This MMWR presents important information that public health officials and others can use to help understand and address the needs of people with disabilities in the United States.

Report Limitation: Currently, the BRFSS does not assess deafness or serious difficulty hearing. Therefore, data on the number of people who have hearing difficulties at the state level was not collected. This results in a likely underestimate of the total number of people with disabilities in the U.S. presented in this report.

Main Findings:

1 in 5 adults or over 53 million people in the United States have a disability of one form or another, with state-level estimates ranging from 1 in 6 (16.4%; Minnesota) to nearly 1 in 3 (31.5%; Alabama).

- The most common functional disability type was mobility disability, reported by about 1 in 8 adults.

- Over a third of adults 65 years or older reported any disability.

- Adults 45–64 years of age were more likely than other age group adults to report a cognitive disability.

- Individuals reporting a higher household income or education level were less likely to report having a disability, compared to individuals in lower income or education levels.

- Women were more likely to report any disability when compared with men (24.4% versus 19.8%). This was also seen for most of the disability types.

- Disability was more frequently reported by non-Hispanic blacks (29.0%) and Hispanic (25.9%) adults than by white non-Hispanic (20.6%) adults.

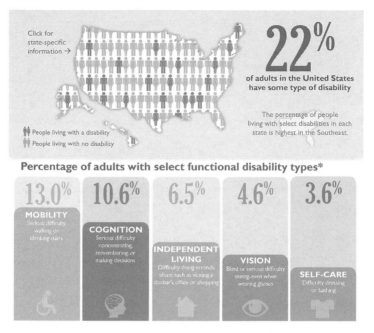

Figure 2.1. *Impact of Disability in the United States*

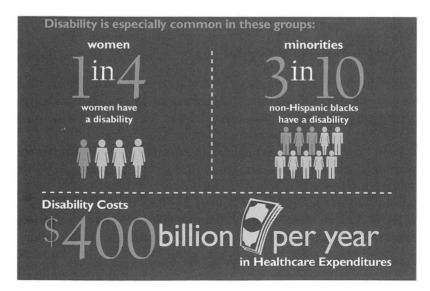

Figure 2.2. *Disability and Communities*

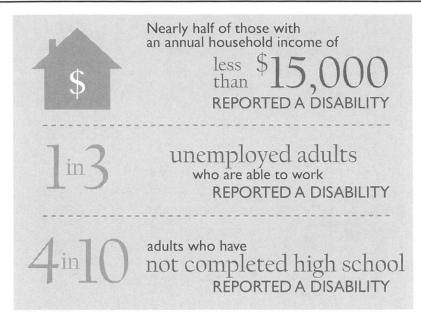

Figure 2.3. *Disability and Livelihood*

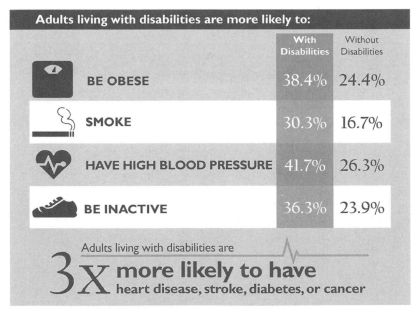

Figure 2.4. *Disability and Health*

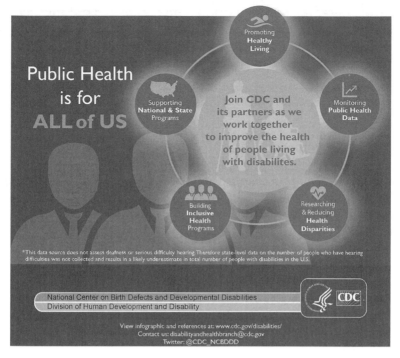

Figure 2.5. *Public Health for All*

Implications:

- Although disability information has been collected in national surveys for many years, this is the first time functional disability type is included in a state-based health survey. This new information can help researchers and public health professionals better understand the makeup of adults with disabilities at a state level, and therefore, better plan programs to address the needs of the different disability populations.

- Variation among states in the percentage of people who reported a disability, with the highest percentage of disability generally found in states in the southern U.S., reinforces the importance of assuring that all people with disabilities receive the health care and support they need to improve the health and wellbeing of the entire population.

- Because middle-aged adults (45-64 years old) were more likely to report cognitive disabilities than adults in other age groups, further research can be used to help better understand reasons for this, and ways in which their unique needs can be addressed.

- Since the percentage of disability is higher among certain groups such as women, older people, and racial and ethnic minorities, it is important that the programs and resources available for people with disabilities address the needs of these populations.

- The ADA has made a positive difference in the lives of those who have disabilities, providing better access to buildings, transportation, and employment. However, health disparities (differences in health) between people with and without disability are still present. Furthermore, disadvantaged people, namely those with lower education or income and those who are unemployed, are still more likely to report a disability. Working together we can help ensure that children and adults with disabilities receive needed programs, services and health care throughout their lives so that they can achieve their full potential, live a quality life, and experience independence in their communities.

What is CDC doing to improve the lives of people with disabilities?

CDC supports 18 state-based disability and health programs and four National Public Health Practice and Resource Centers which promote healthy lifestyles and work to improve quality of life for people with disabilities. The primary goals of the state programs are to

- Increase health promotion opportunities for people with disabilities;

- Improve access to healthcare services for people with disabilities; and

- Improve emergency preparedness for people with disabilities.

The CDC's Disability and Health website also provides information and resources that public health practitioners, healthcare providers and people interested in the health and wellbeing of people with disabilities can use to increase awareness about disability inclusion. This information and the resources can help ensure that everybody, with and without disabilities, can live, work, learn, and play in their communities.

You may to visit the newly updated Disability and Health website to find helpful information about disability inclusion and learn more about

- Barriers that people with disabilities usually experience in their communities;

- Strategies to create inclusive communities; and

- Resources to include people with disabilities in public health programs and activities.

CDC also maintains the Disability and Health Data System (DHDS), an online interactive tool that provides instant access to state-level, disability-specific health data. Users can customize the disability and health data they view, making it easy to identify health differences between adults with and without disabilities. In a future update of the system, users will be able to find health data by functional disability type.

Americans with Disabilities

Table 2.1. Prevalence of Disability for Selected Age Groups: 2005 and 2010

Category	2005[1]				2010				Difference	
	Number	Margin of error (±)[2]	Percent	Margin of error (±)[2]	Number	Margin of error (±)[2]	Percent	Margin of error (±)[2]	Number	Percent
All ages	291,099	*****	100.0	(X)	303,858	*****	100.0	(X)	**12,760	(X)
With a disability	54,425	894	18.7	0	56,672	905	18.7	0	*2,247	-
Severe disability	34,947	601	12.0	0	38,284	654	12.6	0	*3,337	*0.6
Aged 6 and older	266,752	84	100.0	(X)	278,222	88	100.0	(X)	*11,469	(X)
Needed personal assistance	10,996	336	4.1	0	12,349	396	4.4	0	*1,353	*0.6
Aged 15 and older	230,391	*****	100.0	(X)	241,682	*****	100.0	(X)	**11,291	(X)
With a disability	49,069	794	21.3	0	51,454	838	21.3	0	*2,385	-
Severe disability	32,771	567	14.2	0	35,683	631	14.8	0	*2,918	*0.5
Difficulty seeing	7,793	350	3.4	0	8,077	354	3.3	0	284	-

Table 2.1. Continued

Category	2005[1]				2010				Difference	
	Number	Margin of error (±)[2]	Percent	Margin of error (±)[2]	Number	Margin of error (±)[2]	Percent	Margin of error (±)[2]	Number	Percent
Severe	1,783	129	0.8	0	2,010	139	0.8	0	*228	0.1
Difficulty hearing	7,809	325	3.4	0	7,572	320	3.1	0	-237	*-0.3
Severe	993	103	0.4	-	1,096	122	0.5	0	103	-
Aged 21 to 64	170,349	185	100.0	(X)	177,295	193	100.0	(X)	*6945	(X)
With a disability	28,141	622	16.5	0	29,479	705	16.6	0	*1,338	0.1
Employed	12,838	495	45.6	1	12,115	432	41.1	1	*-723	*-4.5
Severe disability	18,705	469	11.0	0	20,286	566	11.4	0	*1,581	*0.5
Employed	5,738	277	30.7	1	5,570	261	27.5	1	-167	*-3.2
Nonsevere disability	9,436	403	5.5	0	9,193	374	5.2	0	-243	*-0.4
Employed	7,100	356	75.2	2	6,544	311	71.2	2	*-556	*-4.1
No disability	142,208	636	83.5	0	147,816	733	83.4	0	*5,607	-0.1
Employed	118,707	678	83.5	0	116,881	862	79.1	0	*-1,826	*-4.4
Aged 65 and older	35,028	*****	100.0	(X)	38,599	*****	100.0	(X)	**3,571	(X)

15

Table 2.1. Continued

Category	2005[1]				2010				Difference	
	Number	Margin of error (±)[2]	Percent	Margin of error (±)[2]	Number	Margin of error (±)[2]	Percent	Margin of error (±)[2]	Number	Percent
With a disability	18,132	324	51.8	1	19,234	327	49.8	1	*1,102	*-1.9
Severe disability	12,942	273	36.9	1	14,138	276	36.6	1	*1,196	-0.3

(X) Not applicable.

– Represents or rounds to zero.

* Denotes a statistically significant difference at the 90 percent confidence level.

** Denotes a difference between two controlled estimates. By definition, this difference is statistically significant.

***** Indicates (in margin of error column) that the estimate is controlled to independent population estimates. A statistical test for sampling variability is not appropriate.

[1] Estimates of disability prevalence for 2005 may differ from the estimates presented in "Americans With Disabilities: 2005, P70-117" due to changes in the survey weighting since the report's publication. Furthermore, the margins of error in the 2005 report were calculated using the generalized variance formula method. The estimates of variance shown here use the successive differences replication method.

[2] A margin of error is a measure of an estimate's variability. The larger the margin of error in relation to the size of the estimate, the less reliable the estimate.

The margins of error shown in this table are for the 90 percent confidence level. For more information about the source and accuracy of the estimates, including margins of error, standard errors, and confidence intervals, see the Source and Accuracy Statement at www.census.gov/sipp/sourceac/S&A08 _W1toW6(S&A-13).pdf.

Source: U.S. Census Bureau, Survey of Income and Program Participation, June–September 2005 and May–August 2010.

Table 2.2. Age-Adjusted and Unadjusted Disability Rates by Gender, Race, Hispanic Origin: 2005 and 2010

Category	Age-adjusted disability rate[1]				Unadjusted disability rate				
	2010		2005		2010		Difference	2005	
	Estimate	Margin of error (±)[2]	Estimate	Margin of error (±)[2]	Estimate	Margin of error (±)[2]		Estimate	Margin of error (±)[2]
All people	**18.7**	**0.3**	**18.7**	**0.3**	**18.6**	**0.3**	**–**	**18.1**	**0.3**
Male	17.3	0.4	17.4	0.4	19.0	0.4	0.2	18.3	0.3
Female	18.6	0.3	18.5	0.3	18.1	0.4		17.6	0.4
White alone	20.1	0.4	19.8	0.4	18.1	0.3	-0.2	17.9	0.3
Black alone	19.7	0.4	19.8	0.4	22.3	0.7	23.2	22.2	0.7
Asian alone	20.7	0.7	20.3	0.7	12.5	13.0	14.5	13.0	12.4
Not Hispanic	20.4	0.3	18.4	0.3	14.6	1.3	14.4	20.7	13.0
Hispanic or Latino	13.0	1.0	0.9	0.6	13.2	17.8	13.1	0.6	13.2

– Represents or rounds to zero.

* Denotes a statistically significant difference at the 90 percent confidence level.

[1] Age-adjustments followed the methodology described in Anderson and Rosenberg (1998) using the year 2000 standard population by 5-year age groups from Day (1996).

[2] A margin of error is a measure of an estimate's variability. The larger the margin of error in relation to the size of the estimate, the less reliable the estimate.

The margins of error shown in this table are for the 90 percent confidence level. For more information about the source and accuracy of the estimates, including margins of error, standard errors, and confidence intervals, see the Source and Accuracy Statement at www.census.gov/sipp/sourceac/S&A08_W1toW6(S&A-13).pdf.

Source: U.S. Census Bureau, Survey of Income and Program Participation, June–September 2005 and May–August 2010.

Chapter 3

Common Barriers Experienced by People with Disabilities

Nearly everyone faces hardships and difficulties at one time or another. But for people with disabilities, barriers can be more frequent and have greater impact. The World Health Organization (WHO) describes barriers as being more than just physical obstacles. Here is the WHO definition of barriers:

"Factors in a person's environment that, through their absence or presence, limit functioning and create disability. These include aspects such as:

- a physical environment that is not accessible,

- lack of relevant assistive technology (assistive, adaptive, and rehabilitative devices),

This chapter includes excerpts from "Common Barriers to Participation Experienced by People with Disabilities," National Center on Birth Defects and Developmental Disabilities, Centers for Disease Control and Prevention (CDC), July 22, 2015; text from "Inclusion Strategies," National Center on Birth Defects and Developmental Disabilities, Centers for Disease Control and Prevention (CDC), July 22, 2015; and text from "Rehabilitative and Assistive Technology: Overview," National Institute of Child Health and Human Development (NICHD), November 30, 2012.

- negative attitudes of people towards disability,

- services, systems and policies that are either nonexistent or that hinder the involvement of all people with a health condition in all areas of life."

Often there are multiple barriers that can make it extremely difficult or even impossible for people with disabilities to function. Here are the seven most common barriers. Often, more than one barrier occurs at a time.

- Attitudinal

- Communication

- Physical

- Policy

- Programmatic

- Social

- Transportation

Attitudinal Barriers

Attitudinal barriers are the most basic and contribute to other barriers. For example, some people may not be aware that difficulties in getting to or into a place can limit a person with a disability from participating in everyday life and common daily activities. Examples of attitudinal barriers include:

- Stereotyping: People sometimes stereotype those with disabilities, assuming their quality of life is poor or that they are unhealthy because of their impairments.

- Stigma, prejudice, and discrimination: Within society, these attitudes may come from people's ideas related to disability— people may see disability as a personal tragedy, as something that needs to be cured or prevented, or as a sign of a lack of ability to behave as expected in society.

Today, society's understanding of disability is improving as we recognize "disability" as what occurs when a person's functional needs are not addressed in his or her physical and social environment. By not considering disability a personal deficit or shortcoming, and instead thinking of it as a social responsibility in which all people can be supported to live independent and full lives, it becomes easier to recognize and address challenges that all people – including those with disabilities – experience.

Communication Barriers

Communication barriers are experienced by people who have disabilities that affect hearing, speaking, reading, writing, and or understanding, and who use different ways to communicate than people who do not have these disabilities. Examples of communication barriers include:

- Written health promotion messages with barriers that prevent people with vision impairments from receiving the message. These include

  - Use of small print or no large-print versions of material, and

  - No Braille or versions for people who use screen readers.

- Auditory health messages may be inaccessible to people with hearing impairments, including

  - Videos that do not include captioning, and

  - Oral communications without accompanying manual interpretation (such as, American Sign Language).

- The use of technical language, long sentences, and words with many syllables may be significant barriers to understanding for people with cognitive impairments.

Physical barriers

Physical barriers are structural obstacles in natural or manmade environments that prevent or block mobility (moving around in the environment) or access. Examples of physical barriers include:

- Steps and curbs that block a person with mobility impairment from entering a building or using a sidewalk;

- Mammography equipment that requires a woman with mobility impairment to stand; and

- Absence of a weight scale that accommodates wheelchairs or others who have difficulty stepping up.

Policy Barriers

Policy barriers are frequently related to a lack of awareness or enforcement of existing laws and regulations that require programs and activities be accessible to people with disabilities. Examples of policy barriers include:

- Denying qualified individuals with disabilities the opportunity to participate in or benefit from federally funded programs, services, or other benefits;

- Denying individuals with disabilities access to programs, services, benefits, or opportunities to participate as a result of physical barriers; and

- Denying reasonable accommodations to qualified individuals with disabilities, so they can perform the essential functions of the job for which they have applied or have been hired to perform.

Programmatic Barriers

Programmatic barriers limit the effective delivery of a public health or healthcare program for people with different types of impairments. Examples of programmatic barriers include:

- Inconvenient scheduling;

- Lack of accessible equipment (such as mammography screening equipment);

- Insufficient time set aside for medical examination and procedures;

- Little or no communication with patients or participants; and

- Provider's attitudes, knowledge, and understanding of people with disabilities.

Social Barriers

Social barriers are related to the conditions in which people are born, grow, live, learn, work and age – or social determinants of health – that can contribute to decreased functioning among people with disabilities. Here are examples of social barriers:

- People with disabilities are far less likely to be employed. The unemployment rate in 2012 for people with disabilities was more than 1 in 10 (13.9%) compared to less than 1 in 10 (6.0%) for those without disabilities.

- Adults age 25 years and older with disabilities are less likely to have completed high school compared to their peers without disabilities (23.5% compared to 11.1%).

- People with disabilities are more likely to live in poverty compared to people without disabilities (21.6% compare to 12.8%).

- Children with disabilities are almost four times more likely to experience violence than children without disabilities.

Transportation Barriers

Transportation barriers are due to a lack of adequate transportation that interferes with a person's ability to be independent and to function in society. Examples of transportation barriers include:

- Lack of access to accessible or convenient transportation for people who are not able to drive because of vision or cognitive impairments, and

- Public transportation may be unavailable or at inconvenient distances or locations.

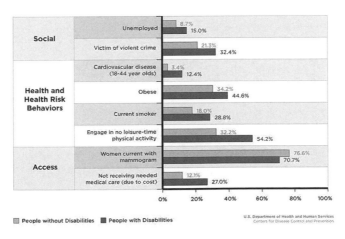

Figure 3.1. *Factors Affecting the Health of People with Disabilities and without Disabilities—Transportation Barriers*

Inclusion Strategies

Inclusion of people with disabilities into everyday activities involves practices and policies designed to identify and remove barriers such as physical, communication, and attitudinal, that hamper individuals' ability to have full participation in society, the same as people without disabilities. Inclusion involves:

- Getting fair treatment from others (non-discrimination);

- Making products, communications, and the physical environment more usable by as many people as possible (universal design);

- Modifying items, procedures, or systems to enable a person with a disability to use them to the maximum extent possible (reasonable accommodations); and

- Eliminating the belief that people with disabilities are unhealthy or less capable of doing things (stigma, stereotypes).

Disability inclusion involves input from people with disabilities, generally through disability-focused and independent living organizations, in program or structural design, implementation, monitoring, and evaluation.

Chapter 4

Women with Disabilities

Persons with disabilities are the world's largest minority, representing **15% of the global population**. 80% of this population live in developing countries.

Women and girls with disabilities are subjected to multiple layers of discrimination. Based on their gender and disability status they often face "double discrimination." This inequality is exacerbated for women and girls with disabilities who are members of marginalized ethnic or racial groups or part of the lesbian, gay, bisexual, transgender, and intersex community.

Unemployment rates are highest among women with disabilities. The United Nations estimates that 75 percent of women with disabilities are unemployed and women with disabilities who are employed often earn less than their male counterparts and women without disabilities. Gender disparities also exist in education. While the overall literacy rate for persons with disabilities is 3 percent, UNESCO estimates that it is just 1 percent for women and girls with disabilities.

Women and girls with disabilities often face disproportionately high rates of gender-based violence, sexual abuse, neglect, maltreatment,

---

This chapter includes excerpts from "Advancing Women and Girls with Disabilities," USAID, August 24, 2015; text from "Violence Against Women with Disabilities," Office on Women's Health (OWH), January 22, 2015; and text from "16 Day Challenge: Invisible Women: Violence Against Women with Disabilities," USAID, December 3, 2012.

and exploitation. Studies show that women and girls with disabilities are twice as likely to experience gender-based violence compared to women and girls without disabilities. Women with disabilities are often denied reproductive healthcare and at times are even subjected to forced sterilization. When healthcare services are available, they may not be physically accessible for women with varying types of disabilities, or healthcare providers don't know how to accommodate them.

The exclusion and violence against women and girls with disabilities in any country carries heavy financial and social consequences. Discrimination against persons with disabilities hinders economic development, limits democracy, and erodes societies. Perhaps because of the challenges they face, women and girls with disabilities are poised to be leaders within their communities and can greatly contribute to the economic development of their countries.

Violence against women with disabilities

Research suggests that women with disabilities are more likely to suffer domestic violence and sexual assault than women without disabilities. And women with disabilities report abuse that lasts longer and is more intense than women without disabilities.

Like other women, women with disabilities usually are abused by someone they know, such as a partner or family member. In addition, women with disabilities face the risk of abuse by health care providers or caregivers. Caregivers can withhold medicine and assistive devices, such as wheelchairs or braces. They can also refuse to help with daily needs like bathing, dressing, or eating.

If you are being abused by someone you rely on to take care of you, you may feel trapped. If you can, reach out for help to someone you trust, such as a doctor, family member, friend or neighbor.

There are over a billion people with disabilities on the planet. Approximately half of them are women with disabilities. They are grandmothers, mothers, partners, lovers, and sisters. They are seldom seen in market places, the fields, the classrooms, at the health clinics or in the workplace. Women with disabilities are by and large an invisible group in society. Their invisibility is partly due to the multiple forms of discrimination and the intersectionality of disability and gender.

Violence against women and girls with disabilities is an important, and often overlooked, aspect of gender-based violence. A reflection of attitudes ingrained in all cultural systems of the world where women are seen as lesser human beings – and women with disabilities as even less worthy – makes it easy for abusive power and control over them.

Research by Women's Aid indicates that one in four women experience domestic violence. For women with a disability, this figure doubles. Be it at the hands of their partner, family, or caregiver, almost one in two women with disabilities will be abused in their lifetime.

The experiences of women with disabilities fit within traditional definitions of domestic violence, but some do not—they are disability-specific, such as having medicine withheld, being physically assaulted, deliberately not being assisted to go to the toilet, or having their assistive devices taken away. Also women with disabilities may fear reporting or leaving an abuser because of emotional, financial or physical dependence, or fear of loss of parental rights. In situations of conflict where rape is often used as a weapon of war, women with disabilities are seen as easy targets. Conversely, situations of conflict invariably increase the incidence of disability. The United States Government National Action Plan on Women, Peace and Security highlights the need to take special measures to protect women and girls with disabilities from gender-based violence, particularly rape and other forms of sexual abuse, and all other forms of violence in situations of armed conflict.

The Convention on the Rights of Persons with Disabilities (CRPD), adopted by the U.N. General Assembly in 2006, recognized that "women and girls with disabilities are often at greater risk, both within and outside the home of violence, injury or abuse, neglect or negligent treatment, maltreatment or exploitation" and emphasized "the need to incorporate a gender perspective in all efforts to promote the full enjoyment of human rights and fundamental freedoms by persons with disabilities."

Chapter 5

Aging and Disabilities

Almost 16 million Americans aged 65 and older report having at least one disability, according to a new report by the U.S. Census Bureau, commissioned and funded by the NIA. This is the first Census report on disabilities among older people and looks at disability status by age, sex, marital status, education, and poverty status.

The report is based on data from the American Community Survey (ACS) and covers six types of disability, including difficulty in hearing, vision, cognition, walking, self-care, and independent living. People who reported any one of the six disability types are considered to have a disability. The most common type of disability was difficulty in walking or climbing stairs, which was reported by two-thirds of those with a disability.

The report includes information on the geographic distribution of older people with a disability, with data shown at the county level. The prevalence of disability at older ages varies widely across counties; the Appalachian region, the lower Mississippi Valley, and parts of the upper South have particularly high rates. The report includes a number of maps, including one showing the percentage of older people living alone in poverty with a disability.

This chapter includes excerpts from "NIH-commissioned report highlights disability among older population," National Institute on Aging (NIA), December 10, 2014; and text from "Older Americans With a Disability: 2008–2012," U.S. Census Bureau, American Community Survey Reports, December 2014.

The oldest old – those aged 85 and older – had the highest prevalence of disability. While this group represented 13.6 percent of the total older population, they accounted for 25.4 percent of those with a disability.

Introduction

Disability, as defined by the Americans with Disabilities Act (ADA), is an individual's physical or mental impairment that substantially limits one or more major life activities of that individual. Studies consistently find that disability rates rise with age. Beyond age 65, the oldest old (aged 85 and over) are at highest risk for disease and disability, and among them, disability prevalence increases rapidly with age.

Changes in population age structure are contributing to a growing number of older people with a disability. In the past several decades, the U.S. older population itself has been aging—the proportion of the oldest-old segment (aged 85 and over) of the older population has increased from 8.8 percent in 1980 to 13.6 percent in 2010. Given higher prevalence rates among the oldest old, this changing composition of the older population has increased the number with a disability.

Baby Boomers started to enter the older age ranks in 2011, and they will swell the size of the older population in the next 2 decades. The number of older people with a disability could also expand rapidly. Thus, it is important to identify those among the older population most at risk for disability in order to help older people with a disability and their families plan strategies to deal with daily activity difficulties.

In recent decades, the concept of disability has shifted from an individual, medical perspective to a social model in which disability is viewed as the result of social and physical barriers. The International Classification of Functioning, Disability, and Health recognizes the value of both models and views disability as arising from the interaction of health conditions and environmental and personal factors. The U.S. Census Bureau modified the American Community Survey (ACS) questions on disability starting in 2008 to better reflect this new paradigm.

How the ACS Measures Disability

The ACS questions cover six disability types:

1. **Hearing difficulty**—deaf or having serious difficulty hearing.

2. **Vision difficulty**—blind or having serious difficulty seeing, even when wearing glasses.

3. **Cognitive difficulty**—because of a physical, mental, or emotional problem, having difficulty remembering, concentrating, or making decisions.

4. **Ambulatory difficulty**—having serious difficulty walking or climbing stairs.

5. **Self-care difficulty**—having difficulty bathing or dressing.

6. **Independent living difficulty**—because of a physical, mental, or emotional problem, having difficulty doing errands alone, such as visiting a doctor's office or shopping.

Respondents who report any one of the six disability types are considered to have a disability.

The ACS identifies serious difficulty with four basic areas of functioning—hearing, vision, cognition, and ambulation. The ACS supplements the functional limitations with questions about selected activities from the Katz Activities of Daily Living (ADL) – difficulty dressing and bathing; and from the Lawton Instrumental Activities of Daily Living (IADL) scales – difficulty

performing errands, such as visiting a doctor's office or shopping. However, the ACS does not gather information on the severity or timing of onset of the disability, or on the use of technology or assistance.

Status, Number, and Type of Disability

Disability status

In 2008–2012, there were 40.7 million people aged 65 and over in the United States, representing 13.2 percent of the total population. Among this older population, about 15.7 million, or 38.7 percent, reported having one or more disabilities.

The older population with a disability was disproportionately concentrated among the oldest old—those aged 85 and older represented 13.6 percent of the total older population, but accounted for 25.4 percent of the older population with a disability, with 65- to 74-year-olds and 75- to 84-year olds about evenly split for the remainder (37.0 percent and 37.6 percent, respectively). Furthermore, women composed 59.0 percent of the older population experiencing disabilities (higher than their 56.8 percent share of the total older population).

31

This translates into a sex ratio of 69 men per 100 women for the older population with a disability.

Number of disabilities

Among the older population, 61.3 percent reported having no disabilities among the six types defined on the ACS questionnaire, 15.9 percent reported having only one type of disability, 8.0 percent reported two types of disabilities, and 14.7 percent reported three or more types of disabilities (Figure 4.1.). The patterns of the number of disabilities differed by age. When this percentage distribution was examined by three broad age groups, the share without a disability declined as age rose, while the shares with one, two, and three or more disabilities generally rose with age. The contrast is particularly salient when it comes to three or more types of disabilities. For the youngest age group (65 to 74), only 7.0 percent reported three or more types of disabilities, the proportion more than doubled to 16.5 percent for those aged 75 to 84, and reached 41.5 percent for those aged 85 and older.

Type of disability

Of the six ACS disability items, ambulatory difficulty was the most frequently reported by the older population in 2008–2012. About 10 million people, or two-thirds (66.5 percent) of the total older population with a disability, reported having serious difficulty walking or climbing stairs (Table 5.1.). Difficulty with independent living, such as visiting a

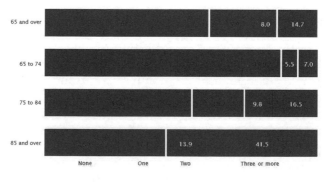

Source: U.S. Census Bureau, American Community Survey, 5-year estimates, 2008–2012.

Figure 5.1. *Population Aged 65 and Over by Number of Disabilities and Age: 2008–2012*

doctor's office or shopping, was a distant second (47.8 percent), followed by serious difficulty hearing (40.4 percent).

The order for these top three types of disability was consistent across age groups, except for those aged 65 to 74, where the prevalence of hearing difficulty (34.9 percent) was higher than that of independent living (34.0 percent). The prevalence rate for all disability types increased with age as expected, but interesting contrasts existed between men and women. Older women were more likely than older men to have five of the six types of disability included in the ACS, especially that of ambulatory difficulty (73.1 percent for women versus 57.1 percent for men). Older women's higher prevalence rates for disability may partly be a function of their age composition compared with that of older men. Older men, however, stood out with a higher proportion reporting serious difficulty hearing (52.0 percent, compared with 32.3 percent for women). Men's higher likelihood for having a hearing disability may reflect the life-long occupational differentials between men and women, that men may be more likely to have worked in industries such as mining, manufacturing, or construction—industries documented to cause noise-induced hearing loss. Some of these studies also pointed to smoking as having a possible correlation with hearing impairment at older ages.

Conclusion

With the improvements in life expectancy, the focus of population aging in the United States has now moved to quality of life for the older population in their late life. Increases in both total life expectancy and disability-free life expectancy have been linked to delays in the onset of disability and increases in the rates of recovery from disability. Disability can be reduced with improved medical treatment, positive behavioral changes, wider use of assistive technologies, rising education levels, and improvements in socioeconomic status.

With the first Baby Boomers having entered the 65-and-older ranks in 2011, the United States may experience a rapid expansion in the number of older people with a disability in the next 2 decades. The future of disability among older Americans will be affected by how this country prepares for and manages a complex array of demographic, fiscal, medical, technological, and other developments that will unfold in the next several decades.

Chapter 6

Abuse of Children with Disabilities

Bullying of Children with Intellectual Disabilities

Understanding Bullying

Bullying is a form of youth violence. CDC defines bullying as any unwanted aggressive behavior(s) by another youth or group of youths who are not siblings or current dating partners that involves an observed or perceived power imbalance and is repeated multiple times or is highly likely to be repeated. Bullying may inflict harm or distress on the targeted youth including physical, psychological, social, or educational harm. Bullying can include aggression that is physical (hitting, tripping), verbal (name calling, teasing), or relational/social (spreading rumors, leaving out of group). A young person can be a perpetrator, a victim, or both (also known as "bully/victim"). Bullying can also occur through technology and is called electronic aggression or cyber-bullying. Electronic aggression is bullying that occurs through e-mail, a chat room, instant messaging, a Website or blog, text messaging, or videos or pictures posted on Website or blog or sent through cell phones.

This chapter includes excerpts from "Understanding Bullying Fact Sheet," Centers for Disease Control (CDC), 2015; and text from "Bullying and Children and Youth with Disabilities and Special Health Needs," U.S. Department of Health & Human Services (HHS), July 13, 2012.

Why is bullying a public health problem?

Bullying is widespread in the United States.

- In a 2013 nationwide survey, 20% of high school students reported being bullied on school property in the 12 months preceding the survey.

- An estimated 15% of high school students reported in 2013 that they were bullied electronically in the 12 months before the survey

- During the 2012-2013 school year, 8% of public school students ages 12-18 reported being bullied on a weekly basis.

How does bullying affect health?

Bullying can result in physical injury, social and emotional distress, and even death. Victimized youth are at increased risk for depression, anxiety, sleep difficulties, and poor school adjustment. Youth who bully others are at increased risk for substance use, academic problems, and violence later in adolescence and adulthood. Compared to youth who only bully, or who are only victims, bully-victims suffer the most serious consequences and are at greater risk for both mental health and behavior problems.

Who is at risk for bullying?

Different factors can increase a youth's risk of engaging in or experiencing bullying. However, the presence of these factors does not always mean that a young person will bully others or be bullied.

Some of the factors associated with a higher likelihood of engaging in bullying behavior include:

- Externalizing problems, such as defiant and disruptive behavior

- Harsh parenting by caregivers

- Attitudes accepting of violence

Some of the factors associated with a higher likelihood of victimization include:

- Poor peer relationships

- Low self-esteem

- Perceived by peers as different or quiet

How can we prevent bullying?

The ultimate goal is to stop bullying before it starts. Research on preventing and addressing bullying is still developing. School-based bullying prevention programs are widely implemented, but infrequently evaluated. Based on a review of the limited research on school based bullying prevention, the following program elements are promising:

- Improving supervision of students

- Using school rules and behavior management techniques in the classroom and throughout the school to detect and address bullying by providing consequences for bullying

- Having a whole school anti-bullying policy, and enforcing that policy consistently

- Promoting cooperation among different professionals and between school staff and parents

How does CDC approach bullying prevention?

CDC uses a four-step approach to address public health problems like bullying.

Step 1: Define and monitor the problem

Before we can prevent bullying, we need to know how big the problem is, where it is, and who it affects. CDC learns about a problem by gathering and studying data. These data are critical because they help us know where prevention is most needed.

Step 2: Identify risk and protective factors

It is not enough to know that bullying is affecting a certain group of people in a certain area. We also need to know why. CDC conducts and supports research to answer this question. We can then develop programs to reduce or get rid of risk factors and increase protective factors.

Step 3: Develop and test prevention strategies

Using information gathered in research, CDC develops and tests strategies to prevent bullying.

Step 4: Ensure widespread adoption

In this final step, CDC shares the best prevention strategies. CDC may also provide funding or technical help so communities can adopt these strategies.

Bullying and Children and Youth with Disabilities and Special Health Needs

Children with physical, developmental, intellectual, emotional, and sensory disabilities are more likely to be bullied than their peers. Any number of factors—physical vulnerability, social skill challenges, or intolerant environments—may increase their risk. Research suggests that some children with disabilities may bully others as well.

Kids with special health needs, such as epilepsy or food allergies, may also be at higher risk of being bullied. For kids with special health needs, bullying can include making fun of kids because of their allergies or exposing them to the things they are allergic to. In these cases, bullying is not just serious; it can mean life or death.

A small but growing amount of research shows that:

- Children with attention deficit or hyperactivity disorder (ADHD) are more likely than other children to be bullied. They also are somewhat more likely than others to bully their peers.

- Children with autism spectrum disorder (ASD) are at increased risk of being bullied and left out by peers. In a study of 8–17-year-olds, researchers found that children with ASD were more than three times as likely to be bullied as their peers.

- Children with epilepsy are more likely to be bullied by peers, as are children with medical conditions that affect their appearance, such as cerebral palsy, muscular dystrophy, and spina bifida. These children frequently report being called names related to their disability.

- Children with hemiplagia (paralysis of one side of their body) are more likely than other children their age to be bullied and have fewer friends.

- Children who have diabetes and are dependent on insulin may be especially vulnerable to peer bullying.

- Children who stutter may be more likely to be bullied. In one study, 83 percent of adults who stammered as children said that they were teased or bullied; 71 percent of those who had been bullied said it happened at least once a week.

- Children with learning disabilities (LD) are at a greater risk of being bullied. At least one study also has found that children with LD may also be more likely than other children to bullying their peers.

Effects of Bullying

Kids who are bullied are more likely to have:

- Depression and anxiety. Signs of these include increased feelings of sadness and loneliness, changes in sleep and eating patterns, and loss of interest in activities they used to enjoy. These issues may persist into adulthood.

- Health complaints.

- Decreased academic achievement – GPA and standardized test scores – and school participation. They are more likely to miss, skip or drop out of school.

Bullying, Disability Harassment, and the Law

Bullying behavior can become "disability harassment," which is prohibited under Section 504 of the Rehabilitation Act of 1973 and Title II of the Americans with Disabilities Act of 1990. According to the U.S. Department of Education, disability harassment is "intimidation or abusive behavior toward a student based on disability that creates a hostile environment by interfering with or denying a student's participation in or receipt of benefits, services, or opportunities in the institution's program." (U.S. Department of Education, 2000)

Disability harassment can take different forms including verbal harassment, physical threats, or threatening written statements.

When a school learns that disability harassment may have occurred, the school must investigate the incident(s) promptly and respond appropriately. Disability harassment can occur in any location that is connected with school—classrooms, the cafeteria, hallways, the playground, athletic fields, or school buses. It also can occur during school-sponsored events. (Education Law Center, 2002)

What Parents Can Do

If you believe a child with special needs is being bullied:

- Be supportive of the child and encourage him or her to describe who was involved and how and where the bullying happened. Be sure to tell the child that it is not his or her fault and that nobody deserves to be bullied or harassed. Do not encourage the child to fight back. This may make the problem worse.

- Ask the child specific questions about his or her friendships. Be aware of signs of bullying, even if the child doesn't call it that.

Children with disabilities do not always realize they are being bullied. They may, for example, believe that they have a new friend although this "friend" is making fun of them.

- Talk with the child's teacher immediately to see whether he or she can help to resolve the problem.

- Put your concerns in writing and contact the principal if the bullying or harassment is severe or the teacher doesn't fix the problem. Explain what happened in detail and ask for a prompt response. Keep a written record of all conversations and communications with the school.

- Ask the school district to convene a meeting of the Individualized Education Program (IEP) or the Section 504 teams. These groups ensure that the school district is meeting the needs of its students with disabilities. This meeting will allow parents to explain what has been happening and will let the team review the child's IEP or 504 plans and make sure that the school is taking steps to stop the harassment. Work with the school to help establish a system-wide bullying prevention program that includes support systems for bullied children. As the U.S. Department of Education (2000) recognizes, "creating a supportive school climate is the most important step in preventing harassment."

- Explore whether the child may also be bullying other younger, weaker students at school. If so, his or her IEP may need to be modified to include help to change the aggressive behavior.

- Be persistent. Talk regularly with the child and with school staff to see whether the behavior has stopped.

Getting Additional Support

If a school district does not take reasonable, appropriate steps to end the bullying or harassment of a child with special needs, the district may be violating federal, state, and local laws.

For more information, contact:

The U.S. Department of Education
Office for Civil Rights
Phone: (800)-421-3481
Website: www2.ed.gov/about/offices/list/ocr/complaintintro.html

The U.S. Department of Education
Office of Special Education Programs
Phone: (202) 245-7468
Website: www.ed.gov/about/offices/list/osers/osep/index.html

The U.S. Department of Justice
Civil Rights Division
Phone: 1-877-292-3804
Website: www.justice.gov/crt/complaint/#three

Part Two

Types of Disabilities

Chapter 7

Birth Defects

Facts about Birth Defects

Birth defects are serious conditions that are changes to the structure of one or more parts of the body. Birth defects affect 1 in every 33 babies born in the United States each year. Read further below about what we have learned about birth defects and how women can improve their chances of having a baby born without a birth defect.

Birth Defects Are Common

Every 4 ½ minutes, a baby is born with a birth defect in the United States. That translates into nearly 120,000 babies affected by birth defects each year.

Birth defects can affect almost any part of the body (e.g., heart, brain, foot). They may affect how the body looks, works, or both. Birth defects can vary from mild to severe. The well-being of each child affected with a birth defect depends mostly on which organ or body part is involved and how much it is affected. Depending on the severity of the defect and what body part is affected, the expected lifespan of a person with a birth defect may or may not be affected.

This chapter includes excerpts from "Facts about Birth Defects," Centers for Disease Control and Prevention (CDC), September 21, 2015; text from "Guidance for Preventing Birth Defects," Centers for Disease Control and Prevention (CDC), November 24, 2014; and text from "Ten Things You Need to Know About Birth Defects," Centers for Disease Control and Prevention (CDC), October 20, 2014.

Identifying Birth Defects

A birth defect can be found before birth, at birth, or any time after birth. Most birth defects are found within the first year of life. Some birth defects (such as cleft lip) are easy to see, but others (such as heart defects or hearing loss) are found using special tests, such as echocardiograms (an ultrasound picture of the heart), X-rays or hearing tests.

Causes

Birth defects can occur during any stage of pregnancy. Most birth defects occur in the first 3 months of pregnancy, when the organs of the baby are forming. This is a very important stage of development. However, some birth defects occur later in pregnancy. During the last six months of pregnancy, the tissues and organs continue to grow and develop.

Most birth defects are thought to be caused by a complex mix of factors. These factors include our genes (information inherited from our parents), our behaviors, and things in the environment. For some birth defects, we know the cause. But for most, we don't.

Certain things can increase the chance that a pregnancy will be affected by a birth defect. These are called risk factors. There are some things that you can change to reduce your chances, while other things cannot be changed. Some risk factors that can increase the chances of having a baby with a birth defect: include:

- Smoking, drinking alcohol, or taking certain "street" drugs during pregnancy.

- Having certain medical conditions, such as being obese or having uncontrolled diabetes before and during pregnancy.

- Taking certain medications, such as isotretinoin (a drug used to treat severe acne).

- Having someone in your family with a birth defect. To learn more about your risk of having a baby with a birth defect, you can talk with a clinical geneticist or a genetic counselor.

- Being an older mother, typically over the age of 34 years.

Having one or more of these risks doesn't mean you'll have a pregnancy affected by a birth defect.

Also, women can have a baby born with a birth defect even when they don't have any of these risks. It is important to talk to your doctor about what you can do to lower your risk.

Living with a Birth Defect

Babies who have birth defects often need special care and interventions to survive and to thrive developmentally. State birth defects tracking programs provide one way to identify and refer children as early as possible for services they need. Early intervention is vital to improving outcomes for these babies. If your child has a birth defect, you should ask his or her doctor about local resources and treatment. Geneticists, genetic counselors, and other specialists are another resource.

Guidance for Preventing Birth Defects

Not all birth defects can be prevented. But a woman can increase her own chances of having a healthy baby by managing health conditions and adopting healthy behaviors before becoming pregnant. This is important because many birth defects happen very early during pregnancy, sometimes before a woman even knows she is pregnant. Read below for some steps a woman can take to get ready for a healthy pregnancy.

Women should:

1. Get 400 micrograms (mcg) of folic acid every day.

Folic acid is a B vitamin. If a woman has enough folic acid in her body at least one month before and during pregnancy, it can help prevent major birth defects of the baby's brain and spine (anencephaly and spina bifida). Women can get folic acid from fortified foods or supplements, or a combination of the two, in addition to a varied diet rich in folate.

2. Avoid alcohol at any time during pregnancy.

When a pregnant woman drinks alcohol, so does her baby. Alcohol that's in the woman's blood passes to the baby through the umbilical cord. There is no known safe amount of alcohol use during pregnancy or while trying to get pregnant. There is also no safe time during pregnancy to drink. All types of alcohol are equally harmful, including all wines and beer. Drinking alcohol during pregnancy can cause miscarriage, stillbirth, and a range of lifelong physical, behavioral, and intellectual disabilities. These disabilities are known as fetal alcohol spectrum disorders (FASDs). The best advice is to stop drinking alcohol when you start trying to get pregnant.

3. Avoid smoking cigarettes or using "street" drugs.

The dangers of smoking during pregnancy include premature birth, certain birth defects (cleft lip or cleft palate), and infant death. Even being around tobacco smoke puts a woman and her unborn baby at risk for problems. A woman who uses illegal—or "street"—drugs during pregnancy can have a baby who is born premature; is low birth weight; or has other health problems, such as birth defects.

Quitting smoking before getting pregnant is best. For a woman who is already pregnant, quitting as early as possible can still help protect against some health problems for the baby, such as low birth weight.

It's never too late to quit smoking.

4. Prevent infections.

Some infections that a woman can get during pregnancy can be harmful to the unborn baby and can even cause birth defects. Some easy steps to prevent infections include washing her hands, cooking meat until its well done, and staying away from people who have an infection. Learn how to help prevent infections.

5. Talk to a health care provider about taking any medications.

We know certain medications can cause serious birth defects if they are taken during pregnancy. But for many medications taken by pregnant women, the safety has been difficult to determine. If a woman is pregnant or planning a pregnancy, she should not stop taking medications she needs or begin taking new medications without first talking with her doctor. This includes prescription and over-the-counter medications and dietary or herbal products.

6. Talk to your doctor about vaccinations (shots).

Most vaccinations are safe and recommended during pregnancy. Some vaccines protect women against infections that can cause birth defects. Having the right vaccinations at the right time can help keep a woman and her baby healthy. She should talk to her doctor about which vaccines are recommended for her during pregnancy.

Pregnant women are more prone to severe illness from the flu, including hospitalizations and even death, than women who are not pregnant. Pregnant woman with flu also have a greater chance for serious problems for their unborn baby, including premature birth. Getting a flu shot is the first and most important step in protecting against flu. The flu shot given during pregnancy has been shown to protect both the mother and her baby (up to 6 months old) from flu.

7. Reach and maintain a healthy weight.

A woman who is obese (a body mass index (BMI) of 30 or higher) before pregnancy is at a higher risk for complications during pregnancy. Obesity also increases a pregnant woman's risk of several serious birth defects for her baby.

If a woman is overweight or obese, she should talk with her doctor about ways to reach a healthy weight **before** she gets pregnant.

8. Keep diabetes under control.

Poor control of diabetes during pregnancy increases the chances for birth defects and other problems for the baby. It can also cause serious complications for the woman. Proper healthcare before and during pregnancy can help prevent birth defects and other poor outcomes.

9. See a health care professional regularly.

A woman should be sure to see her doctor when planning a pregnancy and start prenatal care as soon as she thinks that she is pregnant. It is important to see the doctor regularly throughout pregnancy, so a woman should keep all her prenatal care appointments.

Pregnancy is an exciting time, but it also can be stressful. Knowing that you are doing all that you can to get ready for pregnancy, staying healthy during pregnancy, and giving your baby a healthy start in life will help you to have peace of mind.

Ten Things You Need to Know about Birth Defects

1. Did you know that birth defects are common?

Fact: Birth defects affect 1 in 33 babies every year and cause 1 in 5 infant deaths. For many babies born with a birth defect, there is no family history of the condition.

2. Did you know that a woman should take folic acid during her teens and throughout her life?

Fact: Because half of all pregnancies in the United States are not planned, all women who can become pregnant should take a vitamin with folic acid every day. Folic acid helps a baby's brain and spine develop very early in the first month of pregnancy when a woman might not know she is pregnant.

3. Did you know that many birth defects are diagnosed after a baby leaves the hospital?

Fact: Many birth defects are not found immediately at birth. A birth defect can affect how the body looks, how it works, or both. Some birth defects like cleft lip or spina bifida are easy to see. Others, like heart defects, are not.

4. Did you know that some birth defects can be diagnosed before birth?

Fact: Tests like an ultrasound and amniocentesis can detect birth defects such as spina bifida, heart defects, or Down syndrome before a baby is born. Prenatal care and screening are important because early diagnosis allows families to make decisions and plan for the future.

5. Did you know that birth defects can greatly affect the finances not only of the families involved, but of everyone?

Fact: In the United States, birth defects have accounted for over 139,000 hospital stays during a single year, resulting in $2.6 billion in hospital costs alone. Families and the government share the burden of these costs. Additional costs due to lost wages or occupational limitations can affect families as well.

6. Did you know that birth defects can be caused by many different things, not just genetics?

Fact: The cause of most birth defects is unknown. Use of cigarettes, alcohol, and other drugs, taking of some medicines; and exposure to chemicals and infectious diseases during pregnancy have been linked to birth defects. Researchers are studying the role of these factors, as well as genetics, as causes of birth defects.

7. Did you know that some birth defects can be prevented?

Fact: A woman can take some important steps before and during pregnancy to help prevent birth defects. She can take folic acid; have regular medical checkups; make sure medical conditions, such as diabetes, are under control; have tests for infectious diseases and get necessary vaccinations; and not use cigarettes, alcohol, or other drugs.

8. Did you know there are ways a pregnant woman can keep her unborn baby safe from infections?

Fact: The best way to keep an unborn baby safe from infections is for a pregnant woman to wash her hands often, especially after using the bathroom; touching raw meat, uncooked eggs, or unwashed vegetables; handling pets; gardening; or caring for small children.

9. Did you know there is no known safe amount of alcohol or safe time to drink during pregnancy?

Fact: Fetal alcohol spectrum disorders (FASDs) are a group of conditions that can occur in a person whose mother drank alcohol during pregnancy. These effects can include physical problems and problems with behavior and learning which can last a lifetime. There is no known safe amount, no safe time, and no safe type of alcohol to drink during pregnancy. FASDs are 100% preventable if a woman does not drink alcohol while pregnant.

10. Did you know that an unborn child is not always protected from the outside world?

Fact: The placenta, which attaches a baby to the mother, is not a strong barrier. When a mother uses cigarettes, alcohol, or other drugs, or is exposed to infectious diseases, her baby is exposed also. Healthy habits like taking folic acid daily and eating nutritious foods can help ensure that a child is born healthy.

Chapter 8

Cerebral Palsy

What is Cerebral Palsy?

Cerebral palsy refers to a group of neurological disorders that appear in infancy or early childhood and permanently affect body movement and muscle coordination cerebral palsy (CP) is caused by damage to or abnormalities inside the developing brain that disrupt the brain's ability to control movement and maintain posture and balance. The term *cerebral* refers to the brain; *palsy* refers to the loss or impairment of motor function.

Cerebral palsy affects the motor area of the brain's outer layer (called the cerebral cortex), the part of the brain that directs muscle movement.

In some cases, the cerebral motor cortex hasn't developed normally during fetal growth. In others, the damage is a result of injury to the brain either before, during, or after birth. In either case, the damage is not repairable and the disabilities that result are permanent.

Children with CP exhibit a wide variety of symptoms, including:

- lack of muscle coordination when performing voluntary movements (ataxia)

- stiff or tight muscles and exaggerated reflexes (spasticity)

- weakness in one or more arm or leg;

Text in this chapter is excerpted from "Cerebral Palsy," National Institute of Neurological Disorders and Stroke (NINDS), July 2, 2015.

- walking on the toes, a crouched gait, or a "scissored" gait;

- variations in muscle tone, either too stiff or too floppy;

- excessive drooling or difficulties swallowing or speaking;

- shaking (tremor) or random involuntary movements;

- delays in reaching motor skill milestones; and

- difficulty with precise movements such as writing or buttoning a shirt.

The symptoms of CP differ in type and severity from one person to the next, and may even change in an individual over time. Symptoms may vary greatly among individuals, depending on which parts of the brain have been injured. All people with cerebral palsy have problems with movement and posture, and some also have some level of intellectual disability, seizures, and abnormal physical sensations or perceptions, as well as other medical disorders. People with CP also may have impaired vision or hearing, and language, and speech problems.

CP is the leading cause of childhood disabilities, but it doesn't always cause profound disabilities. While one child with severe CP might be unable to walk and need extensive, lifelong care, another child with mild CP might be only slightly awkward and require no special assistance. The disorder isn't progressive, meaning it doesn't get worse over time. However, as the child gets older, certain symptoms may become more or less evident.

A study by the Centers for Disease Control and Prevention shows the average prevalence of cerebral palsy is 3.3 children per 1,000 live births.

There is no cure for cerebral palsy, but supportive treatments, medications, and surgery can help many individuals improve their motor skills and ability to communicate with the world.

What are the early signs?

The signs of cerebral palsy usually appear in the early months of life, although specific diagnosis may be delayed until age two years or later. Infants with CP frequently have *developmental delay*, in which they are slow to reach developmental milestones such as learning to roll over, sit, crawl, or walk. Some infants with CP have abnormal muscle tone. Decreased muscle tone (hypotonia) can make them appear relaxed, even floppy. Increased muscle tone (hypertonia) can make them seem stiff or rigid. In some cases, an early period of hypotonia will progress to hypertonia after the first 2 to 3 months of life. Children with CP may also have unusual posture or favor one side of the body when they reach, crawl, or move. It is important to note that some children *without* CP also might have some of these signs.

Some early warning signs:

In a Baby Younger Than 6 Months of Age

- His head lags when you pick him up while he's lying on his back
- He feels stiff
- He feels floppy
- When you pick him up, his legs get stiff and they cross or scissor

In a Baby Older Than 6 Months of Age

- She doesn't roll over in either direction
- She cannot bring her hands together
- She has difficulty bringing her hands to her mouth
- She reaches out with only one hand while keeping the other fisted

In a Baby Older Than 10 Months of Age

- He crawls in a lopsided manner, pushing off with one hand and leg while dragging the opposite hand and leg
- He cannot stand holding onto support

What causes cerebral palsy?

Cerebral palsy is caused by abnormal development of part of the brain or by damage to parts of the brain that control movement. This damage can occur before, during, or shortly after birth. The majority of children have *congenital cerebral palsy* CP (that is, they were born with it), although it may not be detected until months or years later. A small number of children have *acquired cerebral palsy*, which means the disorder begins after birth. Some causes of acquired cerebral palsy include brain damage in the first few months or years of life, brain infections such as bacterial meningitis or viral encephalitis, problems with blood flow to the brain, or head injury from a motor vehicle accident, a fall, or child abuse.

In many cases, the cause of cerebral palsy is unknown. Possible causes include genetic abnormalities, congenital brain malformations, maternal infections or fevers, or fetal injury, for example. The following types of brain damage may cause its characteristic symptoms:

Damage to the white matter of the brain (periventricular leukomalacia, or PVL). The white matter of the brain is responsible for transmitting signals inside the brain and to the rest of the body. Damage from PVL looks like tiny holes in the white matter of an infant's brain. These gaps in brain tissue interfere with the normal transmission of signals. Researchers have identified a period of selective vulnerability in the developing fetal brain, a period of time between 26 and 34 weeks of gestation, in which periventricular white matter is particularly sensitive to insults and injury.

Abnormal development of the brain (cerebral dysgenesis). Any interruption of the normal process of brain growth during fetal development can cause brain malformations that interfere with the transmission of brain signals. Mutations in the genes that control brain development during this early period can keep the brain from developing normally. Infections, fevers, trauma, or other conditions that cause unhealthy conditions in the womb also put an unborn baby's nervous system at risk.

Bleeding in the brain (intracranial hemorrhage). Bleeding inside the brain from blocked or broken blood vessels is commonly caused by fetal stroke. Some babies suffer a stroke while still in the womb because of blood clots in the *placenta* that block blood flow in the brain. Other types of fetal stroke are caused by malformed or weak blood vessels in the brain or by blood-clotting abnormalities. Maternal high blood pressure (hypertension) is a common medical disorder during pregnancy and is more common in babies with fetal stroke. Maternal infection, especially pelvic inflammatory disease, has also been shown to increase the risk of fetal stroke.

Severe lack of oxygen in the brain. Aphyxia, a lack of oxygen in the brain caused by an interruption in breathing or poor oxygen supply, is common for a brief period of time in babies due to the stress of labor and delivery. If the supply of oxygen is cut off or reduced for lengthy periods, an infant can develop a type of brain damage called *hypoxic-ischemic encephalopathy,* which destroys tissue in the cerebral motor cortex and other areas of the brain. This kind of damage can also be caused by severe maternal low blood pressure, rupture of the uterus, detachment of the placenta, or problems involving the umbilical cord, or severe trauma to the head during labor and delivery.

What are the risk factors?

There are some medical conditions or events that can happen during pregnancy and delivery that may increase a baby's risk of being born with cerebral palsy. These risks include:

Low birthweight and premature birth. Premature babies (born less than 37 weeks into pregnancy) and babies weighing less than 5 ½ pounds at birth have a much higher risk of developing cerebral palsy than full-term, heavier weight babies. Tiny babies born at very early gestational ages are especially at risk.

Multiple births. Twins, triplets, and other multiple births – even those born at term – are linked to an increased risk of cerebral palsy. The death of a baby's twin or triplet further increases the risk.

Infections during pregnancy. Infections such as toxoplasmosis, rubella (German measles), cytomegalovirus, and herpes, can infect the womb and placenta. Inflammation triggered by infection may then go on to damage the developing nervous system in an unborn baby. Maternal fever during pregnancy or delivery can also set off this kind of inflammatory response.

Blood type incompatibility between mother and child. R*h incompatibility* is a condition that develops when a mother's Rh blood type (either positive or negative) is different from the blood type of her baby. The mother's system doesn't tolerate the baby's different blood type and her body will begin to make antibodies that will attack and kill her baby's blood cells, which can cause brain damage.

Exposure to toxic substances. Mothers who have been exposed to toxic substances during pregnancy, such as methyl mercury, are at a heightened risk of having a baby with cerebral palsy.

Mothers with thyroid abnormalities, intellectual disability, excess protein in the urine, or seizures. Mothers with any of these conditions are slightly more likely to have a child with CP.

There are also medical conditions during labor and delivery, and immediately after delivery that act as warning signs for an increased risk of CP. However, most of these children will not develop CP. Warning signs include:

Breech presentation. Babies with cerebral palsy are more likely to be in a breech position (feet first) instead of head first at the beginning of labor. Babies who are unusually floppy as fetuses are more likely to be born in the breech position.

Complicated labor and delivery. A baby who has vascular or respiratory problems during labor and delivery may already have suffered brain damage or abnormalities.

Small for gestational age. Babies born smaller than normal for their gestational age are at risk for cerebral palsy because of factors that kept them from growing naturally in the womb.

Low Apgar score. The Apgar score is a numbered rating that reflects a newborn's physical health. Doctors periodically score a baby's heart rate, breathing, muscle tone, reflexes, and skin color during the first minutes after birth. A low score at 10-20 minutes after delivery is often considered an important sign of potential problems such as CP.

Jaundice. More than 50 percent of newborns develop jaundice (a yellowing of the skin or whites of the eyes) after birth when *bilirubin*, a substance normally found in bile, builds up faster than their livers can break it down and pass it from the body. Severe, untreated jaundice can kill brain cells and can cause deafness and CP.

Seizures. An infant who has seizures faces a higher risk of being diagnosed later in childhood with CP.

Can cerebral palsy be prevented?

Cerebral palsy related to genetic abnormalities cannot be prevented, but a few of the risk factors for congenital cerebral palsy can be managed or avoided. For example, *rubella*, or German measles, is preventable if women are vaccinated against the disease before becoming pregnant. Rh incompatibilities can also be managed early in pregnancy. Acquired cerebral palsy, often due to head injury, is often preventable using common safety tactics, such as using car seats for infants and toddlers.

How is cerebral palsy diagnosed?

Most children with cerebral palsy are diagnosed during the first 2 years of life. But if a child's symptoms are mild, it can be difficult for a doctor to make a reliable diagnosis before the age of 4 or 5.

Doctors will order a series of tests to evaluate the child's motor skills. During regular visits, the doctor will monitor the child's development, growth, muscle tone, age-appropriate motor control, hearing and vision, posture, and coordination, in order to rule out other disorders that could cause similar symptoms. Although symptoms may change over time, CP is not progressive. If a child is continuously losing motor skills, the problem more likely is a condition other than CP—such as a genetic or muscle disease, metabolism disorder, or tumors in the nervous system.

Lab tests can identify other conditions that may cause symptoms similar to those associated with CP.

Neuroimaging techniques that allow doctors to look into the brain (such as an MRI scan) can detect abnormalities that indicate a potentially treatable movement disorder. Neuroimaging methods include:

- **Cranial ultrasound** uses high-frequency sound waves to produce pictures of the brains of young babies. It is used for high-risk premature infants because it is the least intrusive of the imaging techniques, although it is not as successful as computed tomography or magnetic resonance imaging at capturing subtle changes in white matter—the type of brain tissue that is damaged in CP.

- **Computed tomography (CT)** uses X-rays to create images that show the structure of the brain and the areas of damage.

- **Magnetic resonance imaging (MRI)** uses a computer, a magnetic field, and radio waves to create an anatomical picture of the brain's tissues and structures. MRI can show the location and type of damage and offers finer levels of details than CT.

Another test, an **electroencephalogram**, uses a series of electrodes that are either taped or temporarily pasted to the scalp to detect electrical activity in the brain. Changes in the normal electrical pattern may help to identify epilepsy.

Some metabolic disorders can masquerade as CP. Most of the childhood metabolic disorders have characteristic brain abnormalities or malformations that will show up on an MRI.

Other types of disorders can also be mistaken for CP or can cause specific types of CP. For example, coagulation disorders (which prevent blood from clotting or lead to excessive clotting) can cause prenatal or perinatal strokes that damage the brain and produce symptoms characteristic of CP, most commonly hemiparetic CP. Referrals to specialists such as a child neurologist, developmental pediatrician, ophthalmologist, or otologist aid in a more accurate diagnosis and help doctors develop a specific treatment plan.

How is cerebral palsy treated?

Cerebral palsy can't be cured, but treatment will often improve a child's capabilities. Many children go on to enjoy near-normal adult lives if their disabilities are properly managed. In general, the earlier treatment begins, the better chance children have of overcoming developmental disabilities or learning new ways to accomplish the tasks that challenge them.

There is no standard therapy that works for every individual with cerebral palsy. Once the diagnosis is made, and the type of CP is determined, a team of health care professionals will work with a child and his or her parents to identify specific impairments and needs, and then develop an appropriate plan to tackle the core disabilities that affect the child's quality of life.

Physical therapy, usually begun in the first few years of life or soon after the diagnosis is made, is a cornerstone of CP treatment. Specific sets of exercises (such as resistive, or strength training programs) and activities can maintain or improve muscle strength, balance, and motor skills, and prevent contractures. Special braces (called orthotic devices) may be used to improve mobility and stretch spastic muscles.

Occupational therapy focuses on optimizing upper body function, improving posture, and making the most of a child's mobility. Occupational therapists help individuals address new ways to meet everyday activities such as dressing, going to school, and participating in day-to-day activities.

Recreation therapy encourages participation in art and cultural programs, sports, and other events that help an individual expand physical and cognitive skills and abilities. Parents of children who participate in recreational therapies usually notice an improvement in their child's speech, self-esteem, and emotional well-being.

Speech and language therapy can improve a child's ability to speak, more clearly, help with swallowing disorders, and learn new ways to communicate—using sign language and/or special communication devices such as a computer with a voice synthesizer, or a special board covered with symbols of everyday objects and activities to which a child can point to indicate his or her wishes.

Treatments for problems with eating and drooling are often necessary when children with CP have difficulty eating and drinking because they have little control over the muscles that move their mouth, jaw, and tongue. They are also at risk for breathing food or fluid into the lungs, as well as for malnutrition, recurrent lung infections, and progressive lung disease.

Do adults with cerebral palsy face special health challenges?

Premature aging. The majority of individuals with CP will experience some form of premature aging by the time they reach their 40s because of the extra stress and strain the disease puts upon their bodies. The developmental delays that often accompany CP keep some organ systems from developing to their full capacity and level of performance. As a consequence, organ systems such as the cardiovascular system (the heart, veins, and arteries) and pulmonary system (lungs) have to work harder and they age prematurely.

Functional issues at work. The day-to-day challenges of the workplace are likely to increase as an employed individual with CP reaches middle age. Some individuals will be able to continue working with accommodations such as an adjusted work schedule, assistive equipment, or frequent rest periods.

Depression. Mental health issues can also be of concern as someone with cerebral palsy grows older. The rate of depression is three to four times higher in people with disabilities such as cerebral palsy. It appears to be related not so much to the severity of their disabilities, but to how well they cope with them. The amount of emotional support someone has, how successful they are at coping with disappointment and stress, and whether or not they have an optimistic outlook about the future all have a significant impact on mental health.

Post-impairment syndrome. This syndrome is marked by a combination of pain, fatigue, and weakness due to muscle abnormalities, bone deformities, *overuse syndromes* (sometimes also called repetitive motion injuries), and arthritis. Fatigue is often a challenge, since individuals with CP may use up to three to five times the amount of energy that able-bodied people use when they walk and move about.

Osteoarthritis and degenerative arthritis. Musculoskeletal abnormalities that may not produce discomfort during childhood can cause pain in adulthood. For example, the abnormal relationships between joint surfaces and excessive joint compression can lead to the early development of painful osteoarthritis and degenerative arthritis. Individuals with CP also may have limited strength and restricted patterns of movement, which puts them at risk for overuse syndromes and *nerve entrapments*.

Pain. Individuals with CP may have pain that can be acute (usually comes on quickly and lasts a short while) or chronic, and is experienced most commonly in the hips, knees, ankles, and the upper and lower back. Individuals with spastic CP may have an increased number of painful sites and worse pain than those with other types of cerebral palsy. Preventive treatment aimed at correcting skeletal and muscle abnormalities early in life may help to avoid the progressive accumulation of stress and strain that causes pain. Dislocated hips, which are particularly likely to cause pain, can be surgically repaired.

Other medical conditions. Adults have higher than normal rates of other medical conditions secondary to their cerebral palsy, such as hypertension, incontinence, bladder dysfunction, and swallowing difficulties. Scoliosis is likely to progress after puberty, when bones have matured into their final shape and size. People with CP also have a higher incidence of bone fractures, occurring most frequently during physical therapy sessions.

Chapter 9

Cleft Lip and Palate

Cleft lip and cleft palate are birth defects that occur when a baby's lip or mouth do not form properly during pregnancy. Together, these birth defects commonly are called "orofacial clefts." These birth defects happen early during pregnancy. A baby can have a cleft lip, a cleft palate, or both a cleft lip and cleft palate.

Facial Development

Figure 9.1. *Baby with Cleft Lip*

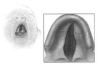

Figure 9.2. *Baby with Cleft Palate*

A baby's head forms early during pregnancy. To make the face, body tissue and special cells from each side of the head grow toward

This chapter includes excerpts from "Facts about Cleft Lip and Cleft Palate," National Center on Birth Defects and Developmental Disabilities at Centers for Disease Control and Prevention (CDC), October 20, 2014.

the center of the face and join together. This joining of tissue forms the facial features, like the lips and mouth.

Cleft Lip

The lip forms between the fourth and seventh weeks of pregnancy. A cleft lip happens if the tissue that makes up the lip does not join completely before birth. This results in an opening in the upper lip. The opening in the lip can be a small slit or it can be a large opening that goes through the lip into the nose. A cleft lip can be on one or both sides of the lip or in the middle of the lip, which occurs very rarely. Children with a cleft lip also can have a cleft palate.

Cleft Palate

The roof of the mouth (palate) is formed between the sixth and ninth weeks of pregnancy. A cleft palate happens if the tissue that makes up the roof of the mouth does not join together completely during pregnancy. For some babies, both the front and back parts of the palate are open. For other babies, only part of the palate is open.

Occurrence

CDC recently estimated that, each year in the United States, about 2,650 babies are born with a cleft palate and 4,440 babies are born with a cleft lip with or without a cleft palate. Isolated orofacial clefts, or clefts that occur with no other major birth defects, are one of the most common types of birth defects in the United States. Depending on the cleft type, the rate of isolated orofacial clefts can vary from 50% to 80%.

Causes

Like the many families of children with birth defects, CDC wants to find out what causes them. Understanding the factors that can increase the chance of having a baby with a birth defect will help us learn more about the causes. CDC coordinates, funds, and collaborates on one of the largest studies in the United States–the National Birth Defects Prevention Study–to understand the causes of and risks for birth defects, including orofacial clefts.

The causes of orofacial clefts among most infants are unknown. Some children have a cleft lip or cleft palate because of changes in their genes. Cleft lip and cleft palate are thought to be caused by a combination of genes and other factors, such as things the mother comes in contact with in her environment, or what the mother eats or drinks, or certain medications she uses during pregnancy.

Recently, CDC reported on important findings from research studies about some factors that increase the chance of having a baby with an orofacial cleft:

- Smoking – Women who smoke during pregnancy are more likely to have a baby with an orofacial cleft than women who do not smoke.

- Diabetes – Women with diabetes diagnosed before pregnancy have an increased risk of having a child with a cleft lip with or without cleft palate, compared to women who did not have diabetes.

- Use of certain medicines – Women who used certain medicines to treat epilepsy, such as topiramate or valproic acid, during the first trimester (the first 3 months) of pregnancy have an increased risk of having a baby with cleft lip with or without cleft palate, compared to women who didn't take these medicines.

Diagnosis

Orofacial clefts, especially cleft lip with or without cleft palate, can be diagnosed during pregnancy by a routine ultrasound. They can also be diagnosed after the baby is born, especially cleft palate. However, sometimes certain types of cleft palate (for example, submucous cleft palate and bifid uvula) might not be diagnosed until later in life.

Management and Treatment

Children with a cleft lip with or without a cleft palate or a cleft palate alone often have problems with feeding and speaking clearly, and can have ear infections. They also might have hearing problems and problems with their teeth. Services and treatment for children with orofacial clefts can vary depending on the severity of the cleft; the child's age and needs; and the presence of associated syndromes or other birth defects, or both.

Surgery to repair a cleft lip usually occurs in the first few months of life and is recommended within the first 12 months of life. Surgery to repair a cleft palate is recommended within the first 18 months of life or earlier if possible. Many children will need additional surgical procedures as they get older. Surgical repair can improve the look and appearance of a child's face and might also improve breathing, hearing, and speech and language development. Children born with orofacial clefts might need other types of treatments and services, such as special dental or orthodontic care or speech therapy.

Because children with orofacial clefts often require a variety of services that need to be provided in a coordinated manner throughout childhood and into adolescence and sometimes adulthood, the American Cleft Palate – Craniofacial Association recommends services and treatment by cleft and craniofacial teams. Cleft and craniofacial teams provide a coordinated approach to care for children with orofacial clefts. These teams usually consist of experienced and qualified physicians and health care providers from different specialties. Cleft and craniofacial teams and centers are located throughout the United States and other countries. Resources are available to help in choosing a cleft and craniofacial team.

With treatment, most children with orofacial clefts do well and lead a healthy life. Some children with orofacial clefts may have issues with self-esteem if they are concerned with visible differences between themselves and other children. Parent-to-parent support groups can prove to be useful for families of babies with birth defects of the head and face, such as orofacial clefts.

Chapter 10

Cystic Fibrosis

What Is Cystic Fibrosis?

Cystic fibrosis (CF), or CF, is an inherited disease of the secretory glands. Secretory glands include glands that make mucus and sweat.

"Inherited" means the disease is passed from parents to children through genes. People who have CF inherit two faulty genes for the disease—one from each parent. The parents likely don't have the disease themselves.

CF mainly affects the lungs, pancreas, liver, intestines, sinuses, and sex organs.

Overview

Mucus is a substance made by tissues that line some organs and body cavities, such as the lungs and nose. Normally, mucus is a slippery, watery substance. It keeps the linings of certain organs moist and prevents them from drying out or getting infected.

If you have CF, your mucus becomes thick and sticky. It builds up in your lungs and blocks your airways. (Airways are tubes that carry air in and out of your lungs.)

The buildup of mucus makes it easy for bacteria to grow. This leads to repeated, serious lung infections. Over time, these infections can severely damage your lungs.

Text in this chapter is excerpted from "Cystic Fibrosis," National Heart, Lung, and Blood Institute (NHLBI), December 26, 2013.

The thick, sticky mucus also can block tubes, or ducts, in your pancreas (an organ in your abdomen). As a result, the digestive enzymes that your pancreas makes can't reach your small intestine.

These enzymes help break down food. Without them, your intestines can't fully absorb fats and proteins. This can cause vitamin deficiency and malnutrition because nutrients pass through your body without being used. You also may have bulky stools, intestinal gas, a swollen belly from severe constipation, and pain or discomfort.

CF also causes your sweat to become very salty. Thus, when you sweat, you lose large amounts of salt. This can upset the balance of minerals in your blood and cause many health problems. Examples of these problems include dehydration (a lack of fluid in your body), increased heart rate, fatigue (tiredness), weakness, decreased blood pressure, heat stroke, and, rarely, death.

If you or your child has CF, you're also at higher risk for diabetes or two bone-thinning conditions called osteoporosis and osteopenia.

CF also causes infertility in men, and the disease can make it harder for women to get pregnant. (The term "infertility" refers to the inability to have children.)

Outlook

The symptoms and severity of CF vary. If you or your child has the disease, you may have serious lung and digestive problems. If the disease is mild, symptoms may not show up until the teen or adult years.

The symptoms and severity of CF also vary over time. Sometimes you'll have few symptoms. Other times, your symptoms may become more severe. As the disease gets worse, you'll have more severe symptoms more often.

Lung function often starts to decline in early childhood in people who have CF. Over time, damage to the lungs can cause severe breathing problems. Respiratory failure is the most common cause of death in people who have CF.

As treatments for CF continue to improve, so does life expectancy for those who have the disease. In recent days, some people who have CF are living into their forties or fifties, or longer.

Early treatment for CF can improve your quality of life and increase your lifespan. Treatments may include nutritional and respiratory therapies, medicines, exercise, and other treatments.

Your doctor also may recommend pulmonary rehabilitation (PR). PR is a broad program that helps improve the well-being of people who have chronic (ongoing) breathing problems.

Other Names for Cystic Fibrosis

- Cystic fibrosis of the pancreas
- Fibrocystic disease of the pancreas
- Mucoviscidosis
- Mucoviscidosis of the pancreas
- Pancreas fibrocystic disease
- Pancreatic cystic fibrosis

What Causes Cystic Fibrosis?

A defect in the CFTR gene causes cystic fibrosis (CF). This gene makes a protein that controls the movement of salt and water in and out of your body's cells. In people who have CF, the gene makes a protein that doesn't work well. This causes thick, sticky mucus and very salty sweat.

Research suggests that the CFTR protein also affects the body in other ways. This may help explain other symptoms and complications of CF.

More than a thousand known defects can affect the CFTR gene. The type of defect you or your child has may affect the severity of CF. Other genes also may play a role in the severity of the disease.

How Is Cystic Fibrosis Inherited?

Every person inherits two CFTR genes—one from each parent. Children who inherit a faulty CFTR gene from each parent will have CF.

Children who inherit one faulty CFTR gene and one normal CFTR gene are "CF carriers." CF carriers usually have no symptoms of CF and live normal lives. However, they can pass the faulty CFTR gene to their children.

The image below shows how two parents who are both CF carriers can pass the faulty CFTR gene to their children.

Who Is at Risk for Cystic Fibrosis?

Cystic fibrosis (CF) affects both males and females and people from all racial and ethnic groups. However, the disease is most common among Caucasians of Northern European descent.

CF also is common among Latinos and American Indians, especially the Pueblo and Zuni. The disease is less common among African Americans and Asian Americans.

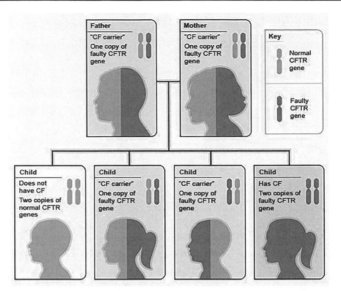

Figure 10.1. *Example of an Inheritance Pattern for Cystic Fibrosis: The image shows how CFTR genes are inherited. A person inherits two copies of the CFTR gene—one from each parent. If each parent has a normal CFTR gene and a faulty CFTR gene, each child has a 25 percent chance of inheriting two normal genes; a 50 percent chance of inheriting one normal gene and one faulty gene; and a 25 percent chance of inheriting two faulty genes.*

More than 10 million Americans are carriers of a faulty CF gene. Many of them don't know that they're CF carriers.

What Are the Signs and Symptoms of Cystic Fibrosis?

The signs and symptoms of cystic fibrosis (CF) vary from person to person and over time. Sometimes you'll have few symptoms. Other times, your symptoms may become more severe.

One of the first signs of CF that parents may notice is that their baby's skin tastes salty when kissed, or the baby doesn't pass stool when first born.

Most of the other signs and symptoms of CF happen later. They're related to how CF affects the respiratory, digestive, or reproductive systems of the body.

Respiratory System Signs and Symptoms

People who have CF have thick, sticky mucus that builds up in their airways. This buildup of mucus makes it easier for bacteria to

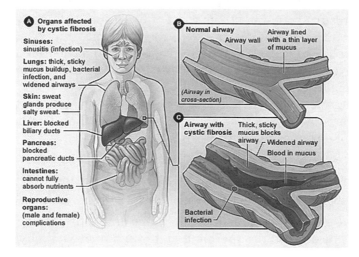

Figure 10.2. *Cystic Fibrosis: "A" shows the organs that cystic fibrosis can affect. "B" shows a cross-section of a normal airway. "C" shows an airway with cystic fibrosis. The widened airway is blocked by thick, sticky mucus that contains blood and bacteria.*

grow and cause infections. Infections can block the airways and cause frequent coughing that brings up thick sputum (spit) or mucus that's sometimes bloody.

People who have CF tend to have lung infections caused by unusual germs that don't respond to standard antibiotics. For example, lung infections caused by bacteria called mucoid Pseudomonas are much more common in people who have CF than in those who don't. An infection caused by these bacteria may be a sign of CF.

People who have CF have frequent bouts of sinusitis, an infection of the sinuses. The sinuses are hollow air spaces around the eyes, nose, and forehead. Frequent bouts of bronchitis and pneumonia also can occur. These infections can cause long-term lung damage.

As CF gets worse, you may have more serious problems, such as pneumothorax or bronchiectasis.

Some people who have CF also develop nasal polyps (growths in the nose) that may require surgery.

Digestive System Signs and Symptoms

In CF, mucus can block tubes, or ducts, in your pancreas (an organ in your abdomen). These blockages prevent enzymes from reaching your intestines.

71

As a result, your intestines can't fully absorb fats and proteins. This can cause ongoing diarrhea or bulky, foul-smelling, greasy stools. Intestinal blockages also may occur, especially in newborns. Too much gas or severe constipation in the intestines may cause stomach pain and discomfort.

A hallmark of CF in children is poor weight gain and growth. These children are unable to get enough nutrients from their food because of the lack of enzymes to help absorb fats and proteins.

As CF gets worse, other problems may occur, such as:

- Pancreatitis. This is a condition in which the pancreas become inflamed, which causes pain.

- Rectal prolapse. Frequent coughing or problems passing stools may cause rectal tissue from inside you to move out of your rectum.

- Liver disease due to inflamed or blocked bile ducts.

- Diabetes.

- Gallstones.

Reproductive System Signs and Symptoms

Men who have CF are infertile because they're born without a vas deferens. The vas deferens is a tube that delivers sperm from the testes to the penis.

Women who have CF may have a hard time getting pregnant because of mucus blocking the cervix or other CF complications.

Other Signs, Symptoms, and Complications

Other signs and symptoms of CF are related to an upset of the balance of minerals in your blood.

CF causes your sweat to become very salty. As a result, your body loses large amounts of salt when you sweat. This can cause dehydration (a lack of fluid in your body), increased heart rate, fatigue (tiredness), weakness, decreased blood pressure, heat stroke, and, rarely, death.

CF also can cause clubbing and low bone density. Clubbing is the widening and rounding of the tips of your fingers and toes. This sign develops late in CF because your lungs aren't moving enough oxygen into your bloodstream.

Low bone density also tends to occur late in CF. It can lead to bone-thinning disorders called osteoporosis and osteopenia.

How Is Cystic Fibrosis Diagnosed?

Doctors diagnose cystic fibrosis (CF) based on the results from various tests.

Newborn Screening

All States screen newborns for CF using a genetic test or a blood test. The genetic test shows whether a newborn has faulty CFTR genes. The blood test shows whether a new born's pancreas is working properly.

Sweat Test

If a genetic test or blood test suggests CF, a doctor will confirm the diagnosis using a sweat test. This test is the most useful test for diagnosing CF. A sweat test measures the amount of salt in sweat.

For this test, the doctor triggers sweating on a small patch of skin on an arm or leg. He or she rubs the skin with a sweat-producing chemical and then uses an electrode to provide a mild electrical current. This may cause a tingling or warm feeling.

Sweat is collected on a pad or paper and then analyzed. The sweat test usually is done twice. High salt levels confirm a diagnosis of CF.

Other Tests

If you or your child has CF, your doctor may recommend other tests, such as:

- Genetic tests to find out what type of CFTR defect is causing your CF.

- A chest X-ray. This test creates pictures of the structures in your chest, such as your heart, lungs, and blood vessels. A chest X-ray can show whether your lungs are inflamed or scarred, or whether they trap air.

- A sinus X-ray. This test may show signs of sinusitis, a complication of CF.

- Lung function tests. These tests measure how much air you can breathe in and out, how fast you can breathe air out, and how well your lungs deliver oxygen to your blood.

- A sputum culture. For this test, your doctor will take a sample of your sputum (spit) to see whether bacteria are growing in it.

If you have bacteria called mucoid Pseudomonas, you may have more advanced CF that needs aggressive treatment.

Prenatal Screening

If you're pregnant, prenatal genetic tests can show whether your fetus has CF. These tests include amniocentesis and chorionic villus sampling (CVS).

In amniocentesis, your doctor inserts a hollow needle through your abdominal wall into your uterus. He or she removes a small amount of fluid from the sac around the baby. The fluid is tested to see whether both of the baby's CFTR genes are normal.

In CVS, your doctor threads a thin tube through the vagina and cervix to the placenta. The doctor removes a tissue sample from the placenta using gentle suction. The sample is tested to see whether the baby has CF.

Cystic Fibrosis Carrier Testing

People who have one normal CFTR gene and one faulty CFTR gene are CF carriers. CF carriers usually have no symptoms of CF and live normal lives. However, carriers can pass faulty CFTR genes on to their children.

If you have a family history of CF or a partner who has CF (or a family history of it) and you're planning a pregnancy, you may want to find out whether you're a CF carrier.

A genetics counselor can test a blood or saliva sample to find out whether you have a faulty CF gene. This type of testing can detect faulty CF genes in 9 out of 10 cases.

How Is Cystic Fibrosis Treated?

Cystic fibrosis (CF) has no cure. However, treatments have greatly improved in recent years. The goals of CF treatment include:

- Preventing and controlling lung infections
- Loosening and removing thick, sticky mucus from the lungs
- Preventing or treating blockages in the intestines
- Providing enough nutrition
- Preventing dehydration (a lack of fluid in the body)

Depending on the severity of CF, you or your child may be treated in a hospital.

Specialists Involved

If you or your child has CF, you may be treated by a CF specialist. This is a doctor who is familiar with the complex nature of CF.

Often, a CF specialist works with a medical team of nurses, physical therapists, dietitians, and social workers. CF specialists often are located at major medical centers.

The United States also has more than 100 CF Care Centers. These centers have teams of doctors, nurses, dietitians, respiratory therapists, physical therapists, and social workers who have special training related to CF care. Most CF Care Centers have pediatric and adult programs or clinics.

Treatment for Lung Problems

The main treatments for lung problems in people who have CF are chest physical therapy (CPT), exercise, and medicines. Your doctor also may recommend a pulmonary rehabilitation (PR) program.

Chest Physical Therapy

CPT also is called chest clapping or percussion. It involves pounding your chest and back over and over with your hands or a device to loosen the mucus from your lungs so that you can cough it up.

You might sit down or lie on your stomach with your head down while you do CPT. Gravity and force help drain the mucus from your lungs.

Some people find CPT hard or uncomfortable to do. Several devices have been developed that may help with CPT, such as:

- An electric chest clapper, known as a mechanical percussor.

- An inflatable therapy vest that uses high-frequency airwaves to force the mucus that's deep in your lungs toward your upper airways so you can cough it up.

- A small, handheld device that you exhale through. The device causes vibrations that dislodge the mucus.

- A mask that creates vibrations that help break the mucus loose from your airway walls.

Breathing techniques also may help dislodge mucus so you can cough it up. These techniques include forcing out a couple of short breaths or deeper breaths and then doing relaxed breathing. This may help loosen the mucus in your lungs and open your airways.

Exercise

Aerobic exercise that makes you breathe harder can help loosen the mucus in your airways so you can cough it up. Exercise also helps improve your overall physical condition.

However, CF causes your sweat to become very salty. As a result, your body loses large amounts of salt when you sweat. Thus, your doctor may recommend a high-salt diet or salt supplements to maintain the balance of minerals in your blood.

If you exercise regularly, you may be able to cut back on your CPT. However, you should check with your doctor first.

Medicines

If you have CF, your doctor may prescribe antibiotics, anti-inflammatory medicines, bronchodilators, or medicines to help clear the mucus. These medicines help treat or prevent lung infections, reduce swelling and open up the airways, and thin mucus. If you have mutations in a gene called G551D, which occurs in about 5 percent of people who have CF, your doctor may prescribe the oral medicine ivacaftor (approved for people with CF who are 6 years of age and older).

Antibiotics are the main treatment to prevent or treat lung infections. Your doctor may prescribe oral, inhaled, or intravenous (IV) antibiotics.

Oral antibiotics often are used to treat mild lung infections. Inhaled antibiotics may be used to prevent or control infections caused by the bacteria mucoid Pseudomonas. For severe or hard-to-treat infections, you may be given antibiotics through an IV tube (a tube inserted into a vein). This type of treatment may require you to stay in a hospital.

Anti-inflammatory medicines can help reduce swelling in your airways due to ongoing infections. These medicines may be inhaled or oral.

Bronchodilators help open the airways by relaxing the muscles around them. These medicines are inhaled. They're often taken just before CPT to help clear mucus out of your airways. You also may take bronchodilators before inhaling other medicines into your lungs.

Your doctor may prescribe medicines to reduce the stickiness of your mucus and loosen it up. These medicines can help clear out mucus, improve lung function, and prevent worsening lung symptoms.

Treatments for Advanced Lung Disease

If you have advanced lung disease, you may need oxygen therapy. Oxygen usually is given through nasal prongs or a mask.

If other treatments haven't worked, a lung transplant may be an option if you have severe lung disease. A lung transplant is surgery to remove a person's diseased lung and replace it with a healthy lung from a deceased donor.

Pulmonary Rehabilitation

Your doctor may recommend PR as part of your treatment plan. PR is a broad program that helps improve the well-being of people who have chronic (ongoing) breathing problems.

PR doesn't replace medical therapy. Instead, it's used with medical therapy and may include:

- Exercise training

- Nutritional counseling

- Education on your lung disease or condition and how to manage it

- Energy-conserving techniques

- Breathing strategies

- Psychological counseling and/or group support

PR has many benefits. It can improve your ability to function and your quality of life. The program also may help relieve your breathing problems. Even if you have advanced lung disease, you can still benefit from PR.

Treatment for Digestive Problems

CF can cause many digestive problems, such as bulky stools, intestinal gas, a swollen belly, severe constipation, and pain or discomfort. Digestive problems also can lead to poor growth and development in children.

Nutritional therapy can improve your strength and ability to stay active. It also can improve growth and development in children. Nutritional therapy also may make you strong enough to resist some lung infections. A nutritionist can help you create a nutritional plan that meets your needs.

In addition to having a well-balanced diet that's rich in calories, fat, and protein, your nutritional therapy may include:

- Oral pancreatic enzymes to help you digest fats and proteins and absorb more vitamins.

- Supplements of vitamins A, D, E, and K to replace the fat-soluble vitamins that your intestines can't absorb.

- High-calorie shakes to provide you with extra nutrients.

- A high-salt diet or salt supplements that you take before exercising.

- A feeding tube to give you more calories at night while you're sleeping. The tube may be threaded through your nose and throat and into your stomach. Or, the tube may be placed directly into your stomach through a surgically made hole. Before you go to bed each night, you'll attach a bag with a nutritional solution to the entrance of the tube. It will feed you while you sleep.

Other treatments for digestive problems may include enemas and mucus-thinning medicines to treat intestinal blockages. Sometimes surgery is needed to remove an intestinal blockage.

Your doctor also may prescribe medicines to reduce your stomach acid and help oral pancreatic enzymes work better.

Treatments for Cystic Fibrosis Complications

A common complication of CF is diabetes. The type of diabetes associated with CF often requires different treatment than other types of diabetes.

Another common CF complication is the bone-thinning disorder osteoporosis. Your doctor may prescribe medicines that prevent your bones from losing their density.

Living with Cystic Fibrosis

If you or your child has cystic fibrosis (CF), you should learn as much as you can about the disease. Work closely with your doctors to learn how to manage CF.

Ongoing Care

Having ongoing medical care by a team of doctors, nurses, and respiratory therapists who specialize in CF is important. These specialists often are located at major medical centers or CF Care Centers.

The United States has more than 100 CF Care Centers. Most of these centers have pediatric and adult programs or clinics.

It's standard to have CF checkups every 3 months. Talk with your doctor about whether you should get an annual flu shot and other vaccines. Take all of your medicines as your doctor prescribes. In between checkups, be sure to contact your doctor if you have:

- Blood in your mucus, increased amounts of mucus, or a change in the color or consistency of your mucus.

- Decreased energy or appetite.

- Severe constipation or diarrhea, severe abdominal pain, or vomit that's dark green.

- A fever, which is a sign of infection. (However, you may still have a serious infection that needs treatment even if you don't have a fever.)

Chapter 11

Muscular Dystrophy

Introduction

The first historical account of muscular dystrophy appeared in 1830, when Sir Charles Bell wrote an essay about an illness that caused progressive weakness in boys. Six years later, another scientist reported on two brothers who developed generalized weakness, muscle damage, and replacement of damaged muscle tissue with fat and connective tissue. At that time the symptoms were thought to be signs of tuberculosis.

In the 1850s, descriptions of boys who grew progressively weaker, lost the ability to walk, and died at an early age became more prominent in medical journals. In the following decade, French neurologist Guillaume Duchenne gave a comprehensive account of 13 boys with the most common and severe form of the disease (which now carries his name—Duchenne muscular dystrophy). It soon became evident that the disease had more than one form, and that these diseases affected people of either sex and of all ages.

What is muscular dystrophy?

Muscular dystrophy (MD) refers to a group of more than 30 genetic diseases that cause progressive weakness and degeneration of skeletal muscles used during voluntary movement. The word dystrophy is

Text in this chapter is excerpted from "Muscular Dystrophy: Hope Through Research," National Institute of Neurological Disorders and Stroke (NINDS), September 24, 2015.

derived from the Greek *dys*, which means "difficult" or "faulty," and *troph*, or "nourish." These disorders vary in age of onset, severity, and pattern of affected muscles. All forms of MD grow worse as muscles progressively degenerate and weaken. Many individuals eventually lose the ability to walk.

Some types of MD also affect the heart, gastrointestinal system, endocrine glands, spine, eyes, brain, and other organs. Respiratory and cardiac diseases may occur, and some people may develop a swallowing disorder. MD is not contagious and cannot be brought on by injury or activity.

What causes MD?

All of the muscular dystrophies are inherited and involve a mutation in one of the thousands of genes that program proteins critical to muscle integrity. The body's cells don't work properly when a protein is altered or produced in insufficient quantity (or sometimes missing completely). Many cases of MD occur from spontaneous mutations that are not found in the genes of either parent, and this defect can be passed to the next generation.

Genes are like blueprints: they contain coded messages that determine a person's characteristics or traits. They are arranged along 23 rod-like pairs of *chromosomes*, with one half of each pair being inherited from each parent. Each half of a chromosome pair is similar to the other, except for one pair, which determines the sex of the individual. Muscular dystrophies can be inherited in three ways:

- *Autosomal dominant* inheritance occurs when a child receives a normal gene from one parent and a defective gene from the other parent. Autosomal means the genetic mutation can occur on any of the 22 non-sex chromosomes in each of the body's cells. Dominant means only one parent needs to pass along the abnormal gene in order to produce the disorder. In families where one parent carries a defective gene, each child has a 50 percent chance of inheriting the gene and therefore the disorder. Males and females are equally at risk and the severity of the disorder can differ from person to person.

- *Autosomal recessive* inheritance means that both parents must carry and pass on the faulty gene. The parents each have one defective gene but are not affected by the disorder. Children in these families have a 25 percent chance of inheriting both copies of the defective gene and a 50 percent chance of inheriting one gene and therefore becoming a carrier, able to pass along the defect to their children. Children of either sex can be affected by this pattern of inheritance.

* *X-linked* (or sex-linked) recessive inheritance occurs when a mother carries the affected gene on one of her two X chromosomes and passes it to her son (males always inherit an X chromosome from their mother and a Y chromosome from their father, while daughters inherit an X chromosome from each parent). Sons of carrier mothers have a 50 percent chance of inheriting the disorder. Daughters also have a 50 percent chance of inheriting the defective gene but usually are not affected, since the healthy X chromosome they receive from their father can offset the faulty one received from their mother. Affected fathers cannot pass an X-linked disorder to their sons but their daughters will be carriers of that disorder. Carrier females occasionally can exhibit milder symptoms of MD.

How does MD affect muscles?

Muscles are made up of thousands of muscle fibers. Each fiber is actually a number of individual cells that have joined together during development and are encased by an outer membrane. Muscle fibers that make up individual muscles are bound together by connective tissue.

Muscles are activated when an impulse, or signal, is sent from the brain through the spinal cord and peripheral nerves (nerves that connect the central nervous system to sensory organs and muscles) to the neuromuscular junction (the space between the nerve fiber and the muscle it activates). There, a release of the chemical acetylcholine triggers a series of events that cause the muscle to contract.

The muscle fiber membrane contains a group of proteins—called the *dystrophin-glycoprotein* complex—which prevents damage as muscle fibers contract and relax. When this protective membrane is damaged, muscle fibers begin to leak the protein *creatine kinase* (needed for the chemical reactions that produce energy for muscle contractions) and take on excess calcium, which causes further harm. Affected muscle fibers eventually die from this damage, leading to progressive muscle degeneration.

Although MD can affect several body tissues and organs, it most prominently affects the integrity of muscle fibers. The disease causes muscle degeneration, progressive weakness, fiber death, fiber branching and splitting, phagocytosis (in which muscle fiber material is broken down and destroyed by scavenger cells), and, in some cases, chronic or permanent shortening of tendons and muscles. Also, overall muscle strength and tendon reflexes are usually lessened or lost due to replacement of muscle by connective tissue and fat.

Are there other MD-like conditions?

There are many other heritable diseases that affect the muscles, the nerves, or the neuromuscular junction. Such diseases as inflammatory *myopathy*, progressive muscle weakness, and cardiomyopathy (heart muscle weakness that interferes with pumping ability) may produce symptoms that are very similar to those found in some forms of MD), but they are caused by different genetic defects. The differential diagnosis for people with similar symptoms includes congenital myopathy, spinal muscular atrophy, and congenital myasthenic syndromes. The sharing of symptoms among multiple neuromuscular diseases, and the prevalence of sporadic cases in families not previously affected by MD, often makes it difficult for people with MD to obtain a quick diagnosis. Gene testing can provide a definitive diagnosis for many types of MD, but not all genes have been discovered that are responsible for some types of MD. Some individuals may have signs of MD, but carry none of the currently recognized genetic mutations. Studies of other related muscle diseases may, however, contribute to what we know about MD.

How do the muscular dystrophies differ?

There are nine major groups of the muscular dystrophies. The disorders are classified by the extent and distribution of muscle weakness, age of onset, rate of progression, severity of symptoms, and family history (including any pattern of inheritance). Although some forms of MD become apparent in infancy or childhood, others may not appear until middle age or later. Overall, incidence rates and severity vary, but each of the dystrophies causes progressive skeletal muscle deterioration, and some types affect cardiac muscle.

How are the muscular dystrophies treated?

There is no specific treatment that can stop or reverse the progression of any form of MD. All forms of MD are genetic and cannot be prevented at this time, aside from the use of prenatal screening interventions. However, available treatments are aimed at keeping the person independent for as long as possible and prevent complications that result from weakness, reduced mobility, and cardiac and respiratory difficulties. Treatment may involve a combination of approaches, including physical therapy, drug therapy, and surgery. The available treatments are sometimes quite effective and can have a significant impact on life expectancy and quality of life.

Assisted ventilation is often needed to treat respiratory muscle weakness that accompanies many forms of MD, especially in the later stages. Air that includes supplemental oxygen is fed through a flexible mask (or, in some cases, a tube inserted through the esophagus and into the lungs) to help the lungs inflate fully. Since respiratory difficulty may be most extreme at night, some individuals may need overnight ventilation. Many people prefer non-invasive ventilation, in which a mask worn over the face is connected by a tube to a machine that generates intermittent bursts of forced air that may include supplemental oxygen. Some people with Duchenne MD, especially those who are overweight, may develop obstructive sleep apnea and require nighttime ventilation. Individuals on a ventilator may also require the use of a gastric feeding tube.

Drug therapy may be prescribed to delay muscle degeneration. Corticosteroids such as prednisone can slow the rate of muscle deterioration in Duchenne MD and help children retain strength and prolong independent walking by as much as several years. However, these medicines have side effects such as weight gain, facial changes, loss of linear (height) growth, and bone fragility that can be especially troubling in children. Immunosuppressive drugs such as cyclosporine and azathioprine can delay some damage to dying muscle cells. Drugs that may provide short-term relief from myotonia (muscle spasms and weakness) include mexiletine; phenytoin; baclofen, which blocks signals sent from the spinal cord to contract the muscles; dantrolene, which interferes with the process of muscle contraction; and quinine. (Drugs for myotonia may not be effective in myotonic MD but work well for myotonia congenita, a genetic neuromuscular disorder characterized by the slow relaxation of the muscles.) Respiratory infections may be treated with antibiotics.

Physical therapy can help prevent deformities, improve movement, and keep muscles as flexible and strong as possible. Options include passive stretching, postural correction, and exercise. A program is developed to meet the individual's needs. Therapy should begin as soon as possible following diagnosis, before there is joint or muscle tightness.

- Passive stretching can increase joint flexibility and prevent contractures that restrict movement and cause loss of function. When done correctly, passive stretching is not painful. The therapist or other trained health professional slowly moves the joint as far as possible and maintains the position for about 30 seconds. The movement is repeated several times during the session. Passive stretching on children may be easier following a warm bath or shower.

- Regular, moderate exercise can help people with MD maintain range of motion and muscle strength, prevent muscle atrophy, and delay the development of contractures. Individuals with a weakened diaphragm can learn coughing and deep breathing exercises that are designed to keep the lungs fully expanded.

- Postural correction is used to counter the muscle weakness, contractures, and spinal irregularities that force individuals with MD into uncomfortable positions. When possible, individuals should sit upright, with feet at a 90-degree angle to the floor. Pillows and foam wedges can help keep the person upright, distribute weight evenly, and cause the legs to straighten. Armrests should be at the proper height to provide support and prevent leaning.

- Support aids such as wheelchairs, splints and braces, other orthopedic appliances, and overhead bed bars (trapezes) can help maintain mobility. Braces are used to help stretch muscles and provide support while keeping the person ambulatory. Spinal supports can help delay scoliosis. Night splints, when used in conjunction with passive stretching, can delay contractures. Orthotic devices such as standing frames and swivel walkers help people remain standing or walking for as long as possible, which promotes better circulation and improves calcium retention in bones.

- Repeated low-frequency bursts of electrical stimulation to the thigh muscles may produce a slight increase in strength in some boys with Duchenne MD, though this therapy has not been proven to be effective.

Occupational therapy may help some people deal with progressive weakness and loss of mobility. Some individuals may need to learn new job skills or new ways to perform tasks while other persons may need to change jobs. Assistive technology may include modifications to home and workplace settings and the use of motorized wheelchairs, wheelchair accessories, and adaptive utensils.

Speech therapy may help individuals whose facial and throat muscles have weakened. Individuals can learn to use special communication devices, such as a computer with voice synthesizer

Dietary changes have not been shown to slow the progression of MD. Proper nutrition is essential, however, for overall health. Limited mobility or inactivity resulting from muscle weakness can contribute to obesity, dehydration, and constipation. A high-fiber, high-protein, low-calorie diet combined with recommended fluid intake may help. Feeding techniques can help people with MD who have a swallowing disorder and find it difficult to pass from or liquid from the mouth to the stomach.

Corrective surgery is often performed to ease complications from MD.

- Tendon or muscle-release surgery is recommended when a contracture becomes severe enough to lock a joint or greatly impair movement. The procedure, which involves lengthening a tendon or muscle to free movement, is usually performed under general anesthesia. Rehabilitation includes the use of braces and physical therapy to strengthen muscles and maintain the restored range of motion. A period of immobility is often needed after these orthopedic procedures, thus the benefits of the procedure should be weighed against the risk of this period of immobility, as the latter may lead to a setback.

- Individuals with either Emery-Dreifuss or myotonic dystrophy may require a pacemaker at some point to treat cardiac problems.

- Surgery to reduce the pain and postural imbalance caused by scoliosis may help some individuals. Scoliosis occurs when the muscles that support the spine begin to weaken and can no longer keep the spine straight. The spinal curve, if too great, can interfere with breathing and posture, causing pain. One or more metal rods may need to be attached to the spine to increase strength and improve posture. Another option is spinal fusion, in which bone is inserted between the vertebrae in the spine and allowed to grow, fusing the vertebrae together to increase spinal stability.

- People with myotonic dystrophy often develop cataracts, a clouding of the lens of the eye that blocks light. Cataract surgery involves removing the cloudy lens to improve the person's ability to see.

What is the prognosis?

The prognosis varies according to the type of MD and the speed of progression. Some types are mild and progress very slowly, allowing normal life expectancy, while others are more severe and result in functional disability and loss of ambulation. Life expectancy often depends on the degree of muscle weakness, as well as the presence and severity of respiratory and/or cardiac complications.

Chapter 12

Spina Bifida

Introduction

The human nervous system develops from a small, specialized plate of cells along the back of an embryo (called the neural plate). Early in development, the edges of this plate begin to curl up toward each other, creating the neural tube—a narrow sheath that closes to form the brain and spinal cord of the embryo. As development progresses, the top of the tube becomes the brain and the remainder becomes the spinal cord. This process is usually complete by the 28th day of pregnancy. But if problems occur during this process, the result can be brain disorders called *neural tube defects*, including *spina bifida*.

What is spina bifida?

Spina bifida, which literally means "cleft spine," is characterized by the incomplete development of the brain, spinal cord, and/or meninges (the protective covering around the brain and spinal cord). It is the most common neural tube defect in the United States—affecting 1,500 to 2,000 of the more than 4 million babies born in the country each year. An estimated 166,000 individuals with spina bifida live in the United States.

Text in this chapter is excerpted from "Spina Bifida Fact Sheet," National Institute of Neurological Disorders and Stroke (NINDS), June 2013.

What are the different types of spina bifida?

There are four types of spina bifida: occulta, closed neural tube defects, meningocele, and myelomeningocele.

Occulta is the mildest and most common form in which one or more vertebrae are malformed. The name "occulta," which means "hidden," indicates that a layer of skin covers the malformation, or opening in the vertebrae. This form of spina bifida, present in 10-20 percent of the general population, rarely causes disability or symptoms.

Closed neural tube defects make up the second type of spina bifida. This form consists of a diverse group of defects in which the spinal cord is marked by malformations of fat, bone, or meninges. In most instances there are few or no symptoms; in others the malformation causes incomplete paralysis with urinary and bowel dysfunction.

In the third type, *meningocele*, spinal fluid and meninges protrude through an abnormal vertebral opening; the malformation contains no neural elements and may or may not be covered by a layer of skin. Some individuals with meningocele may have few or no symptoms while others may experience such symptoms as complete paralysis with bladder and bowel dysfunction.

Myelomeningocele, the fourth form, is the most severe and occurs when the spinal cord/neural elements are exposed through the opening in the spine, resulting in partial or complete paralysis of the parts of the body below the spinal opening. The impairment may be so severe that the affected individual is unable to walk and may have bladder and bowel dysfunction.

What causes spina bifida?

The exact cause of spina bifida remains a mystery. No one knows what disrupts complete closure of the neural tube, causing this malformation to develop. Scientists suspect the factors that cause spina bifida are multiple: genetic, nutritional, and environmental factors all play a role. Research studies indicate that insufficient intake of folic acid—a common B vitamin—in the mother's diet is a key factor in causing spina bifida and other neural tube defects. Prenatal vitamins typically contain folic acid as well as other vitamins.

What are the signs and symptoms of spina bifida?

The symptoms of spina bifida vary from person to person, depending on the type and level of involvement. Closed neural tube defects are often recognized early in life due to an abnormal tuft or clump of hair

90

or a small dimple or birthmark on the skin at the site of the spinal malformation.

Meningocele and myelomeningocele generally involve a fluid-filled sac—visible on the back—protruding from the spinal canal. In meningocele, the sac may be covered by a thin layer of skin. In most cases of myelomeningocele, there is no layer of skin covering the sac and an area of abnormally developed spinal cord tissue is usually exposed.

What are the complications of spina bifida?

Complications of spina bifida can range from minor physical problems with little functional impairment to severe physical and mental disabilities. It is important to note, however, that most people with spina bifida are of normal intelligence. Spina bifida's impact is determined by the size and location of the malformation, whether it covered, and which spinal nerves are involved. All nerves located below the malformation are affected to some degree. Therefore, the higher the malformation occurs on the back, the greater the amount of nerve damage and loss of muscle function and sensation.

In addition to abnormal sensation and paralysis, another neurological complication associated with spina bifida is Chiari II malformation—a condition common in children with myelomeningocele—in which the brain stem and the cerebellum (hindbrain) protrude downward into the spinal canal or neck area. This condition can lead to compression of the spinal cord and cause a variety of symptoms including difficulties with feeding, swallowing, and breathing control; choking; and changes in upper arm function (stiffness, weakness).

Chiari II malformation may also result in a blockage of cerebrospinal fluid, causing a condition called *hydrocephalus*, which is an abnormal buildup of cerebrospinal fluid in and around the brain. Cerebrospinal fluid is a clear liquid that surrounds the brain and spinal cord. The buildup of fluid puts damaging pressure on these structures. Hydrocephalus is commonly treated by surgically implanting a shunt—a hollow tube—in the brain to drain the excess fluid into the abdomen.

Some newborns with myelomeningocele may develop meningitis, an infection in the meninges. Meningitis may cause brain injury and can be life-threatening.

Children with both myelomeningocele and hydrocephalus may have learning disabilities, including difficulty paying attention, problems with language and reading comprehension, and trouble learning math.

Additional problems such as latex allergies, skin problems, gastrointestinal conditions, and depression may occur as children with spina bifida get older.

How is it diagnosed?

In most cases, spina bifida is diagnosed prenatally, or before birth. However, some mild cases may go unnoticed until after birth (postnatal). Very mild forms (spinal bifida occulta), in which there are no symptoms, may never be detected.

How is spina bifida treated?

There is no cure for spina bifida. The nerve tissue that is damaged cannot be repaired, nor can function be restored to the damaged nerves. Treatment depends on the type and severity of the disorder. Generally, children with the mildest form need no treatment, although some may require surgery as they grow.

The key early priorities for treating myelomeningocele are to prevent infection from developing in the exposed nerves and tissue through the spinal defect, and to protect the exposed nerves and structures from additional trauma. Typically, a child born with spina bifida will have surgery to close the defect and minimize the risk of infection or further trauma within the first few days of life.

Selected medical centers continue to perform fetal surgery for treatment of myelomeningocele through a National Institutes of Health experimental protocol (Management of Myelomeningocele Study, or MOMS). Fetal surgery is performed in utero (within the uterus) and involves opening the mother's abdomen and uterus and sewing shut the abnormal opening over the developing baby's spinal cord. Some doctors believe the earlier the defect is corrected, the better the baby's outcome. Although the procedure cannot restore lost neurological function, it may prevent additional loss from occurring.

The surgery is considered experimental and there are risks to the fetus as well as to the mother. The major risks to the fetus are those that might occur if the surgery stimulates premature delivery, such as organ immaturity, brain hemorrhage, and death. Risks to the mother include infection, blood loss leading to the need for transfusion, gestational diabetes, and weight gain due to bed rest.

Still, the benefits of fetal surgery are promising, and include less exposure of the vulnerable spinal nerve tissue and bone to the intra-uterine environment, in particular the amniotic fluid, which is considered toxic. As an added benefit, doctors have discovered that the procedure may affect the way the fetal hindbrain develops in utero, decreasing the severity of certain complications—such as Chiari II and hydrocephalus—and in some cases, eliminating the need for surgery to implant a shunt.

Twenty to fifty percent of children with myelomeningocele develop a condition called progressive tethering, or tethered cord syndrome; their spinal cord become fastened to an immovable structure—such as overlying membranes and vertebrae—causing the spinal cord to become abnormally stretched with the child's growth. This condition can cause loss of muscle function to the legs, as well as changes in bowel and bladder function. Early surgery on a tethered spinal cord may allow the child to return to their baseline level of functioning and prevent further neurological deterioration.

Some children will need subsequent surgeries to manage problems with the feet, hips, or spine. Individuals with hydrocephalus generally will require additional surgeries to replace the shunt, which can be outgrown or become clogged or infected.

Some individuals with spina bifida require assistive devices such as braces, crutches, or wheelchairs. The location of the malformation on the spine often indicates the type of assistive devices needed. Children with a defect high on the spine will have more extensive paralysis and will often require a wheelchair, while those with a defect lower on the spine may be able to use crutches, leg braces, or walkers. Beginning special exercises for the legs and feet at an early age may help prepare the child for walking with those braces or crutches when he or she is older.

Treatment for bladder and bowel problems typically begins soon after birth, and may include bladder catheterizations and bowel management regimens.

Can the disorder be prevented?

Folic acid, also called folate, is an important B vitamin in the development of a healthy fetus. Although taking this vitamin cannot guarantee having a healthy baby, it can help. Recent studies have shown that by adding folic acid to their diets, women of childbearing age significantly reduce the risk of having a child with a neural tube defect, such as spina bifida. Therefore, it is recommended that all women of childbearing age consume 400 micrograms of folic acid daily. Foods high in folic acid include dark green vegetables, egg yolks, and some fruits. Many foods—such as some breakfast cereals, enriched breads, flours, pastas, rice, and other grain products—are now fortified with folic acid. Many multivitamins contain the recommended dosage of folic acid as well.

Women who already have a child with spina bifida, who have spina bifida themselves, or who have already had a pregnancy affected by any neural tube defect are at greater risk of having another child with spina bifida or another neural tube defect; 5-10 times the risk to the general population. These women may benefit from taking a higher daily dose of folic acid before they consider becoming pregnant.

What is the prognosis?

Children with spina bifida can lead active lives. Prognosis, activity, and participation depend on the number and severity of abnormalities and associated personal and environmental factors. Most children with the disorder have normal intelligence and can walk, often with assistive devices. If learning problems develop, appropriate educational interventions are helpful.

Chapter 13

Arthritis

Why are disabilities and limitations important for people with arthritis?

Arthritis impacts function and mobility that can result in activity and other limitations, and is the most common cause of disability among U.S. adults.

Arthritis-Related Disabilities among U.S. Adults

A CDC study showed that 47.5 million U.S. adults (21.8%) reported a disability. Arthritis or rheumatism was the most common cause of disability, while back or spine problems and heart trouble round out the top three causes. Among adults reporting a disability, the most commonly identified limitations were difficulty climbing a flight of stairs (21.7 million, 10.0%) and walking 3 city blocks (22.5 million, 10.3%). That means that 1 in 10 adults have trouble walking a distance equal to walking from the parking lot to the back of a large store or through a mall.

What Is Arthritis?

Many people start to feel pain and stiffness in their bodies over time. Sometimes their hands or knees or shoulders get sore and are

This chapter includes excerpts from "About Arthritis Disabilities and Limitations," Centers for Disease Control and Prevention (CDC), November 5, 2014; text from "Living With Arthritis: Health Information Basics for You and Your Family," National Institute of Arthritis and Musculoskeletal and Skin Diseases (NIAMS), July 2014.

hard to move and may become swollen. These people may have arthritis. Arthritis may be caused by inflammation of the tissue lining the joints. Some signs of inflammation include redness, heat, pain, and swelling. These problems are telling you that something is wrong.

Joints are places where two bones meet, such as your elbow or knee. Over time, in some types of arthritis but not in all, the joints involved can become severely damaged.

There are different types of arthritis. In some diseases in which arthritis occurs, other organs, such as your eyes, your chest, or your skin, can also be affected. Some people may worry that arthritis means they won't be able to work or take care of their children and their family. Others think that you just have to accept things like arthritis.

It's true that arthritis can be painful. But there are things you can do to feel better. This publication tells you some facts about arthritis and gives you some ideas about what to do so you can keep doing many of the things you enjoy.

What Are the Types of Arthritis?

There are several types of arthritis. The two most common ones are osteoarthritis and rheumatoid arthritis.

Osteoarthritis is the most common form of arthritis. This condition usually comes with age and most often affects the fingers, knees, and hips. Sometimes osteoarthritis follows an injury to a joint. For example, a young person might hurt his knee badly playing soccer. Or someone might fall or be injured in a car accident. Then, years after the individual's knee has apparently healed, he might get arthritis in his knee joint.

Rheumatoid arthritis happens when the body's own defense system doesn't work properly. It affects joints and bones (often of the hands and feet), and may also affect internal organs and systems. You may feel sick or tired, and you may have a fever.

Another common type of arthritis, gout, is caused by crystals that build up in the joints. It usually affects the big toe, but many other joints may be affected.

Arthritis is seen with many other conditions. These include:

- **lupus**, in which the body's defense system can harm the joints, the heart, the skin, the kidneys, and other organs

- **an infection** that gets into a joint and destroys the cushion between the bones.

Do I Have Arthritis?

Pain is the way your body tells you that something is wrong. Most types of arthritis cause pain in your joints. You might have trouble moving around. Some kinds of arthritis can affect different parts of your body. So, along with pain in your joints, you may:

- have a fever
- lose weight
- have trouble breathing
- get a rash or itch.

These symptoms may also be signs of other illnesses.

What Can I Do?

Go see a doctor. Many people use herbs or medicines that you can buy without a prescription for pain. You should tell your doctor if you do. Only a doctor can tell if you have arthritis or a related condition and what to do about it. It's important not to wait.

You'll need to tell the doctor how you feel and where you hurt. The doctor will examine you and may take X-rays (pictures) of your bones or joints. The X-rays don't hurt and aren't dangerous. You may also have to give a little blood for tests that will help the doctor decide what kind of arthritis you may have.

How Will the Doctor Help?

After the doctor knows what kind of arthritis you have, he or she will talk with you about the best way to treat it. The doctor may give you a prescription for medicine that will help with the pain, stiffness, and inflammation. Health insurance or public assistance may help you pay for the medicine, doctor visits, tests, and X-rays.

How Should I Use Arthritis Medicine?

Before you leave the doctor's office, make sure you ask about the best way to take the medicine the doctor prescribes. For example, you may need to take some medicines with milk, or you may need to eat something just before or after taking them, to make sure they don't upset your stomach.

You should also ask how often to take the medicine or to put cream on the spots that bother you. Creams might make your skin and joints feel better. Sometimes, though, they can make your skin burn or break out in a rash. If this happens, call the doctor.

What If I Still Hurt?

Sometimes you might still have pain after using your medicine. Here are some things to try.

- Take a warm shower.

- Do some gentle stretching exercises.

- Use an ice pack on the sore area.

- Rest the sore joint.

If you still hurt after using your medicine correctly and doing one or more of these things, call your doctor. Another kind of medicine might work better for you. Some people can also benefit from surgery, such as joint replacement.

You Can Feel Better!

Arthritis can damage your joints, internal organs, and skin. There are things you can do to keep the damage from getting worse. They might also make you feel better:

- Try to keep your weight down. Too much weight can make your knees and hips hurt.

- Exercise. Moving all of your joints will help you. The doctor or nurse can show you how to move more easily. Going for a walk every day will help, too.

- Take your medicines when and how you are supposed to. They can help reduce pain and stiffness.

- Try taking a warm shower in the morning.

- See your doctor regularly.

Chapter 14

Disability Caused by Injury and Trauma

Chapter Contents

Section 14.1

Back Pain

Text in this section is excerpted from "Low Back Pain Fact Sheet,"
National Institute of Neurological Disorders and Stroke (NINDS),
August 3, 2015.

If you have lower back pain, you are not alone. About 80 percent of adults experience low back pain at some point in their lifetimes. It is the most common cause of job-related disability and a leading contributor to missed work days. In a large survey, more than a quarter of adults reported experiencing low back pain during the past 3 months.

Men and women are equally affected by low back pain, which can range in intensity from a dull, constant ache to a sudden, sharp sensation that leaves the person incapacitated. Pain can begin abruptly as a result of an accident or by lifting something heavy, or it can develop over time due to age-related changes of the spine. Sedentary lifestyles also can set the stage for low back pain, especially when a weekday routine of getting too little exercise is punctuated by strenuous weekend workout.

Most low back pain is acute, or short term, and lasts a few days to a few weeks. It tends to resolve on its own with self-care and there is no residual loss of function. The majority of acute low back pain is mechanical in nature, meaning that there is a disruption in the way the components of the back (the spine, muscle, intervertebral discs, and nerves) fit together and move.

Subacute low back pain is defined as pain that lasts between 4 and 12 weeks.

Chronic back pain is defined as pain that persists for 12 weeks or longer, even after an initial injury or underlying cause of acute low back pain has been treated. About 20 percent of people affected by acute low back pain develop chronic low back pain with persistent symptoms at one year. In some cases, treatment successfully relieves chronic low back pain, but in other cases pain persists despite medical and surgical treatment.

The magnitude of the burden from low back pain has grown worse in recent years. In 1990, a study ranking the most burdensome conditions in the U.S. in terms of mortality or poor health as a result of disease put low back pain in sixth place; in 2010, low back pain jumped to third place, with only ischemic heart disease and chronic obstructive pulmonary disease ranking higher.

What structures make up the back?

The lower back where most back pain occurs includes the five vertebrae (referred to as L1-L5) in the lumbar region, which supports much of the weight of the upper body. The spaces between the vertebrae are maintained by round, rubbery pads called intervertebral discs that act like shock absorbers throughout the spinal column to cushion the bones as the body moves. Bands of tissue known as ligaments hold the vertebrae in place, and tendons attach the muscles to the spinal column. Thirty-one pairs of nerves are rooted to the spinal cord and they control body movements and transmit signals from the body to the brain.

What causes lower back pain?

The vast majority of low back pain is mechanical in nature. In many cases, low back pain is associated with spondylosis, a term that refers to the general degeneration of the spine associated with normal wear and tear that occurs in the joints, discs, and bones of the spine as people get older. Some examples of mechanical causes of low back pain include:

- **Sprains and strains** account for most acute back pain. Sprains are caused by overstretching or tearing ligaments, and strains are tears in tendon or muscle. Both can occur from twisting or lifting something improperly, lifting something too heavy, or overstretching. Such movements may also trigger spasms in back muscles, which can also be painful.

- **Intervertebral disc degeneration** is one of the most common mechanical causes of low back pain, and it occurs when the usually rubbery discs lose integrity as a normal process of aging. In a healthy back, intervertebral discs provide height and allow bending, flexion, and torsion of the lower back. As the discs deteriorate, they lose their cushioning ability.

- **Herniated or ruptured discs** can occur when the intervertebral discs become compressed and bulge outward (herniation) or rupture, causing low back pain.

- **Radiculopathy** is a condition caused by compression, inflammation and/or injury to a spinal nerve root. Pressure on the nerve root results in pain, numbness, or a tingling sensation that travels or radiates to other areas of the body that are served by that nerve. Radiculopathy may occur when spinal stenosis or a herniated or ruptured disc compresses the nerve root.

- **Sciatica** is a form of radiculopathy caused by compression of the sciatic nerve, the large nerve that travels through the buttocks and extends down the back of the leg. This compression causes shock-like or burning low back pain combined with pain through the buttocks and down one leg, occasionally reaching the foot. In the most extreme cases, when the nerve is pinched between the disc and the adjacent bone, the symptoms may involve not only pain, but numbness and muscle weakness in the leg because of interrupted nerve signaling. The condition may also be caused by a tumor or cyst that presses on the sciatic nerve or its roots.

- **Spondylolisthesis** is a condition in which a vertebra of the lower spine slips out of place, pinching the nerves exiting the spinal column.

- **A traumatic injury**, such as from playing sports, car accidents, or a fall can injure tendons, ligaments or muscle resulting in low back pain. Traumatic injury may also cause the spine to become overly compressed, which in turn can cause an intervertebral disc to rupture or herniate, exerting pressure on any of the nerves rooted to the spinal cord. When spinal nerves become compressed and irritated, back pain and sciatica may result.

- **Spinal stenosis** is a narrowing of the spinal column that puts pressure on the spinal cord and nerves that can cause pain or numbness with walking and over time leads to leg weakness and sensory loss.

- **Skeletal irregularities** include scoliosis, a curvature of the spine that does not usually cause pain until middle age; lordosis, an abnormally accentuated arch in the lower back; and other congenital anomalies of the spine.

Low back pain is rarely related to serious underlying conditions, but when these conditions do occur, they require immediate medical attention. Serious underlying conditions include:

- **Infections** are not a common cause of back pain. However, infections can cause pain when they involve the vertebrae, a condition called osteomyelitis; the intervertebral discs, called discitis; or the sacroiliac joints connecting the lower spine to the pelvis, called sacroiliitis.

- **Tumors** are a relatively rare cause of back pain. Occasionally, tumors begin in the back, but more often they appear in the back as a result of cancer that has spread from elsewhere in the body.

- **Cauda equina syndrome** is a serious but rare complication of a ruptured disc. It occurs when disc material is pushed into the spinal canal and compresses the bundle of lumbar and sacral nerve roots, causing loss of bladder and bowel control. Permanent neurological damage may result if this syndrome is left untreated.

- **Abdominal aortic aneurysms** occur when the large blood vessel that supplies blood to the abdomen, pelvis, and legs becomes abnormally enlarged. Back pain can be a sign that the aneurysm is becoming larger and that the risk of rupture should be assessed.

- **Kidney stones** can cause sharp pain in the lower back, usually on one side.

Other underlying conditions that predispose people to low back pain include:

- **Inflammatory diseases of the joints** such as arthritis, including osteoarthritis and rheumatoid arthritis as well as spondylitis, an inflammation of the vertebrae, can also cause low back pain. Spondylitis is also called spondyloarthritis or spondyloarthropathy.

- **Osteoporosis** is a metabolic bone disease marked by a progressive decrease in bone density and strength, which can lead to painful fractures of the vertebrae.

- **Endometriosis** is the buildup of uterine tissue in places outside the uterus.

- **Fibromyalgia**, a chronic pain syndrome involving widespread muscle pain and fatigue.

What are the risk factors for developing low back pain?

Beyond underlying diseases, certain other risk factors may elevate one's risk for low back pain, including:

Age: The first attack of low back pain typically occurs between the ages of 30 and 50, and back pain becomes more common with advancing age. As people grow older, loss of bone strength from osteoporosis can lead to fractures, and at the same time, muscle elasticity and tone decrease. The intervertebral discs begin to lose fluid and flexibility with age, which decreases their ability to cushion the vertebrae. The risk of spinal stenosis also increases with age.

Fitness level: Back pain is more common among people who are not physically fit. Weak back and abdominal muscles may not properly support the spine. "Weekend warriors"—people who go out and exercise a lot after being inactive all week—are more likely to suffer painful back injuries than people who make moderate physical activity a daily habit. Studies show that low-impact aerobic exercise is beneficial for the maintaining the integrity of intervertebral discs.

Pregnancy is commonly accompanied by low back pain, which results from pelvic changes and alterations in weight loading. Back symptoms almost always resolve postpartum.

Weight gain: Being overweight, obese, or quickly gaining significant amounts of weight can put stress on the back and lead to low back pain.

Genetics: Some causes of back pain, such as ankylosing spondylitis, a form of arthritis that involves fusion of the spinal joints leading to some immobility of the spine, have a genetic component.

Occupational risk factors: Having a job that requires heavy lifting, pushing, or pulling, particularly when it involves twisting or vibrating the spine, can lead to injury and back pain. An inactive job or a desk job may also lead to or contribute to pain, especially if you have poor posture or sit all day in a chair with inadequate back support.

Mental health factors: Pre-existing mental health issues such as anxiety and depression can influence how closely one focuses on their pain as well as their perception of its severity. Pain that becomes chronic also can contribute to the development of such psychological factors. Stress can affect the body in numerous ways, including causing muscle tension.

Backpack overload in children: Low back pain unrelated to injury or other known cause is unusual in pre-teen children. However, a backpack overloaded with schoolbooks and supplies can strain the back and cause muscle fatigue. The American Academy of Orthopaedic Surgeons recommends that a child's backpack should weigh no more than 15 to 20 percent of the child's body weight.

How is back pain treated?

Treatment for low back pain generally depends on whether the pain is acute or chronic. In general, surgery is recommended only if there is evidence of worsening nerve damage and when diagnostic tests indicate structural changes for which corrective surgical procedures have been developed.

Conventionally used treatments and their level of supportive evidence include:

Hot or cold packs have never been proven to quickly resolve low back injury; however, they may help ease pain and reduce inflammation for people with acute, subacute, or chronic pain, allowing for greater mobility among some individuals.

Activity: Bed rest should be limited. Individuals should begin stretching exercises and resume normal daily activities as soon as possible, while avoiding movements that aggravate pain. Strong evidence shows that persons who continue their activities without bed rest following onset of low back pain appeared to have better back flexibility than those who rested in bed for a week. Other studies suggest that bed rest alone may make back pain worse and can lead to secondary complications such as depression, decreased muscle tone, and blood clots in the legs.

Strengthening exercises, beyond general daily activities, are not advised for acute low back pain, but may be an effective way to speed recovery from chronic or subacute low back pain. Maintaining and building muscle strength is particularly important for persons with skeletal irregularities. Health care providers can provide a list of beneficial exercises that will help improve coordination and develop proper posture and muscle balance. Evidence supports short- and long-term benefits of yoga to ease chronic low back pain.

Physical therapy programs to strengthen core muscle groups that support the low back, improve mobility and flexibility, and promote proper positioning and posture are often used in combinations with other interventions.

Medications: A wide range of medications are used to treat acute and chronic low back pain. Some are available over the counter (OTC); others require a physician's prescription. Certain drugs, even those available OTC, may be unsafe during pregnancy, may interact with other medications, cause side effects, or lead to serious adverse effects such as liver damage or gastrointestinal ulcers and bleeding. Consultation with a health care provider is advised before use.

Can back pain be prevented?

Recurring back pain resulting from improper body mechanics is often preventable by avoiding movements that jolt or strain the back, maintaining correct posture, and lifting objects properly. Many work-related injuries are caused or aggravated by stressors such as heavy lifting, contact stress (repeated or constant contact between soft body tissue and a hard or sharp object), vibration, repetitive motion, and awkward posture. Using ergonomically designed furniture and equipment to protect the body from injury at home and in the workplace may reduce the risk of back injury.

The use of lumbar supports in the form of wide elastic bands that can be tightened to provide support to the lower back and abdominal muscles to prevent low back pain remains controversial. Such supports are widely used despite a lack of evidence showing that they actually prevent pain. Multiple studies have determined that the use of lumbar supports provides no benefit in terms of the prevention and treatment of back pain. Although there have been anecdotal case reports of injury reduction among workers using lumbar support belts, many companies that have back belt programs also have training and ergonomic awareness programs. The reported injury reduction may be related to a combination of these or other factors. Furthermore, some caution is advised given that wearing supportive belts may actually lead to or aggravate back pain by causing back muscles to weaken from lack of use.

Recommendations for keeping one's back healthy

Following any period of prolonged inactivity, a regimen of low-impact exercises is advised. Speed walking, swimming, or stationary bike riding 30 minutes daily can increase muscle strength and flexibility. Yoga also can help stretch and strengthen muscles and improve posture. Consult a physician for a list of low-impact, age-appropriate exercises that are specifically targeted to strengthening lower back and abdominal muscles.

- Always stretch before exercise or other strenuous physical activity.

- Don't slouch when standing or sitting. The lower back can support a person's weight most easily when the curvature is reduced. When standing, keep your weight balanced on your feet.

- At home or work, make sure work surfaces are at a comfortable height.

- Sit in a chair with good lumbar support and proper position and height for the task. Keep shoulders back. Switch sitting positions often and periodically walk around the office or gently stretch muscles to relieve tension. A pillow or rolled-up towel placed behind the small of the back can provide some lumbar support. During prolonged periods of sitting, elevate feet on a low stool or a stack of books.

- Wear comfortable, low-heeled shoes.

- Sleeping on one's side with the knees drawn up in a fetal position can help open up the joints in the spine and relieve pressure by reducing the curvature of the spine. Always sleep on a firm surface.

- Don't try to lift objects that are too heavy. Lift from the knees, pull the stomach muscles in, and keep the head down and in line with a straight back. When lifting, keep objects close to the body. Do not twist when lifting.

- Maintain proper nutrition and diet to reduce and prevent excessive weight gain, especially weight around the waistline that taxes lower back muscles. A diet with sufficient daily intake of calcium, phosphorus, and vitamin D helps to promote new bone growth.

- Quit smoking. Smoking reduces blood flow to the lower spine, which can contribute to spinal disc degeneration. Smoking also increases the risk of osteoporosis and impedes healing. Coughing due to heavy smoking also may cause back pain.

Section 14.2

Spinal Cord Injury: Understanding Paralysis, Paraplegia, and Quadriplegia

Text in this section is excerpted from "Spinal Cord Injury: Hope
Through Research," National Institute of Neurological Disorders and
Stroke (NINDS), July 2013.

Introduction

Until World War II, a serious spinal cord injury (SCI) usually meant
certain death. Anyone who survived such injury relied on a wheelchair
for mobility in a world with few accommodations and faced an ongoing
struggle to survive secondary complications such as breathing problems, blood clots, kidney failure, and pressure sores. By the middle of
the twentieth century, new antibiotics and novel approaches to preventing and treating bed sores and urinary tract infections revolution-
ized care after spinal cord injury. This greatly expanded life expectancy
and required new strategies to maintain the health of people living
with chronic paralysis. New standards of care for treating spinal cord
injuries were established: reposition the spine, fix the bones in place
to prevent further damage, and rehabilitate disabilities with exercise.

Recently, improved emergency care for people with spinal cord injuries, antibiotics to treat infections, and aggressive rehabilitation can
minimize damage to the nervous system and restore function to varying degrees. Advances in research are giving doctors and people living
with SCI hope that spinal cord injuries will eventually be repairable.
With new surgical techniques and developments in spinal nerve regen-
eration, cell replacement, neuroprotection, and neurorehabilitation,
the future for spinal cord injury survivors looks brighter than ever.

Facts and Figures about Spinal Cord Injury

- There are an estimated 12,000 spinal cord injuries every year in
  the United States alone.

- More than a quarter of a million Americans are currently living
  with spinal cord injuries.

- The cost of managing the care of spinal cord injury patients is $3 billion each year.

- The largest proportion of spinal cord injuries (36.5 percent) occurs during car accidents; more than a quarter are the result of falls; and the rest are due to acts of violence (primarily gunshot wounds), sporting accidents, and other less common causes.

- The average age at injury has risen and is now 42.6 years.

- 80 percent of spinal cord injury patients are men.

What is a spinal cord injury?

The vertebrae normally protect the soft tissues of the spinal cord, but they can be broken or dislocated in a variety of ways that puts harmful pressure on the spinal cord. Injuries can occur at any level of the spinal cord. The segment of the cord that is injured, and the severity of the damage to the nervous tissue, will determine which body functions are compromised or lost. An injury to a part of the spinal cord causes physiological consequences to parts of the body controlled by nerves at and below the level of the injury.

Motor vehicle accidents and catastrophic falls are the most common causes of physical trauma that breaks, crushes, or presses on the vertebrae and can cause irreversible damage at the corresponding level of the spinal cord and below. Severe trauma to the cervical cord results in paralysis of most of the body, including the arms and legs, and is called *tetraplegia* (though the older term, *quadriplegia*, is still in common use). Trauma to the thoracic nerves in the upper, middle, or lower back results in paralysis of the trunk and lower extremities, called *paraplegia*.

Penetrating injuries, such as gunshot or knife wounds, damage the spinal cord; however, most traumatic injuries do not completely sever the spinal cord. Instead, an injury is more likely to cause fractures and compression of the vertebrae, which then crush and destroy the axons that carry signals up and down the spinal cord. A spinal cord injury can damage a few, many, or almost all of the axons that cross the site of injury. A variety of cells located in and around the injury site may also die. Some injuries in which there is little or no nerve cell death but only pressure-induced blockage of nerve signaling or only demyelination without axonal damage will allow almost complete recovery. Others in which there is complete cell death across even a thin horizontal level of the spinal cord will result in complete paralysis.

What immediate treatments are available?

Injury to the spine isn't always obvious. Any injury that involves the head and neck, pelvic fractures, penetrating injuries in the area of the spine, or injuries that result from falling from heights should raise concerns regarding an unstable spinal column. Until imaging of the spine is done at an emergency or trauma center, people who might have spine injury should be cared for as if any significant movement of the neck or back could cause further damage.

At the accident scene, emergency personnel will immobilize the head and neck to prevent movement, put a rigid collar around the neck, and carefully place the person on a rigid backboard to prevent further damage to the spinal cord. Sedation may be given to relax the person and prevent movement. A breathing tube may be inserted if the injury is to the high cervical cord and the individual is at risk of respiratory arrest.

At the hospital or trauma center, realigning the spine using a rigid brace or axial traction (using a mechanical force to stretch the spine and relieve pressure on the spinal cord) is usually done as soon as possible to stabilize the spine and prevent additional damage. Fractured vertebrae, bone fragments, herniated discs, or other objects compressing the spinal column may need to be surgically removed. Spinal decompression surgery to relieve pressure within the spinal column also may be necessary in the days after injury. Results of a neurosurgical study show that, in some cases, earlier surgery is associated with better functional recovery.

Section 14.3

Traumatic Brain Injury

This section includes excerpts from "Traumatic Brain Injury in the United States: Fact Sheet," Centers for Disease Control and Prevention (CDC), February 24, 2014; text from "Severe Traumatic Brain Injury," Centers for Disease Control and Prevention (CDC), March 4, 2014; and text from "Prevention," Centers for Disease Control and Prevention (CDC), April 15, 2013.

Overview

Traumatic brain injury (TBI) is a major cause of death and disability in the United States, contributing to about 30% of all injury deaths. Every day, 138 people in the United States die from injuries that include TBI. Those who survive a TBI can face effects lasting a few days to disabilities which may last the rest of their lives. Effects of TBI can include impaired thinking or memory, movement, sensation (e.g., vision or hearing), or emotional functioning (e.g., personality changes, depression). These issues not only affect individuals but can have lasting effects on families and communities.

What is a TBI?

A TBI is caused by a bump, blow, or jolt to the head or a penetrating head injury that disrupts the normal function of the brain. Not all blows or jolts to the head result in a TBI. The severity of a TBI may range from "mild" (i.e., a brief change in mental status or consciousness) to "severe" (i.e., an extended period of unconsciousness or memory loss after the injury). Most TBIs that occur each year are mild, commonly called concussions.

How big is the problem?

- In 2010, about 2.5 million emergency department (ED) visits, hospitalizations, or deaths were associated with TBI—either alone or in combination with other injuries—in the United States.

- TBI contributed to the deaths of more than 50,000 people.

- TBI was a diagnosis in more than 280,000 hospitalizations and 2.2 million ED visits. These consisted of TBI alone or TBI in combination with other injuries.

- Over the past decade (2001–2010), while rates of TBI-related ED visits increased by 70%, hospitalization rates only increased by 11% and death rates decreased by 7%.

- In 2009, an estimated 248,418 children (age 19 or younger) were treated in U.S. EDs for sports and recreation-related injuries that included a diagnosis of concussion or TBI.3

- From 2001 to 2009, the rate of ED visits for sports and recreation-related injuries with a diagnosis of concussion or TBI, alone or in combination with other injuries, rose 57% among children (age 19 or younger).

What are the leading causes of TBI?

- From 2006–2010, falls were the leading cause of TBI, accounting for 40% of all TBIs in the United States that resulted in an ED visit, hospitalization, or death. Falls disproportionately affect the youngest and oldest age groups:

- More than half (55%) of TBIs among children 0 to 14 years were caused by falls.

- More than two-thirds (81%) of TBIs in adults aged 65 and older are caused by falls.

- Unintentional blunt trauma (e.g., being hit by an object) was the second leading cause of TBI, accounting for about 15% of TBIs in the United States for 2006–2010.

- Close to a quarter (24%) of all TBIs in children less than 15 years of age were related to blunt trauma

- Among all age groups, motor vehicle crashes were the third overall leading cause of TBI (14%). When looking at just TBI-related deaths, motor vehicle crashes were the second leading cause of TBI-related deaths (26%) for 2006–2010.

- About 10% of all TBIs are due to assaults. They accounted for 3% of TBIs in children less than 15 years of age and 1.4% of TBIs in adults 65 years and older for 2006–2010. About 75% of all assaults associated with TBI occur in persons 15 to 44 years of age.

Risk factors for TBI

Among TBI-related deaths in 2006–2010:

- Men were nearly three times as likely to die as women.

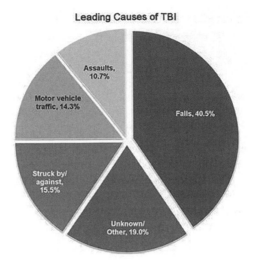

Figure 14.1. *Leading causes of TBI*

- Rates were highest for persons 65 years and older.
- The leading cause of TBI-related death varied by age.
- Falls were the leading cause of death for persons 65 years or older.
- Motor vehicle crashes were the leading cause for children and young adults ages 5-24 years.
- Assaults were the leading cause for children ages 0-4.

Among non-fatal TBI-related injuries for 2006–2010:
- Men had higher rates of TBI hospitalizations and ED visits than women.
- Hospitalization rates were highest among persons aged 65 years and older.
- Rates of ED visits were highest for children aged 0-4 years.
- Falls were the leading cause of TBI-related ED visits for all but one age group.
- Assaults were the leading cause of TBI-related ED visits for persons 15 to 24 years of age.

The leading cause of TBI-related hospitalizations varied by age:
- Falls were the leading cause among children ages 0-14 and adults 45 years and older.

- Motor vehicle crashes were the leading cause of hospitalizations for adolescents and persons ages 15-44 years.

Severe Traumatic Brain Injury

Each year, TBIs contribute to a substantial number of deaths and cases of permanent disability. In fact, TBI is a contributing factor to a third (30%) of all injury-related deaths in the United States. In 2010, approximately 2.5 million people sustained a traumatic brain injury.

A severe TBI not only impacts the life of an individual and their family, but it also has a large societal and economic toll. The estimated economic cost of TBI in 2010, including direct and indirect medical costs, is estimated to be approximately $76.5 billion. Additionally, the cost of fatal TBIs and TBIs requiring hospitalization, many of which are severe, account for approximately 90% of the total TBI medical costs.

Types of Severe TBI

There are two types of severe TBI, each described below by associated causes:

Closed – an injury to the brain caused by movement of the brain within the skull. Causes may include falls, motor vehicle crash, or being struck by or with an object.

Penetrating – an injury to the brain caused by a foreign object entering the skull. Causes may include firearm injuries or being struck with a sharp object.

> The Glasgow Coma Scale (GCS), a clinical tool designed to assess coma and impaired consciousness, is one of the most commonly used severity scoring systems. Persons with GCS scores of 3 to 8 are classified with a severe TBI, those with scores of 9 to 12 are classified with a moderate TBI, and those with scores of 13 to 15 are classified with a mild TBI. Other classification systems include the Abbreviated Injury Scale (AIS), the Trauma Score, and the Abbreviated Trauma Score. Despite their limitations, these systems are crucial to understanding the clinical management and the likely outcomes of this injury as the prognosis for milder forms of TBIs is better than for moderate or severe TBIs.

Potential Affects of Severe TBI

A non-fatal severe TBI may result in an extended period of uncon-sciousness (coma) or amnesia after the injury. For individuals hospi-talized after a TBI, almost half (43%) have a related disability one year after the injury. A TBI may lead to a wide range of short- or long-term issues affecting:

- **Cognitive Function** (e.g., attention and memory)

- **Motor function** (e.g., extremity weakness, impaired coordina-tion and balance)

- **Sensation** (e.g., hearing, vision, impaired perception and touch)

- **Emotion** (e.g., depression, anxiety, aggression, impulse control, personality changes)

Approximately 5.3 million Americans are living with a TBI-related disability and the consequences of severe TBI can affect all aspects of an individual's life. This can include relationships with family and friends, as well as their ability to work or be employed, do household tasks, drive, and/or participate in other activities of daily living.

Fast Facts

Falls are the leading cause of TBI and recent data shows that the number of fall-related TBIs among children aged 0-4 years and in older adults aged 75 years or older is increasing.

Among all age groups, motor vehicle crashes and traffic-re-lated incidents result in the largest percentage of TBI-related deaths (31.8%).

People aged 65 years old and older have the highest rates of TBI-related hospitalizations and death.

Shaken Baby Syndrome (SBS), a form of abusive head trauma (AHT) and inflicted traumatic brain injury (ITBI), is a leading cause of child maltreatment deaths in the United States.

CDC's research and programs work to reduce severe TBI and its consequences by developing and evaluating clinical guidelines, con-ducting surveillance, implementing primary prevention and education strategies, and developing evidence-based interventions to save lives and reduce morbidity from this injury.

Chapter 15

Sensory Disabilities

Chapter Contents

Section 15.1

Hearing Loss

This section includes excerpts from "Hearing Loss," National Institute on Aging (NIA), March 2, 2015; and text from "Age-Related Hearing Loss," National Institute on Deafness and Other Communication Disorders (NIDCD), November 2013.

How Do I Know If I Have Hearing Loss?

See your doctor if you:

- Have trouble hearing over the telephone

- Find it hard to follow conversations when two or more people are talking

- Often ask people to repeat what they are saying

- Need to turn up the TV volume so loud that others complain

- Have a problem hearing because of background noise

- Think that others seem to mumble

- Can't understand when women and children speak to you

Types of Hearing Loss

Hearing loss can have many different causes. Here are two kinds of hearing loss common in older people:

Presbycusis is a common type of hearing loss that comes on slowly as a person gets older. It seems to run in families and affects hearing in both ears. The degree of hearing loss varies from person to person. Are you starting to have trouble hearing someone on the phone? That could be an early sign of this type of hearing loss.

Tinnitus causes a ringing, roaring, or hissing noise in your ear. Tinnitus can go hand-in-hand with many types of hearing loss. It can also be a sign of other health problems, such as high blood pressure or allergies. Often it is unclear what causes tinnitus, which may come and go, disappear quickly, or be permanent.

Other Hearing Loss Problems

Loud noise is one of the most common causes of hearing loss. Noise from lawn mowers, snow blowers, or loud music can damage the inner ear. This can result in permanent hearing loss. You can prevent most noise-related hearing loss. Protect yourself by turning down the sound on your stereo, television, or headphones; move away from loud noise; or use earplugs or other ear protection.

Ear wax or fluid buildup can block sounds that are carried from the eardrum to the inner ear. If wax blockage is a problem, try using mild treatments, such as mineral oil, baby oil, glycerin, or commercial ear drops to soften ear wax. A punctured eardrum can also cause hearing loss. The eardrum can be damaged by infection, pressure, or putting objects in the ear, including cotton-tipped swabs. See your doctor if you have pain or fluid draining from the ear.

Viruses and bacteria, a heart condition, stroke, brain injury, or a tumor may affect your hearing. If you have hearing problems caused by a new medication, check with your doctor to see if another medicine can be used.

Sudden deafness is a medical emergency that may be curable if treated in time. See a doctor right away.

Talk to Your Doctor

Your family doctor may be able to diagnose and treat your hearing problem. Or, your doctor may refer you to other experts. For example:

- A doctor who specializes in medical problems of the ear, nose, and throat is an otorhinolaryngologist, also called an ENT doctor.

- An audiologist has special training in hearing loss and treatment options.

- A hearing aid specialist conducts and evaluates basic hearing tests, offers counseling, and fits and tests hearing aids.

What Devices Can Help?

Hearing aids. Hearing aids are electronic, battery-run devices that make sounds louder. There are many types of hearing aids. Before buying a hearing aid, ask if your health insurance will cover the cost. Also ask if you can have a trial period so you can make sure the device is right for you. An audiologist or hearing aid specialist will show you how to use your hearing aid.

119

Hearing aids should fit comfortably in your ear. You may need several visits with the hearing aid specialist to get it right. Hearing aids may need repairs, and batteries have to be changed on a regular basis. Remember, when you buy a hearing aid, you are buying both a product and a service.

Assistive devices. Other products can also help improve your hearing:

- Alert systems can work with doorbells, smoke detectors, and alarm clocks to send you visual signals or vibrations. For example, a flashing light could let you know someone is at the door or the phone is ringing, or a vibrating alarm clock under your pillow could wake you in the morning. Some people rely on the vibration setting on their cell phones to alert them to calls.

- Telephone amplifying devices can make it easier to use the phone.

- TV and radio listening systems can let you hear the TV or radio without being bothered by background noise or needing to turn up the volume.

Cochlear implants. These electronic devices are for people with severe hearing loss. They don't work for all types of hearing loss.

Devices That Help You Hear Better

Analog hearing aids make certain sounds louder and other sounds lower, making it easier to follow conversations.

Digital hearing aids give you some choice over what sounds are louder or softer. By controlling some background noise, you may hear conversations more easily.

Telecoil refers to magnetic coil in a hearing aid that helps you hear when talking on the telephone or in buildings that have special sound systems.

Induction loop systems work if you have a hearing aid or a cochlear implant with telecoils. Ask if this type of system is available at public places such as auditoriums, movie theaters, churches, synagogues, and meeting spaces where microphones are used.

What Can I Do If I Have Trouble Hearing?

- Let people know you have a hearing problem.

- Ask people to face you and to speak more slowly and clearly. Also, ask them to speak louder without shouting.

- Pay attention to what is being said and to facial expressions or gestures.

- Let the person talking know if you do not understand what he or she said.

- Ask the person speaking to reword a sentence and try again.

How Can I Help a Person with Hearing Loss?

Here are some tips you can use when talking with someone who has a hearing problem:

- In a group, include people with hearing loss in the conversation.

- Find a quiet place to talk to help reduce background noise, especially in restaurants and at social gatherings.

- Stand in good lighting and use facial expressions or gestures to give clues.

- Face the person and speak clearly.

- Speak a little more loudly than normal, but don't shout.

- Speak at a reasonable speed.

- Do not hide your mouth, eat, or chew gum while speaking.

- Repeat yourself if necessary, using different words.

- Try to make sure only one person talks at a time.

- Be patient. Stay positive and relaxed.

- Ask how you can help.

Many people develop hearing problems as they grow older. Currently, there are many ways to improve your hearing. The best way to handle the problem is to find professional help as soon as you notice you are having trouble hearing.

What is age-related hearing loss?

Age-related hearing loss (presbycusis) is the loss of hearing that gradually occurs in most of us as we grow older. It is one of the most common conditions affecting older and elderly adults.

Approximately one in three people in the United States between the ages of 65 and 74 has hearing loss, and nearly half of those older than 75 have difficulty hearing. Having trouble hearing can make it hard to understand and follow a doctor's advice, respond to warnings, and hear phones, doorbells, and smoke alarms. Hearing loss can also make it hard to enjoy talking with family and friends, leading to feelings of isolation.

Age-related hearing loss most often occurs in both ears, affecting them equally. Because the loss is gradual, if you have age-related hearing loss you may not realize that you've lost some of your ability to hear.

There are many causes of age-related hearing loss. Most commonly, it arises from changes in the inner ear as we age, but it can also result from changes in the middle ear, or from complex changes along the nerve pathways from the ear to the brain. Certain medical conditions and medications may also play a role.

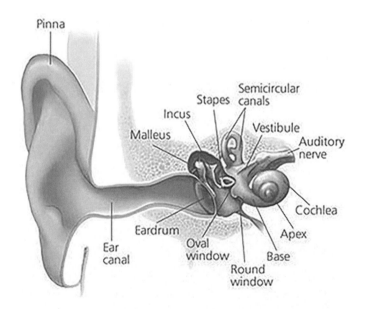

Figure 15.1. *The auditory system*

Why do we lose our hearing as we get older?

Many factors can contribute to hearing loss as you get older. It can be difficult to distinguish age-related hearing loss from hearing loss that can occur for other reasons, such as long-term exposure to noise.

Noise-induced hearing loss is caused by long-term exposure to sounds that are either too loud or last too long. This kind of noise exposure can damage the sensory hair cells in your ear that allow you to hear. Once these hair cells are damaged, they do not grow back and your ability to hear is diminished.

Conditions that are more common in older people, such as high blood pressure or diabetes, can contribute to hearing loss. Medications that are toxic to the sensory cells in your ears (for example, some chemotherapy drugs) can also cause hearing loss.

Rarely, age-related hearing loss can be caused by abnormalities of the outer ear or middle ear. Such abnormalities may include reduced function of the tympanic membrane (the eardrum) or reduced function of the three tiny bones in the middle ear that carry sound waves from the tympanic membrane to the inner ear.

Most older people have a combination of both age-related hearing loss and noise-induced hearing loss.

Can I prevent age-related hearing loss?

At this time, scientists don't know how to prevent age-related hearing loss. However, you can protect yourself from noise-induced hearing loss by protecting your ears from sounds that are too loud and last too long. It's important to be aware of potential sources of damaging noises, such as loud music, firearms, snowmobiles, lawn mowers, and leaf blowers. Avoiding loud noises, reducing the amount of time you're exposed to loud noise, and protecting your ears with ear plugs or ear muffs are easy things you can do to protect your hearing and limit the amount of hearing you might lose as you get older.

How can I tell if I have a hearing problem?

Ask yourself the following questions. If you answer "yes" to three or more of these questions, you could have a hearing problem and may need to have your hearing checked.

Table 15.1. Hearing Problem Questionnaire

Do I have a problem hearing on the telephone or cell phone?	YES	NO
Do I have trouble hearing when there is noise in the background?	YES	NO
Is it hard for me to follow a conversation when two or more people talk at the same time?	YES	NO
Do I have to strain to understand a conversation?	YES	NO
Do many people I talk to seem to mumble (or not speak clearly)?	YES	NO
Do I misunderstand what others are saying?	YES	NO
Do I often ask people to repeat themselves?	YES	NO
Do people complain that I turn the TV volume up too high?	YES	NO

What should I do if I have trouble hearing?

Hearing problems can be serious. The most important thing you can do if you think you have a hearing problem is to seek advice from a health care provider. There are several types of professionals who can help you. Each has a different type of training and expertise. Each can be an important part of your hearing health care.

- An otolaryngologist or ENT is a doctor who specializes in diagnosing and treating diseases of the ear, nose, throat, and neck. The otolaryngologist will try to find out why you're having trouble hearing and offer treatment options.

- An audiologist has specialized training in identifying and measuring the type and degree of hearing loss. Some audiologists may be licensed to fit hearing aids.

- A hearing aid specialist is someone who is licensed by your state to conduct and evaluate basic hearing tests, offer counseling, and fit and test hearing aids. You must be examined by a physician before you can be fitted for a hearing aid, although federal law allows you to sign a waiver if you don't wish to be examined before you purchase an aid.

What treatments and devices can help?

Your treatment will depend on the severity of your hearing loss, so some treatments will work better for you than others. There are a number of devices and aids that help you hear better when you have hearing loss. Here are the most common ones:

- **Hearing aids** are electronic instruments you wear in or behind your ear. They make sounds louder. To find the hearing aid that works best for you, you may have to try more than one. Be sure to ask for a trial period with your hearing aid and understand the terms and conditions of the trial period. Work with your hearing aid provider until you are comfortable with putting on and removing the hearing aid, adjusting the volume level, and changing the batteries.

- **Cochlear implants.** Cochlear implants are small electronic devices surgically implanted in the inner ear that help provide a sense of sound to people who are profoundly deaf or hard-of-hearing. If your hearing loss is severe, your doctor may recommend a cochlear implant in one or both ears.

- **Bone anchored hearing systems** bypass the ear canal and middle ear, and are designed to use your body's natural ability to transfer sound through bone conduction. The sound processor picks up sound, converts it into vibrations, and then relays the vibrations through your skull bone to your inner ear.

- **Assistive listening devices** include telephone and cell phone amplifying devices, smart phone or tablet "apps," and closed-circuit systems (hearing loop systems) in places of worship, theaters, and auditoriums.

- **Lip reading or speech reading** is another option that helps people with hearing problems follow conversational speech. People who use this method pay close attention to others when they talk by watching the speaker's mouth and body movements. Special trainers can help you learn how to lip read or speech read.

Can my friends and family help me?

You and your family can work together to make living with hearing loss easier. Here are some things you can do:

- Tell your friends and family about your hearing loss. The more friends and family you tell, the more people there will be to help you cope with your hearing loss.

- Ask your friends and family to face you when they talk so that you can see their faces. If you watch their faces move and see their expressions, it may help you to understand them better.

- Ask people to speak louder, but not shout. Tell them they do not have to talk slowly, just more clearly.

- Turn off the TV or the radio when you aren't actively listening to it.

- Be aware of noise around you that can make hearing more diffi-cult. When you go to a restaurant, for example, don't sit near the kitchen or near a band playing music. Background noise makes it hard to hear people talk.

Working together to hear better may be tough on everyone for a while. It will take time for you to get used to watching people as they talk and for people to get used to speaking louder and more clearly. Be patient and continue to work together. Hearing better is worth the effort.

Section 15.2

Vision Loss

This section includes excerpts from "Healthy Vision," National Eye Institute (NEI), April 23, 2013; text from "Common Eye Disorders," Centers for Disease Control and Prevention (CDC), April 23, 2013; and text from "Healthy Vision: Make It Last a Lifetime," Centers for Disease Control and Prevention (CDC), May 11, 2015.

What You Should Know

What is low vision?

When you have low vision, eyeglasses, contact lenses, medicine, or surgery may not help. Activities like reading, shopping, cooking, writing, and watching TV may be hard to do.

In fact, millions of Americans lose some of their sight every year. While vision loss can affect anyone at any age, low vision is most com-mon for those over age 65.

Low vision is usually caused by eye diseases or health conditions. Some of these include age-related macular degeneration (AMD), cataract, diabetes, and glaucoma. Eye injuries and birth defects are some other causes. Whatever the cause, lost vision cannot be restored. It can, however, be managed with proper treatment and vision rehabilitation.

You should visit an eye care professional if you experience any changes to your eyesight.

How do I know if I have low vision?

Below are some signs of low vision. Even when wearing your glasses or contact lenses, do you still have difficulty with—

- Recognizing the faces of family and friends?

- Reading, cooking, sewing, or fixing things around the house?

- Selecting and matching the color of your clothes?

- Seeing clearly with the lights on or feeling like they are dimmer than normal?

- Reading traffic signs or the names of stores?

These could all be early warning signs of vision loss or eye disease. The sooner vision loss or eye disease is detected by an eye care professional, the greater your chances of keeping your remaining vision.

How do I know when to get an eye exam?

Visit your eye care professional regularly for a comprehensive dilated eye exam. However, if you notice changes to your eyes or eyesight, visit your eye care professional right away!

What can I do if I have low vision?

To cope with vision loss, you must first **have an excellent support team**. This team should include you, your primary eye care professional, and an optometrist or ophthalmologist specializing in low vision.

Occupational therapists, orientation and mobility specialists, certified low vision therapists, counselors, and social workers are also available to help.

Together, the low vision team can help you make the most of your remaining vision and maintain your independence.

Second, **talk with your eye care professional** about your vision problems. Even though it may be difficult, ask for help. Find out where you can get more information about support services and adaptive devices. Also, find out which services and devices are best for you and which will give you the most independence. Remember, Erin, Joma, Lawrence, and Ruth each had different types of vision loss, but they all talked with their eye care professional and are now living fulfilling and independent lives.

Third, **ask about vision rehabilitation**, even if your eye care professional says that "nothing more can be done for your vision."

Vision rehabilitation programs offer a wide range of services, including training for magnifying and adaptive devices, ways to complete daily living skills safely and independently, guidance on modifying your home, and information on where to locate resources and support to help you cope with your vision loss.

Medicare may cover part or all of a patient's occupational therapy, but the therapy must be ordered by a doctor and provided by a Medicare-approved healthcare provider. To see if you are eligible for Medicare-funded occupational therapy, call 1800MEDICARE (1-800-633-4227).

Finally, **be persistent**. Remember that you are your best healthcare advocate. Explore your options, learn as much as you can, and keep asking questions about vision rehabilitation. In fact, write down questions to ask your doctor before your exam, and bring along a notepad to jot down answers.

There are many resources to help people with low vision, and many of these programs, devices, and technologies can help you maintain your normal, everyday way of life.

What questions should I ask my eye care team?

An important part of any doctor patient relationship is effective communication. Here are some questions to ask your eye care professional or specialist in low vision to jumpstart the discussion about vision loss.

Questions to ask your eye care professional:

- What changes can I expect in my vision?

- Will my vision loss get worse? How much of my vision will I lose?

- Will regular eyeglasses improve my vision?

- What medical or surgical treatments are available for my condition?

- What can I do to protect or prolong my vision?
- Will diet, exercise, or other lifestyle changes help?
- If my vision can't be corrected, can you refer me to a specialist in low vision?
- Where can I get vision rehabilitation services?

Questions to ask your specialist in low vision:
- How can I continue my normal, routine activities?
- Are there resources to help me in my job?
- Will any special devices help me with daily activities like reading, sewing, cooking, or fixing things around the house?
- What training and services are available to help me live better and more safely with low vision?
- Where can I find individual or group support to cope with my vision loss?

Common Eye Disorders

Approximately 11 million Americans aged 12 years and older could improve their vision through proper refractive correction. More than 3.3 million Americans aged 40 years and older are either legally blind (having best-corrected visual acuity of 6/60 or worse (=20/200) in the better-seeing eye) or are with low vision (having best-corrected visual acuity less than 6/12 (<20/40) in the better-seeing eye, excluding those who were categorized as being blind). The leading causes of blindness and low vision in the United States are primarily age-related eye diseases such as age-related macular degeneration, cataract, diabetic retinopathy, and glaucoma. Other common eye disorders include amblyopia and strabismus.

Refractive Errors

Refractive errors are the most frequent eye problems in the United States. Refractive errors include myopia (near-sightedness), hyperopia (farsightedness), astigmatism (distorted vision at all distances), and presbyopia that occurs between age 40–50 years (loss of the ability to focus up close, inability to read letters of the phone book, need to hold newspaper farther away to see clearly) can be corrected by eyeglasses, contact lenses, or in some cases surgery. Recent studies conducted by the National Eye Institute showed that proper refractive correction could improve vision among 11 million Americans aged 12 years and older.

Age-Related Macular Degeneration

Macular degeneration, often called age-related macular degeneration (AMD), is an eye disorder associated with aging and results in damaging sharp and central vision. Central vision is needed for seeing objects clearly and for common daily tasks such as reading and driving. AMD affects the macula, the central part the retina that allows the eye to see fine details. There are two forms of AMD—wet and dry.

1. Wet AMD is when abnormal blood vessel behind the retina start to grow under the macula, ultimately leading to blood and fluid leakage. Bleeding, leaking, and scarring from these blood vessels cause damage and lead to rapid central vision loss. An early symptom of wet AMD is that straight lines appear wavy.

2. Dry AMD is when the macula thins overtime as part of aging process, gradually blurring central vision. The dry form is more common and accounts for 70–90% of cases of AMD and it progresses more slowly than the wet form. Over time, as less of the macula functions, central vision is gradually lost in the affected eye. Dry AMD generally affects both eyes. One of the most common early signs of dry AMD is drusen.

Drusen are tiny yellow or white deposits under the retina. They often are found in people aged 60 years and older. The presence of small drusen is normal and does not cause vision loss. However, the presence of large and more numerous drusen raises the risk of developing advanced dry AMD or wet AMD.

It is estimated that 1.8 million Americans aged 40 years and older are affected by AMD and an additional 7.3 million with large drusen are at substantial risk of developing AMD. The number of people with AMD is estimated to reach 2.95 million in 2020. AMD is the leading cause of permanent impairment of reading and fine or close-up vision among people aged 65 years and older.

Cataract

Cataract is a clouding of the eye's lens and is the leading cause of blindness worldwide, and the leading cause of vision loss in the United States. Cataracts can occur at any age because of a variety of causes, and can be present at birth. Although treatment for the removal of cataract is widely available, access barriers such as insurance coverage, treatment costs, patient choice, or lack of awareness prevent many people from receiving the proper treatment.

An estimated 20.5 million (17.2%) Americans aged 40 years and older have cataract in one or both eyes, and 6.1 million (5.1%) have had their lens removed operatively. The total number of people who have cataracts is estimated to increase to 30.1 million by 2020.

Diabetic Retinopathy

Diabetic retinopathy (DR) is a common complication of diabetes. It is the leading cause of blindness in American adults. It is characterized by progressive damage to the blood vessels of the retina, the light-sensitive tissue at the back of the eye that is necessary for good vision. DR progresses through four stages, mild nonproliferative retinopathy (microaneurysms), moderate nonproliferative retinopathy (blockage in some retinal vessels), severe nonproliferative retinopathy (more vessels are blocked leading to deprived retina from blood supply leading to growing new blood vessels), and proliferative retinopathy (most advanced stage). Diabetic retinopathy usually affects both eyes.

The risks of DR are reduced through disease management that includes good control of blood sugar, blood pressure, and lipid abnormalities. Early diagnosis of DR and timely treatment reduce the risk of vision loss; however, as many as 50% of patients are not getting their eyes examined or are diagnosed too late for treatment to be effective.

It is the leading cause of blindness among U.S. working-aged adults aged 20–74 years. An estimated 4.1 million and 899,000 Americans are affected by retinopathy and vision-threatening retinopathy, respectively.

Glaucoma

Glaucoma is a group of diseases that can damage the eye's optic nerve and result in vision loss and blindness. Glaucoma occurs when the normal fluid pressure inside the eyes slowly rises. However, recent findings now show that glaucoma can occur with normal eye pressure. With early treatment, you can often protect your eyes against serious vision loss.

There are two major categories "open angle" and "closed angle" glaucoma. Open angle, is a chronic condition that progress slowly over long period of time without the person noticing vision loss until the disease is very advanced, that is why it is called "sneak thief of sight." Angle closure can appear suddenly and is painful. Visual loss can progress quickly; however, the pain and discomfort lead patients to seek medical attention before permanent damage occurs.

Amblyopia

Amblyopia, also referred to as "lazy eye," is the most common cause of vision impairment in children. Amblyopia is the medical term used when the vision in one of the eyes is reduced because the eye and the brain are not working together properly. The eye itself looks normal, but it is not being used normally because the brain is favoring the other eye. Conditions leading to amblyopia include strabismus, an imbalance in the positioning of the two eyes; more nearsighted, far-sighted, or astigmatic in one eye than the other eye, and rarely other eye conditions such as cataract.

Unless it is successfully treated in early childhood amblyopia usually persists into adulthood, and is the most common cause of permanent one-eye vision impairment among children and young and middle-aged adults. An estimated 2%–3% of the population suffer from amblyopia.

Strabismus

Strabismus involves an imbalance in the positioning of the two eyes. Strabismus can cause the eyes to cross in (esotropia) or turn out (exotropia). Strabismus is caused by a lack of coordination between the eyes. As a result, the eyes look in different directions and do not focus simultaneously on a single point. In most cases of strabismus in children, the cause is unknown. In more than half of these cases, the problem is present at or shortly after birth (congenital strabismus). When the two eyes fail to focus on the same image, there is reduced or absent depth perception and the brain may learn to ignore the input from one eye, causing permanent vision loss in that eye (one type of amblyopia).

Healthy Vision: Make It Last a Lifetime

To keep your eyes healthy, get a comprehensive dilated eye exam: if you haven't had a comprehensive dilated eye exam for some time, schedule one now.

Taking care of your eyes is a priority just like eating well and being physically active. Healthy vision can help keep you safe and healthy. To keep your eyes healthy, get a comprehensive dilated eye exam: an eye care professional will use drops to widen the pupils to check for common vision problems and eye diseases. It's the best way to find out if you need glasses or contacts, or are in the early stages of an eye disease.

Vision Health for All Ages

You can have a dilated eye exam regularly to check for common eye problems. If you haven't had an exam for some time, schedule one this month. Don't forget to take care of your children's eyes as well.

- Although older adults tend to have more vision problems, pre-schoolers may also not see as well as they should.

- The U.S. Preventive Services Task Force recommends vision screening for all children aged 3 to 5 years to find conditions such as amblyopia, or lazy eye, which can be treated effectively if caught early.

Some eye conditions can cause vision loss and even blindness. These include:

- Cataracts, a clouding of the eye.

- Diabetic retinopathy, which causes damage to the blood vessels in the back of the eye.

- Glaucoma, damage to the optic nerve, often with increased eye pressure.

- Age-related macular degeneration, which gradually affects central vision.

Other eye conditions, such as refractive errors, which happen when the shape of your eye doesn't bend light correctly, are common problems easily corrected with glasses, contact lenses, or laser surgery. An estimated 11 million Americans aged 12 years and older could see better if they used corrective lenses, or had eye surgery, if appropriate.

Nine ways you can help protect your vision

1. Get regular comprehensive dilated eye exams.

2. Know your family's eye health history. It's important to know if anyone has been diagnosed with an eye disease or condition, since some are hereditary.

3. Eat right to protect your sight. In particular, eat plenty of dark leafy greens such as spinach, kale, or collard greens, and fish

that is high in omega-3 fatty acids such as salmon, albacore tuna, trout, and halibut.

4. Maintain a healthy weight.

5. Wear protective eyewear when playing sports or doing activities around the home, such as painting, yard work, and home repairs.

6. Quit smoking or never start.

7. Wear sunglasses that block 99 percent-100 percent of ultraviolet A (UVA) and ultraviolet B (UVB) radiation.

8. Wash your hands before taking out your contacts and cleanse your contact lenses properly to avoid infection.

9. Practice workplace eye safety.

Eyes and Overall Health

Taking care of your eyes also may benefit your overall health. People with vision problems are more likely than those with good vision to have diabetes, poor hearing, heart problems, high blood pressure, lower back pain and strokes, as well as have increased risk for falls, injury and depression. Among people aged 65 and older, more than 50 percent of those who are blind, and more than 40 percent of those with impaired vision say their overall health is fair or poor. But more than 20 percent of older Americans without vision problems reported fair to poor health.

In addition to your comprehensive dilated eye exams, visit an eye care professional if you have

- Decreased vision.

- Eye pain.

- Drainage or redness of the eye.

- Double vision.

- Diabetes.

- Floaters (tiny specks that appear to float before your eyes).

- Circles (halos) around light sources.

- Flashes of light.

Diabetes and Your Eyes

If you have diabetes, there's a lot you can do to prevent eye problems. Keeping your blood glucose under control can prevent or delay the onset of diabetic eye diseases. Keeping your blood pressure under control is also important.

Diabetic retinopathy (as noted previously) is a common complication of diabetes and usually affects both eyes. It is the leading cause of blindness in American adults. Early diagnosis of diabetic retinopathy and timely treatment reduce the risk of vision loss; however, as many as 50 percent of patients are not getting their eyes examined or are diagnosed too late for treatment to be effective. Finding and treating eye problems early can help save your sight.

Chapter 16

Speech Disorders

Chapter Contents

Section 16.1

Aphasia

Text in this section is excerpted from "Ninds Aphasia Information Page," National Institute of Neurological Disorder and Stroke (NINDS), September 11, 2015.

What is Aphasia?

Aphasia is a neurological disorder caused by damage to the portions of the brain that are responsible for language. Primary signs of the disorder include difficulty in expressing oneself when speaking, trouble understanding speech, and difficulty with reading and writing. Aphasia is not a disease, but a symptom of brain damage. Most commonly seen in adults who have suffered a stroke, aphasia can also result from a brain tumor, infection, head injury, or dementia that damages the brain. It is estimated that about 1 million people in the United States suffer from aphasia. The type and severity of language dysfunction depends on the precise location and extent of the damaged brain tissue.

Generally, aphasia can be divided into four broad categories:

1. *Expressive aphasia* involves difficulty in conveying thoughts through speech or writing. The patient knows what he wants to say, but cannot find the words he needs.

2. *Receptive aphasia* involves difficulty understanding spoken or written language. The patient hears the voice or sees the print but cannot make sense of the words.

3. Patients with *anomic or amnesia aphasia*, the least severe form of aphasia, have difficulty in using the correct names for particular objects, people, places, or events.

4. *Global aphasia* results from severe and extensive damage to the language areas of the brain. Patients lose almost all language function, both comprehension and expression. They cannot speak or understand speech, nor can they read or write.

Is there any treatment?

In some instances, an individual will completely recover from aphasia without treatment. In most cases, however, language therapy should begin as soon as possible and be tailored to the individual needs of the patient. Rehabilitation with a speech pathologist involves extensive exercises in which patients read, write, follow directions, and repeat what they hear. Computer-aided therapy may supplement standard language therapy.

What is the prognosis?

The outcome of aphasia is difficult to predict given the wide range of variability of the condition. Generally, people who are younger or have less extensive brain damage fare better. The location of the injury is also important and is another clue to prognosis. In general, patients tend to recover skills in language comprehension more completely than those skills involving expression.

Section 16.2

Apraxia

Text in this section is excerpted from "Ninds Apraxia Information Page," National Institute of Neurological Disorder and Stroke (NINDS), September 11, 2015.

What is Apraxia?

Apraxia (called "dyspraxia" if mild) is a neurological disorder characterized by loss of the ability to execute or carry out skilled movements and gestures, despite having the desire and the physical ability to perform them. Apraxia results from dysfunction of the cerebral hemispheres of the brain, especially the parietal lobe, and can arise from many diseases or damage to the brain.

There are several kinds of apraxia, which may occur alone or together. The most common is buccofacial or orofacial apraxia, which causes the inability to carry out facial movements on command such as licking lips, whistling, coughing, or winking. Other types of apraxia include limb-kinetic apraxia (the inability to make fine, precise movements with an arm or leg), ideomotor apraxia (the inability to make the proper movement in response to a verbal command), ideational apraxia (the inability to coordinate activities with multiple, sequential movements, such as dressing, eating, and bathing), verbal apraxia (difficulty coordinating mouth and speech movements), constructional apraxia (the inability to copy, draw, or construct simple figures), and oculomotor apraxia (difficulty moving the eyes on command). Apraxia may be accompanied by a language disorder called aphasia. Corticobasal ganglionic degeneration is a disease that causes a variety of types of apraxia, especially in elderly adults.

Is there any treatment?

Generally, treatment for individuals with apraxia includes physical, speech, or occupational therapy. If apraxia is a symptom of another disorder, the underlying disorder should be treated.

What is the prognosis?

The prognosis for individuals with apraxia varies and depends partly on the underlying cause. Some individuals improve significantly while others may show very little improvement.

Chapter 17

Intellectual and Cognitive Disabilities

Chapter Contents

Section 17.1

Down Syndrome

Text in this section is excerpted from "Facts about Down Syndrome," Centers for Disease Control and Prevention (CDC), October 20, 2014.

Down syndrome is a condition in which a person has an extra chromosome. Chromosomes are small "packages" of genes in the body. They determine how a baby's body forms during pregnancy and how the baby's body functions as it grows in the womb and after birth. Typically, a baby is born with 46 chromosomes. Babies with Down syndrome have an extra copy of one of these chromosomes, chromosome 21. A medical term for having an extra copy of a chromosome is 'trisomy.' Down syndrome is also referred to as Trisomy 21. This extra copy changes how the baby's body and brain develop, which can cause both mental and physical challenges for the baby.

Even though people with Down syndrome might act and look similar, each person has different abilities. People with Down syndrome usually have an IQ (a measure of intelligence) in the mildly-to-moderately low range and are slower to speak than other children.

Some common physical features of Down syndrome include:

- A flattened face, especially the bridge of the nose

- Almond-shaped eyes that slant up

- A short neck

- Small ears

- A tongue that tends to stick out of the mouth

- Tiny white spots on the iris (colored part) of the eye

- Small hands and feet

- A single line across the palm of the hand (palmar crease)

- Small pinky fingers that sometimes curve toward the thumb

- Poor muscle tone or loose joints

142

- Shorter in height as children and adults

Down syndrome remains the most common chromosomal condition diagnosed in the United States. Each year, about 6,000 babies born in the United States have Down syndrome. This means that Down syndrome occurs in about 1 out of every 700 babies.

Types of Down Syndrome

There are three types of Down syndrome. People often can't tell the difference between each type without looking at the chromosomes because the physical features and behaviors are similar.

1. **Trisomy 21:** About 95% of people with Down syndrome have Trisomy 21. With this type of Down syndrome, each cell in the body has 3 separate copies of chromosome 21 instead of the usual 2 copies.

2. **Translocation Down syndrome:** This type accounts for a small percentage of people with Down syndrome (about 3%). This occurs when an extra part or a whole extra chromosome 21 is present, but it is attached or "trans-located" to a different chromosome rather than being a separate chromosome 21.

3. **Mosaic Down syndrome:** This type affects about 2% of the people with Down syndrome. Mosaic means mixture or combination. For children with mosaic Down syndrome, some of their cells have 3 copies of chromosome 21, but other cells have the typical two copies of chromosome 21. Children with mosaic Down syndrome may have the same features as other children with Down syndrome. However, they may have fewer features of the condition due to the presence of some (or many) cells with a typical number of chromosomes.

Causes and Risk Factors

The extra chromosome 21 leads to the physical features and developmental challenges that can occur among people with Down syndrome. Researchers know that Down syndrome is caused by an extra chromosome, but no one knows for sure why Down syndrome occurs or how many different factors play a role. One factor that increases the risk for having a baby with Down syndrome is the mother's age. Women who are 35 years or older when they become pregnant are more likely to have a pregnancy affected by Down syndrome than women who become pregnant at a younger age. However, the majority of babies with Down syndrome are born to mothers less than 35 years old, because there are many more births among younger women.

Diagnosis

Doctors can diagnose Down syndrome during pregnancy or after the baby is born. Some families want to know during pregnancy whether their baby has Down syndrome. Diagnosis of Down syndrome during pregnancy can allow parents and families to prepare for their baby's special needs.

During pregnancy

There are two basic types of tests available to detect Down syndrome during pregnancy. Screening tests are one type and diagnostic tests are another type. A screening test can tell a woman and her health care provider whether her pregnancy has a lower or higher chance of having Down syndrome. So screening tests help decide whether a diagnostic test might be needed. Screening tests do not provide an absolute diagnosis, but they are safer for the mother and the baby. Diagnostic tests can typically detect whether or not a baby will have Down syndrome, but they can be more risky for the mother and baby. Neither screening nor diagnostic tests can predict the full impact of Down syndrome on a baby; no one can predict this.

Screening tests

Screening tests often include a combination of a blood test, which measures the amount of various substances in the mother's blood (e.g., MS-AFP, Triple Screen, Quad-screen), and an ultrasound, which creates a picture of the baby. During an ultrasound, one of the things the technician looks at is the fluid behind the baby's neck. Extra fluid in this region could indicate a genetic problem. These screening tests can help determine the baby's risk of Down syndrome. Rarely, screening tests can give an abnormal result even when there is nothing wrong with the baby. Sometimes, the test results are normal and yet they miss a problem that does exist.

Another test available since 2010 for certain chromosome problems, including Down syndrome, screens the mother's blood to detect small pieces of the developing baby's DNA that are circulating in the mother's blood. This test is recommended for women who are more likely to have a pregnancy affected by Down syndrome. The test is typically completed during the first trimester (first 3 months of pregnancy) and it is becoming more widely available.

Diagnostic tests

Diagnostic tests are usually performed after a positive screening test in order to confirm a Down syndrome diagnosis. Types of diagnostic tests include:

- Chorionic villus sampling (CVS)—examines material from the placenta

- Amniocentesis—examines the amniotic fluid (the fluid from the sac surrounding the baby)

- Percutaneous umbilical blood sampling (PUBS)—examines blood from the umbilical cord

These tests look for changes in the chromosomes that would indicate a Down syndrome diagnosis.

After birth

Once a baby is born, a doctor will examine the baby and most likely will be able to diagnose a baby with Down syndrome. Doctors usually order tests of the baby's blood to confirm whether there is an extra chromosome (chromosome 21) in the baby's cells.

Because almost half of babies born with Down syndrome have a heart defect, all newborns with Down syndrome should receive an echocardiogram (an ultrasound picture of the heart).

Other health problems among children with Down syndrome

Many people with Down syndrome have the common facial features and no other major birth defects. However, some people with Down syndrome might have one or more major birth defects or other medical problems. Some of the more common health problems among children with Down syndrome are listed below:

- Hearing loss (up to 75% of people with Down syndrome may be affected)

- Obstructive sleep apnea, which is a condition where the person's breathing temporarily stops while asleep (between 50–75%)

- Ear infections (between 50–70%)

- Eye diseases (up to 60%), like cataracts and eye issues requiring glasses

- Heart defects present at birth (50%)

Other less common health problems among people with Down syndrome include:

- Intestinal blockage at birth requiring surgery

- Hip dislocation

- Thyroid disease

- Anemia (red blood cells can't carry enough oxygen to the body) and iron deficiency (anemia where the red blood cells don't have enough iron)

- Leukemia in infancy or early childhood

- Hirschsprung disease

Health care providers routinely monitor children with Down syndrome for these conditions. If they are diagnosed, treatment is offered.

Living with Down syndrome

Down syndrome is a lifelong condition. Services early in life will often help babies and children with Down syndrome to improve their physical and intellectual abilities. Most of these services focus on helping children with Down syndrome develop to their full potential. These services include speech, occupational, and physical therapy, and they are typically offered through early intervention programs in each state. Children with Down syndrome may also need extra help or attention in school, although many children are included in regular classes.

Many people with Down syndrome lead productive and fulfilling lives well into adulthood. They can have jobs and live independently. However, it is important for people with Down syndrome to be involved in their community, take good care of themselves, and see a healthcare provider regularly. Families of people with Down syndrome often can help their loved ones by connecting with other families that have had children with Down syndrome. This may help families gain insight into overcoming potential differences in caring for their child with Down syndrome.

Section 17.2

Fetal Alcohol Spectrum Disorders

This section includes excerpted from "Facts about FASDs," Centers for Disease Control and Prevention (CDC), April 16, 2015; and text from "About FASD," Substance Abuse and Mental Health Services Administration (SAMHSA), July 30, 2015.

Fetal alcohol spectrum disorders (FASDs) are a group of conditions that can occur in a person whose mother drank alcohol during pregnancy. These effects can include physical problems and problems with behavior and learning. Often, a person with an FASD has a mix of these problems.

Cause and Prevention

FASDs are caused by a woman drinking alcohol during pregnancy. Alcohol in the mother's blood passes to the baby through the umbilical cord. When a woman drinks alcohol, so does her baby.

There is no known safe amount of alcohol during pregnancy or when trying to get pregnant. There is also no safe time to drink during pregnancy. Alcohol can cause problems for a developing baby throughout pregnancy, including before a woman knows she's pregnant. All types of alcohol are equally harmful, including all wines and beer.

To prevent FASDs, a woman should not drink alcohol while she is pregnant, or when she might get pregnant. This is because a woman could get pregnant and not know for up to 4 to 6 weeks. In the United States, nearly half of pregnancies are unplanned.

If a woman is drinking alcohol during pregnancy, it is never too late to stop drinking. Because brain growth takes place throughout pregnancy, the sooner a woman stops drinking the safer it will be for her and her baby.

FASDs are completely preventable if a woman does not drink alcohol during pregnancy—so why take the risk?

Signs and Symptoms

FASDs refer to the whole range of effects that can happen to a person whose mother drank alcohol during pregnancy. These conditions can affect each person in different ways, and can range from mild to severe.

A person with an FASD might have:

- Abnormal facial features, such as a smooth ridge between the nose and upper lip (this ridge is called the philtrum)

- Small head size

- Shorter-than-average height

- Low body weight

- Poor coordination

- Hyperactive behavior

- Difficulty with attention

- Poor memory

- Difficulty in school (especially with math)

- Learning disabilities

- Speech and language delays

- Intellectual disability or low IQ

- Poor reasoning and judgment skills

- Sleep and sucking problems as a baby

- Vision or hearing problems

- Problems with the heart, kidneys, or bones

Types of FASDs

Different terms are used to describe FASDs, depending on the type of symptoms.

- **Fetal Alcohol Syndrome (FAS):** FAS represents the most involved end of the FASD spectrum. Fetal death is the most extreme outcome from drinking alcohol during pregnancy. People with FAS might have abnormal facial features, growth problems, and central nervous system (CNS) problems. People with FAS can have problems with learning, memory, attention span, communication, vision, or hearing. They might have a mix of these problems. People with FAS often have a hard time in school and trouble getting along with others.

- **Alcohol-Related Neurodevelopmental Disorder (ARND):** People with ARND might have intellectual disabilities and problems with behavior and learning. They might do poorly in school and have difficulties with math, memory, attention, judgment, and poor impulse control.

- **Alcohol-Related Birth Defects (ARBD):** People with ARBD might have problems with the heart, kidneys, or bones or with hearing. They might have a mix of these.

> The term fetal alcohol effects (FAE) was previously used to describe intellectual disabilities and problems with behavior and learning in a person whose mother drank alcohol during pregnancy. In 1996, the Institute of Medicine (IOM) replaced FAE with the terms alcohol-related neurodevelopmental disorder (ARND) and alcohol-related birth defects (ARBD).

Diagnosis

The term FASDs is not meant for use as a clinical diagnosis. CDC worked with a group of experts and organizations to review the research and develop guidelines for diagnosing FAS. The guidelines were developed for FAS only. CDC and its partners are working to put together diagnostic criteria for other FASDs, such as ARND.

Diagnosing FAS can be hard because there is no medical test, like a blood test, for it. And other disorders, such as ADHD (attention-deficit/hyperactivity disorder) and Williams syndrome, have some symptoms like FAS.

To diagnose FAS, doctors look for:

- Abnormal facial features (e.g., smooth ridge between nose and upper lip)

- Lower-than-average height, weight, or both

- Central nervous system problems (e.g., small head size, problems with attention and hyperactivity, poor coordination)

- Prenatal alcohol exposure; although confirmation is not required to make a diagnosis

Treatment

FASDs last a lifetime. There is no cure for FASDs, but research shows that early intervention treatment services can improve a child's development.

There are many types of treatment options, including medication to help with some symptoms, behavior and education therapy, parent training, and other alternative approaches. No one treatment is right for every child. Good treatment plans will include close monitoring, follow-ups, and changes as needed along the way.

Also, "protective factors" can help reduce the effects of FASDs and help people with these conditions reach their full potential.

Protective factors include:

- Diagnosis before 6 years of age

- Loving, nurturing, and stable home environment during the school years

- Absence of violence

- Involvement in special education and social services

Get Help!

If you or the doctor thinks there could be a problem, **ask the doctor for a referral to a specialist** (someone who knows about FASDs), such as a developmental pediatrician, child psychologist, or clinical geneticist. In some cities, there are clinics whose staffs have special training in diagnosing and treating children with FASDs. To find doctors and clinics in your area visit the National and State Resource Directory from the National Organization on Fetal Alcohol Syndrome (NOFAS).

At the same time as you ask the doctor for a referral to a specialist, **call your state's public early childhood system** to request a free evaluation to find out if your child qualifies for intervention services. This is sometimes called a Child Find evaluation. You do not need to wait for a doctor's referral or a medical diagnosis to make this call.

Where to call for a free evaluation from the state depends on your child's age:

- **If your child is younger than 3 years old,** contact your local early intervention system.

- **If your child is 3 years old or older,** contact your local public school system.

Even if your child is not old enough for kindergarten or enrolled in a public school, call your local elementary school or board of education and ask to speak with someone who can help you have your child evaluated.

Section 17.3

Head Trauma in Infants (Shaken Baby Syndrome)

This section includes excerpted from "Preventing Abusive Head Trauma in Children," Centers for Disease Control and Prevention (CDC), August 10, 2015; and text from "Pediatric Abusive Head Trauma," Centers for Disease Control and Prevention (CDC), April 2012.

Know the Facts About AHT

- Abusive head trauma is the leading cause of physical child abuse deaths in the United States.
- Babies less than one year old are at greatest risk of injury from abusive head trauma.
- The most common trigger for abusive head trauma is inconsolable or excessive crying.

What Is Abusive Head Trauma?

Abusive head trauma (AHT), which includes shaken baby syndrome, is a preventable and severe form of physical child abuse that results in an injury to the brain of an infant or child. AHT is most common in children under age five, with children under one year of age at most risk. It is caused by violent shaking or blunt impact. The resulting injury can cause bleeding around the brain or on the inside back layer of the eyes.

Nearly all victims of AHT suffer serious, long-term health consequences such as vision problems, developmental delays, physical disabilities, and hearing loss. At least one of every four babies who experience AHT dies from this form of child abuse.

Research shows that AHT often happens when a parent or caregiver becomes angry or frustrated from a child's crying. The caregiver then shakes the child, hitting or slamming the child's head into something in an effort to stop the crying.

Crying—including long bouts of inconsolable crying—is normal behavior in infants. Shaking, throwing, hitting, or hurting a baby is never the right response to crying.

How Can Abusive Head Trauma Be Prevented?

You can play a key role in preventing AHT by understanding the dangers of violently shaking or hitting a baby's head into something, knowing the risk factors and the triggers for abuse, and finding ways to support parents and caregivers in your community.

If you are a parent or caregiver

- Understand that infant crying is worse in the first few months of life, but it will get better as the child grows.

- Try calming a crying baby by rocking gently, offering a pacifier, singing or talking softly, taking a walk with a stroller, or going for a drive in the car.

- If the baby won't stop crying, check for signs of illness and call the doctor if you suspect the child is sick.

- If you are getting upset or losing control, focus on calming yourself down. Put the baby in a safe place and walk away to calm down, checking on the baby every 5 to 10 minutes.

- Call a friend, relative, neighbor, or parent helpline for support.

If you are a friend, family member, or observer of a parent or caregiver

- Be aware of new parents in your family and community who may need help or support.

- Provide support by offering to give a parent or caregiver a break when needed.

- Let the parent know that dealing with a crying baby can be very frustrating—especially when you are tired or stressed, but infant crying is normal and it will get better soon.

- Encourage parents and caregivers to take a calming break if needed while the baby is safe in the crib.

- Be sensitive and supportive in situations when parents are trying to calm a crying baby.

The Problem of Abusive Head Trauma in Children

Serious traumatic brain injury in young children is largely the result of abuse and results in significant morbidity and mortality. Among United States children, abuse is the third leading cause of all head injuries, after falls and motor vehicle crashes. For children in the first year of life, the majority of serious head injuries result from abuse. Estimates of the incidence of abusive head trauma vary, but most range from 20 to 30 cases per 100,000 children under 1 year of age. The incidence rate has been observed to decrease with increasing age with substantially higher incidence among those 1 year of age and younger. The peak incidence and rapid decrease with age are thought to be related to episodes of prolonged, inconsolable, and unpredictable crying that are developmentally normal for infants.

Episodes of crying that can trigger shaking behavior among parents and caregivers are known to increase in the first month after birth, peak in the second month, and decrease thereafter. While the majority of victims are under 2 years of age and the peak incidence is typically found from 2-3 months, injuries consistent with abusive head trauma have been found in children as old as 5 years of age. The case fatality rate for abusive head trauma has been estimated to exceed 20%, with significant disability for nearly two-thirds of the survivors. Deaths due to abusive head trauma also peak at 1 to 2 months of age, most likely due to higher physiologic vulnerability during early infancy. Infants who have assault-related head injuries at 3-4 months of age or older may be more resilient and more likely to survive their injuries. These children often have long-term consequences of their injuries. Neurologic, behavioral, and cognitive sequelae have been observed in victims of abusive head trauma. Serious brain injury in children has been estimated to consume billions of dollars in health care costs each year, with significantly higher costs for abused versus non-abused children.

Chapter 18

Learning Disabilities

What are the indicators of learning disabilities?

Many children have difficulty with reading, writing, or other learning-related tasks at some point, but this does not mean they have learning disabilities. A child with a learning disability often has several related signs, and these persist over time. The signs of learning disabilities vary from person to person. Common signs that a person may have learning disabilities include the following:

- Difficulty with reading and/or writing

- Problems with math skills

- Difficulty remembering

- Problems paying attention

- Trouble following directions

- Difficulty with concepts related to time

- Problems staying organized

A child with a learning disability also may exhibit one or more of the following:

- Impetuous behavior

Text in this chapter is excerpted from "Condition Information," National Institute of Child Health and Human Development (NICHD), February 28, 2014.

- Inappropriate responses in school or social situations
- Difficulty staying on task (easily distracted)
- Difficulty finding the right way to say something
- Inconsistent school performance
- Immature way of speaking
- Difficulty listening well
- Problems dealing with new things in life
- Problems understanding words or concepts

These signs alone are not enough to determine that a person has a learning disability. A professional assessment is necessary to diagnose a learning disability.

Each learning disability has its own signs. Also, not every person with a particular disability will have all of the signs of that disability.

Children being taught in a second language that they are learning sometimes act in ways that are similar to the behaviors of someone with a learning disability. For this reason, learning disability assessment must take into account whether a student is bilingual or a second language learner.

Below are some common learning disabilities and the signs associated with them:

- Dyslexia
- Dysgraphia
- Dyscalculia
- Dyspraxia

Dyslexia

People with dyslexia usually have trouble making the connections between letters and sounds and with spelling and recognizing words.

People with dyslexia often show other signs of the condition. These may include:

- Failure to fully understand what others are saying
- Difficulty organizing written and spoken language
- Delayed ability to speak

- Poor self-expression (for example, saying "thing" or "stuff" for words not recalled)

- Difficulty learning new vocabulary, either through reading or hearing

- Trouble learning foreign languages

- Slowness in learning songs and rhymes

- Slow reading as well as giving up on longer reading tasks

- Difficulty understanding questions and following directions

- Poor spelling

- Difficulty recalling numbers in sequence (for example, telephone numbers and addresses)

- Trouble distinguishing left from right

Dysgraphia

Dysgraphia is characterized by problems with writing. This disorder may cause a child to be tense and awkward when holding a pen or pencil, even to the extent of contorting his or her body. A child with very poor handwriting that he or she does not outgrow may have dysgraphia.

Other signs of this condition may include:

- A strong dislike of writing and/or drawing

- Problems with grammar

- Trouble writing down ideas

- A quick loss of energy and interest while writing

- Trouble writing down thoughts in a logical sequence

- Saying words out loud while writing

- Leaving words unfinished or omitting them when writing sentences

Dyscalculia

Signs of this disability include problems understanding basic arithmetic concepts, such as fractions, number lines, and positive and negative numbers.

Other symptoms may include:

- Difficulty with math-related word problems

- Trouble making change in cash transactions

- Messiness in putting math problems on paper

- Trouble recognizing logical information sequences (for example, steps in math problems)

- Trouble with understanding the time sequence of events

- Difficulty with verbally describing math processes

Dyspraxia

A person with dyspraxia has problems with motor tasks, such as hand-eye coordination, that can interfere with learning.
Some other symptoms of this condition include:

- Problems organizing oneself and one's things

- Breaking things

- Trouble with tasks that require hand-eye coordination, such as coloring within the lines, assembling puzzles, and cutting precisely

- Poor balance

- Sensitivity to loud and/or repetitive noises, such as the ticking of a clock

- Sensitivity to touch, including irritation over bothersome-feeling clothing

How many people are affected/at risk for learning disabilities?

There is a wide range in estimates of the number of people affected by learning disabilities and disorders. Some of the variation results from differences in requirements for diagnosis in different states.

Some reports estimate that as many as 15% to 20% of Americans are affected by learning disabilities and disorders. In contrast, a major national study found that approximately 5% of children in the United States had learning disabilities. It also found that approximately 4% had both a learning disability and attention deficit/hyperactivity disorder (ADHD). Other research, conducted in 2006, estimated that 4.6

million school-age children in the United States have been diagnosed with learning disabilities.

What causes learning disabilities?

Researchers do not know exactly what causes learning disabilities, but they appear to be related to differences in brain structure. These differences are present from birth and often are inherited. To improve understanding of learning disabilities, researchers at the NICHD and elsewhere are studying areas of the brain and how they function. Scientists have found that learning disabilities are related to areas of the brain that deal with language and have used imaging studies to show that the brain of a dyslexic person develops and functions differently from a typical brain.

Sometimes, factors that affect a developing fetus, such as alcohol or drug use, can lead to a learning disability. Other factors in an infant's environment may play a role as well. These can include poor nutrition and exposure to toxins such as lead in water or paint. In addition, children who do not receive the support necessary to promote their intellectual development early on may show signs of learning disabilities once they start school.

Sometimes a person may develop a learning disability later in life. Possible causes in such a case include dementia or a traumatic brain injury (TBI).

How are learning disabilities diagnosed?

Learning disabilities are often identified when a child begins to attend school. Educators may use a process called "response to intervention" (RTI) to help identify children with learning disabilities. Specialized testing is required to make a clear diagnosis, however.

RTI

RTI usually involves the following:

- Monitoring all students' progress closely to identify possible learning problems

- Providing a child identified as having problems with help on different levels, or tiers

- Moving this youngster through the tiers as appropriate, increasing educational assistance if the child does not show progress

159

Students who are struggling in school can also have individual evaluations. An evaluation can:

- Identify whether a child has a learning disability

- Determine a child's eligibility under federal law for special education services

- Help construct an individualized education plan (IEP) that outlines supports for a youngster who qualifies for special education services

- Establish a benchmark for measuring the child's educational progress

A full evaluation for a learning disability includes the following:

- A medical examination, including a neurological exam, to identify or rule out other possible causes of the child's difficulties, including emotional disorders, intellectual and developmental disabilities, and brain diseases

- Exploration of the youngster's developmental, social, and school performance

- A discussion of family history

- Academic achievement testing and psychological assessment

Usually, several specialists work as a team to perform an evaluation. The team may include a psychologist, special education expert, and speech-language pathologist (SLP). Many schools also have reading specialists on staff who can help diagnosis a reading disability.

Role of School Psychologists

School psychologists are trained in both education and psychology. They can help to identify students with learning disabilities and can diagnose the learning disability. They can also help the student with the disability, parents, and teachers come up with plans that improve learning.

Role of SLPs

All SLPs are trained in diagnosing and treating speech- and language-related disorders. A SLP can provide a complete language evaluation as well as an assessment of the child's ability to organize his or her thoughts and possessions. The SLP may evaluate various age-appropriate learning-related skills in the child, such as understanding directions, manipulating sounds, and reading and writing.

Is there a cure for learning disabilities?

Learning disabilities have no cure, but early intervention can provide tools and strategies to lessen their effects. People with learning disabilities can be successful in school and work and in their personal lives. More information is available about interventions for learning disabilities.

What are the treatments for learning disabilities?

People with learning disabilities and disorders can learn strategies for coping with their disabilities. Getting help earlier increases the likelihood for success in school and later in life. If learning disabilities remain untreated, a child may begin to feel frustrated with schoolwork, which can lead to low self-esteem, depression, and other problems.

Usually, experts work to help a child learn skills by building on the child's strengths and developing ways to compensate for the child's weaknesses. Interventions vary depending on the nature and extent of the disability.

Chapter 19

Autism Spectrum Disorders

Autism spectrum disorder (ASD) is a developmental disability that can cause significant social, communication and behavioral challenges. There is often nothing about how people with ASD look that sets them apart from other people, but people with ASD may communicate, interact, behave, and learn in ways that are different from most other people. The learning, thinking, and problem-solving abilities of people with ASD can range from gifted to severely challenged. Some people with ASD need a lot of help in their daily lives; others need less.

A diagnosis of ASD now includes several conditions that used to be diagnosed separately: autistic disorder, pervasive developmental disorder not otherwise specified (PDD-NOS), and Asperger syndrome. These conditions are now all called autism spectrum disorder.

Signs and Symptoms

People with ASD often have problems with social, emotional, and communication skills. They might repeat certain behaviors and might not want change in their daily activities. Many people with ASD also have different ways of learning, paying attention, or reacting to things. Signs of ASD begin during early childhood and typically last throughout a person's life.

This chapter includes excerpts from "Facts About ASD," Centers for Disease Control and Prevention (CDC), August 12, 2015.

Children or adults with ASD might:

- not point at objects to show interest (for example, not point at an airplane flying over)

- not look at objects when another person points at them

- have trouble relating to others or not have an interest in other people at all

- avoid eye contact and want to be alone

- have trouble understanding other people's feelings or talking about their own feelings

- prefer not to be held or cuddled, or might cuddle only when they want to

- appear to be unaware when people talk to them, but respond to other sounds

- be very interested in people, but not know how to talk, play, or relate to them

- repeat or echo words or phrases said to them, or repeat words or phrases in place of normal language

- have trouble expressing their needs using typical words or motions

- not play "pretend" games (for example, not pretend to "feed" a doll)

- repeat actions over and over again

- have trouble adapting when a routine changes

- have unusual reactions to the way things smell, taste, look, feel, or sound

- lose skills they once had (for example, stop saying words they were using)

Diagnosis

Diagnosing ASD can be difficult since there is no medical test, like a blood test, to diagnose the disorders. Doctors look at the child's behavior and development to make a diagnosis.

ASD can sometimes be detected at 18 months or younger. By age 2, a diagnosis by an experienced professional can be considered very reliable. However, many children do not receive a final diagnosis until much older. This delay means that children with ASD might not get the early help they need.

Treatment

There is currently no cure for ASD. However, research shows that early intervention treatment services can improve a child's development. Early intervention services help children from birth to 3 years old (36 months) learn important skills. Services can include therapy to help the child talk, walk, and interact with others. Therefore, it is important to talk to your child's doctor as soon as possible if you think your child has ASD or other developmental problem.

Even if your child has not been diagnosed with an ASD, he or she may be eligible for early intervention treatment services. The Individuals with Disabilities Education Act (IDEA) says that children under the age of 3 years (36 months) who are at risk of having developmental delays may be eligible for services. These services are provided through an early intervention system in your state. Through this system, you can ask for an evaluation.

In addition, treatment for particular symptoms, such as speech therapy for language delays, often does not need to wait for a formal ASD diagnosis.

Causes and Risk Factors

We do not know all of the causes of ASD. However, we have learned that there are likely many causes for multiple types of ASD. There may be many different factors that make a child more likely to have an ASD, including environmental, biologic and genetic factors.

- Most scientists agree that genes are one of the risk factors that can make a person more likely to develop ASD.

- Children who have a sibling with ASD are at a higher risk of also having ASD.

- ASD tends to occur more often in people who have certain genetic or chromosomal conditions, such as fragile X syndrome or tuberous sclerosis.

- When taken during pregnancy, the prescription drugs valproic acid and thalidomide have been linked with a higher risk of ASD.

- There is some evidence that the critical period for developing ASD occurs before, during, and immediately after birth.

- Children born to older parents are at greater risk for having ASD.

ASD continues to be an important public health concern. Like the many families living with ASD, CDC wants to find out what causes the disorder. Understanding the factors that make a person more likely to develop ASD will help us learn more about the causes. One of the largest U.S. studies to date, called Study to Explore Early Development (SEED) is currently being carried out. SEED is looking at many possible risk factors for ASD, including genetic, environmental, pregnancy, and behavioral factors.

Who Is Affected

ASD occurs in all racial, ethnic, and socioeconomic groups, but is almost five times more common among boys than among girls. CDC estimates that about 1 in 68 children has been identified with autism spectrum disorder (ASD).

More people than ever before are being diagnosed with ASD. It is unclear exactly how much of this increase is due to a broader definition of ASD and better efforts in diagnosis. However, a true increase in the number of people with an ASD cannot be ruled out. The increase in ASD diagnosis is likely due to a combination of these factors.

For over a decade, CDC's Autism and Developmental Disabilities Monitoring (ADDM) Network has been estimating the number of children with ASD in the United States. It will be important to use the same methods to track how the number of children with ASD is changing over time in order to learn more about the disorder.

If You're Concerned

If you think your child might have ASD or you think there could be a problem with the way your child plays, learns, speaks, or acts, **contact your child's doctor, and share your concerns.**

If you or the doctor is still concerned, **ask the doctor for a referral to a specialist** who can do a more in-depth evaluation of your child. Specialists who can do a more in-depth evaluation and make a diagnosis include:

- Developmental Pediatricians (doctors who have special training in child development and children with special needs)

- Child Neurologists (doctors who work on the brain, spine, and nerves)

- Child Psychologists or Psychiatrists (doctors who know about the human mind)

Chapter 20

Attention Deficit Hyperactivity Disorder

Attention Deficit Hyperactivity Disorder (ADHD) is one of the most common *neurodevelopmental* disorders of childhood. It is usually first diagnosed in childhood and often lasts into adulthood. Children with ADHD may have trouble paying attention, controlling impulsive behaviors (may act without thinking about what the result will be), or be overly active.

Signs and Symptoms

It is normal for children to have trouble focusing and behaving at one time or another. However, children with ADHD do not just grow out of these behaviors. The symptoms continue and can cause difficulty at school, at home, or with friends.

A child with ADHD might:

- daydream a lot

- forget or lose things a lot

This chapter includes excerpts from "Facts About ADHD," Centers for Disease Control and Prevention (CDC), June 26, 2015; text from "Dealing with ADHD: What You Need to Know," U.S. Food and Drug Administration (FDA), August 6, 2015.

- squirm or fidget

- talk too much

- make careless mistakes or take unnecessary risks

- have a hard time resisting temptation

- have trouble taking turns

- have difficulty getting along with others

Causes of ADHD

Scientists are studying cause(s) and risk factors in an effort to find better ways to manage and reduce the chances of a person having ADHD. The cause(s) and risk factors for ADHD are unknown, but current research shows that genetics plays an important role. Recent studies of twins link genes with ADHD.

In addition to genetics, scientists are studying other possible causes and risk factors including:

- Brain injury

- Environmental exposures (e.g., lead)

- Alcohol and tobacco use during pregnancy

- Premature delivery

- Low birth weight

Research does not support the popularly held views that ADHD is caused by eating too much sugar, watching too much television, parenting, or social and environmental factors such as poverty or family chaos. Of course, many things, including these, might make symptoms worse, especially in certain people. But the evidence is not strong enough to conclude that they are the main causes of ADHD.

Diagnosis

Deciding if a child has ADHD is a several step process. There is no single test to diagnose ADHD, and many other problems, like anxiety, depression, and certain types of learning disabilities, can have similar symptoms. One step of the process involves having a medical exam, including hearing and vision tests, to rule out other problems with symptoms like ADHD. Another part of the process may include a checklist for rating ADHD symptoms and taking a history of the child from parents, teachers, and sometimes, the child.

Treatments

In most cases, ADHD is best treated with a combination of behavior therapy and medication. For preschool-aged children (4-5 years of age) with ADHD, behavior therapy is recommended as the first line of treatment. No single treatment is the answer for every child and good treatment plans will include close monitoring, follow-ups and any changes needed along the way.

Consequences of Not Treating

Left untreated, ADHD can have serious consequences.

A child may fall behind in school, encounter difficulties in friendships, and have conflicts with parents, says the American Academy of Child and Adolescent Psychiatry.

Studies show that children with untreated ADHD have more emergency room visits and are more likely to have self-inflicted injuries than those treated for the disorder. Untreated adolescents with ADHD are more likely to take risks, such as drinking and driving. And they have twice as many motor vehicle accidents as those who are treated.

ADHD: Not Just for Kids

Studies suggest that approximately 4% of adults may have attention deficit hyperactivity disorder (ADHD). The symptoms of ADHD in adults are the same as those in children, but they manifest somewhat differently. Adults with ADHD may have poor time management skills and trouble with multi-tasking, become restless with downtime, and avoid activities that require sustained concentration.

A diagnosis of ADHD in an adult is given only when it's known that some of the symptoms were present early in childhood, usually under the age of seven.

"For some adults, a diagnosis of ADHD can bring a sense of relief," says psychiatrist Tiffany Farchione. Receiving a diagnosis allows adults to understand the reasons for their problems, and treatment can help them to deal with challenges more effectively.

Chapter 21

Psychiatric Disability and Mental Disorders

The following are descriptions of the most common categories of mental illness in the United States.

Anxiety Disorders

Anxiety disorders are characterized by excessive fear or anxiety that is difficult to control and negatively and substantially impacts daily functioning. Fear refers to the emotional response to a real or perceived threat while anxiety is the anticipation of a future threat. These disorders can range from specific fears (called phobias), such as the fear of flying or public speaking, to more generalized feelings of worry and tension. Anxiety disorders typically develop in childhood and persist to adulthood. Specific anxiety disorders include generalized anxiety disorder (GAD), panic disorder, separation anxiety disorder, and social anxiety disorder (social phobia).

Evidence suggests that many anxiety disorders may be caused by a combination of genetics, biology, and environmental factors. Adverse

This chapter includes excerpts from "Mental Disorders," Substance Abuse and Mental Health Services Administration (SAMHSA), October 9, 2015; and text from "Behavioral Health Treatments and Services," Substance Abuse and Mental Health Services Administration (SAMHSA), October 9, 2015.

childhood experiences may also contribute to risk for developing anxiety disorders.

Attention Deficit Hyperactivity Disorder

Attention deficit hyperactivity disorder (ADHD) is defined by a persistent pattern of inattention (for example, difficulty keeping focus) and/or hyperactivity-impulsivity (for example, difficulty controlling behavior, excessive and inappropriate motor activity). Children with ADHD have difficulty performing well in school, interacting with other children, and following through on tasks. Adults with ADHD are often extremely distractible and have significant difficulties with organization. There are three sub-types of the disorder:

1. Predominantly hyperactive/impulsive

2. Predominantly inattentive

3. Combined hyperactive/inattentive

Current research suggests that ADHD has a high degree of heritability, however, the exact gene or constellation of genes that give rise to the disorder are not known. Environmental risk factors may include low birth weight, smoking and alcohol use during pregnancy, exposure to lead, and history of child maltreatment.

The three overarching features of ADHD include inattention, hyperactivity, and impulsivity. Inattentive children may have trouble paying close attention to details, make careless mistakes in schoolwork, are easily distracted, have difficulty following through on tasks, such as homework assignments, or quickly become bored with a task. Hyperactivity may be defined by fidgeting or squirming, excessive talking, running about, or difficulty sitting still. Finally, impulsive children may be impatient, may blurt out answers to questions prematurely, have trouble waiting their turn, may frequently interrupt conversations, or intrude on others' activities.

Bipolar and Related Disorders

People with bipolar and related disorders experience atypical, dramatic swings in mood, and activity levels that go from periods of feeling intensely happy, irritable, and impulsive to periods of intense sadness and feelings of hopelessness. Individuals with this disorder experience discrete mood episodes, characterized as either a:

- Manic episode—abnormally elevated, expansive, or irritable mood accompanied by increased energy or activity that substantially impairs functioning

- Hypomanic episode—similar to a manic episode, however not severe enough to cause serious social or occupational problems

- Major depressive episode—persistent depressed mood or loss of interest or pleasure

- Mixed state—includes symptoms of both a manic episode and a major depressive episode

People exhibiting these symptoms are most frequently identified as having one of two types of bipolar disorders: bipolar I disorder or bipolar II disorder.

The bipolar I diagnosis is used when there has been at least one manic episode in a person's life. The bipolar II diagnosis is used when there has been a more regular occurrence of depressive episodes along with a hypomanic episode, but not a full-blown manic episode. Cyclothymic disorder, or cyclothymia, is a diagnosis used for a mild form of bipolar disorder.

A family history of bipolar disorder is the strongest risk factor for the condition, and the level of risk increases with the degree of kinship.

As mentioned previously, bipolar disorders are characterized by manic and depressive episodes. In children, manic episodes may present as an excessively silly or joyful mood that is unusual for the child or an uncharacteristically irritable temperament and are accompanied by unusual behavioral changes, such as decreased need for sleep, risk-seeking behavior, and distractibility. Depressive episodes may present as a persistent, sad mood, feelings of worthlessness or guilt, and loss of interest in previously enjoyable activities. Behavioral changes associated with depressive episodes may include fatigue or loss of energy, gaining or losing a significant amount of weight, complaining about pain, or suicidal thoughts or plans.

Depressive Disorders (Including Major Depressive Disorder)

Depressive disorders are among the most common mental health disorders in the United States. They are characterized by a sad, hopeless, empty, or irritable mood, and somatic and cognitive changes that significantly interfere with daily life. Major depressive disorder (MDD) is defined as having a depressed mood for most of the day and a marked loss of interest or pleasure, among other symptoms present nearly every day for at least a two-week period. In children and adolescents, MDD may manifest as an irritable rather than a sad disposition.

MDD is thought to have many possible causes, including genetic, biological, and environmental factors. Adverse childhood experiences and stressful life experiences are known to contribute to risk for MDD. In addition, those with closely related family members (for example, parents or siblings) who are diagnosed with the disorder are at increased risk.

A diagnosis for MDD at a minimum requires that symptoms of depressed mood (for example, feelings of sadness, emptiness, hopelessness) and loss of interest or pleasure in activities are present. Additional symptoms may include significant weight loss or gain, insomnia or hypersomnia, feelings of restlessness, lethargy, feelings of worthlessness or excessive guilt, distractibility, and recurrent thoughts of death, including suicidal ideation. Symptoms must be present for at least two-weeks and cause significant impairment or dysfunction in daily life.

Disruptive, Impulse Control, and Conduct Disorders

This class of disorders is characterized by problems with self-control of emotions or behaviors that violate the rights of others and/or bring a person into conflict with societal norms or authority figures. Oppositional defiant disorder and conduct disorder are the most prominent of this class of disorders in children.

Oppositional Defiant Disorder

Children with oppositional defiant disorder (ODD) display a frequent and persistent pattern of angry or irritable mood, argumentative/defiant behavior, or vindictiveness. Symptoms are typically first seen in the preschool years, and often precede the development of conduct disorder.

Children who experienced harsh, inconsistent, or neglectful child-rearing practices are at increased risk for developing ODD.

Symptoms of ODD include angry/irritable mood, argumentative/defiant behavior, or vindictiveness. A child with an angry/irritable mood may often lose their temper, be frequently resentful, or easily annoyed. Argumentative or defiant children are frequently combative with authority figures or adults and often refuse to comply with rules. They may also deliberately annoy others or blame others for their mistakes or misbehavior. These symptoms must be evident for at least six months and observed when interacting with at least one individual who is not a sibling.

Conduct Disorder

Occurring in children and teens, conduct disorder is a persistent pattern of disruptive and violent behaviors that violate the basic rights of others or age-appropriate social norms or rules, and causes significant impairment in the child or family's daily life.

Conduct disorder may be preceded by temperamental risk factors, such as behavioral difficulties in infancy and below-average intelligence. Similar to ODD, environmental risk factors may include harsh or inconsistent child-rearing practices and/or child maltreatment. Parental criminality, frequent changes of caregivers, large family size, familial psychopathology, and early institutional living may also contribute to risk for developing the disorder. Community-level risk factors may include neighborhood exposure to violence, peer rejection, and association with a delinquent peer group. Children with a parent or sibling with conduct disorder or other behavioral health disorders (for example, ADHD, schizophrenia, severe alcohol use disorder) are more likely to develop the condition. Children with conduct disorder often present with other disorders as well, including ADHD, learning disorders, and depression.

The primary symptoms of conduct disorder include aggression to people and animals (for example, bullying or causing physical harm), destruction of property (for example, fire-setting), deceitfulness or theft (for example, breaking and entering), and serious violations of rules (for example, truancy, elopement). Symptoms must be present for 12 months and fall into one of three subtypes depending on the age at onset (childhood, adolescent, or unspecified).

Obsessive-Compulsive and Related Disorders

Obsessive-compulsive disorder (OCD) is defined by the presence of persistent thoughts, urges, or images that are intrusive and unwanted (obsessions), or repetitive and ritualistic behaviors that a person feels are necessary in order to control obsessions (compulsions). OCD tends to begin in childhood or adolescence, with most individuals being diagnosed by the age of 19.

The causes of OCD are largely unknown, however there is some evidence that it runs in families and is associated with environmental risk factors, such as child maltreatment or traumatic childhood events.

Prerequisites for OCD include the presence of obsessions, compulsions, or both. Obsessions may include persistent thoughts (for example, of contamination), images (for example, of horrific scenes), or urges (for example, to jump from a window) and are perceived as unpleasant and involuntary. Compulsions include repetitive behaviors that the person is compelled to carry out ritualistically in response to an obsession or according to a rigid set of rules. Compulsions are carried out in an effort to prevent or reduce anxiety or distress, and yet are clearly excessive or unrealistic. A common example of an OCD symptom is a person who is obsessed with germs and feels compelled to wash their hands excessively. OCD symptoms are time-consuming and cause significant dysfunction in daily life.

Schizophrenia Spectrum and Other Psychotic Disorders

The defining characteristic of schizophrenia and other psychotic disorders is abnormalities in one or more of five domains: delusions, hallucinations, disorganized thinking, grossly disorganized or abnormal motor behavior, and negative symptoms, which include diminished emotional expression and a decrease in the ability to engage in self-initiated activities. Disorders in this category include schizotypal disorder, schizoaffective disorder, and schizophreniform disorder. The most common diagnosis in this category is schizophrenia.

Schizophrenia

Schizophrenia is a brain disorder that impacts the way a person thinks (often described as a "thought disorder"), and is characterized by a range of cognitive, behavioral, and emotional experiences that can include: delusions, hallucinations, disorganized thinking, and grossly disorganized or abnormal motor behavior. These symptoms are chronic and severe, significantly impairing occupational and social functioning.

While family history of psychosis is often not predictive of schizophrenia, genetic predisposition correlates to risk for developing the disease. Physiological factors, such as certain pregnancy and birth complications and environmental factors, such as season of birth (late winter/early spring) and growing up in an urban environment may be associated with increased risk for schizophrenia.

People with schizophrenia can experience what are termed positive or negative symptoms. Positive symptoms are psychotic behaviors including:

- Delusions of false and persistent beliefs that are not part of the individual's culture. For example, people with schizophrenia may believe that their thoughts are being broadcast on the radio.

Hallucinations that include hearing, seeing, smelling, or feeling things that others cannot. Most commonly, people with the disorder hear voices that talk to them or order them to do things.

- Disorganized speech that involves difficulty organizing thoughts, thought-blocking, and making up nonsensical words.

- Grossly disorganized or catatonic behavior.

Negative symptoms may include flat affect, disillusionment with daily life, isolating behavior, lack of motivation, and infrequent speaking, even when forced to interact. As with other forms of serious mental illness, schizophrenia is related to homelessness, involvement with the criminal justice system, and other negative outcomes.

Trauma- and Stressor-Related Disorders

The defining characteristic of trauma- and stressor-related disorders is previous exposure to a traumatic or stressful event. The most common disorder in this category is post-traumatic stress disorder (PTSD).

Post-Traumatic Stress Disorder

Post-traumatic stress disorder (PTSD) is characterized as the development of debilitating symptoms following exposure to a traumatic or dangerous event. These can include re-experiencing symptoms from an event, such as flashbacks or nightmares, avoidance symptoms, changing a personal routine to escape having to be reminded of an event, or being hyper-aroused (easily startled or tense) that makes daily tasks nearly impossible to complete. PTSD was first identified as a result of symptoms experienced by soldiers and those in war; however, other traumatic events, such as rape, child abuse, car accidents, and natural disasters have also been shown to give rise to PTSD.

Risk for PTSD is separated into three categories, including pre-traumatic, peri-traumatic, and post traumatic factors.

1. Pre-traumatic factors include childhood emotional problems by age 6, lower socioeconomic status, lower education, prior exposure to trauma, childhood adversity, lower intelligence, minority racial/ethnic status, and a family psychiatric history. Female gender and younger age at exposure may also contribute to pre-traumatic risk.

2. Peri-traumatic factors include the severity of the trauma, perceived life threat, personal injury, interpersonal violence, and dissociation during the trauma that persists afterwards.

3. Post-traumatic risk factors include negative appraisals, ineffective coping strategies, subsequent exposure to distressing reminders, subsequent adverse life events, and other trauma-related losses.

Diagnosis of PTSD must be preceded by exposure to actual or threatened death, serious injury, or violence. This may entail directly experiencing or witnessing the traumatic event, learning that the traumatic event occurred to a close family member or friend, or repeated exposure to distressing details of the traumatic event. Individuals diagnosed with PTSD experience intrusive symptoms (for example, recurrent upsetting dreams, flashbacks, distressing memories, intense psychological distress), avoidance of stimuli associated with the traumatic event, and negative changes in cognition and mood corresponding with the traumatic event (for example, dissociative amnesia, negative beliefs about oneself, persistent negative affect, feelings of detachment or estrangement). They also experience significant changes in arousal and reactivity associated with the traumatic events, such as hyper vigilance, distractibility, exaggerated startle response, and irritable or self-destructive behavior.

Chapter 22

Degenerative Diseases That Cause Disabilities

Chapter Contents

Section 22.1

Alzheimer's Disease

Text in this section is excerpted from "Alzheimer's Disease Fact
Sheet," National Institute on Aging (NIA), May 2015.

Alzheimer's disease is an irreversible, progressive brain disorder
that slowly destroys memory and thinking skills, and eventually
the ability to carry out the simplest tasks. In most people with Alzheimer's, symptoms first appear in their mid-60s. Estimates vary,
but experts suggest that more than 5 million Americans may have
Alzheimer's.

Alzheimer's disease is currently ranked as the sixth leading cause
of death in the United States, but recent estimates indicate that the
disorder may rank third, just behind heart disease and cancer, as a
cause of death for older people.

Alzheimer's is the most common cause of dementia among older
adults. Dementia is the loss of cognitive functioning—thinking,
remembering, and reasoning—and behavioral abilities to such an
extent that it interferes with a person's daily life and activities.
Dementia ranges in severity from the mildest stage, when it is just
beginning to affect a person's functioning, to the most severe stage,
when the person must depend completely on others for basic activities
of daily living.

The causes of dementia can vary, depending on the types of brain
changes that may be taking place. Other dementias include Lewy
body dementia, frontotemporal disorders, and vascular dementia. It is
common for people to have mixed dementia—a combination of two or
more disorders, at least one of which is dementia. For example, some
people have both Alzheimer's disease and vascular dementia.

Alzheimer's disease is named after Dr. Alois Alzheimer. In 1906,
Dr. Alzheimer noticed changes in the brain tissue of a woman who had
died of an unusual mental illness. Her symptoms included memory
loss, language problems, and unpredictable behavior. After she died,
he examined her brain and found many abnormal clumps (now called
amyloid plaques) and tangled bundles of fibers (now called neurofibril-
lary, or tau, tangles).

These plaques and tangles in the brain are still considered some of the main features of Alzheimer's disease. Another feature is the loss of connections between nerve cells (neurons) in the brain. Neurons transmit messages between different parts of the brain, and from the brain to muscles and organs in the body.

Changes in the Brain

Scientists continue to unravel the complex brain changes involved in the onset and progression of Alzheimer's disease. It seems likely that damage to the brain starts a decade or more before memory and other cognitive problems appear. During this preclinical stage of Alzheimer's disease, people seem to be symptom-free, but toxic changes are taking place in the brain. Abnormal deposits of proteins form amyloid plaques and tau tangles throughout the brain, and once-healthy neurons stop functioning, lose connections with other neurons, and die.

The damage initially appears to take place in the hippocampus, the part of the brain essential in forming memories. As more neurons die, additional parts of the brain are affected, and they begin to shrink. By the final stage of Alzheimer's, damage is widespread, and brain tissue has shrunk significantly.

Signs and Symptoms

Memory problems are typically one of the first signs of cognitive impairment related to Alzheimer's disease. Some people with memory problems have a condition called mild cognitive impairment (MCI). In MCI, people have more memory problems than normal for their age, but their symptoms do not interfere with their everyday lives. Movement difficulties and problems with the sense of smell have also been linked to MCI. Older people with MCI are at greater risk for developing Alzheimer's, but not all of them do. Some may even go back to normal cognition.

The first symptoms of Alzheimer's vary from person to person. For many, decline in non-memory aspects of cognition, such as word-finding, vision/spatial issues, and impaired reasoning or judgment, may signal the very early stages of Alzheimer's disease. Researchers are studying biomarkers (biological signs of disease found in brain images, cerebrospinal fluid, and blood) to see if they can detect early changes in the brains of people with MCI and in cognitively normal people who may be at greater risk for Alzheimer's. Studies indicate that such early detection may be possible, but more research is needed before these techniques can be relied upon to diagnose Alzheimer's disease in everyday medical practice.

Mild Alzheimer's Disease

As Alzheimer's disease progresses, people experience greater memory loss and other cognitive difficulties. Problems can include wandering and getting lost, trouble handling money and paying bills, repeating questions, taking longer to complete normal daily tasks, and personality and behavior changes. People are often diagnosed in this stage.

Moderate Alzheimer's Disease

In this stage, damage occurs in areas of the brain that control language, reasoning, sensory processing, and conscious thought. Memory loss and confusion grow worse, and people begin to have problems recognizing family and friends. They may be unable to learn new things, carry out multistep tasks such as getting dressed, or cope with new situations. In addition, people at this stage may have hallucinations, delusions, and paranoia and may behave impulsively.

Severe Alzheimer's Disease

Ultimately, plaques and tangles spread throughout the brain, and brain tissue shrinks significantly. People with severe Alzheimer's cannot communicate and are completely dependent on others for their care. Near the end, the person may be in bed most or all of the time as the body shuts down.

What Causes Alzheimer's

Scientists don't yet fully understand what causes Alzheimer's disease in most people. In people with early-onset Alzheimer's, a genetic mutation is usually the cause. Late-onset Alzheimer's arises from a complex series of brain changes that occur over decades. The causes probably include a combination of genetic, environmental, and lifestyle factors. The importance of any one of these factors in increasing or decreasing the risk of developing Alzheimer's may differ from person to person.

Diagnosis of Alzheimer's Disease

Doctors use several methods and tools to help determine whether a person who is having memory problems has "possible Alzheimer's dementia" (dementia may be due to another cause) or "probable Alzheimer's dementia" (no other cause for dementia can be found).

To diagnose Alzheimer's, doctors may:

- ask the person and a family member or friend questions about overall health, past medical problems, ability to carry out daily activities, and changes in behavior and personality

- conduct tests of memory, problem solving, attention, counting, and language

- carry out standard medical tests, such as blood and urine tests, to identify other possible causes of the problem

- perform brain scans, such as computed tomography (CT), magnetic resonance imaging (MRI), or positron emission tomography (PET), to rule out other possible causes for symptoms

These tests may be repeated to give doctors information about how the person's memory and other cognitive functions are changing over time.

Alzheimer's disease can be definitely diagnosed only after death, by linking clinical measures with an examination of brain tissue in an autopsy.

People with memory and thinking concerns should talk to their doctor to find out whether their symptoms are due to Alzheimer's or another cause, such as stroke, tumor, Parkinson's disease, sleep disturbances, side effects of medication, an infection, or a non-Alzheimer's dementia. Some of these conditions may be treatable and possibly reversible.

If the diagnosis is Alzheimer's, beginning treatment early in the disease process may help preserve daily functioning for some time, even though the underlying disease process cannot be stopped or reversed. An early diagnosis also helps families plan for the future. They can take care of financial and legal matters, address potential safety issues, learn about living arrangements, and develop support networks.

In addition, an early diagnosis gives people greater opportunities to participate in clinical trials that are testing possible new treatments for Alzheimer's disease or other research studies.

Treatment of Alzheimer's Disease

Alzheimer's disease is complex, and it is unlikely that any one drug or other intervention can successfully treat it. Recent approaches focus on helping people maintain mental function, manage behavioral symptoms, and slow or delay the symptoms of disease. Researchers hope to develop therapies targeting specific genetic, molecular, and cellular mechanisms so that the actual underlying cause of the disease can be stopped or prevented.

Maintaining Mental Function

Several medications are approved by the U.S. Food and Drug Administration (FDA) to treat symptoms of Alzheimer's. Donepezil (Aricept®), rivastigmine (Exelon®), and galantamine (Razadyne®) are used to treat mild to moderate Alzheimer's (donepezil can be used for severe Alzheimer's as well). Memantine (Namenda®) is used to treat moderate to severe Alzheimer's. These drugs work by regulating neurotransmitters, the chemicals that transmit messages between neurons. They may help maintain thinking, memory, and communication skills, and help with certain behavioral problems. However, these drugs don't change the underlying disease process. They are effective for some but not all people, and may help only for a limited time.

Managing Behavior

Common behavioral symptoms of Alzheimer's include sleeplessness, wandering, agitation, anxiety, and aggression. Scientists are learning why these symptoms occur and are studying new treatments—drug and non-drug—to manage them. Research has shown that treating behavioral symptoms can make people with Alzheimer's more comfortable and makes things easier for caregivers.

Looking for New Treatments

Alzheimer's disease research has developed to a point where scientists can look beyond treating symptoms to think about addressing underlying disease processes. In ongoing clinical trials, scientists are developing and testing several possible interventions, including immunization therapy, drug therapies, cognitive training, physical activity, and treatments used for cardiovascular and diabetes.

Section 22.2

Amyotrophic Lateral Sclerosis

Text in this section is excerpted from "Amyotrophic Lateral Sclerosis
(ALS) Fact Sheet," National Institute of Neurological Disorders and
Stroke (NINDS), July 15, 2015.

What is amyotrophic lateral sclerosis?

Amyotrophic lateral sclerosis (ALS), sometimes called Lou Gehrig's
disease, is a rapidly progressive, invariably fatal neurological disease
that attacks the nerve cells (neurons) responsible for controlling voluntary muscles (muscle action we are able to control, such as those in
the arms, legs, and face). The disease belongs to a group of disorders
known as motor neuron diseases, which are characterized by the gradual degeneration and death of motor neurons.

Motor neurons are nerve cells located in the brain, brain stem, and
spinal cord that serve as controlling units and vital communication
links between the nervous system and the voluntary muscles of the
body. Messages from motor neurons in the brain (called upper motor
neurons) are transmitted to motor neurons in the spinal cord (called
lower motor neurons) and from them to particular muscles. In ALS,
both the upper motor neurons and the lower motor neurons degenerate
or die, and stop sending messages to muscles. Unable to function, the
muscles gradually weaken, waste away (atrophy), and have very fine
twitches (called fasciculations). Eventually, the ability of the brain to
start and control voluntary movement is lost.

ALS causes weakness with a wide range of disabilities. Eventually,
all muscles under voluntary control are affected, and individuals lose
their strength and the ability to move their arms, legs, and body. When
muscles in the diaphragm and chest wall fail, people lose the ability
to breathe without ventilatory support. Most people with ALS die
from respiratory failure, usually within 3 to 5 years from the onset of
symptoms. However, about 10 percent of those with ALS survive for
10 or more years.

Although the disease usually does not impair a person's mind or
intelligence, several recent studies suggest that some persons with

ALS may have depression or alterations in cognitive functions involving decision-making and memory.

ALS does not affect a person's ability to see, smell, taste, hear, or recognize touch. Patients usually maintain control of eye muscles and bladder and bowel functions, although in the late stages of the disease most individuals will need help getting to and from the bathroom.

Who gets ALS?

More than 12,000 people in the U.S. have a definite diagnosis of ALS, for a prevalence of 3.9 cases per 100,000 persons in the U.S. general population, according to a report on data from the National ALS Registry. ALS is one of the most common neuromuscular diseases worldwide, and people of all races and ethnic backgrounds are affected. ALS is more common among white males, non-Hispanics, and persons aged 60–69 years, but younger and older people also can develop the disease. Men are affected more often than women.

In 90 to 95 percent of all ALS cases, the disease occurs apparently at random with no clearly associated risk factors. Individuals with this sporadic form of the disease do not have a family history of ALS, and their family members are not considered to be at increased risk for developing it.

About 5 to 10 percent of all ALS cases are inherited. The familial form of ALS usually results from a pattern of inheritance that requires only one parent to carry the gene responsible for the disease. Mutations in more than a dozen genes have been found to cause familial ALS.

About one-third of all familial cases (and a small percentage of sporadic cases) result from a defect in a gene known as "chromosome 9 open reading frame 72," or C9orf72. The function of this gene is still unknown. Another 20 percent of familial cases result from mutations in the gene that encodes the enzyme copper-zinc superoxide dismutase 1 (SOD1).

What are the symptoms?

The onset of ALS may be so subtle that the symptoms are overlooked. The earliest symptoms may include fasciculations, cramps, tight and stiff muscles (spasticity), muscle weakness affecting an arm or a leg, slurred and nasal speech, or difficulty chewing or swallowing. These general complaints then develop into more obvious weakness or atrophy that may cause a physician to suspect ALS.

The parts of the body showing early symptoms of ALS depend on which muscles in the body are affected. Many individuals first see the effects of the disease in a hand or arm as they experience difficulty with simple tasks requiring manual dexterity such as buttoning a shirt, writing, or turning a key in a lock. In other cases, symptoms initially affect one of the legs, and people experience awkwardness when walking or running or they notice that they are tripping or stumbling more often. When symptoms begin in the arms or legs, it is referred to as "limb onset" ALS. Other individuals first notice speech problems, termed "bulbar onset" ALS.

Regardless of the part of the body first affected by the disease, muscle weakness and atrophy spread to other parts of the body as the disease progresses. Individuals may develop problems with moving, swallowing (dysphagia), and speaking or forming words (dysarthria). Symptoms of upper motor neuron involvement include spasticity and exaggerated reflexes (hyperreflexia) including an overactive gag reflex. An abnormal reflex commonly called Babinski's sign (the large toe extends upward as the sole of the foot is stimulated in a certain way) also indicates upper motor neuron damage. Symptoms of lower motor neuron degeneration include muscle weakness and atrophy, muscle cramps, and fasciculations.

To be diagnosed with ALS, people must have signs and symptoms of both upper and lower motor neuron damage that cannot be attributed to other causes.

Although the sequence of emerging symptoms and the rate of disease progression vary from person to person, eventually individuals will not be able to stand or walk, get in or out of bed on their own, or use their hands and arms. Difficulty swallowing and chewing impair the person's ability to eat normally and increase the risk of choking. Maintaining weight will then become a problem. Because cognitive abilities are relatively intact, people are aware of their progressive loss of function and may become anxious and depressed. A small percentage of individuals may experience problems with memory or decision-making, and there is growing evidence that some may even develop a form of dementia over time.

Health care professionals need to explain the course of the disease and describe available treatment options so that people can make informed decisions in advance. In later stages of the disease, individuals have difficulty breathing as the muscles of the respiratory system weaken. They eventually lose the ability to breathe on their own and must depend on ventilatory support for survival. Affected individuals also face an increased risk of pneumonia during later stages of ALS.

How is ALS diagnosed?

No one test can provide a definitive diagnosis of ALS, although the presence of upper and lower motor neuron signs is strongly suggestive. Instead, the diagnosis of ALS is primarily based on the symptoms and signs the physician observes in the patient and a series of tests to rule out other diseases. Physicians obtain the individual's full medical history and usually conduct a neurologic examination at regular intervals to assess whether symptoms such as muscle weakness, atrophy of muscles, hyperreflexia, and spasticity are getting progressively worse.

Since ALS symptoms in the early stages of the disease can be similar to those of a wide variety of other, more treatable diseases or disorders, appropriate tests must be conducted to exclude the possibility of other conditions. One of these tests is electromyography (EMG), a special recording technique that detects electrical activity in muscles. Certain EMG findings can support the diagnosis of ALS. Another common test is a nerve conduction study (NCS), which measures electrical energy by assessing the nerve's ability to send a signal).

Specific abnormalities in the NCS and EMG may suggest, for example, that the individual has a form of peripheral neuropathy (damage to peripheral nerves) or myopathy (muscle disease) rather than ALS. The physician may order magnetic resonance imaging (MRI), a non-invasive procedure that uses a magnetic field and radio waves to take detailed images of the brain and spinal cord. Standard MRI scans are normal in people with ALS. However, they can reveal evidence of other problems that may be causing the symptoms, such as a spinal cord tumor, a herniated disk in the neck that compresses the spinal cord, syringomyelia (a cyst in the spinal cord), or cervical spondylosis (abnormal wear affecting the spine in the neck).

Based on the person's symptoms and findings from the examination and from these tests, the physician may order tests on blood and urine samples to eliminate the possibility of other diseases as well as routine laboratory tests. In some cases, for example, if a physician suspects that the individual may have a myopathy rather than ALS, a muscle biopsy may be performed.

Infectious diseases such as human immunodeficiency virus (HIV), human T-cell leukemia virus (HTLV), polio, West Nile virus, and Lyme disease can in some cases cause ALS-like symptoms. Neurological disorders such as multiple sclerosis, post-polio syndrome, multifocal motor neuropathy, and spinal muscular atrophy also can mimic certain facets of the disease and should be considered by physicians attempting to make a diagnosis. Fasciculations, the fine rippling movements in the muscle, and muscle cramps also occur in benign conditions.

Because of the prognosis carried by this diagnosis and the variety of diseases or disorders that can resemble ALS in the early stages of the disease, individuals may wish to obtain a second neurological opinion.

How is ALS treated?

No cure has yet been found for ALS. However, the U.S. Food and Drug Administration (FDA) approved the first drug treatment for the disease—riluzole (Rilutek)—in 1995. Riluzole is believed to reduce damage to motor neurons by decreasing the release of glutamate. Clinical trials with ALS patients showed that riluzole prolongs survival by several months, mainly in those with difficulty swallowing. The drug also extends the time before an individual needs ventilation support. Riluzole does not reverse the damage already done to motor neurons, and persons taking the drug must be monitored for liver damage and other possible side effects. However, this first disease-specific therapy offers hope that the progression of ALS may one day be slowed by new medications or combinations of drugs.

Other treatments for ALS are designed to relieve symptoms and improve the quality of life for individuals with the disorder. This supportive care is best provided by multidisciplinary teams of health care professionals such as physicians; pharmacists; physical, occupational, and speech therapists; nutritionists; and social workers and home care and hospice nurses. Working with patients and caregivers, these teams can design an individualized plan of medical and physical therapy and provide special equipment aimed at keeping patients as mobile and comfortable as possible.

Physicians can prescribe medications to help reduce fatigue, ease muscle cramps, control spasticity, and reduce excess saliva and phlegm. Drugs also are available to help patients with pain, depression, sleep disturbances, and constipation. Pharmacists can give advice on the proper use of medications and monitor a patient's prescriptions to avoid risks of drug interactions.

Physical therapy and special equipment can enhance an individual's independence and safety throughout the course of ALS. Gentle, low-impact aerobic exercise such as walking, swimming, and stationary bicycling can strengthen unaffected muscles, improve cardiovascular health, and help patients fight fatigue and depression. Range of motion and stretching exercises can help prevent painful spasticity and shortening (contracture) of muscles. Physical therapists can recommend exercises that provide these benefits without overworking muscles. Occupational therapists can suggest devices such as ramps, braces, walkers, and wheelchairs that help individuals conserve energy and remain mobile.

People with ALS who have difficulty speaking may benefit from working with a speech therapist. These health professionals can teach individuals adaptive strategies such as techniques to help them speak louder and more clearly. As ALS progresses, speech therapists can help people develop ways for responding to yes-or-no questions with their eyes or by other nonverbal means and can recommend aids such as speech synthesizers and computer-based communication systems. These methods and devices help people communicate when they can no longer speak or produce vocal sounds.

Nutritional support is an important part of the care of people with ALS. Individuals and caregivers can learn from speech therapists and nutritionists how to plan and prepare numerous small meals throughout the day that provide enough calories, fiber, and fluid and how to avoid foods that are difficult to swallow. People may begin using suction devices to remove excess fluids or saliva and prevent choking. When individuals can no longer get enough nourishment from eating, doctors may advise inserting a feeding tube into the stomach. The use of a feeding tube also reduces the risk of choking and pneumonia that can result from inhaling liquids into the lungs. The tube is not painful and does not prevent individuals from eating food orally if they wish.

When the muscles that assist in breathing weaken, use of nocturnal ventilatory assistance (intermittent positive pressure ventilation [IPPV] or bilevel positive airway pressure [BIPAP]) may be used to aid breathing during sleep. Such devices artificially inflate the person's lungs from various external sources that are applied directly to the face or body. Individuals with ALS will have breathing tests on a regular basis to determine when to start non-invasive ventilation (NIV). When muscles are no longer able to maintain normal oxygen and carbon dioxide levels, these devices may be used full-time. The NeuRx Diaphragm Pacing System, which uses implanted electrodes and a battery pack to cause the diaphragm (breathing muscle) to contract, has been approved by the Food and Drug Administration to help certain individuals who have ALS and breathing problems an average benefit of up to 16 months before onset of severe respiratory failure.

Individuals may eventually consider forms of mechanical ventilation (respirators) in which a machine inflates and deflates the lungs. To be effective, this may require a tube that passes from the nose or mouth to the windpipe (trachea) and for long-term use, an operation such as a tracheostomy, in which a plastic breathing tube is inserted directly in the patient's windpipe through an opening in the neck. Patients and their families should consider several factors when deciding whether and when to use one of these options. Ventilation devices differ in their effect on the person's quality of life and in cost. Although ventilation support can ease problems with breathing and prolong survival, it does not affect the progression of ALS. People need to be fully informed about these considerations and the long-term effects of life without movement before they make decisions about ventilation support.

Social workers and home care and hospice nurses help patients, families, and caregivers with the medical, emotional, and financial challenges of coping with ALS, particularly during the final stages of the disease. Respiratory therapists can help caregivers with tasks such as operating and maintaining respirators, and home care nurses are available not only to provide medical care but also to teach caregivers about giving tube feedings and moving patients to avoid painful skin problems and contractures. Home hospice nurses work in consultation with physicians to ensure proper medication and pain control.

Section 22.3

Multiple Sclerosis

Text in this chapter is excerpted from "Multiple Sclerosis," National Institute of Neurological Disorders and Stroke (NINDS), June 2012.

Introduction

Multiple sclerosis (MS) is the most common disabling neurological disease of young adults. It most often appears when people are between 20 to 40 years old. However, it can also affect children and older people.

The course of MS is unpredictable. A small number of those with MS will have a mild course with little to no disability, while another smaller group will have a steadily worsening disease that leads to increased disability over time. Most people with MS, however, will have short periods of symptoms followed by long stretches of relative relief, with partial or full recovery. There is no way to predict, at the beginning, how an individual person's disease will progress.

Researchers have spent decades trying to understand why some people get MS and others don't, and why some individuals with MS have symptoms that progress rapidly while others do not. How does the disease begin? Why is the course of MS so different from person to person? Is there anything we can do to prevent it? Can it be cured?

What is Multiple Sclerosis?

Multiple sclerosis (MS) is a neuroinflammatory disease that affects myelin, a substance that makes up the membrane (called the myelin sheath) that wraps around nerve fibers (axons). Myelinated axons are commonly called *white matter*. Researchers have learned that MS also damages the nerve cell bodies, which are found in the brain's *gray matter*, as well as the axons themselves in the brain, spinal cord, and optic nerve (the nerve that transmits visual information from the eye to the brain). As the disease progresses, the brain's cortex shrinks (cortical atrophy).

The term multiple sclerosis refers to the distinctive areas of scar tissue (sclerosis or plaques) that are visible in the white matter of people who have MS. Plaques can be as small as a pinhead or as large as the size of a golf ball. Doctors can see these areas by examining the brain and spinal cord using a type of brain scan called *magnetic resonance imaging* (MRI).

While MS sometimes causes severe disability, it is only rarely fatal and most people with MS have a normal life expectancy.

What are plaques made of and why do they develop?

Plaques, or *lesions*, are the result of an inflammatory process in the brain that causes immune system cells to attack myelin. The myelin sheath helps to speed nerve impulses traveling within the nervous system. Axons are also damaged in MS, although not as extensively, or as early in the disease, as myelin.

Under normal circumstances, cells of the immune system travel in and out of the brain patrolling for infectious agents (viruses, for example) or unhealthy cells. This is called the "surveillance" function of the immune system.

Surveillance cells usually won't spring into action unless they recognize an infectious agent or unhealthy cells. When they do, they produce substances to stop the infectious agent. If they encounter unhealthy cells, they either kill them directly or clean out the dying area and produce substances that promote healing and repair among the cells that are left.

Researchers have observed that immune cells behave differently in the brains of people with MS. They become active and attack what appears to be healthy myelin. It is unclear what triggers this attack. MS is one of many autoimmune disorders, such as rheumatoid arthritis and lupus, in which the immune system mistakenly attacks a person's healthy tissue as opposed to performing its normal role of attacking foreign invaders like viruses and bacteria. Whatever the reason, during these periods of immune system activity, most of the myelin within the affected area is damaged or destroyed. The axons also may be damaged. The symptoms of MS depend on the severity of the immune reaction as well as the location and extent of the plaques, which primarily appear in the brain stem, cerebellum, spinal cord, optic nerves, and the white matter of the brain around the brain ventricles (fluid-filled spaces inside of the brain).

What are the signs and symptoms of MS?

The symptoms of MS usually begin over one to several days, but in some forms, they may develop more slowly. They may be mild or severe and may go away quickly or last for months. Sometimes the initial symptoms of MS are overlooked because they disappear in a day or so and normal function returns. Because symptoms come and go in the majority of people with MS, the presence of symptoms is called an attack, or in medical terms, an exacerbation. Recovery from symptoms is referred to as remission, while a return of symptoms is called a relapse. This form of MS is therefore called *relapsing-remitting* MS, in contrast to a more slowly developing form called primary progressive MS. Progressive MS can also be a second stage of the illness that follows years of relapsing-remitting symptoms.

A diagnosis of MS is often delayed because MS shares symptoms with other neurological conditions and diseases.

The first symptoms of MS often include:

- vision problems such as blurred or double vision or optic neuritis, which causes pain in the eye and a rapid loss of vision.

- weak, stiff muscles, often with painful muscle spasms

- tingling or numbness in the arms, legs, trunk of the body, or face

195

- clumsiness, particularly difficulty staying balanced when walking

- bladder control problems, either inability to control the bladder or urgency

- dizziness that doesn't go away

MS may also cause later symptoms such as:

- mental or physical fatigue which accompanies the above symptoms during an attack

- mood changes such as depression or euphoria

- changes in the ability to concentrate or to multitask effectively

- difficulty making decisions, planning, or prioritizing at work or in private life.

Some people with MS develop transverse myelitis, a condition caused by inflammation in the spinal cord. Transverse myelitis causes loss of spinal cord function over a period of time lasting from several hours to several weeks. It usually begins as a sudden onset of lower back pain, muscle weakness, or abnormal sensations in the toes and feet, and can rapidly progress to more severe symptoms, including paralysis. In most cases of transverse myelitis, people recover at least some function within the first 12 weeks after an attack begins. Transverse myelitis can also result from viral infections, arteriovenous malformations, or neuroinflammatory problems unrelated to MS. In such instances, there are no plaques in the brain that suggest previous MS attacks.

Neuro-myelitis optica is a disorder associated with transverse myelitis as well as optic nerve inflammation. Patients with this disorder usually have antibodies against a particular protein in their spinal cord, called the aquaporin channel. These patients respond differently to treatment than most people with MS.

Most individuals with MS have muscle weakness, often in their hands and legs. Muscle stiffness and spasms can also be a problem. These symptoms may be severe enough to affect walking or standing. In some cases, MS leads to partial or complete paralysis. Many people with MS find that weakness and fatigue are worse when they have a fever or when they are exposed to heat. MS exacerbations may occur following common infections.

Tingling and burning sensations are common, as well as the opposite, numbness and loss of sensation. Moving the neck from side to side or flexing it back and forth may cause "Lhermitte's sign," a characteristic sensation of MS that feels like a sharp spike of electricity coursing down the spine.

While it is rare for pain to be the first sign of MS, pain often occurs with optic neuritis and trigeminal neuralgia, a neurological disorder that affects one of the nerves that runs across the jaw, cheek, and face. Painful spasms of the limbs and sharp pain shooting down the legs or around the abdomen can also be symptoms of MS.

Most individuals with MS experience difficulties with coordination and balance at some time during the course of the disease. Some may have a continuous trembling of the head, limbs, and body, especially during movement, although such trembling is more common with other disorders such as Parkinson's disease.

Fatigue is common, especially during exacerbations of MS. A person with MS may be tired all the time or may be easily fatigued from mental or physical exertion.

Urinary symptoms, including loss of bladder control and sudden attacks of urgency, are common as MS progresses. People with MS sometimes also develop constipation or sexual problems.

Depression is a common feature of MS. A small number of individuals with MS may develop more severe psychiatric disorders such as bipolar disorder and paranoia, or experience inappropriate episodes of high spirits, known as euphoria.

People with MS, especially those who have had the disease for a long time, can experience difficulty with thinking, learning, memory, and judgment. The first signs of what doctors call cognitive dysfunction may be subtle. The person may have problems finding the right word to say, or trouble remembering how to do routine tasks on the job or at home. Day-to-day decisions that once came easily may now be made more slowly and show poor judgment. Changes may be so small or happen so slowly that it takes a family member or friend to point them out.

How is MS diagnosed?

There is no single test used to diagnose MS. Doctors use a number of tests to rule out or confirm the diagnosis. There are many other disorders that can mimic MS. Some of these other disorders can be cured, while others require different treatments than those used for MS. Therefore, it is very important to perform a thorough investigation before making a diagnosis.

In addition to a complete medical history, physical examination, and a detailed neurological examination, a doctor will order an MRI scan of the head and spine to look for the characteristic lesions of MS. MRI is used to generate images of the brain and/or spinal cord. Then a special dye or contrast agent is injected into a vein and the MRI is repeated. In regions with active inflammation in MS, there is disruption of the blood-brain barrier and the dye will leak into the active MS lesion.

Doctors may also order evoked potential tests, which use electrodes on the skin and painless electric signals to measure how quickly and accurately the nervous system responds to stimulation. In addition, they may request a lumbar puncture (sometimes called a "spinal tap") to obtain a sample of cerebrospinal fluid. This allows them to look for proteins and inflammatory cells associated with the disease and to rule out other diseases that may look similar to MS, including some infections and other illnesses. MS is confirmed when positive signs of the disease are found in different parts of the nervous system at more than one time interval and there is no alternative diagnosis.

Are there treatments available for MS?

There is still no cure for MS, but there are treatments for initial attacks, medications and therapies to improve symptoms, and recently developed drugs to slow the worsening of the disease. These new drugs have been shown to reduce the number and severity of relapses and to delay the long term progression of MS.

How do doctors treat the symptoms of MS?

MS causes a variety of symptoms that can interfere with daily activities but which can usually be treated or managed to reduce their impact. Many of these issues are best treated by neurologists who have advanced training in the treatment of MS and who can prescribe specific medications to treat the problems.

Vision problems

Eye and vision problems are common in people with MS but rarely result in permanent blindness. Inflammation of the optic nerve or damage to the myelin that covers the optic nerve and other nerve fibers can cause a number of symptoms, including blurring or graying of vision, blindness in one eye, loss of normal color vision, depth perception, or a dark spot in the center of the visual field (scotoma).

Uncontrolled horizontal or vertical eye movements (nystagmus) and "jumping vision" (opsoclonus) are common to MS, and can be either mild or severe enough to impair vision.

Double vision (diplopia) occurs when the two eyes are not perfectly aligned. This occurs commonly in MS when a pair of muscles that control a specific eye movement aren't coordinated due to weakness in one or both muscles. Double vision may increase with fatigue or as the result of spending too much time reading or on the computer. Periodically resting the eyes may be helpful.

Weak muscles, stiff muscles, painful muscle spasms, and weak reflexes

Muscle weakness is common in MS, along with muscle spasticity. Spasticity refers to muscles that are stiff or that go into spasms without any warning. Spasticity in MS can be as mild as a feeling of tightness in the muscles or so severe that it causes painful, uncontrolled spasms. It can also cause pain or tightness in and around the joints. It also frequently affects walking, reducing the normal flexibility or "bounce" involved in taking steps.

Tremor

People with MS sometimes develop tremor, or uncontrollable shaking, often triggered by movement. Tremor can be very disabling. Assistive devices and weights attached to limbs are sometimes helpful for people with tremor. Deep brain stimulation& and drugs such as clonazepam also may be useful.

Problems with walking and balance

Many people with MS experience difficulty walking. In fact, studies indicate that half of those with relapsing-remitting MS will need some kind of help walking within 15 years of their diagnosis if they remain untreated. The most common walking problem in people with MS experience is ataxia—unsteady, uncoordinated movements—due to damage with the areas of the brain that coordinate movement of muscles. People with severe ataxia generally benefit from the use of a cane, walker, or other assistive device. Physical therapy can also reduce walking problems in many cases.

In 2010, the FDA approved the drug dalfampridine to improve walking in patients with MS. It is the first drug approved for this use. Clinical trials showed that patients treated with dalfampridine had faster walking speeds than those treated with a placebo pill.

Fatigue

Fatigue is a common symptom of MS and may be both physical (for example, tiredness in the legs) and psychological (due to depression). Probably the most important measures people with MS can take to counter physical fatigue are to avoid excessive activity and to stay out of the heat, which often aggravates MS symptoms. On the other hand, daily physical activity programs of mild to moderate intensity can significantly reduce fatigue. An antidepressant such as fluoxetine may be prescribed if the fatigue is caused by depression. Other drugs that may reduce fatigue in some individuals include amantadine and modafinil.

Fatigue may be reduced if the person receives occupational therapy to simplify tasks and/or physical therapy to learn how to walk in a way that saves physical energy or that takes advantage of an assistive device. Some people benefit from stress management programs, relaxation training, membership in an MS support group, or individual psychotherapy. Treating sleep problems and MS symptoms that interfere with sleep (such as spastic muscles) may also help.

Pain

People with MS may experience several types of pain during the course of the disease.

Trigeminal neuralgia is a sharp, stabbing, facial pain caused by MS affecting the trigeminal nerve as it exits the brainstem on its way to the jaw and cheek. It can be treated with anticonvulsant or antispasmodic drugs, alcohol injections, or surgery.

People with MS occasionally develop central pain, a syndrome caused by damage to the brain and/or spinal cord. Drugs such as gabapentin and nortryptiline sometimes help to reduce central pain.

Burning, tingling, and prickling (commonly called "pins and needles") are sensations that happen in the absence of any stimulation. The medical term for them is dysesthesias" They are often chronic and hard to treat.

Chronic back or other musculoskeletal pain may be caused by walking problems or by using assistive aids incorrectly. Treatments may include heat, massage, ultrasound treatments, and physical therapy to correct faulty posture and strengthen and stretch muscles.

Problems with bladder control and constipation

The most common bladder control problems encountered by people with MS are urinary frequency, urgency, or the loss of bladder control.

The same spasticity that causes spasms in legs can also affect the bladder. A small number of individuals will have the opposite problem—retaining large amounts of urine. Urologists can help with treatment of bladder-related problems. A number of medical treatments are available. Constipation is also common and can be treated with a high-fiber diet, laxatives, and other measures.

Sexual issues

People with MS sometimes experience sexual problems. Sexual arousal begins in the central nervous system, as the brain sends messages to the sex organs along nerves running through the spinal cord. If MS damages these nerve pathways, sexual response—including arousal and orgasm—can be directly affected. Sexual problems may also stem from MS symptoms such as fatigue, cramped or spastic muscles, and psychological factors related to lowered self-esteem or depression. Some of these problems can be corrected with medications. Psychological counseling also may be helpful.

Depression

Studies indicate that clinical depression is more frequent among people with MS than it is in the general population or in persons with many other chronic, disabling conditions. MS may cause depression as part of the disease process, since it damages myelin and nerve fibers inside the brain. If the plaques are in parts of the brain that are involved in emotional expression and control, a variety of behavioral changes can result, including depression. Depression can intensify symptoms of fatigue, pain, and sexual dysfunction. It is most often treated with selective serotonin reuptake inhibitor (SSRI) antidepressant medications, which are less likely than other antidepressant medications to cause fatigue.

Inappropriate laughing or crying

MS is sometimes associated with a condition called pseudobulbar affect that causes inappropriate and involuntary expressions of laughter, crying, or anger. These expressions are often unrelated to mood; for example, the person may cry when they are actually very happy, or laugh when they are not especially happy. In 2010, the U.S. Food and Drug Administration (FDA) approved the first treatment specifically for pseudobulbar affect, a combination of the drugs dextromethorphan and quinidine. The condition can also be treated with other drugs such as amitriptyline or citalopram.

201

Cognitive changes

Half- to three-quarters of people with MS experience cognitive impairment, which is a phrase doctors use to describe a decline in the ability to think quickly and clearly and to remember easily. These cognitive changes may appear at the same time as the physical symptoms or they may develop gradually over time. Some individuals with MS may feel as if they are thinking more slowly, are easily distracted, have trouble remembering, or are losing their way with words. The right word may often seem to be on the tip of their tongue.

Some experts believe that it is more likely to be cognitive decline, rather than physical impairment, that causes people with MS to eventually withdraw from the workforce. A number of neuropsychological tests have been developed to evaluate the cognitive status of individuals with MS. Based on the outcomes of these tests, a neuropsychologist can determine the extent of strengths and weaknesses in different cognitive areas. Drugs such as donepezil, which is usually used for Alzheimer's disease, may be helpful in some cases.

Complementary and Alternative Therapies (CAM)

Many people with MS use some form of complementary or alternative medicine. These therapies come from many disciplines, cultures, and traditions and encompass techniques as different as acupuncture, aromatherapy, ayurvedic medicine, touch and energy therapies, physical movement disciplines such as yoga and tai chi, herbal supplements, and biofeedback.

Because of the risk of interactions between alternative and more conventional therapies, people with MS should discuss all the therapies they are using with their doctor, especially herbal supplements. Although herbal supplements are considered "natural," they have biologically-active ingredients that could have harmful effects on their own or interact harmfully with other medications.

Section 22.4

Parkinson's Disease

Text in this section is excerpted from "Parkinson's Disease," National Institute of Neurological Disorders and Stroke (NINDS), December 2014.

What is Parkinson's disease?

Parkinson's disease (PD) is a degenerative disorder of the central nervous system that belongs to a group of conditions called movement disorders. It is both chronic, meaning it persists over a long period of time, and progressive, meaning its symptoms grow worse over time. As nerve cells (neurons) in parts of the brain become impaired or die, people may begin to notice problems with movement, tremor, stiffness in the limbs or the trunk of the body, or impaired balance. As these symptoms become more pronounced, people may have difficulty walking, talking, or completing other simple tasks. Not everyone with one or more of these symptoms has PD, as the symptoms appear in other diseases as well.

The precise cause of PD is unknown, although some cases of PD are hereditary and can be traced to specific genetic mutations. Most cases are sporadic—that is, the disease does not typically run in families. It is thought that PD likely results from a combination of genetic susceptibility and exposure to one or more unknown environmental factors that trigger the disease.

PD is the most common form of parkinsonism, in which disorders of other causes produce features and symptoms that closely resemble Parkinson's disease. While most forms of parkinsonism have no known cause, there are cases in which the cause is known or suspected or where the symptoms result from another disorder.

No cure for PD exists at present time, but research is ongoing and medications or surgery can often provide substantial improvement with motor symptoms.

What are the symptoms of the disease?

The four primary symptoms of PD are:

1. **Tremor.** The tremor associated with PD has a characteristic appearance. Typically, the tremor takes the form of a rhythmic back-and-forth motion at a rate of 4-6 beats per second. It may involve the thumb and forefinger and appear as a "pill rolling" tremor. Tremor often begins in a hand, although sometimes a foot or the jaw is affected first. It is most obvious when the hand is at rest or when a person is under stress. Tremor usually disappears during sleep or improves with intentional movement. It is usually the first symptom that causes people to seek medical attention.

2. **Rigidity.** Rigidity, or a resistance to movement, affects most people with PD. The muscles remain constantly tense and contracted so that the person aches or feels stiff. The rigidity becomes obvious when another person tries to move the individual's arm, which will move only in ratchet-like or short, jerky movements known as "cogwheel" rigidity.

3. **Bradykinesia.** This slowing down of spontaneous and automatic movement is particularly frustrating because it may make simple tasks difficult. The person cannot rapidly perform routine movements. Activities once performed quickly and easily—such as washing or dressing—may take much longer. There is often a decrease in facial expressions.

4. **Postural instability.** Postural instability, or impaired balance, causes affected individuals to fall easily.

PD does not affect everyone the same way, and the rate of progression and the particular symptoms differ among individuals.

PD symptoms typically begin on one side of the body. However, the disease eventually affects both sides. Even after the disease involves both sides of the body, the symptoms are often less severe on one side than on the other.

Friends or family members may be the first to notice changes in someone with early PD. They may see that the person's face lacks expression and animation (known as "masked face") or that the person moves more slowly.

Early symptoms of PD may be subtle and occur gradually. Affected people may feel mild tremors or have difficulty getting out of a chair. Activities may take longer to complete than in the past and individuals may note some stiffness in addition to slowness. They may notice that they speak too softly or that their handwriting is slow and looks cramped or small. This very early period may last a long time before the more classical and obvious motor (movement) symptoms appear.

As the disease progresses, the symptoms of Parkinson's disease may begin to interfere with daily activities. Affected individuals may not be able to hold utensils steady or they may find that the shaking makes reading a newspaper difficult. People with PD often develop a so-called parkinsonian gait that includes a tendency to lean forward, taking small quick steps as if hurrying (called festination), and reduced swinging in one or both arms. They may have trouble initiating movement (start hesitation), and they may stop suddenly as they walk (freezing).

A number of other symptoms may accompany PD, and some can be treated with medication or physical therapy.

- *Depression.* This common disorder may appear early in the course of the disease, even before other symptoms are noticed. Some people lose their motivation and become dependent on family members. Fortunately, depression typically can be treated successfully with antidepressant medications such as amytriptyline or fluoxetine.

- *Emotional changes.* Some people with PD become fearful and insecure, while others may become irritable or uncharacteristically pessimistic.

- *Difficulty with swallowing and chewing.* Muscles used in swallowing may work less efficiently in later stages of the disease. Food and saliva may collect in the mouth and back of the throat, which can result in choking or drooling. These problems may also make it difficult to get adequate nutrition. Speech-language therapists, occupational therapists (who help people learn new ways to perform activities of daily living), and dieticians can often help with these problems.

- *Speech changes.* About half of all individuals with PD have speech difficulties that may be characterized as speaking too softly or in a monotone. Some may hesitate before speaking, slur, or speak too fast. A speech therapist may be able to help these individuals reduce some of these problems.

- *Urinary problems or constipation.* In some people with PD, bladder and bowel problems can occur due to the improper functioning of the autonomic nervous system, which is responsible for regulating smooth muscle activity. Medications can effectively treat some of these symptoms.

- *Skin problems.* In PD, the skin on the face may become oily, particularly on the forehead and at the sides of the nose. The scalp may become oily too, resulting in dandruff. In other cases, the skin can become very dry. Standard treatments for skin problems can help.

- *Sleep problems.* Sleep problems are common in PD and include difficulty staying asleep at night, restless sleep, nightmares and emotional dreams, and drowsiness or sudden sleep onset during the day. Another common problem is "REM behavior disorder," in which people act out their dreams, potentially resulting in injury to themselves or their bed partners. The medications used to treat PD may contribute to some of these sleep issues. Many of these problems respond to specific therapies.

- *Dementia or other cognitive problems.* Some people with PD may develop memory problems and slow thinking. Cognitive problems become more severe in late stages of PD, and a diagnosis of Parkinson's disease dementia (PDD) may be given. Memory, social judgment, language, reasoning, or other mental skills may be affected. There is currently no way to halt PD dementia, but drugs such as rivastigmine, donepezil, or memantine may help. The medications used to treat the motor symptoms of PD may cause confusion and hallucinations.

- *Orthostatic hypotension.* Orthostatic hypotension is a sudden drop in blood pressure when a person stands up from a lying-down or seated position. This may cause dizziness, lightheadedness, and, in extreme cases, loss of balance or fainting. Studies have suggested that, in PD, this problem results from a loss of nerve endings in the sympathetic nervous system that controls heart rate, blood pressure, and other automatic functions in the body. The medications used to treat PD may also contribute to this symptom. Orthostatic hypotension may improve by increasing salt intake. Physicians treating the disorder may also reduce anti-hypertension drug dosage or by prescribing medications such as fludrocortisone.

- *Muscle cramps and dystonia.* The rigidity and lack of normal movement associated with PD often causes muscle cramps, especially in the legs and toes. Massage, stretching, and applying heat may help with these cramps. PD can also be associated with dystonia—sustained muscle contractions that cause forced or twisted positions. Dystonia in PD is often caused by fluctuations in the body's level of dopamine. Management strategies may involve adjusting medications.

- *Pain.* Many people with PD develop aching muscles and joints because of the rigidity and abnormal postures often associated with the disease. Treatment with levodopa and other dopaminergic drugs often alleviates these pains to some extent. Certain exercises may help.

- *Fatigue and loss of energy.* Many people with PD often have fatigue, especially late in the day. Fatigue may be associated with depression or sleep disorders, but it may also result from muscle stress or from overdoing activity when the person feels well. Fatigue may also result from akinesia—trouble initiating or carrying out movement. Exercise, good sleep habits, staying mentally active, and not forcing too many activities in a short time may help to alleviate fatigue.

- *Sexual dysfunction.* Because of its effects on nerve signals from the brain, PD may cause sexual dysfunction. PD-related depression or use of certain medications may also cause decreased sex drive and other problems. People should discuss these issues with their physician as they may be treatable.

Hallucinations, delusions, and other psychotic symptoms can be caused by the drugs prescribed for PD. Reducing PD medications dosages or changing medications may be necessary if hallucinations occur. If such measures are not effective, doctors sometimes prescribe drugs called atypical antipsychotics, which include clozapine and quetiapine. The typical antipsychotic drugs, which include haloperidol, worsen the motor symptoms of PD and should not be used.

How is Parkinson's disease diagnosed?

There are currently no blood or laboratory tests that diagnose sporadic PD. Therefore, the diagnosis is based on medical history and a neurological examination. In some cases PD can be difficult to diagnose accurately early on in the course of the disease. Early signs and symptoms of PD may sometimes be dismissed as the effects of normal aging. Doctors may sometimes request brain scans or laboratory tests in order to rule out other disorders. However, computed tomography (CT) and magnetic resonance imaging (MRI) brain scans of people with

PD usually appear normal. Since many other diseases have similar features but require different treatments, making a precise diagnosis is important so that people can receive the proper treatment.

What is the prognosis?

The average life expectancy of a person with PD is generally the same as for people who do not have the disease. Fortunately, there are many treatment options available for people with PD. However, in the late stages, PD may no longer respond to medications and can become associated with serious complications such as choking, pneumonia, and falls.

PD is a slowly progressive disorder. It is not possible to predict what course the disease will take for an individual person. One commonly used scale neurologists use for describing how the symptoms of PD have progressed in a patient is the Hoehn and Yahr scale.

Hoehn and Yahr Staging of Parkinson's Disease

Stage one – symptoms on one side of the body only.

Stage two – symptoms on both sides of the body. No impairment of balance.

Stage three – balance impairment. Mild to moderate disease. Physically independent.

Stage four – severe disability, but still able to walk or stand unassisted.

Stage five – wheelchair-bound or bedridden unless assisted.

Another commonly used scale is the Movement Disorders Society-Unified Parkinson's Disease Rating Scale (MDS-UPDRS). This four-part scale measures motor movement in PD: non-motor experiences of daily living, motor experiences of daily living, motor examination, and motor complications. Both the Hoehn and Yahr scale and the MDS-UPDRS are used to describe how individuals are faring and to help assess treatment response.

How is the disease treated?

At present, there is no cure for PD, but medications or surgery can often provide improvement in the motor symptoms.

Drug Therapy

Medications for PD fall into three categories.

The first category includes drugs that increase the level of dopamine in the brain. The most common drugs for PD are dopamine precursors—substances such as levodopa that cross the blood-brain barrier and are then changed into dopamine. Other drugs mimic dopamine or prevent or slow its breakdown.

The second category of PD drugs affects other neurotransmitters in the body in order to ease some of the symptoms of the disease. For example, anticholinergic drugs interfere with production or uptake of the neurotransmitter acetylcholine. These can be effective in reducing tremors.

The third category of drugs prescribed for PD includes medications that help control the non-motor symptoms of the disease, that is, the symptoms that don't affect movement. For example, people with PD-related depression may be prescribed antidepressants

Surgery

Before the discovery of levodopa, surgery was an option for treating PD. Studies in the past few decades have led to great improvements in surgical techniques, and surgery is again considered for people with PD for whom drug therapy is no longer sufficient.

Pallidotomy and Thalamotomy. The earliest types of surgery for PD involved selectively destroying specific parts of the brain that contribute to PD symptoms. Surgical techniques have been refined and can be very effective for the motor symptoms of PD. The most common lesion surgery is called pallidotomy. In this procedure, a surgeon selectively destroys a portion of the brain called the globus pallidus. Pallidotomy can improve symptoms of tremor, rigidity, and bradykinesia, possibly by interrupting the connections between the globus pallidus and the striatum or thalamus. Some studies have also found that pallidotomy can improve gait and balance and reduce the amount of levodopa people require, thus reducing drug-induced dyskinesias. Another procedure, called thalamotomy, involves surgically destroying part of the thalamus; this approach is useful primarily to reduce tremor.

Because these procedures cause permanent destruction of small amounts of brain tissue, they have largely been replaced by deep brain stimulation for treatment of PD. However, a new method using focused ultrasound from outside the head is being tested because it creates lesions without the need for surgery.

Deep Brain Stimulation. Deep brain stimulation, or DBS, uses an electrode surgically implanted into part of the brain, typically the subthalamic nucleus or the globus pallidus. Similar to a cardiac pacemaker, a pulse generator (battery pack) that is implanted in the chest area under the collarbone sends finely controlled electrical signals to the electrode(s) via a wire placed under the skin. When turned on using an external wand, the pulse generator and electrodes painlessly stimulate the brain in a way that helps to block signals that cause many of the motor symptoms of PD. DBS is approved by the U.S. Food and Drug Administration and is widely used as a treatment for PD.

DBS can be used on one or both sides of the brain. If it is used on just one side, it will affect symptoms on the opposite side of the body. DBS is primarily used to stimulate one of three brain regions: the subthalamic nucleus, the globus pallidus interna, or the thalamus. Stimulation of either the globus pallidus or the subthalamic nucleus can reduce tremor, bradykinesia, and rigidity. Stimulation of the thalamus is useful primarily for reducing tremor.

People who initially responded well to treatment with levodopa tend to respond well to DBS. While the motor function benefits of DBS can be substantial, it usually does not help with speech problems, "freezing," posture, balance, anxiety, depression, or dementia.

One advantage of DBS compared to pallidotomy and thalamotomy is that the electrical current can be turned off using a handheld device. The pulse generator also can be externally programmed.

Individuals must return to the medical center frequently for several months after DBS surgery in order to have the stimulation adjusted very carefully to give the best results. After a few months, the number of medical visits usually decreases significantly, though individuals may occasionally need to return to the center to have their stimulator checked. Currently, the battery for the pulse generator must be surgically replaced every three to five years. DBS does not stop PD from progressing, and some problems may gradually return. DBS is not a good option for everyone. It is generally appropriate for people with levodopa-responsive PD who have developed dyskinesias or other disabling "off" symptoms despite drug therapy. It is not generally an option for people with memory problems, hallucinations, severe depression, poor health, or a poor response to levodopa. DBS has not been demonstrated to be of benefit for "atypical" parkinsonian syndromes such as multiple system atrophy, progressive supranuclear palsy, or post-traumatic parkinsonism, which also do not improve with Parkinson's medications.

As with any brain surgery, DBS has potential complications, including stroke or brain hemorrhage. These complications are rare, however. There is also a risk of infection, which may require antibiotics or even replacement of parts of the DBS system.

Complementary and Supportive Therapies

A wide variety of complementary and supportive therapies may be used for PD. Among these therapies are standard physical, occupational, and speech therapy techniques, which can help with such problems as gait and voice disorders, tremors and rigidity, and cognitive decline.

Part Three

Assistive Technology and Treatment Options That Help People with Disabilities

Chapter 23

What Is Assistive Technology?

Assistive Technology

Assistive technology is any service or tool which can help an older person or a person with a disability perform activities that might otherwise be difficult or not be possible. Such technology may be something as simple as a walker to make moving around easier or an amplification device to make sounds easier to hear (for talking on the telephone or watching television, for instance). It could also include a magnifying glass that helps someone who has poor vision read the newspaper or a scooter that makes it possible to travel over distances that are too far to walk. In short, anything that helps the elderly continue to participate in daily activities is considered assistive technology.

For many seniors, assistive technology makes the difference between being able to live independently and having to get long-term nursing or home-health care. For others, assistive technology is critical to the ability to perform simple activities of daily living, such as bathing and going to the bathroom.

This chapter includes excerpts from "Assistive Technology," U.S. Department of Health & Human Services (HHS), April 13, 2012; text from "Rehabilitative and Assistive Technology: Condition Information," National Institute of Child Health and Human Development (NICHD), November 30, 2012; and text from "Rehabilitation Engineering," National Institute Of Biomedical Imaging And Bioengineering (NIBIB), June 2013.

How can I tell if assistive technology is right for me?

Older adults must carefully evaluate their needs before deciding to purchase assistive technology. Using assistive technology may change the mix of services that a senior requires or may affect the way that those services are provided. For this reason, the process of needs assessment and planning is important.

Usually, needs assessment has the most value when it is done by a team working with the senior in the place where the assistive technology will be used. For example, an older person who has trouble communicating or is hard of hearing should consult with his or her doctor, an audiology specialist, a speech-language therapist, along with family and friends. Together, these people can identify the problem precisely and can help select the most effective devices available at the lowest cost. A professional member of the team, such as the audiology specialist, can also arrange for any training that the senior and his or her family may require to use the equipment needed.

When considering all the options of assistive technology, it is often useful to look at the issue in terms of high-tech and low-tech solutions. Seniors must also remember to plan ahead and think about how their needs might change over time. High-tech devices tend to be more expensive but may be able to assist with many different needs. Low-tech equipment is usually cheaper but less adaptable for multiple purposes.

How Can I Pay For Assistive Technology?

Right now, no single private insurance plan or public program will pay for all types of assistive technology under any circumstances. However, Medicare Part B will cover up to 80% of the cost of assistive technology if the items being purchased meet the definition of "durable medical equipment." This is defined as devices that are "primarily and customarily used to serve a medical purpose, and generally are not useful to a person in the absence of illness or injury." To find out if Medicare will cover the cost of a particular piece of assistive technology, call 1-800-MEDICARE (1-800-633-4227, TTY/TDD: 1-877-486-2048).

Depending on where you live, the state-run Medicaid program may pay for some assistive technology. Keep in mind, though, that even when Medicaid does cover part of the cost, the benefits usually do not provide the amount of financial aid needed to buy an expensive piece of equipment, such as a power wheelchair.

Seniors who are eligible for veterans' benefits should definitely look into whether they can receive assistance from the Department of Veterans Affairs (DVA). Many people consider the DVA to have a model payment system for assistive technology because the agency has a structure in place to pay for the large volume of equipment that it buys. The DVA also invests in training people in how to use assistive devices.Subsidy programs provide some types of assistive technology at a reduced cost or for free. Many businesses and not-for-profit groups have set up subsidy programs that include discounts, grants, or rebates to get consumers to try a specific product. The idea is that by offering this benefit, the program sponsors can encourage seniors and people with disabilities to use an item that they otherwise might not consider. Obviously, older adults should be careful about participating in subsidy programs that are run by businesses with commercial interests in the product or service because of the potential for fraud.

What is rehabilitation engineering?

Rehabilitation engineering is the use of engineering science and principles to 1) develop technological solutions and devices to assist individuals with disabilities and 2) aid the recovery of physical and cognitive functions lost because of disease or injury.

Rehabilitation engineers design and build devices and systems to meet a wide range of needs that can assist individuals with mobility, communication, hearing, vision, and cognition. These tools help people with day-to-day activities and tasks related to employment, independent living, and education.

Rehabilitation engineering may involve relatively simple observations of how workers perform tasks, and then making accommodations to eliminate further injuries and discomfort. On the other end of the spectrum, more complex rehabilitation engineering is the design of sophisticated brain computer interfaces that allow a severely disabled individual to operate computers, and other assistive devices simply by thinking about the task they want to perform.

Rehabilitation engineers also develop and improve rehabilitation methods used by individuals to regain functions lost due to disease or injury, such as limb (arm and or leg) mobility following a stroke or a joint replacement.

What types of assistive devices have been developed through rehabilitation engineering?

The following are examples of the many types of assistive devices.

- Wheelchairs; scooters; and prosthetic devices, such as artificial limbs that provide mobility for people with physical disabilities that affect movement.

- Kitchen implements with large, cushioned grips to help people with weakness or arthritis in their hands with everyday living tasks.

- Automatic page-turners, book holders, and adapted pencil grips, that allow participation in educational activities in school and at home.

- Medication dispensers with alarms that can help people remember to take their medicine on time.

- Specially engineered computer programs that provide voice recognition to help people with sensory impairments use computer technology.

What are NIBIB-funded researchers developing in the area of rehabilitation engineering?

Promising research currently supported by NIBIB includes a wide range of approaches and technological development. Several examples are described below.

Wireless Tongue Drive System for Paralyzed Patients: NIBIB-funded researchers are developing an assistive technology called the Tongue Drive System (TDS). The core TDS technology exploits the fact that even individuals with severe paralysis that impairs limb movement, breathing, and speech can still move their tongue. Simple tongue movements send commands to the computer allowing users to steer their wheelchairs, operate their computers, and generally control their environment in an independent fashion.

Neurostimulation in Individuals with Spinal Cord Injury (SCI) for Recovery of Voluntary Control of Standing and Movement, and Involuntary Control of Blood Pressure, Bladder and Sexual Function: Through the NIBIB Rehabilitation Engineering program, researchers are developing the next generation of high density electrode arrays for stimulation of the spinal cord. The first patient received a current generation electrical stimulator implant in his lower back. The electrical stimulation and locomotor training resulted in the ability to stand independently for several minutes, some voluntary leg control, and regained blood pressure control, bladder, bowel, and sexual function. Three more patients have received this treatment and had similar results.

Smart Environment Technologies: As the population ages, increasing numbers of Americans are unable to live independently. NIBIB-funded researchers are working on creating smart environments that aid with home health monitoring and intervention allowing individuals with health issues to remain safely at home. For example, researchers are analyzing the needs and limitations of Alzheimer's patients to develop automated and reminder-based technologies that can be integrated into the home to help with everyday tasks.

Artificial Hands Capable of Complex Movements and Sensation: Persons with hand amputations expect modern hand prostheses to function like intact hands. Current state-of-the-art prosthetic hands simply control two movements "open" and "close." As a result, NIBIB researchers are developing new artificial hand systems that would perform complex hand motions based on measurements of the residual electrical signals from the remaining muscles of an amputee's forearm. Signals from the muscles (in one project) and nerves (from another project) have the potential to result in much finer control of the fingers in the artificial hand. In addition, one of the teams is working on capturing the sense of touch, so in the future the users will be able to also "feel" what they are holding with their artificial hand.

Chapter 24

Home Use Medical Devices and Living Space Modifications

Chapter Contents

Section 24.1

Home Use Devices

This section includes excerpts from "Home Use Devices," U.S. Food
and Drug Administration (FDA), July 21, 2015; text from "Specific
Devices for Home Use," U.S. Food and Drug Administration (FDA),
December 10, 2014; text from "Unique Considerations in the Home,"
U.S. Food and Drug Administration (FDA), July 22, 2014; and text
from "Frequently Asked Questions About Home Use Devices," U.S.
Food and Drug Administration (FDA), December 10, 2014.

What is a Home Use Device?

A **home use medical device** is a medical device intended for
users in any environment outside of a professional health care facility.
This includes devices intended for use in both professional health care
facilities and homes.

- A user is a patient (care recipient), caregiver, or family member
  that directly uses the device or provides assistance in using the
  device.

- A qualified health care professional is a licensed or non-licensed
  health care professional with proficient skill and experience with
  the use of the device so that they can aid or train care recipients
  and caregivers to use and maintain the device

Unique considerations in the home

The home care setting is a challenging environment. Because it is
very different from the hospital setting, it often presents additional
risks to patients and providers. This section outlines environmental
considerations and potential safety hazards providers and patients
should be alert to when using—or considering using—a medical device
in the home setting.

Geographic Location

Where a person lives makes a difference in the type of home health
care services they receive. For example, home health care providers and

222

support staff may not be readily available in a rural setting, where it may also be difficult to obtain needed back-up supplies or equipment.

Different parts of the country experience power outages more frequently than others, especially during public emergencies like Hurricane Katrina. During these uncontrollable events, patients should have back-up plans and extra supplies when using certain medical devices.

Age and Structure of a Home

A home's age and structure can affect the quality of care, especially when using medical devices. For example, older homes may not have the electrical outlets needed for some medical devices. Older homes may also have smaller doorways, hallways, and rooms that do not accommodate large medical equipment. Smaller homes may not allow for wheelchairs to pass through the entranceway, forcing patients to use walkers, crutches, or canes instead.

Before a medical device goes home with a patient, check to see if the medical device is compatible with the patient's home.

- **Pets**

Pets may directly interfere with device operation. For example, they may chew through an electrical cord or play with an accessory, such as tubing. Pets may also contribute to unsanitary conditions where the medical device is used. They may walk over an area that is supposed to be clean, and pet fur/hair may find its way into a device.

- **Unsanitary Conditions**

Unhealthy conditions may result from dirty surface areas, wet towels on the bathroom floor, dirty dishes, and open or scattered garbage. For example, trash that is not properly contained or removed may attract insects and rodents.

The ability to manage medical waste properly and establish safe cleaning practices also requires attention. For instance, the improper disposal of sharps, such as needles, can lead to needle stick injuries in caregivers, patients, and household members. Each state or local government regulates the storage, transportation, and disposal of medical waste. Check with your local government to learn more.

- **Children at Play**

Children may interfere with medical device operation. They may change the dial, settings, and on/off switches, twist tubing, adjust machine vents, or remove electrical cords from the outlet. They can also injure themselves while playing with devices they think are toys.

- **Plumbing**

Clean, running water is critical to the use of a medical device in the home. Some medical devices and equipment, such as dialyzers or infusion pumps, require safe water during use, cleaning, and maintenance. Even if water is not required for a device to operate, it may be necessary for cleaning its accessories.

- **Temperature Extremes**

Extreme heat and humidity can negatively affect a working device. Unusually high levels of heat and humidity may:

- Cause instruments to operate in unexpected or unusual ways;

- Reduce the expected life span of devices or totally destroy products;

- Cause laboratory substances used in chemical analysis to lose strength; or

- Compromise the cleanliness of packaged devices.For example, high humidity becomes a problem when a low flow of air causes moisture to build up on a medical device, resulting in a malfunction. Excess moisture may also cause mold to grow on a device.

- **Dust**

Carpets and drapes can hold allergen-containing dust. If dust gets into a medical device, it may affect the way it works.

- **Fire Hazards**

Fire hazards are a concern when considering a home use medical device. Electrical problems with device equipment such as their potential to overheat or short–circuit may increase the likelihood for home fires. Home care patients who receive supplemental oxygen therapy are also at increased risk. Wherever there is a high concentration of oxygen gas, there is also an increased risk of fire initiated from electrical faults. Taking appropriate fire safety precautions is important.

- **Tripping Hazards**

Too much clutter, loose carpeting, and slippery floor surfaces may cause people to fall. Patients who have trouble moving around without the use of a walker, crutch, or cane have a higher risk of falling when these hazards are present.

- **Poor Lighting**

Poor lighting has been shown to result in injuries, especially from patient falls. Inadequate lighting wcan also make it more difficult for a patient or caregiver to see and operate a medical device.

- **Background Noise**

There is a lot of noise in the home environment–from vacuum cleaners, televisions, telephones, to people arguing. Outside noise, such as trash pick-up trucks and emergency sirens, is also common. All loud noise can interfere with the ability to hear whether a medical device is operating correctly or whether an alarm has sounded.

Frequently Asked Questions about Home Use Devices

What devices does FDA recommend for home use?

FDA is responsible for regulating companies that manufacture, repackage, re-label, and import medical devices sold in the United States. This is accomplished through scientific review of premarket data submitted by a medical device manufacturer to establish a device's safety and efficacy and then once on the market, monitoring medical device adverse event reports to detect and correct device-related problems in a timely manner.

It is important to note because the FDA's scope of work is to regulate the medical device industry, the FDA cannot and does not recommend specific medical devices for use in any setting. Review the instructions for use for a device you plan to use in the home before deciding on the one best for a particular patient population.

I have a patient who lives in a rural area and is being discharged from the hospital. She will be two hours from the nearest clinic. What medical device associated risks should I consider?

There are many risks to consider when caring for a patient who requires a medical device in their home environment, especially in rural areas. It is important to consider:

- What the device needs to operate safely and effectively, (for example: electricity, running water, computer connections, back up supplies)

- Power sources and outlets, (for example: are they compatible with one another?)

- Patient capabilities

Where can I buy home use devices?

Home Use devices are often sold to patients who have a prescription for that given device at hospitals or at pharmacies. Medical devices are also cleared or approved for sale directly to the consumer and these are called Over-the-Counter (OTC) products. Medical devices are also available at many online retailers. If you buy a home use device online, make sure you are buying from a reliable source. Also check the store's return policy and customer support statement before you place an order.

Who do I contact if my device breaks or doesn't work properly?

Make sure you have phone numbers for your homecare agency, doctor, or the device manufacturer to call if your device is not working properly.

Who can write a prescription for a medical device?

Each state has laws and regulations that determine who can write a prescription for a medical device in that state. FDA defers to the states on determining who can write a valid prescription.

How can I find out if my medical device has been recalled?

You can search FDA's online public recall database (www.access-data.fda.gov/scripts/cdrh/cfdocs/cfres/textsearch.cfm).

Do I need a prescription for my device?

Not all medical devices require a prescription; however, many medical devices do require a prescription (for example, contact lenses).

Section 24.2

Home Modifications

This section includes excerpts from "Home Modifications," U.S. Department of Health and Human Services (HHS), July 23, 2012.

Home modifications are changes made to adapt living spaces to meet the needs of people with physical limitations so that they can continue to live independently and safely. These modifications may include adding assistive technology or making structural changes to a home. Modifications can range from something as simple as replacing cabinet doorknobs with pull handles to full-scale construction projects that require installing wheelchair ramps and widening doorways.

The main benefit of making home modifications is that they promote independence and prevent accidents. According to a 2000 AARP housing survey, "89% of older Americans want to stay in their current homes for as long as possible," but other studies show that most homes are not designed to accommodate the needs of people over age 65. A house that was perfectly suitable for a senior at age 55, for example, may have too many stairs or slippery surfaces for a person who is 70 or 80.

How can I tell what home modifications are right for me?

The best way to begin planning for home modifications is by defining the basic terms used and asking some simple questions. According to the Rehabilitation Engineering and Assistive Technology Society of North America (RESNA), home modifications should improve the following features of a home:

- Accessibility. Improving accessibility means making doorways wider, clearing spaces to make sure a wheelchair can pass through, lowering countertop heights for sinks and kitchen cabinets, installing grab bars, and placing light switches and electrical outlets at heights that can be reached easily.

- Adaptability. Adaptability features are changes that can be made quickly to accommodate the needs of seniors or individuals with disabilities without having to completely redesign the home or use different materials for essential fixtures. Examples include installing grab bars in bathroom walls and movable cabinets under the sink so that someone in a wheelchair can use the space.

- Universal Design. Universal design features are usually built into a home when the first blueprints or architectural plans are drawn. These features include appliances, fixtures, and floor plans that are easy for all people to use, flexible enough so that they can be adapted for special needs, sturdy and reliable, and functional with a minimum of effort and understanding of the mechanisms involved.

Where do I begin?

Before you make home modifications, you should evaluate your current and future needs by going through your home room by room and answering a series of questions to highlight where changes might be made. Several checklists are available to help you conduct this review. The National Resource Center on Supportive Housing and Home Modifications is a good place to start.

You can begin your survey by examining areas of your home. Here are some questions to ask:

Appliances, Kithchen, Bathroom

- Are cabinet doorknobs easy to use?
- Are stove controls easy to use and clearly marked?
- Are faucets easy to use?
- Are there grab bars where needed?

Doors, Windows

- Are your doors and windows easy to open and close?
- Are your door locks sturdy and easy to operate?
- Are your doors wide enough to accommodate a walker or wheelchair?
- Do your doors have peepholes or viewing?

Electrical Outlets, Swicthes, Safety Devices

- Are light or power switches easy to turn on and off?

- Are electrical outlets easy to reach?
- Are the electrical outlets properly grounded to prevent shocks?
- Are your extension cords in good condition?
- Can you hear the doorbell in every part of the house?
- Do you have smoke detectors throughout your home?
- Do you have an alarm system?
- Is the telephone readily available for emergencies?
- Would you benefit from having an assistive device to make it easier to hear and talk on the telephone?

Floors

- Are all of the floors in your home on the same level?
- Are steps up and down marked in some way?
- Are all floor surfaces safe and covered with non-slip or non-skid materials?
- Do you have scatter rugs or doormats that could be hazardous?

Hallways, Steps, Stairways

- Are hallways and stairs in good condition?
- Do all of your hallways and stairs have smooth, safe surfaces?
- Do your stairs have steps that are big enough for your whole foot?
- Do you have handrails on both sides of the stairway?
- Are your stair rails wide enough for you to grasp them securely?
- Would you benefit from building a ramp to replace the stairs or steps inside or outside of your home?

Lighting, Ventilation

- Do you have night lights where they are needed?
- Is the lighting in each room sufficient for the use of the room?
- Is the lighting bright enough to ensure safety?
- Is each room well-ventilated with good air circulation?

- Once you have explored all the areas of your home that could benefit from remodeling, you might make a list of potential problems and possible solutions.

- Are all appliances and utensils conveniently and safely located?

- Can the oven and refrigerator be opened easily?

- Can you sit down while working?

- Can you get into and out of the bathtub or shower easily?

- Is the kitchen counter height and depth comfortable for you?

- Is the water temperature regulated to prevent scalding or burning?

- Would you benefit from having convenience items, such as a handheld showerhead, a garbage disposal, or a trash compactor?

Chapter 25

Devices for Improving Communication and Hearing

Chapter Contents

Section 25.1

Captions for Deaf and Hard-of-Hearing Viewers

Text in this section is excerpted from "Closed Captioning on
Television," Federal Communications Commission (FCC),
December 30, 2014.

Closed captioning displays the audio portion of a television program
as text on the TV screen, providing a critical link to news, entertain-
ment and information for individuals who are deaf or hard-of-hearing. Congress requires video programming distributors (VPDs)—cable
operators, broadcasters, satellite distributors and other multi-channel
video programming distributors—to close caption their TV programs.
FCC closed captioning rules

FCC rules for TV closed captioning ensure that viewers who are
deaf and hard of hearing have full access to programming, address
captioning quality and provide guidance to video programming distributors and programmers. The rules apply to all television programming
with captions, requiring that captions be:

- Accurate: Captions must match the spoken words in the dialogue and convey background noises and other sounds to the
  fullest extent possible.

- Synchronous: Captions must coincide with their corresponding
  spoken words and sounds to the greatest extent possible and must
  be displayed on the screen at a speed that can be read by viewers.

- Complete: Captions must run from the beginning to the end of
  the program to the fullest extent possible.

- Properly placed: Captions should not block other important
  visual content on the screen, overlap one another or run off the
  edge of the video screen.

The rules distinguish between pre-recorded, live, and near-live
programming and explain how the standards apply to each type of
programming, recognizing the greater hurdles involved with captioning live and near-live programming.

(The FCC does not regulate captioning of home videos, DVDs or video games.)

Exempt programming

Currently, there are two categories of exemptions from the closed captioning rules, self-implementing and economically burdensome:

- Self-implementing exemptions include public service announcements shorter than 10 minutes and not paid for with federal dollars, programming shown from 2 a.m. to 6 a.m., and programming primarily textual. There is also an exemption for locally produced non-news programming with no repeat value.

- The FCC has established procedures for petitioning for an exemption from the closed captioning rules when compliance would be economically burdensome.

What if you experience closed captioning problems

You may contact your VPD to report the problem at the time that the problem occurs to see if you can get the problem fixed. You can find your VPD's contact information on your bill, or, if you have broadcast only TV, the contact information for the TV station should be in the phone directory. VPDs must provide the FCC with contact information for the receipt and handling of immediate closed captioning concerns by consumers, and contact information for written closed captioning complaints.

For captioning problems during non-emergency programming, you may file a written complaint with either the FCC or your VPD. If you file your complaint with the FCC, the FCC will forward the complaint to your VPD. FCC rules require that your written complaint must be filed within 60 days of the captioning problem. After receiving a complaint, either directly from you or from the FCC, the VPD has 30 days to respond to the complaint. If you filed your complaint with your VPD and they do not respond within 30 days, or if a dispute remains, you can send your complaint to the FCC.

Section 25.2

Cochlear Implants

Text in this section is excerpted from "Cochlear Implants," National Institute on Deafness and Other Communication Disorders (NIDCD), August 2014.

What is a cochlear implant?

A cochlear implant is a small, complex electronic device that can help to provide a sense of sound to a person who is profoundly deaf or severely hard-of-hearing. The implant consists of an external portion that sits behind the ear and a second portion that is surgically placed under the skin (see figure). An implant has the following parts:

- A microphone, which picks up sound from the environment.

- A speech processor, which selects and arranges sounds picked up by the microphone.

- A transmitter and receiver/stimulator, which receive signals from the speech processor and convert them into electric impulses.

- An electrode array, which is a group of electrodes that collects the impulses from the stimulator and sends them to different regions of the auditory nerve.

An implant does not restore normal hearing. Instead, it can give a deaf person a useful representation of sounds in the environment and help him or her to understand speech.

How does a cochlear implant work?

A cochlear implant is very different from a hearing aid. Hearing aids amplify sounds so they may be detected by damaged ears. Cochlear implants bypass damaged portions of the ear and directly stimulate the auditory nerve. Signals generated by the implant are sent by way of the auditory nerve to the brain, which recognizes the signals as sound. Hearing through a cochlear implant is different from normal

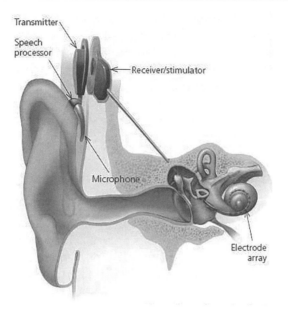

Figure 25.1. *Ear with cochlear implant*

hearing and takes time to learn or relearn. However, it allows many people to recognize warning signals, understand other sounds in the environment, and enjoy a conversation in person or by telephone.

Who gets cochlear implants?

Children and adults who are deaf or severely hard-of-hearing can be fitted for cochlear implants. According to the Food and Drug Administration (FDA), as of December 2012, approximately 324,200 people worldwide have received implants. In the United States, roughly 58,000 adults and 38,000 children have received them.

Since 2000, cochlear implants have been FDA-approved for use in eligible children beginning at 12 months of age. For young children who are deaf or severely hard-of-hearing, implantation while young exposes them to sounds during an optimal period to develop speech and language skills. A growing body of research, much of it funded by the NIDCD, has shown that when these children receive a cochlear implant followed by intensive therapy before 18 months of age, they are better able to hear, comprehend sound and music, and speak than their peers who receive implants when they are older. Studies have also shown that eligible children who receive a cochlear implant at a young age develop language skills at a rate comparable to children with normal hearing, and many succeed in mainstream classrooms.

Some adults who have lost all or most of their hearing later in life can also benefit from cochlear implants. They learn to associate the signal provided by an implant with sounds they remember. This often provides these individuals with the ability to understand speech solely by listening through the implant, without requiring any visual cues such as those provided by lip-reading or sign language.

How does someone receive a cochlear implant?

Use of a cochlear implant requires both a surgical procedure and significant therapy to learn or relearn the sense of hearing. Not everyone performs at the same level with this device. The decision to receive an implant should involve discussions with medical specialists, including an experienced cochlear-implant surgeon. The process can be expensive. For example, a person's health insurance may cover the expense, but not always. Some individuals may choose not to have a cochlear implant for a variety of personal reasons. Surgical implantations are almost always safe, although complications are a risk factor, just as with any kind of surgery. An additional consideration is learning to interpret the sounds created by an implant. This process takes time and practice. Speech-language pathologists and audiologists are frequently involved in this learning process. Prior to implantation, all of these factors need to be considered.

What does the future hold for cochlear implants?

With advancements in technology and continued follow-up studies with people who already have received implants, researchers are evaluating how cochlear implants might be used for other types of hearing loss.

NIDCD is supporting research to improve upon the benefits provided by cochlear implants. It may be possible to use a shortened electrode array, inserted into a portion of the cochlea, for individuals whose hearing loss is limited to the higher frequencies. Other studies are exploring ways to make a cochlear implant convey the sounds of speech more clearly. Researchers also are looking at the potential benefits of pairing a cochlear implant in one ear with either another cochlear implant or a hearing aid in the other ear.

Section 25.3

Hearing Aids

Text in this section is excerpted from "Hearing Aids," National
Institute on Deafness and Other Communication Disorders (NIDCD),
September 2013.

What is a hearing aid?

A hearing aid is a small electronic device that you wear in or behind
your ear. It makes some sounds louder so that a person with hearing loss can listen, communicate, and participate more fully in daily
activities. A hearing aid can help people hear more in both quiet and
noisy situations. However, only about one out of five people who would
benefit from a hearing aid actually uses one.

A hearing aid has three basic parts: a microphone, amplifier, and
speaker. The hearing aid receives sound through a microphone, which
converts the sound waves to electrical signals and sends them to an
amplifier. The amplifier increases the power of the signals and then
sends them to the ear through a speaker.

How can hearing aids help?

Hearing aids are primarily useful in improving the hearing and
speech comprehension of people who have hearing loss that results
from damage to the small sensory cells in the inner ear, called hair
cells. This type of hearing loss is called sensorineural hearing loss. The
damage can occur as a result of disease, aging, or injury from noise or
certain medicines.

A hearing aid magnifies sound vibrations entering the ear. Surviv-
ing hair cells detect the larger vibrations and convert them into neural
signals that are passed along to the brain. The greater the damage to
a person's hair cells, the more severe the hearing loss, and the greater
the hearing aid amplification needed to make up the difference. However, there are practical limits to the amount of amplification a hearing
aid can provide. In addition, if the inner ear is too damaged, even large
vibrations will not be converted into neural signals. In this situation,
a hearing aid would be ineffective.

How can I find out if I need a hearing aid?

If you think you might have hearing loss and could benefit from a hearing aid, visit your physician, who may refer you to an otolaryngologist or audiologist. An otolaryngologist is a physician who specializes in ear, nose, and throat disorders and will investigate the cause of the hearing loss. An audiologist is a hearing health professional who identifies and measures hearing loss and will perform a hearing test to assess the type and degree of loss.

Are there different styles of hearing aids?

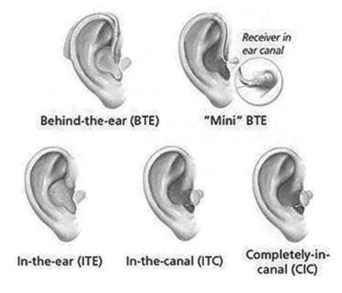

Behind-the-ear (BTE)   "Mini" BTE

Receiver in ear canal

In-the-ear (ITE)   In-the-canal (ITC)   Completely-in-canal (CIC)

Figure 25.2. *Styles of hearing aids*

Behind-the-ear (BTE) hearing aids consist of a hard plastic case worn behind the ear and connected to a plastic earmold that fits inside the outer ear. The electronic parts are held in the case behind the ear. Sound travels from the hearing aid through the earmold and into the ear. BTE aids are used by people of all ages for mild to profound hearing loss. A new kind of BTE aid is an open-fit hearing aid. Small, open-fit aids fit behind the ear completely, with only a narrow tube inserted into the ear canal, enabling the canal to remain open. For this reason, open-fit hearing aids may be a good choice for people who experience a buildup of earwax, since this type of aid is less likely to be damaged by such substances. In addition, some people may prefer the open-fit hearing aid because their perception of their voice does not sound "plugged up.

- **In-the-ear** (ITE) hearing aids fit completely inside the outer ear and are used for mild to severe hearing loss. The case holding the electronic components is made of hard plastic. Some ITE aids may have certain added features installed, such as a telecoil. A telecoil is a small magnetic coil that allows users to receive sound through the circuitry of the hearing aid, rather than through its microphone. This makes it easier to hear conversations over the telephone. A telecoil also helps people hear in public facilities that have installed special sound systems, called induction loop systems. Induction loop systems can be found in many churches, schools, airports, and auditoriums. ITE aids usually are not worn by young children because the casings need to be replaced often as the ear grows.

- **Canal** aids fit into the ear canal and are available in two styles. The in-the-canal (ITC) hearing aid is made to fit the size and shape of a person's ear canal. A completely-in-canal (CIC) hearing aid is nearly hidden in the ear canal. Both types are used for mild to moderately severe hearing loss. Because they are small, canal aids may be difficult for a person to adjust and remove. In addition, canal aids have less space available for batteries and additional devices, such as a telecoil. They usually are not recommended for young children or for people with severe to profound hearing loss because their reduced size limits their power and volume.

Do all hearing aids work the same way?

Hearing aids work differently depending on the electronics used. The two main types of electronics are analog and digital.

Analog aids convert sound waves into electrical signals, which are amplified. Analog/adjustable hearing aids are custom built to meet the needs of each user. The aid is programmed by the manufacturer according to the specifications recommended by your audiologist. Analog/programmable hearing aids have more than one program or setting. An audiologist can program the aid using a computer, and you can change the program for different listening environments—from a small, quiet room to a crowded restaurant to large, open areas, such as a theater or stadium. Analog/programmable circuitry can be used in all types of hearing aids. Analog aids usually are less expensive than digital aids.

Digital aids convert sound waves into numerical codes, similar to the binary code of a computer, before amplifying them. Because the code also includes information about a sound's pitch or loudness, the aid can be specially programmed to amplify some frequencies more than others. Digital circuitry gives an audiologist more flexibility in adjusting the aid to a user's needs and to certain listening environments. These aids also can be programmed to focus on sounds coming from a specific direction. Digital circuitry can be used in all types of hearing aids.

Which hearing aid will work best for me?

The hearing aid that will work best for you depends on the kind and severity of your hearing loss. If you have a hearing loss in both of your ears, two hearing aids are generally recommended because two aids provide a more natural signal to the brain. Hearing in both ears also will help you understand speech and locate where the sound is coming from.

You and your audiologist should select a hearing aid that best suits your needs and lifestyle. Price is also a key consideration because hearing aids range from hundreds to several thousand dollars. Similar to other equipment purchases, style and features affect cost. However, don't use price alone to determine the best hearing aid for you. Just because one hearing aid is more expensive than another does not necessarily mean that it will better suit your needs.

A hearing aid will not restore your normal hearing. With practice, however, a hearing aid will increase your awareness of sounds and their sources. You will want to wear your hearing aid regularly, so select one that is convenient and easy for you to use. Other features to consider include parts or services covered by the warranty, estimated schedule and costs for maintenance and repair, options and upgrade opportunities, and the hearing aid company's reputation for quality and customer service.

What questions should I ask before buying a hearing aid?

Before you buy a hearing aid, ask your audiologist these important questions:

- What features would be most useful to me?
- What is the total cost of the hearing aid? Do the benefits of newer technologies outweigh the higher costs?

- Is there a trial period to test the hearing aids? (Most manufacturers allow a 30- to 60-day trial period during which aids can be returned for a refund.) What fees are nonrefundable if the aids are returned after the trial period?

- How long is the warranty? Can it be extended? Does the warranty cover future maintenance and repairs?

- Can the audiologist make adjustments and provide servicing and minor repairs? Will loaner aids be provided when repairs are needed?

- What instruction does the audiologist provide?

Can I obtain financial assistance for a hearing aid?

Hearing aids are generally not covered by health insurance companies, although some do. For eligible children and young adults ages 21 and under, Medicaid will pay for the diagnosis and treatment of hearing loss, including hearing aids, under the Early and Periodic Screening, Diagnostic, and Treatment (EPSDT) service. Also, children may be covered by their state's early intervention program or State Children's Health Insurance Program.

Medicare does not cover hearing aids for adults; however, diagnostic evaluations are covered if they are ordered by a physician for the purpose of assisting the physician in developing a treatment plan. Since Medicare has declared the BAHA a prosthetic device and not a hearing aid, Medicare will cover the BAHA if other coverage policies are met.

Some nonprofit organizations provide financial assistance for hearing aids, while others may help provide used or refurbished aids.

Chapter 26

Low Vision Devices and Services

Chapter Contents

Section 26.1

Living with Low Vision

Text in this section is excerpted from "Living With Low Vision,"
National Eye Institute (NEI), September 2012.

What is low vision?

When you have low vision, eyeglasses, contact lenses, medicine, or surgery may not help. Activities like reading, shopping, cooking, writing, and watching TV may be hard to do.

In fact, millions of Americans lose some of their sight every year. While vision loss can affect anyone at any age, low vision is most common for those over age 65.

Low vision is usually caused by eye diseases or health conditions. Some of these include age-related macular degeneration (AMD), cataract, diabetes, and glaucoma. Eye injuries and birth defects are some other causes. Whatever the cause, lost vision cannot be restored. It can, however, be managed with proper treatment and vision rehabilitation.

You should visit an eye care professional if you experience any changes to your eyesight.

How do I know if I have low vision?

Below are some signs of low vision. Even when wearing your glasses or contact lenses, do you still have difficulty with

- Recognizing the faces of family and friends?

- Reading, cooking, sewing, or fixing things around the house?

- Selecting and matching the color of your clothes?

- Seeing clearly with the lights on or feeling like they are dimmer than normal?

- Reading traffic signs or the names of stores?

These could all be early warning signs of vision loss or eye disease. The sooner vision loss or eye disease is detected by an eye care professional, the greater your chances of keeping your remaining vision.

How do I know when to get an eye exam?

Visit your eye care professional regularly for a comprehensive dilated eye exam. However, if you notice changes to your eyes or eyesight, visit your eye care professional right away!

What can I do if I have low vision?

To cope with vision loss, you must first **have an excellent support team**. This team should include you, your primary eye care professional, and an optometrist or ophthalmologist specializing in low vision.

Occupational therapists, orientation and mobility specialists, certified low vision therapists, counselors, and social workers are also available to help.

Together, the low vision team can help you make the most of your remaining vision and maintain your independence.

Second, **talk with your eye care professional** about your vision problems. Even though it may be difficult, ask for help. Find out where you can get more information about support services and adaptive devices. Also, find out which services and devices are best for you and which will give you the most independence.

Third, **ask about vision rehabilitation**, even if your eye care professional says that "nothing more can be done for your vision."

Vision rehabilitation programs offer a wide range of services, including training for magnifying and adaptive devices, ways to complete daily living skills safely and independently, guidance on modifying your home, and information on where to locate resources and support to help you cope with your vision loss.

Medicare may cover part or all of a patient's occupational therapy, but the therapy must be ordered by a doctor and provided by a Medicareapproved healthcare provider. To see if you are eligible for Medicare-funded occupational therapy, call 1–800–MEDICARE or 1– 800–633–4227.

Finally, **be persistent**. Remember that you are your best healthcare advocate. Explore our options, learn as much as you can, and keep asking questions about vision rehabilitation. In fact, write down questions to ask your doctor before your exam, and bring along a notepad to jot down answers.

There are many resources to help people with low vision, and many of these programs, devices, and technologies can help you maintain your normal, everyday way of life.

What questions should I ask my eye care team?

An important part of any doctor–patient relationship is effective communication. Here are some questions to ask your eye care professional or specialist in low vision to jumpstart the discussion about vision loss.

Questions to ask your eye care professional:

- What changes can I expect in my vision?

- Will my vision loss get worse? How much of my vision will I lose?

- Will regular eyeglasses improve my vision?

- What medical or surgical treatments are available for my condition?

- What can I do to protect or prolong my vision?

- Will diet, exercise, or other lifestyle changes help?

- If my vision can't be corrected, can you refer me to a specialist in low vision?

- Where can I get vision rehabilitation services?

Questions to ask your specialist in low vision:

- How can I continue my normal, routine activities?

- Are there resources to help me in my job?

- Will any special devices help me with daily activities like reading, sewing, cooking, or fixing things around the house?

- What training and services are available to help me live better and more safely with low vision?

- Where can I find individual or group support to cope with my vision loss?

Section 26.2

What Is Braille?

Text in this section is excerpted from "NLS Factsheets," U.S. Library
of Congress (LOC), February 4, 2015. About Braille

Reading by Touch

Braille is a system of touch reading and writing in which raised dots
represent the letters of the alphabet and numbers, as well as music
notes and symbols. Braille contains symbols for punctuation marks
and provides a system of contractions and short form words to save
space, making it an efficient method of tactile reading.

Braille is read by moving one or more fingers along each line.
Both hands are usually involved in the reading process, and reading
is generally done with the index fingers. Usually, one hand reads
the majority of one line while the other hand locates the beginning
of the next. Average reading speed is approximately 125 words
per minute, but greater speeds of up to 200 words per minute are
possible.

By using braille, blind people can review and study the written
word. They may become aware of conventions such as spelling, punctuation, paragraphing, and footnotes. Most important, braille provides
blind individuals access to a wide range of reading materials—educational and recreational reading as well as informational manuals.
Blind people also are able to pursue hobbies and cultural enrichment
with such braille materials as music scores, hymnals, playing cards,
and board games.

The History of Braille

The system of embossed writing invented by Louis Braille in 1821
gradually came to be accepted throughout the world as the fundamental form of written communication for blind individuals.

Various methods—many of them raised versions of print letters—
had been attempted over the years to enable blind people to read. The
braille system has succeeded because it is based on a rational sequence

of signs devised for the fingertips, rather than imitating signs devised for the eyes. In addition, braille can be written by blind people and used for any notation that follows an accepted sequence, such as numerals, musical notes, or chemical tables.

Braille has undergone many modifications, particularly the addition of contractions representing groups of letters or whole words that appear frequently in a language. The use of contractions permits faster reading and helps reduce the size of braille books, making them less cumbersome.

Several groups have been established over the past century to modify and standardize the braille code. The major goal is to develop easily understood contractions without making the code too complex.

The official braille code, English Braille, American Edition, was first published in 1932 by what is now the Braille Authority of North America (BANA). This organization represents many agencies and consumer groups and has been responsible for updating and interpreting the basic literary braille code and the specialized codes for music, mathematics, computer braille, and other uses in the United States and Canada. Other countries have similar authorities.

The Braille Alphabet

The braille cell, an arrangement of six dots, is the basic unit for reading and writing braille. Sixty-three different patterns are possible from these six dots. For purposes of identification and description, these dots are numbered downward 1-2-3 on the left and 4-5-6 on the right:

$$
\begin{array}{ccc}
1 & \bullet\ \bullet & 4 \\
2 & \bullet\ \bullet & 5 \\
3 & \bullet\ \bullet & 6
\end{array}
$$

Figure 26.1. *The Braille Numbers*

(Note: As shown here, the "•" symbol represents a raised braille dot in the six-dot configuration. The "○" symbol represents a position in the cell where no braille dot occurs.)

The first ten letters of the alphabet (a–j) use only the dots in the upper two rows of the cell.

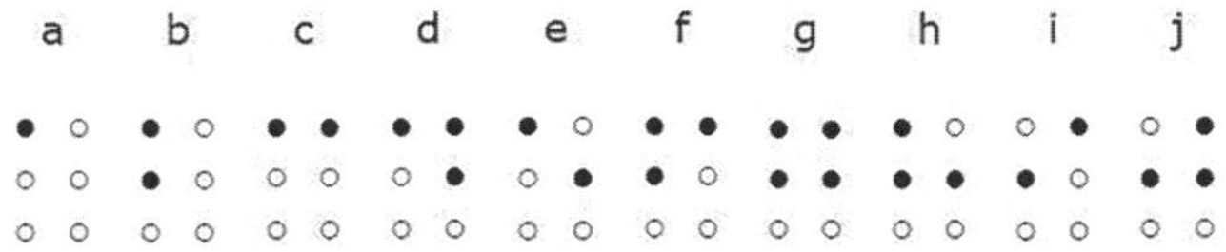

a	b	c	d	e	f	g	h	i	j

Figure 26.2. *The Braille Alphabet (a–i)*

The next ten letters of the alphabet (k–t) are formed by adding dot 3 to each of the first ten letters.

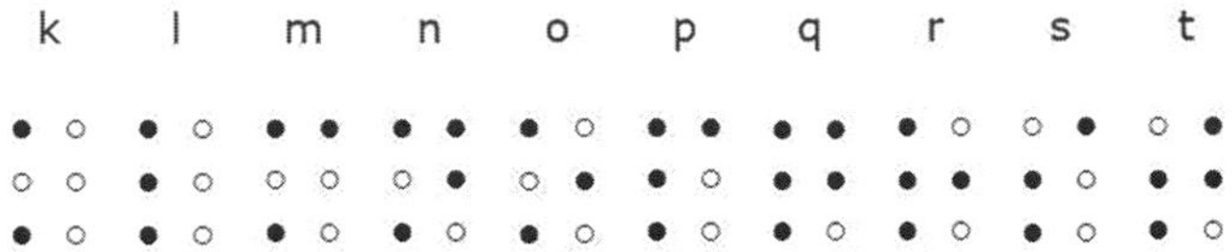

k	l	m	n	o	p	q	r	s	t

Figure 26.3. *The Braille Alphabet (k–t)*

The remaining letters, except for w, are formed by adding dots 3 and 6 to each of the first five letters.

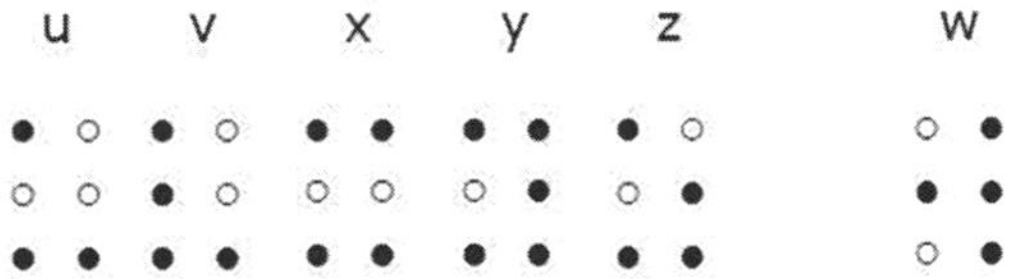

u	v	x	y	z		w

Figure 26.4. *The Braille Alphabet (u–z)*

The letter "w" is an exception because the French alphabet did not contain a "w" when the code was created; the symbol for "w" was added later

Braille and Advances in Technology

Access to information in braille has evolved considerably in recent years. Braille can now be translated and formatted with a computer. Braille characters can be entered directly into a computer with six keys on the computer's keyboard. In addition, text that is entered into a computer via scanning or typing can be put into braille by using special software programs. Braille embossers can take output from a computer and produce single- or double-sided braille materials in a fraction of the time it took to create braille by hand. While this process represents a major advance in braille production, computer-assisted braille translation is not perfect and materials must always be checked by a qualified braille proofreader.

Blind individuals use devices with refreshable braille displays to take notes, read braille materials, prepare school assignments, and perform many other tasks in braille that were not possible even twenty years ago. These advances in braille technology have had a profound impact on educational and professional opportunities available to blind braille readers.

Section 26.3

Low Vision Aids for Computer Users

Text in this section is excerpted from "Assistive Technology Products for Information Access," U.S. Library of Congress (LOC), June, 2015; and text from "Accommodation Solutions," Computer/Electronic Accommodation Program (CAP), March 21, 2013.

Assistive Technology Software for Blind and Low Vision

Screen Magnification

Screen magnification software is used to assist individuals who have vision limitations that prevent them from accomplishing essential job tasks. Screen magnification software accomplishes this by allowing individuals to enlarge text and graphics on a computer screen. The software is loaded onto an individual's computer and functions as a magnifying glass on the computer screen. Screen magnification software often comes with additional capabilities, such as text-to-speech, various color contrast modes and changing the visual display of items on the screen, such as the cursor or insertion point in a document.

Voice Recognition Software

Voice recognition (also called speech recognition) software uses voice commands in place of a mouse and keyboard to enter data into a computer or to navigate a website.

Optical Character Recognition Scanning Software

These software programs allow users to convert scanned documents into accessible text through optical character recognition (OCR). This text can then be read by screen readers or integrated text-to-speech software. The products listed here are specifically designed to meet the needs of persons with visual disabilities.

These programs specifically target the reading and educational needs of people who have learning or reading disabilities. They incorporate special educational tools to assist in reading, writing, and studying.

Reading Machines and Scanners

A reading machine is an electronic device that scans a printed page and, through an internal synthesized voice, reads the printed material aloud. It may also have the capability to save the scanned material for later use. Some reading machines can be connected to computers to allow for magnification of the scanned page. Others come with special features such as alarms or magnification.

Portable Video Magnifiers

These portable devices magnify text in a digital video format. Most run on battery power or can be recharged. Some allow you to save scanned text on the device.

Screen Readers

Screen reading software operates a speech synthesizer, which voices the contents of a computer screen. Screen readers are helpful in navigating programs and word processing documents. The user, through windows-based keystrokes, navigates the electronic environment, hearing the prompts, dialog boxes, etc. Screen readers highlight words as they are read by the computer. Screen readers are compatible with word processing, spreadsheet, commercial web browsers and database packages and can be used in conjunction with screen enlargement and Braille output products.

Large Print Keyboards

Large key keyboards and large print keyboards have keys and/or letters that are larger than those found on standard keyboards.

Braille Displays

The "refreshable" Braille appears one line at a time. Braille displays, used by people who are Braille literate, must be used in conjunction with screen readers, which contain the software necessary to activate the Braille display. Compatible with word processing, database, commercial web browsers, and spreadsheet applications, Braille displays make proofreading, spreadsheet, and database applications more efficient than speech output alone.

Braille Embossers

A Braille embosser is a printer that creates tactile Braille cells instead of written text. Using Braille translation software, a document can be embossed, making Braille production more efficient and available to people who are Braille literate.

Braille Translators

A Braille Translator is a software program that translates a script into Braille cells, and sends it to a Braille embosser, which produces a hard copy in Braille script of the original text.

Chapter 27

Finding Accessible Transportation

Chapter Contents

Section 27.1

Adapting Motor Vehicles for People with Disabilities

Text in this section is excerpted from "Adapting Motor Vehicles
For People With Disabilities," National Highway Traffic Safety
Administration (NHTSA), June 2015.

Introduction

New and existing adaptive technologies continue to broaden opportunities for people with disabilities to drive both comfortably and safely.
Some of these adaptive technologies are as simple as swivel seats for more
convenient access. Others, such as hand controls, may be necessary for a
driver to safely operate a vehicle. Whatever your requirements, chances
are good that adaptive equipment is available to support your special driving needs and allow you to maintain the freedom offered by the open road.

The information in this Section is based on the experience of driver
rehabilitation specialists and other professionals who work with people
who require adaptive devices for their motor vehicles. The steps outlined
here represent a proven process — evaluating your needs, making sure
the vehicle "fits" you properly, choosing appropriate features, installing
and knowing how to use adaptive devices, practicing good vehicle maintenance — that can help you avoid costly mistakes when modifying or
purchasing a vehicle to accommodate your driving requirements.

Also included is general information on cost savings, licensing
requirements, and organizations to contact for additional assistance.
Although the brochure focuses on drivers of modified vehicles, each
section also contains important information for people who drive passengers with disabilities.

Investigate Cost-Saving Opportunities and Licensing Requirements

Cost-Saving Opportunities

With such a wide range of adaptive equipment solutions available, associated costs for modifying a vehicle can vary greatly

depending on an individual's needs. Some adaptive equipment, such as a special seatback cushion, can provide a better view of the road for as little as $50. More complex equipment, such as hand controls, can be purchased for under $1,000. However, a new vehicle modified with adaptive equipment will cost anywhere from $20,000 to $80,000.

Whether you are modifying a vehicle you now own or purchasing a new vehicle with adaptive equipment, it pays to do your homework first. By consulting with a driver rehabilitation specialist before you buy, you can learn what adaptive equipment you need now or may need in the future, avoid paying for equipment you don't need, and learn about opportunities for public and private financial assistance.

Also be aware of the following:

- Some nonprofits that advocate for individuals with disabilities offer programs that may help pay for adaptive devices. Generally, these groups and programs represent local resources. To learn about any available programs in your area, contact your State government office that handles services for persons with disabilities.

- Automotive insurance may cover all or part of the cost of adaptive equipment if your need for such equipment is a result of a motor vehicle crash.

- Workers' compensation typically covers the cost of adaptive equipment if your need for such equipment is a result of a job-related injury.

- Most major vehicle manufacturers offer rebates on adaptive equipment, usually up to $1,000, provided you purchase a vehicle less than one year old. Your local automobile dealer can supply information on these programs and assist you with the application process. Contact information for vehicle manufacturers offering rebates on adaptive equipment is listed in the "Resources" section of this brochure.

- National Mobility Equipment Dealers Association (NMEDA) members are also familiar with vehicle manufacturer rebates, can help you apply for these rebates — and can provide pre-purchase advice about the type of vehicle that will accommodate your adaptive equipment needs.

- Some States waive the sales tax for adaptive devices if you have a doctor's prescription for their use.

- The cost of adaptive equipment may be tax deductible. Check with a qualified tax consultant to learn more.

Licensing Requirements

All States require a valid learner's permit or driver's license to receive an on-the-road driving evaluation. You cannot be denied the opportunity to apply for a permit or license because of age or disability. However, a driver's license with restrictions may be issued based on your need of adaptive equipment.

Evaluate Your Needs

Driver rehabilitation specialists perform comprehensive evaluations to identify the adaptive equipment most suited to your needs and medical condition. As part of this process, a rehabilitation specialist will take into consideration your future equipment needs based on your medical condition and the repetitive stress an adaptive aid may place on a particular muscle group.

In addition, you can expect a complete evaluation to include vision screening as well as:

- Muscle strength, flexibility, and range of motion;
- Coordination and reaction time;
- Judgment and decision-making abilities; and
- Ability to drive with adaptive equipment.

After you finish the evaluation you should receive a report containing specific recommendations on driving requirements or restrictions. You should also be given a complete list of any recommended vehicle requirements or modifications. The recommendations should suggest obtaining on-the-road training to practice safe operation of the equipment and learn safe driving habits.

Finding a Qualified Driver Rehabilitation Specialist

Check with a rehabilitation center in your area to find a qualified driver rehabilitation specialist to perform your evaluation. You'll find rehabilitation centers for each State listed on the Web sites for the Association for Driver Rehabilitation Specialists (ADED) and the American Occupational Therapy Association, Inc. (AOTA). These associations maintain lists of qualified driverrehabilitation specialists in areas across the
United States and Canada.

Paying for an Evaluation

- Vocational rehabilitation agencies and workers' compensation agencies may assist in the cost of a driver evaluation.

- Your health insurance company may pay for part or all of the evaluation. Find out from your insurance company if you need a doctor's prescription or other documentation to receive such benefits.

- If you're a senior citizen, ask if your driver rehabilitation specialist offers a discount to seniors.

Determining the Best Time to Seek a Driving Evaluation

Consult with your doctor to make sure you are physically and psychologically prepared to drive. Being evaluated too soon after an injury, stroke, or other trauma may be misleading because it may show the need for adaptive equipment that you will not need in the future. You want to be functioning at your best when you have a driver evaluation. For the evaluation, you will need to take any equipment you normally use, such as a walker or neck brace. If you use a wheelchair and are planning to modify the wheelchair or obtain a new one, be sure to tell your driver rehabilitation specialist prior to the evaluation.

Evaluating Passengers with Disabilities

Driver rehabilitation specialists may also provide advice on compatibility and transportation safety issues for passengers with special needs. They determine the type of seating needed and the person's ability to enter and exit the vehicle. They provide advice on the purchase of modified vehicles and recommend appropriate wheel chair lifts or other equipment that would work in your vehicle.

If you have a child who requires a special type of safety seat, evaluators make sure the seat fits your child properly. They also make sure you can properly install the seat in your vehicle. The American Academy of Pediatrics (AAP) or your pediatrician can provide information on the safe transportation of children with special needs.

Select the Right Vehicle

Although the purchase or lease of a vehicle is your responsibility, your mobility equipment dealer and driver rehabilitation specialist are qualified to ensure the vehicle you select can be modified to meet your adaptive equipment needs. Take the time to consult with these professionals before you make your purchase decision. To find a qualified dealer in your area, contact the National Mobility Equipment Dealers Association (NMEDA). To find a qualified driver rehabilitation specialist, contact the Association for Driver Rehabilitation Specialists (ADED).

The following questions can help with vehicle selection. They can also help determine if you can modify a vehicle you already own:

- Does the vehicle have the cargo capacity (in pounds) to accommodate the equipment you require?

- Will there be enough space and cargo capacity to accommodate your family or other passengers once the vehicle is modified?

- Is there adequate parking space at home and at work for the vehicle and for loading/unloading a wheelchair?

- Is there adequate parking space to maneuver if you use a walker?

- What additional options are necessary for the safe operation of the vehicle?

If a third party is paying for the vehicle, adaptive devices, or modification costs, find out if there are any limitations or restrictions on what is covered. Always get a written statement on what a funding agency will pay before making your purchase.

Once you select and purchase a vehicle, be aware that you will need to also purchase insurance to cover your vehicle while it's being modified — even though it will be off the road during this period.

Standard Features to Look for in A New Passenger Vehicle

Before purchasing a new vehicle, always sit in it first to make sure you are comfortable. Check to see that you can enter and exit the vehicle with ease. If possible, take it out for a test drive. How well does the car fit your body? To prevent air bag-related injury, you should keep 10 inches between your breast bone and the steering wheel, which contains the driver's side air bag. At the same time, you'll need to be able to easily

reach the pedals while maintaining a comfortable line of sight above the adjusted steering wheel. Also, make sure the vehicle provides you with good visibility in all directions — front, rear, and sides. Your dealer can demonstrate the use of adaptive features, such as adjustable foot pedals and driver seats, which can help ensure a good person-vehicle fit.

When selecting a vehicle, look for and ask about available features designed to improve both the comfort and safety of drivers with disabilities. Some of these features are:

- High or extra-wide doors;

- Adjustable foot pedals;

- Large interior door handles;

- Oversized knobs with clearly visible labels;

- Support handles to assist with entry and exit;

- Large or adjustable-size print for dashboard gauges;

- Seat adjusters that can move the seat in all directions — particularly raising it so the driver's line of sight is 3" above the

- adjusted steering wheel; and

- Dashboard-mounted ignition rather than steering column-mounted ignition.

Choose a Qualified Mobility Dealer to Modify Your Vehicle

Even a half-inch change in the lowering of a van floor can affect a driver's ability to use equipment or to have an unobstructed view of the road. So it's important that you take the time to find a qualified dealer to modify your vehicle. Your driver rehabilitation specialist may be able to provide referrals depending on where you live and your vehicle modification and adaptive equipment needs.

Note: Some State agencies specify the dealer you must use if you want reimbursement. For example, some States require that dealers bidding on State vocational rehabilitation jobs be members of the National Mobility Equipment Dealer's (NMEDA's) Quality Assurance Program.

To find qualified mobility equipment dealers, begin with phone inquiries to learn about credentials, experience, and references. Ask questions about how they operate. Do they work with qualified driver rehabilitation specialists? Will they look at your vehicle before you buy it? Do they require a prescription from a physician or driver evaluation specialist? How long will it take before they can start work on your vehicle?

Also ensure that the dealer you choose to modify your vehicle is registered with the National Highway Traffic Safety Administration

(NHTSA). In order to adapt a vehicle to meet your needs, registered equipment dealers are permitted to modify existing federally mandated safety equipment. In addition, registered mobility equipment dealers must provide you with a written statement regarding the work that was performed, as well as list any Federal Motor Vehicle Safety Standards affected by their modification work on a label adjacent to the original equipment manufacturer's

label or the modifier's certification label.

These labels are often found inside the driver's door.

Questions to consider in evaluating a mobility equipment dealer's qualifications are listed below:

- Is the dealer registered with NHTSA?

- Is the dealer a member of NMEDA — and a participant in this organization's **Quality Assurance Program**?

- What type of training has the staff received?

- What type of warranty is provided on work?

- Does the dealer provide ongoing service and maintenance?

- Are replacement parts stocked and readily available?

If you are satisfied with the answers you receive, check references; then arrange to visit the dealer's facility. Once you are comfortable with a dealer's qualifications, you will want to ask more specific questions, such as:

- How much will the modification cost?

- Are third-party payments accepted?

- How long will it take to modify the vehicle?

- Can the equipment be transferred to a new vehicle in the future?

- Will existing safety features need to be modified to install the adaptive equipment?

While your vehicle is being modified, you will most likely need to be available for fittings. This prevents additional waiting time for adjustments once the equipment is fully installed. Without proper fittings you may have problems with the safe operation of the vehicle and have to go back for adjustments.

Obtain Training on the Use of New Equipment

Both new and experienced drivers need training on how to safely use newly installed adaptive equipment. Your equipment installer and driver rehabilitation specialist should provide information on the new devices and off-road instruction. But literature and off-road instruction aren't enough to equip you to drive safely with your new adaptive equipment. This equipment can be very complex. So it's extremely important to obtain on-the-road training and practice with a driver rehabilitation specialist who has advanced expertise and knowledge of adaptive technologies. If your driver rehabilitation specialist does not offer such training, ask him or her for a referral, or inquire at your local driver licensing office.

State vocational rehabilitation departments and workers' compensation will pay for driver education and training under certain circumstances. At a minimum, their staffs can help you locate a qualified driver rehabilitation specialist to provide training.

Finally, remember to enlist the help of a family member or friend to drive you to all of your training sessions. (It's important to have someone else who can drive your vehicle incase of an emergency.)

Maintain Your Vehicle

Regular maintenance is important for keeping your vehicle and specially installed adaptive features safe and reliable. It may also be mandatory for compliance with the terms of your warranty. Some warranties specify a time period during which adaptive equipment must be inspected. These equipment check-up schedules may differ from those for your vehicle. Make sure you or your modifier submit all warranty cards for all equipment. This will not only ensure coverage, but will also enable manufacturers to contact you in case of a recall.

Section 27.2

Assistance and Accommodation for Air Travel

This section includes excerpts from "Travelers with Disabilities,"
Centers for Disease Control and Prevention (CDC), July 10, 2015;
and text from "Disabilities and Medical Conditions," Transportation
Security Administration (TSA), Aug 11, 2015.

Overview

According to the Americans with Disabilities Act, a person has a disability if he or she has a physical or mental impairment that substantially limits at least 1 major life activity. Some travelers with disabilities, including those experiencing reduced mobility, may require special attention and adaptation of transportation services. With proper preparation, many travelers with disabilities can travel internationally. The following recommendations may assist in ensuring safe, accessible travel:

- Assess each international itinerary on an individual basis, in consultation with specialized travel agencies or tour operators

- Consult travel health providers for additional recommendations

- Plan ahead to ensure that necessary accommodations are available throughout the entire trip

Air Travel

Regulations and Codes

In 1986, Congress passed the Air Carrier Access Act (ACAA) to ensure that people with disabilities are treated without discrimination in a way consistent with the safe carriage of all passengers. The regulations established by the Department of Transportation (DOT) apply to all flights of U.S. airlines as well as flights to or from the United States by foreign carriers.

Because of the act, carriers may not refuse transportation on the basis of a disability. However, there are a few exceptions; for example, the carrier may refuse transportation if the person with a disability would endanger the health or safety of other passengers or if transporting the person would be a violation of Federal Aviation Administration safety rules.

Air carriers are also obliged to accept a declaration by a passenger that he or she is self-reliant. A medical certificate, which is a written statement from the passenger's health care provider saying that the passenger is capable of completing the flight safely without requiring extraordinary medical care or endangering other passengers, can be required only in specific situations (for example, if a person intends to travel with a possible communicable disease, will require a stretcher or oxygen, or if the person's medical condition can be reasonably expected to affect the operation of the flight).

Many airlines voluntarily adhere to codes of practice that are similar to U.S. legislation based on guidelines from the International Civil Aviation Organization. However, these guidelines are not identical to those outlined in U.S. legislation, and the degree of implementation may vary by airline and location. If a traveler's plans include flying between foreign countries while abroad, one must check with the overseas airlines to ensure that the carriers adhere to accessibility standards that are adequate for that traveler's needs.

The Transportation Security Administration (TSA) has established a program for screening travelers with disabilities and their equipment, mobility aids, and devices. TSA permits prescriptions, liquid medications, and other liquids needed by people with disabilities and medical conditions.

Assistance and Accommodations

Under the guidelines of the ACAA, when a traveler with disability requests assistance, the airline is obliged to meet certain accessibility requirements. For example, carriers must provide access to the aircraft door (preferably by a level entry bridge), an aisle seat, and a seat with removable armrests. However, aircraft with <30 seats are generally exempt from these requirements. Any aircraft with >60 seats must have an onboard wheelchair, and personnel must help move the wheelchair from a seat to the lavatory area. However, airline personnel are not required to transfer passengers from wheelchair to wheelchair, wheelchair to aircraft seat, or wheelchair to lavatory seat. In addition, airline personnel are not obliged to assist with feeding, visiting the lavatory, or dispensing medication to travelers. Only wide-body aircraft with ≥2 aisles are required to have fully accessible lavatories. Travelers with disabilities who require assistance should travel with a companion or attendant. However, carriers may not, without reason, require a person with a disability to travel with an attendant.

Airlines may not require advance notice of a passenger with a disability; however, they may require up to 48 hours' advance notice and 1-hour advance check-in for certain accommodations that require preparation time, such as the following services (if they are available on the flight):

- Medical oxygen for use on board the aircraft

- Carriage of an incubator

- Hook-up for a respirator to the aircraft electrical power supply

- Accommodation for a passenger who must travel in a stretcher

- Transportation of an electric wheelchair on a flight scheduled on an aircraft with <60 seats

- Provision by the airline of hazardous material packaging for a battery used in a wheelchair or other assistive devices

- Accommodation for a group of ≥10 people with disabilities who travel as a group

- Provision of an onboard wheelchair to be used on an aircraft that does not have an accessible lavatory

DOT maintains a toll-free hotline (800-778-4838, available 9 am to 5 pm Eastern Time, Monday through Friday, except federal holidays) to provide general information to consumers about the rights of air travelers with disabilities and to assist air travelers with time-sensitive disability-related issues.

Patients with Respiratory Conditions

Travelers with certain respiratory conditions that cause low blood oxygen levels may need supplemental oxygen to make up for the reduced air pressure in the cabin during flight.

Service Animals

Under the ACAA, carriers must permit guide dogs or other service animals with identification to accompany a person with a disability on a flight. Carriers must permit a service animal to accompany a traveler with a disability to any assigned seat, unless the animal obstructs an aisle or other area that must remain clear to facilitate an emergency evacuation, in which case the passenger will be assigned another seat. However, service animals are not exempt from compliance with quarantine regulations and may not be allowed to travel to all international destinations.

Disabilities and Medical Conditions

To ensure your security, all travelers are required to undergo screening at the checkpoint. You or your traveling companion may consult the TSA officer about the best way to relieve any concerns during the screening process. You may provide the officer with the TSA notification card or other medical documentation to describe your condition. If you have other questions or concerns about traveling with a disability please contact passenger support.

If you are approved to use TSA PreV® lane at a participating airport, you do not need to remove shoes, laptops, 3-1-1 liquids, belts, or light jackets during the screening process and TSA officers may swab your hands, mobility aids, equipment and other external medical devices to test for explosives using explosives trace detection technology.

Medications

Medications in pill or other solid form must undergo security screening. It is recommended that medication be clearly labeled to facilitate the screening process. Check with state laws regarding prescription medication labels.

You are responsible for displaying, handling, and repacking the medication when screening is required. Medication can undergo a visual or X-ray screening and may be tested for traces of explosives.

Inform the TSA Officer

Inform the TSA officer that you have medically necessary liquids and/or medications and separate them from other belongings before screening begins. Also declare accessories associated with your liquid medication such as freezer packs, IV bags, pumps and syringes. Labeling these items can help facilitate the screening process.

3-1-1 Liquids Rule Exemption

You may bring medically necessary liquids, medications and creams in excess of 3.4 ounces or 100 milliliters in your carry-on bag. Remove them from your carry-on bag to be screened separately from the rest of your belongings. You are not required to place your liquid medication in a plastic zip-top bag.

Accessories

Ice packs, freezer packs, frozen gel packs, and other accessories required to cool medically necessary liquids must be completely solid at the security checkpoint. If these accessories are partially frozen or slushy, they are subject to the same screening as other medically necessary liquids. Other supplies associated with medically necessary liquids such as IV bags, pumps and syringes must undergo X-ray screening.

Screening

TSA officers may test liquids for explosives or concealed prohibited items. If officers are unable to use X-ray to clear these items, they may ask to open the container and transfer the liquid to a separate empty container or dispose of a small quantity of liquid, if feasible.

Inform the TSA officer if you do not want your liquid medication to be screened by X-ray or opened. Additional steps will be taken to clear the liquid and you will undergo additional screening procedures to include a pat-down and screening of other carry-on property.

Chapter 28

Service Animals and People with Disabilities

What is a service animal?

Under the Americans with Disabilities Act (ADA), a service animal is defined as a dog that has been individually trained to do work or perform tasks for an individual with a disability. The task(s) performed by the dog must be directly related to the person's disability.

What does "do work or perform tasks" mean?

The dog must be trained to take a specific action when needed to assist the person with a disability. For example, a person with diabetes may have a dog that is trained to alert him when his blood sugar reaches high or low levels. A person with depression may have a dog that is trained to remind her to take her medication. Or, a person who has epilepsy may have a dog that is trained to detect the onset of a seizure and then help the person remain safe during the seizure.

Are emotional support, therapy, comfort, or companion animals considered service animals under the ADA?

No. These terms are used to describe animals that provide comfort just by being with a person. Because they have not been trained to

---

Text in this chapter is excerpted from "Frequently Asked Questions about Service Animals and the ADA," Americans with Disabilities Act (ADA), July 2015.

perform a specific job or task, they do not qualify as service animals under the ADA. However, some State or local governments have laws that allow people to take emotional support animals into public places. You may check with your State and local government agencies to find out about these laws.

If someone's dog calms them when having an anxiety attack, does this qualify it as a service animal?

It depends. The ADA makes a distinction between psychiatric service animals and emotional support animals. If the dog has been trained to sense that an anxiety attack is about to happen and take a specific action to help avoid the attack or lessen its impact, that would qualify as a service animal. However, if the dog's mere presence provides comfort, that would not be considered a service animal under the ADA.

Does the ADA require service animals to be professionally trained?

No. People with disabilities have the right to train the dog themselves and are not required to use a professional service dog training program.

Are service-animals-in-training considered service animals under the ADA?

No. Under the ADA, the dog must already be trained before it can be taken into public places. However, some State or local laws cover animals that are still in training.

General Rules

What questions can a covered entity's employees ask to determine if a dog is a service animal?

In situations where it is not obvious that the dog is a service animal, staff may ask only two specific questions: (1) is the dog a service animal required because of a disability? and (2) what work or task has the dog been trained to perform? Staff are not allowed to request any documentation for the dog, require that the dog demonstrate its task, or inquire about the nature of the person's disability.

Do service animals have to wear a vest or patch or special harness identifying them as service animals?

No. The ADA does not require service animals to wear a vest, ID tag, or specific harness.

Who is responsible for the care and supervision of a service animal?

The handler is responsible for caring for and supervising the service animal, which includes toileting, feeding, and grooming and veterinary care. Covered entities are not obligated to supervise or otherwise care for a service animal.

Can a person bring a service animal with them as they go through a salad bar or other self-service food lines?

Yes. Service animals must be allowed to accompany their handlers to and through self-service food lines. Similarly, service animals may not be prohibited from communal food preparation areas, such as are commonly found in shelters or dormitories.

Can hotels assign designated rooms for guests with service animals, out of consideration for other guests?

No. A guest with a disability who uses a service animal must be provided the same opportunity to reserve any available room at the hotel as other guests without disabilities. They may not be restricted to "pet-friendly" rooms.

Can hotels charge a cleaning fee for guests who have service animals?

No. Hotels are not permitted to charge guests for cleaning the hair or dander shed by a service animal. However, if a guest's service animal causes damages to a guest room, a hotel is permitted to charge the same fee for damages as charged to other guests.

Can people bring more than one service animal into a public place?

Generally, yes. Some people with disabilities may use more than one service animal to perform different tasks. For example, a person who has a visual disability and a seizure disorder may use one service animal to assist with way-finding and another that is trained as a seizure alert dog. Other people may need two service animals for the same task, such as a person who needs two dogs to assist him or her with stability when walking. Staff may ask the two permissible questions about each of the dogs. If both dogs can be accommodated, both should be allowed in. In some circumstances, however, it may not be possible to accommodate more than one service animal. For example, in a crowded small restaurant, only one dog may be able to fit under the table. The only other place for the second dog would be in the aisle, which would block the space between tables. In this case, staff may request that one of the dogs be left outside.

Does a hospital have to allow an in-patient with a disability to keep a service animal in his or her room?

Generally, yes. Service animals must be allowed in patient rooms and anywhere else in the hospital the public and patients are allowed to go. They cannot be excluded on the grounds that staff can provide the same services.

What happens if a patient who uses a service animal is admitted to the hospital and is unable to care for or supervise their animal?

If the patient is not able to care for the service animal, the patient can make arrangements for a family member or friend to come to the hospital to provide these services, as it is always preferable that the service animal and its handler not be separated, or to keep the dog during the hospitalization. If the patient is unable to care for the dog and is unable to arrange for someone else to care for the dog, the hospital may place the dog in a boarding facility until the patient is released, or make other appropriate arrangements. However, the hospital must give the patient the opportunity to make arrangements for the dog's care before taking such steps.

Must a service animal be allowed to ride in an ambulance with its handler?

Generally, yes. However, if the space in the ambulance is crowded and the dog's presence would interfere with the emergency medical staff's ability to treat the patient, staff should make other arrangements to have the dog transported to the hospital.

Certification and Registration

Does the ADA require that service animals be certified as service animals?

No. Covered entities may not require documentation, such as proof that the animal has been certified, trained, or licensed as a service animal, as a condition for entry.

There are individuals and organizations that sell service animal certification or registration documents online. These documents do not convey any rights under the ADA and the Department of Justice does not recognize them as proof that the dog is a service animal.

My city requires all dogs to be vaccinated. Does this apply to my service animal?

Yes. Individuals who have service animals are not exempt from local animal control or public health requirements.

My city requires all dogs to be registered and licensed. Does this apply to my service animal?

Yes. Service animals are subject to local dog licensing and registration requirements.

My city requires me to register my dog as a service animal. Is this legal under the ADA?

No. Mandatory registration of service animals is not permissible under the ADA. However, as stated above, service animals are subject to the same licensing and vaccination rules that are applied to all dogs.

My city / college offers a voluntary registry program for people with disabilities who use service animals and provides a special tag identifying the dogs as service animals. Is this legal under the ADA?

Yes. Colleges and other entities, such as local governments, may offer voluntary registries. Many communities maintain a voluntary registry that serves a public purpose, for example, to ensure that emergency staff know to look for service animals during an emergency evacuation process. Some offer a benefit, such as a reduced dog license fee, for individuals who register their service animals. Registries for purposes like this are permitted under the ADA. An entity may not, however, require that a dog be registered as a service animal as a condition of being permitted in public places. This would be a violation of the ADA.

Breeds

Can service animals be any breed of dog?

Yes. The ADA does not restrict the type of dog breeds that can be service animals.

Can individuals with disabilities be refused access to a facility based solely on the breed of their service animal?

No. A service animal may not be excluded based on assumptions or stereotypes about the animal's breed or how the animal might behave. However, if a particular service animal behaves in a way that poses a direct threat to the health or safety of others, has a history of such behavior, or is not under the control of the handler, that animal may be excluded. If an animal is excluded for such reasons, staff must still offer their goods or services to the person without the animal present.

If a municipality has an ordinance that bans certain dog breeds, does the ban apply to service animals?

No. Municipalities that prohibit specific breeds of dogs must make an exception for a service animal of a prohibited breed, unless the dog poses a direct threat to the health or safety of others. Under the "direct threat" provisions of the ADA, local jurisdictions need to determine, on a case-by-case basis, whether a particular service animal can be excluded based on that particular animal's actual behavior or history, but they may not exclude a service animal because of fears or generalizations about how an animal or breed might behave. It is important to note that breed restrictions differ significantly from jurisdiction to jurisdiction. In fact, some jurisdictions have no breed restrictions.

Chapter 29

How Therapists Can Assist People with Disabilities

Chapter Contents

Section 29.1

Occupational Therapists

Text in this section is excerpted from "Occupational Therapists,"
Bureau of Labor Statistics (BLS), January 8, 2014.

What Occupational Therapists Do

Occupational therapists treat injured, ill, or disabled patients through the therapeutic use of everyday activities. They help these patients develop, recover, and improve the skills needed for daily living and working.

Duties

Occupational therapists typically do the following:

- Observe patients doing tasks, ask them questions, and review their medical history

- Evaluate a patient's condition and needs

- Develop a treatment plan for patients, laying out the types of activities and specific goals to be accomplished

- Help people with various disabilities with different tasks, such as leading an autistic child in play activities

- Demonstrate exercises—for example, joint stretches for arthritis relief—that can help relieve pain for people with chronic conditions

- Evaluate a patient's home or workplace and, based on the patient's health needs, identify potential improvements, such as labeling kitchen cabinets for an older person with poor memory

- Educate a patient's family and employer about how to accommodate and care for the patient

- Recommend special equipment, such as wheelchairs and eating aids, and instruct patients on how to use that equipment

- Assess and record patients' activities and progress for patient evaluations, for billing, and for reporting to physicians and other healthcare providers

Patients with permanent disabilities, such as cerebral palsy, often need help performing daily tasks. Therapists show patients how to use appropriate adaptive equipment, such as leg braces, wheelchairs, and eating aids. These devices help patients perform a number of daily tasks, allowing them to function more independently.

Some occupational therapists work with children in educational settings. They evaluate disabled children's abilities, modify classroom equipment to accommodate children with certain disabilities, and help children participate in school activities.

Some therapists provide early intervention therapy to infants and toddlers who have, or are at risk of having, developmental delays.

Therapists who work with the elderly help their patients lead more independent and active lives. They assess patients' abilities and environment and make recommendations. For example, therapists may identify potential fall hazards in a patient's home and recommend their removal.

In some cases, occupational therapists help patients create functional work environments. They evaluate the work space, plan work activities, and meet with the patient's employer to collaborate on changes to the patient's work environment or schedule.

Occupational therapists also may work in mental health settings where they help patients who suffer from developmental disabilities, mental illness, or emotional problems. They help these patients cope with, and engage in, daily life by teaching skills such as time management, budgeting, using public transportation, and doing household chores. In addition, therapists may work with individuals who have problems with drug abuse, alcoholism, depression, or other disorders. They may also work with people who have been through a traumatic event.

Some occupational therapists, such as those employed in hospitals, work as part of a healthcare team along with doctors, registered nurses, and other types of therapists. They may work with patients with chronic conditions, such as diabetes, or help rehabilitate a patient recovering from a hip replacement surgery. Occupational therapists also oversee the work of occupational therapy assistants and aides.

Section 29.2

Physical Therapists

Text in this section is excerpted from "Physical Therapists," Bureau
of Labor Statistics (BLS), January 8, 2014.

What Physical Therapists Do

Physical therapists, sometimes called PTs, help injured or ill people
improve their movement and manage their pain. These therapists are
often an important part of rehabilitation and treatment of patients
with chronic conditions or injuries.

Duties

Physical therapists typically do the following:

- Review patients' medical history and any referrals or notes from
  doctors or surgeons

- Diagnose patients' dysfunctional movements by observing them
  stand or walk and by listening to their concerns, among other
  methods

- Set up a plan of care for patients, outlining the patient's goals
  and the expected outcome of the plan

- Use exercises, stretching maneuvers, hands-on therapy, and
  equipment to ease patients' pain, help them increase their
  mobility, prevent further pain or injury, and facilitate health
  and wellness.

- Evaluate a patient's progress, modifying a plan of care and trying new treatments as needed

- Educate patients and their families about what to expect from
  and how best to cope with the recovery process

Physical therapists provide care to people of all ages who have
functional problems resulting from back and neck injuries; sprains,
strains, and fractures; arthritis; amputations; neurological disorders,

such as stroke or cerebral palsy; injuries related to work and sports; and other conditions.

Physical therapists are trained to use a variety of different techniques—sometimes called modalities—to care for their patients. These techniques include applying heat and cold and using assistive devices such as crutches, wheelchairs, and walkers and equipment, such as adhesive electrodes which apply electric stimulation to treat injuries and pain.

The work of physical therapists varies by type of patient. For example, a patient experiencing loss of mobility due to stroke needs different care from that given to an athlete recovering from an injury. Some physical therapists specialize in one type of care, such as orthopedics or geriatrics. Many physical therapists also work at preventing loss of mobility by developing fitness and wellness programs to encourage healthier and more active lifestyles.

Physical therapists work as part of a healthcare team, overseeing the work of physical therapist assistants and aides and consulting with physicians and surgeons and other specialists.

Section 29.3

Creative Arts Therapists

This section includes excerpts from "Dancing with Disability," National Endowment for the Arts (NEA), Nov 5, 2014.

Creative arts therapies are part of Veterans Health Administration (VHA) Recreation Therapy Service and are direct-care programs that include the following disciplines: Music Therapy, Art Therapy, Dance/Movement Therapy and Drama Therapy.

Creative Arts Therapists

Creative arts therapists are human service professionals who use arts modalities and creative processes to promote wellness, alleviate pain and stress, while offering unique opportunities for interaction. Each creative arts therapy discipline has its own set of professional standards and requisite qualifications. Creative arts therapists are highly skilled, credentialed professionals having completed extensive coursework and clinical training.

Treatment Planning

Qualified creative arts therapists develop treatment goals, provide interventions, document progress, and participate as members of the interdisciplinary team. Therapists plan and carry out treatment programs that are directed to such goals as sensory integration; ambulation; diminishing emotional stress; community reentry; reality orientation; muscular dysfunction reorientation; treatment of psychosocial dysfunction; providing a sense of achievement and progress; and channeling energies into acceptable forms of behavior.

Research

Research supports the effectiveness of creative arts therapies interventions in many areas, including overall physical rehabilitation and facilitating movement. Creative arts therapies further help patients to increase motivation to become engaged in treatment, provide emotional support for Veterans and their families, and create an outlet for expression of feelings. Research results and clinical experiences attest to the viability of creative arts therapies, and often for those who are resistive to other treatment approaches.

Care Standards

Creative arts therapies are listed in Joint Commission standards, Commission on Accreditation of Rehabilitation Facilities and the National Institutes of Health National Center on Complementary and Alternative Medicine. These therapies are recognized as viable, reimbursable treatment options. Creative arts therapists utilize a wide range of techniques of clinical interventions in applying the healing potential and influence of the arts on behavior and quality of life.

Populations Served

Creative arts therapists create non-threatening group and individual art experiences for the exploration of feelings and therapeutic issues, such as self-esteem or personal insight for those with mental health needs. For Alzheimer's disease, interventions are used to trigger short- and long-term memory, decrease agitation, and enhance reality orientation.

Therapeutic Interventions

Interventions are used for persons with chronic illnesses to distract them from pain and facilitate needed relaxation. Creative Arts Therapists organize groups using art experiences to encourage self-expression, communication and socialization, and to facilitate cognitive retraining for Veterans with traumatic brain injury. The use of art-based techniques to break through barriers to the recovery process are utilized in substance abuse. For Veterans with physical disabilities, the creative arts therapists design arts experiences to increase motivation and promote rehabilitative goals.

Part Four

Staying Healthy with a Disability

Chapter 30

Nutrition and Weight Management Issues for People with Disabilities

Chapter Contents

Section 30.1

Nutrition for Swallowing Difficulties

Text in this section is excerpted from "Interventions for Feeding and Nutrition in Cerebral Palsy," Agency for Healthcare Research and Quality (AHRQ), March. 20, 2013; and text from "Safe Swallowing," U.S. Department of Veterans Affairs (VA), May 2013.

What is Dysphagia?

Dysphagia is a swallowing problem that makes eating or drinking certain foods and/or liquids unsafe or difficult. A dysphagia diet includes foods that are softer than regular food. Sometimes liquids need to be thickened. This makes swallowing easier and safer. It also can help prevent food or liquid from going into your lungs.

Table 30.1. Common Causes of Dysphagia

• Stroke	• Chronic lung disease
• Multiple sclerosis, ALS, Parkinson's Disease	• Cancer of the mouth, throat or esophagus
• Surgery to the neck, throat or esophagus	• Radiation to the neck, throat or chest
• Reflux disease	• Dementia, Alzheimer's Disease
• Traumatic Brain Injury	• Aging

Table 30.2. Signs and Symptoms of Dysphagia

• Coughing before, during, and after swallowing	• Change in voice quality – wet, gurgles, or weak
• Choking on foods or liquids	• Drooling
• Repeated swallowing for one bite	• Needing liquids to 'wash' food down
• Taking longer to eat, unable to finish a meal	• Pocketing food in the cheeks or found in the mouth after meals
• Feeling like food is sticking in the throat or chest	• Weight loss

Tips for Safe Swallowing:

- Eat while sitting in an upright position
- Avoid distractions – focus on eating!
- Eat and drink slowly; take small bites
- Chew thoroughly and swallow completely
- Sit upright for 30 minutes after eating

Diet Level and Food Consistency

Your health care provider, dietitian or speech-language pathologist will recommend the right diet level and liquid consistency for you.

- **Dysphagia Pureed**

  Foods on this diet are pureed to a pudding-like consistency.

- **Dysphagia Mechanically-Altered**

  Foods on this diet are soft textured, moist and easy to chew. Meats must be ground or minced into pieces no larger than ¼-inch. Vegetables must smaller than ½-inch pieces, thoroughly cooked and mashed with a fork. Foods from the Dysphagia Pureed diet can also be eaten on this diet.

- **Dysphagia Advanced**

  Foods must be moist and cut into bite-sized pieces. No sticky, chewy, hard, or stringy foods are allowed. Foods from the Dysphagia Pureed and Mechanically-Altered diets can also be eaten on this diet.

Liquid Consistency

- **Nectar Thick**

  Nectar thick liquids are thickened to the consistency of peach or pear nectar. Liquids must stay this thickness at room and body temperature. Nectar thick liquids will coat a spoon lightly.

- **Honey Thick**

  Honey thick liquids are thicker than nectar thick liquids but not as thick as pudding. Liquids should pour slowly off a spoon and coat the spoon like honey. The liquid should not run off like a thin liquid or plop like pudding. Liquids must remain at this consistency at room or body temperature.

Section 30.2

Overweight and Obesity among People with Disabilities

Text in this section is excerpted from "Disability and Obesity,"
Centers for Disease Control and Prevention (CDC), September 14,
2015; and text from "Obesity and Disability," Centers for Disease
Control and Prevention (CDC), October 21, 2013.

Overweight and obesity are terms that identify ranges of weight that are greater than what's generally considered healthy at a given height. Being in the overweight or obese range can be the result of behavioral and environmental factors, or more rarely, genetic factors.

Overweight and obesity are commonly determined by BMI – Body Mass Index. BMI is a number calculated from a person's weight and height. BMI provides a reliable indicator of body fatness for most people and is used to screen for people in weight categories who might have an increased risk of health problems. An adult who has a BMI between 25 and 29.9 is considered overweight, while a BMI of 30 or higher is considered obese. Obesity increases the likelihood of certain diseases and health problems.

Overweight and obesity are both labels for ranges of weight that are greater than what is generally considered healthy for a given height. The terms also identify ranges of weight that have been shown to increase the likelihood of certain diseases and other health problems. Behavior, environment, and genetic factors can affect whether a person is overweight or obese.

Who's at Risk?

Keeping a healthy weight can be challenging for anyone. It requires commitment, support, and access to resources. However, people with disabilities face many challenges to maintaining a healthy weight that go beyond those faced by the general population. These individuals may be at a greater risk of being overweight or obese due to:

- difficulty with chewing or swallowing food, or with its taste or texture;

- medications that can contribute to weight gain, weight loss, and changes in appetite;

- physical limitations that can reduce a person's ability to exercise;

- pain;

- a lack of energy;

- a lack of accessible environments (for example, sidewalks, parks, and exercise equipment) or equipment that can enable exercise;

- a lack of access to healthier food; and

- a lack of resources (for example, money, transportation, and social support from family, friends, neighbors, and community members).

For adults, overweight and obesity ranges are determined by using weight and height to calculate a number called the "body mass index" (BMI). BMI is used because, for most people, it correlates with their amount of body fat.

- An adult who has a BMI between 25 and 29.9 is considered overweight.

- An adult who has a BMI of 30 or higher is considered obese.

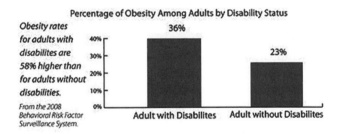

Figure 30.1. *Percentage of Obesity among Adults*

Children

Among children of the same age and sex, overweight is defined on CDC growth charts as a BMI at or above the 85th percentile and lower than the 95th percentile. Obesity is defined as having a BMI at or above the 95th percentile.

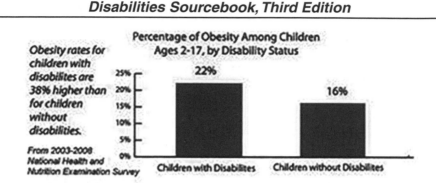

Figure 30.2. *Percentage of Obesity among Children*

The Obesity Epidemic

Obesity affects different people in different ways and may increase the risk for other health conditions among people with and without disabilities.

People with Disabilities

- Children and adults with mobility limitations and intellectual or learning disabilities are at greatest risk for obesity.

- 20% of children 10 through 17 years of age who have special health care needs are obese compared with 15% of children of the same ages without special health care needs.

- Annual health care costs of obesity that are related to disability are estimated at approximately $44 billion.

In the United States

- More than one-third of adults – more than 72 million people – are obese.

- Obesity rates are significantly higher among some racial and ethnic groups. Non-Hispanic Blacks or African Americans have a 51% higher obesity prevalence and Hispanics have a 21% higher obesity prevalence than Non-Hispanic Whites.

- A recent CDC Vital Signs report, titled "State-Specific Obesity Prevalence Among Adults – United States, 2009," points out that people who are obese incurred $1,429 per person extra in medical costs compared to people of normal weight.

- Annual health care costs of obesity for all adults in the United States were estimated to be as high as $147 billion dollars for 2008.

Challenges Faced by People with Disabilities

People with disabilities can find it more difficult to eat healthy, control their weight, and be physically active. This might be due to:

- A lack of healthy food choices.

- Difficulty with chewing or swallowing food, or its taste or texture.

- Medications that can contribute to weight gain, weight loss, and changes in appetite.

- Physical limitations that can reduce a person's ability to exercise.

- Pain.

- A lack of energy.

- A lack of accessible environments (for example, sidewalks, parks, and exercise equipment) that can enable exercise.

- A lack of resources (for example, money, transportation, and social support from family, friends, neighbors, and community members).

Health Consequences of Overweight and Obesity

Overweight and obesity increases the risk of a number of other conditions, including:

- Coronary heart disease

- Type 2 diabetes

- Cancers (endometrial, breast, and colon)

- High blood pressure

- Lipid disorders (for example, high total cholesterol or high levels of triglycerides)

- Stroke

- Liver and gallbladder disease

- Sleep apnea and respiratory problems

- Osteoarthritis (a degeneration of cartilage and its underlying bone within a joint)

- Gynecological problems (abnormal periods, infertility)

What can be done?

Obesity is a complex problem that requires a strong call for action, at many levels, for both adults as well as children. More efforts are needed, and new federal initiatives are helping to change our communities into places that strongly support healthy eating and active living.

All people can:

- Eat more fruits and vegetables and fewer foods high in fat and sugar.

- Drink more water instead of sugary drinks.

- Watch less television.

- Support breastfeeding.

- Promote policies and programs at school, at work, and in the community that make the healthy choice the easy choice.

- Be more physically active.

Everyone, whether they have a disability or not, can maintain a healthy lifestyle by doing a combination of the following:

- eating healthier food in appropriate portion sizes;

- engaging in moderate physical activities on a daily basis, as their condition allows it;

- getting check-ups regularly;

- consulting with health professionals to help with medication or pain management, or to identify appropriate physical activity options.

Given additional challenges that people with disabilities are more likely to face to maintain a healthy lifestyle:

- Health professionals should receive training in how to meet the needs and support healthy lifestyles of people with disabilities.

- Health professionals can ensure that their facilities are accessible and provide services that meet all of the health needs of their patients, beyond the disability.

- Health programs should be designed to include people with disabilities.

- Fitness facilities can ensure that their equipment and programs are accessible and inclusive.

- Accessible transportation options should exist within the community.

- Policies that mandate access to resources and environments can be enforced to facilitate a healthy lifestyle for people with disabilities. Such regulations are provisions of the Rehabilitation Act of 1973, as amended, and the Americans with Disabilities Act of 1990, as amended.

Policies and programs are currently being designed to promote a healthy lifestyle at school, work, and in the community for everyone. These must also be designed in order to address the specific needs of individuals living with a disability.

Section 30.3

Physical Activity among Adults with Disabilities

Text in this section is excerpted from "More Adults with Disabilities Need to Get Physical Activity," Centers for Disease Control and Prevention (CDC), April 29, 2014; and "Weight Loss for Those with Disabilities," U.S. Department of Veterans Affairs (VA), March 20, 2014.

A new CDC Vital Signs™ report shows that aerobic physical activity is important for adults with disabilities and that the federal government, doctors and health professionals, states and communities, and adults with disabilities themselves have a role in increasing physical activity among adults with disabilities. Adults with disabilities who get no physical activity are 50% more likely to have diabetes, stroke, heart disease, or cancer than those who get the recommended amount of physical activity. Adults of all shapes, sizes and abilities can benefit from aerobic physical activity to help avoid these costly and deadly chronic diseases.

10 Important Things You Need to Know about Physical Activity among Adults with Disabilities

1. All adults, including adults with disabilities, need to get regular physical activity for health benefits. Avoid being inactive; some activity is better than none.

2. Doctors and other health professionals can help. Adults with disabilities were 82% more likely to be physically active if their doctor recommended it, than if they did not get a doctor recommendation.

3. Doctors and other health professionals need to know the Physical Activity Guidelines and help their patients with disabilities overcome barriers to reach their physical activity goals.

4. Doctors can ask all patients at every visit, including adults with disabilities, about physical activity.

5. Doctors can recommend physical activity options that match each person's specific abilities, such as hand-crank bicycling, water aerobics and wheelchair basketball. There are a number of resources and programs that can help doctors match physical activities to the abilities of their patients and help them be physically active.

6. Adults with disabilities can talk to their doctor about how much and what kind of physical activity is right for them. Regular aerobic physical activity increases heart and lung function; improves daily living activities and independence; decreases chances of developing chronic diseases; and improves mental health.

7. Adults with disabilities can start physical activity slowly, based on their abilities and fitness level (e.g., active for at least 10 minutes at a time, slowly increasing activity over several weeks if necessary).

8. State and local communities can support physical activity, recreation, and sports-based program opportunities that are accessible to adults with disabilities.

9. State and local communities can improve safe access to public places for physical activity that accommodate users of all abilities by incorporating community features such as proper curb

cuts on sidewalks, ramps for wheelchair access, and well maintained trails.

10. State and local communities can bring together adults with disabilities and their loved ones, doctors and other health professionals, and community leaders to identify available resources and address community needs to increase physical activity.

Key Guidelines for Adults with Disabilities

- When adults with disabilities are not able to meet the above Guidelines, they should engage in regular physical activity according to their abilities and should avoid inactivity.

- Adults with disabilities should talk to their doctor about the amounts and types of physical activity that are appropriate for their abilities.

Weight Loss for Those with Disabilities

It seems simple: Exercise harder. Eat better. Lose those extra few pounds.

But what are the options for a person who can't stand, let alone crank out pushups or run a 5K? How does someone eat healthy when grocery shopping and cooking dinner are both major challenges?

The answer, says VA researcher Dr. Ben Gerber, may be only a telephone call away.

Gerber, of the Jesse Brown VA Medical Center in Chicago, says regular 30-minute targeted phone calls from a trainer can result in significant weight loss for disabled persons. The finding is from a study Gerber worked on along with Dr. James Rimmer of the University of Alabama at Birmingham (UAB).

Gerber says providers often don't know exactly what to tell disabled patients about exercise. "From a provider's perspective, we might tell a patient to walk 30-minutes a day or to eat a certain kind of diet, but for someone with paraplegia, that recommendation becomes a lot more complicated. There also might be competing health priorities," says Gerber. "Who grocery shops and prepares the meals, mobility limitations, pain, depression—all of that plays a role."

All that is part of why people with disabilities have a 66 percent higher rate of obesity than the general population. Intrigued by the challenge, the researchers set out to develop a program to make exercise—and weight loss—more practical and attainable for the disabled population.

One call per week

Their study, published in the December 2013 issue of the American Journal of Physical Medical Rehabilitation, involved more than 100 participants, each with a mobility-limiting disability. The conditions included spinal cord injury, multiple sclerosis, spina bifida, cerebral palsy, stroke, and lupus.

The researchers randomly assigned the volunteers to one of three groups. One group received a physical-activity toolkit along with regular calls from coaches who used a Web-based remote coaching tool called POWERS (Personalized Online Weight and Exercise Response System). The software program was developed by Rimmer's group at UAB through funding from the National Institute on Disability and Rehabilitation Research.

A second group received the toolkit, POWERS calls and nutritional advice. The third group received the physical-activity toolkit only after the study completed and no phone coaching.

For four months, those receiving calls were contacted weekly to develop a plan, monitor progress and troubleshoot any barriers. The calls dropped to every other week after that. At seven months, the calls came only monthly.

After nine months, those on the POWERS plan had lost, on average, nearly five pounds. Participants who also received nutritional advice lost an additional pound. Meanwhile, in the control group, participants actually gained weight—five to six pounds, on average.

Gerber notes that the approach may be a way to reduce not only weight, but health care costs. "Something like this is relatively low-cost," he says. "We can do health behavior promotion and intervention by telephone. That's an easy, cheap, and accessible mechanism to use." He adds the benefits might be especially applicable in VA, with its large population of Veterans, many in rural areas, who have disabilities and other chronic health conditions.

Moving forward

Work remains. Among other tasks, researchers and clinicians have to develop appropriate weight guidelines for those with certain disabilities. Gerber is working now with Dr. Sherri LaVela of the Hines VA

Medical Center on a VA-funded study of weight management among Veterans with spinal cord injuries.

"We're trying to increase the ways we can reach our Veterans," says Gerber. "I think the studies we're doing are showing that people with disabilities can exercise, lose weight, and achieve their goals. Telephone lifestyle coaching is growing in the VA for overweight Veterans. We should also offer services to disabled Veterans that meet their unique needs in weight management."

Chapter 31

Personal Hygiene for People with Disabilities

Chapter Contents

Section 31.1

Dental Care

Text in this section is excerpted from "Dental Care Every Day: A
Caregiver's Guide," National Institute of Dental and Craniofacial
Research (NIDCR), February 2012.

Taking care of someone with a developmental disability requires
patience and skill. As a caregiver, you know this as well as anyone
does. You also know how challenging it is to help that person with dental care. It takes planning, time, and the ability to manage physical,
mental, and behavioral problems. Dental care isn't always easy, but
you can make it work for you and the person you help.

Everyone needs dental care every day. Brushing and flossing
are crucial activities that affect our health. In fact, dental care is
just as important to your client's health and daily routine as taking
medications and getting physical exercise. A healthy mouth helps
people eat well, avoid pain and tooth loss, and feel good about
themselves.

Getting Started

Location. The bathroom isn't the only place to brush someone's
teeth. For example, the kitchen or dining room may be more comfortable. Instead of standing next to a bathroom sink, allow the person to
sit at a table. Place the toothbrush, toothpaste, floss, and a bowl and
glass of water on the table within easy reach.

No matter what location you choose, make sure you have good light.
You can't help someone brush unless you can see inside that person's
mouth. Positioning your body lists ideas on how to sit or stand when
you help someone brush and floss.

Behavior. Problem behavior can make dental care difficult. Try
these ideas and see what works for you.

- At first, dental care can be frightening to some people. Try
  the "tell-show-do" approach to deal with this natural reaction.

Tell your client about each step before you do it. For example, explain how you'll help him or her brush and what it feels like. Show how you're going to do each step before you do it. Also, it might help to let your client hold and feel the toothbrush and floss. Do the steps in the same way that you've explained them.

- Give your client time to adjust to dental care. Be patient as that person learns to trust you working in and around his or her mouth.

- Use your voice and body to communicate that you care. Give positive feedback often to reinforce good behavior.

- Have a routine for dental care. Use the same technique at the same time and place every day. Many people with developmental disabilities accept dental care when it's familiar. A routine might soothe fears or help eliminate problem behavior.

- Be creative. Some caregivers allow their client to hold a favorite toy or special item for comfort. Others make dental care a game or play a person's favorite music. If none of these ideas helps, ask your client's dentist or dental hygienist for advice.

Three Steps to a Healthy Mouth

Like everyone else, people with developmental disabilities can have a healthy mouth if these three steps are followed:

1. Brush every day.
2. Floss every day.
3. Visit a dentist regularly.

Step 1. Brush Every Day

If the person you care for is unable to brush, these suggestions might be helpful.

- First, wash your hands and put on disposable gloves. Sit or stand where you can see all of the surfaces of the teeth.

- Be sure to use a regular or power toothbrush with soft bristles.

- Use a pea-size amount of toothpaste with fluoride, or none at all. Toothpaste bothers people who have swallowing problems. If this is the case for the person you care for, brush with water instead.

- Brush the front, back, and top of each tooth. Gently brush back and forth in short strokes.

- Gently brush the tongue after you brush the teeth.

- Help the person rinse with plain water. Give people who can't rinse a drink of water or consider sweeping the mouth with a finger wrapped in gauze.

Get a new toothbrush with soft bristles every 3 months, after a contagious illness, or when the bristles are worn.

If the person you care for can brush but needs some help, the following ideas might work for you. You may think of other creative ways to solve brushing problems based on your client's special needs.

Make the toothbrush easier to hold.

The same kind of Velcro® strap used to hold food utensils is helpful for some people

Others attach the brush to the hand with a wide elastic or rubber band. Make sure the band isn't too tight.

Make the toothbrush handle bigger.

You can also cut a small slit in the side of a tennis ball and slide it onto the handle of the toothbrush

You can buy a toothbrush with a large handle, or you can slide a bicycle grip onto the handle. Attaching foam tubing, available from home health care catalogs, is also helpful.

Try other toothbrush options.

A power toothbrush might make brushing easier. Take the time to help your client get used to one.

Guide the Toothbrush.

Help brush by placing your hand very gently over your client's hand and guiding the toothbrush. If that doesn't work, you may need to brush the teeth yourself.

Step 2. Floss Every Day

Flossing cleans between the teeth where a toothbrush can't reach. Many people with disabilities need a caregiver to help them floss. Flossing is a tough job that takes a lot of practice. Waxed, unwaxed, flavored, or plain floss all do the same thing. The person you care for might like one more than another, or a certain type might be easier to use.

- Use a string of floss 18 inches long. Wrap that piece around the middle finger of each hand.

- Grip the floss between the thumb and index finger of each hand.

- Start with the lower front teeth, then floss the upper front teeth. Next, work your way around to all the other teeth.

- Work the floss gently between the teeth until it reaches the gumline. Curve the floss around each tooth and slip it under the gum. Slide the floss up and down. Do this for both sides of every tooth, one side at a time.

- Adjust the floss a little as you move from tooth to tooth so the floss is clean for each one.

Try a floss holder

If you have trouble flossing, try using a floss holder instead of holding the floss with your fingers.

The dentist may prescribe a special rinse for your client. Fluoride rinses can help prevent cavities. Chlorhexidine rinses fight germs that cause gum disease. Follow the dentist's instructions and tell your client not to swallow any of the rinse. Ask the dentist for creative ways to use rinses for a client with swallowing problems

Positioning Your Body: Where To Sit or Stand

Keeping people safe when you clean their mouth is important. Experts in providing dental care for people with developmental disabilities recommend the following positions for caregivers. If you work in a group home or related facility, get permission from your supervisor before trying any of these positions.

If the person you're helping is in a wheelchair, sit behind it. Lock the wheels, then tilt the chair into your lap.

Stand behind the person or lean against a wall for additional support. Use your arm to hold the person's head gently against your body.

Step 3. Visit a Dentist Regularly

Your client should have regular dental appointments. Professional cleanings are just as important as brushing and flossing every day. Regular examinations can identify problems before they cause unnecessary pain.

As is the case with dental care at home, it may take time for the person you care for to become comfortable at the dental office. A "get acquainted" visit with no treatment provided might help: The person can meet the dental team, sit in the dental chair if he or she wishes,

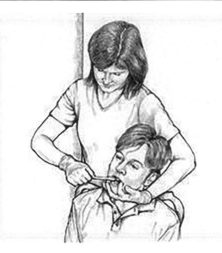

Figure 31.1. *If the person you're helping is in a wheelchair, sit behind it. Lock the wheels, then tilt the chair into your lap.*

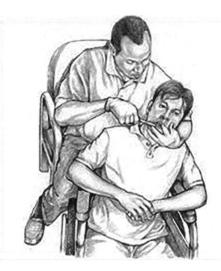

Figure 31.2. *Stand behind the person or lean against a wall for additional support. Use your arm to hold the person's head gently against your body.*

and receive instructions on how to brush and floss. Such a visit can go a long way toward making dental appointments easier.

Prepare for Every Dental Visit: Your Role

- Be prepared for every appointment. You're an important source of information for the dentist. If you have questions about what the dentist will need to know, call the office before the appointment.

- Know the person's dental history. Keep a record of what happens at each visit. Talk to the dentist about what occurred at the last appointment. Remind the dental team of what worked and what didn't.

- Bring a complete medical history. The dentist needs each patient's medical history before treatment can begin. Bring a list of all the medications the person you care for is taking and all known allergies.

- Bring all insurance, billing, and legal information. Know who is responsible for payment. The dentist may need permission, or legal consent, before treatment can begin. Know who can legally give consent.

- Be on time.

Section 31.2

How to Bathe Someone with a Disability

Text in this section is excerpted from "Bathing: Alzheimer's Caregiving Tips," National Institute on Aging. (NIA), October 2012.

Everyday Care

At some point, people with Alzheimer's disease (AD) will need help bathing, combing their hair, brushing their teeth, and getting dressed. Because these are private activities, people may not want help. They may feel embarrassed about being naked in front of caregivers. They also may feel angry about not being able to care for themselves. Below are suggestions that may help with everyday care.

Bathing

Helping someone with AD take a bath or shower can be one of the hardest things you do. Planning can help make the person's bath time better for both of you.

303

The person with AD may be afraid. If so, follow the person's lifelong bathing habits, such as doing the bath or shower in the morning or before going to bed. Here are other tips for bathing.

Main safety tips:

- Never leave a confused or frail person alone in the tub or shower.
- Always check the water temperature before he or she gets in the tub or shower.
- Use plastic containers for shampoo or soap to prevent them from breaking.
- Use a hand-held showerhead.
- Use a rubber bath mat and put safety bars in the tub.
- Use a sturdy shower chair in the tub or shower. This will support a person who is unsteady, and it could prevent falls. You can get shower chairs at drug stores and medical supply stores.

Before a bath or shower:

- Get the soap, washcloth, towels, and shampoo ready.
- Make sure the bathroom is warm and well lighted. Play soft music if it helps to relax the person.
- Be matter-of-fact about bathing. Say, "It's time for a bath now." Don't argue about the need for a bath or shower.
- Be gentle and respectful. Tell the person what you are going to do, step-by-step.
- Make sure the water temperature in the bath or shower is comfortable.
- Don't use bath oil. It can make the tub slippery and may cause urinary tract infections.

During a bath or shower:

- Allow the person with AD to do as much as possible. This protects his or her dignity and helps the person feel more in control.
- Put a towel over the person's shoulders or lap. This helps him or her feel less exposed. Then use a sponge or washcloth to clean under the towel.

- Distract the person by talking about something else if he or she becomes upset.

- Give him or her a washcloth to hold. This makes it less likely that the person will try to hit you.

After a bath or shower:

- Prevent rashes or infections by patting the person's skin with a towel. Make sure the person is completely dry. Be sure to dry between folds of skin.

- If the person has trouble with incontinence, use a protective ointment, such as Vaseline®, around the rectum, vagina, or penis.

- If the person with AD has trouble getting in and out of the bathtub, do a sponge bath instead.

Other bathing tips:

- Give the person a full bath two or three times a week. For most people, a sponge bath to clean the face, hands, feet, underarms, and genital or "private" area is all you need to do every day.

- Washing the person's hair in the sink may be easier than doing it in the shower or bathtub. You can buy a hose attachment for the sink.

- Get professional help with bathing if it becomes too hard for you to do on your own.

Chapter 32

Bowel and Bladder Problems Associated with Disabilities

Studies have shown that individuals with disabilities are more likely than people without disabilities to report:

- Poorer overall health.

- Less access to adequate health care.

- Smoking and physical inactivity.

People with disabilities need health care and health programs for the same reasons anyone else does—to stay well, active, and a part of the community.

Bowel and Bladder

Some disabilities, such as spinal cord injuries, can affect how well a person's bladder and bowel works.

What is a bowel control problem?

You have a bowel control problem if you accidentally pass solid or liquid stool or mucus from your rectum. Bowel control problems

Text in this chapter is excerpted from "Related Conditions," Centers for Disease Control and Prevention (CDC), March 31, 2014; and text from "What I Need to Know about Bowel Control," National Institute of Diabetes and Digestive and Kidney Diseases (NIDDK), December 2012.

include being unable to hold a bowel movement until you reach a toilet and passing stool into your underwear without being aware of it happening. Stool, also called feces, is solid waste that is passed as a bowel movement and includes undigested food, bacteria, mucus, and dead cells. Mucus is a clear liquid that coats and protects tissues in your digestive system.

A bowel control problem—also called fecal incontinence—can be upsetting and embarrassing. Most people with a bowel control problem feel ashamed and try to hide the problem. They may not want to leave the house for fear of losing bowel control in public. They may withdraw from friends and family.

Bowel control problems are often caused by a medical issue and can be treated. If you have a bowel control problem, don't be afraid to talk about it with your doctor. Your doctor may be able to help.

What causes bowel control problems?

Bowel control problems can have many causes. Some common causes are

- diarrhoea

- constipation

- muscle damage or weakness

- nerve damage

- loss of stretch in the rectum

- childbirth by vaginal delivery

- hemorrhoids and rectal prolapse

- rectocele

- inactivity

Diarrhea. Diarrhea causes bowel control problems because loose stool fills your rectum more quickly than your rectum can stretch to hold the stool. This rapid filling can make it harder to reach the bathroom in time.

Constipation. You might be surprised to learn that constipation, a condition in which an adult has fewer than three bowel movements a week or a child has fewer than two bowel movements a week, can lead

308

to bowel control problems. Constipation causes large, hard stools to stretch your rectum and relax your internal sphincters. Then, watery stool can leak out around the hard stool.

The type of constipation that is most likely to lead to a bowel control problem happens when a person squeezes the sphincters and pelvic floor muscles by mistake instead of relaxing them. For example, if you have pain when you have a bowel movement, you may unconsciously learn to squeeze these muscles to delay the bowel movement and avoid pain.

Muscle damage or weakness. If the sphincter muscles are damaged or weakened, they may not be strong enough to keep the anus closed, and stool can leak out. The sphincter muscles can be damaged by

- trauma
- childbirth injuries
- cancer surgery
- surgery to remove hemorrhoids, which are swollen blood vessels in and around your anus and lower rectum

Nerve damage. If the nerves that control your sphincters are damaged, the muscles can't work the way they should. Damage to the nerves that sense stool in your rectum can make it hard to know when you need to use the bathroom.

Nerves can be damaged by

- childbirth
- a long-term habit of straining to pass stool
- stroke
- spinal cord injury
- diseases that affect the nerves, such as diabetes and multiple sclerosis

Brain injuries from stroke, head trauma, or certain diseases can also cause bowel control problems.

Loss of stretch in the rectum. If your rectum is scarred or inflamed, it becomes stiff and can't stretch as much to hold stool. If your rectum gets too full, stool can leak out. Radiation treatment for rectal cancer or other pelvic cancers can cause scarring of the rectum.

309

Inflammatory bowel diseases—chronic disorders that cause irritation and sores on the lining of the digestive system— can cause the rectal wall to become stiff.

Childbirth by vaginal delivery. Childbirth sometimes causes injuries to the muscles and nerves in the pelvic floor. The risk is greater if

- forceps are used to help deliver the baby
- the doctor makes a cut, called an episiotomy, in the vaginal area to prevent the baby's head from tearing the vagina during birth

Bowel control problems related to childbirth may appear soon after delivery or many years later.

Hemorrhoids and rectal prolapse. External hemorrhoids, which develop under the skin around your anus, can prevent your anal sphincter muscles from closing completely. Rectal prolapse, a condition that causes your rectum to drop down through your anus, can also prevent the anal sphincter muscles from closing well enough to prevent leakage. Small amounts of mucus or liquid stool can then leak through your anus.

Rectocele. If you are a woman, you can have rectocele, a condition that causes your rectum to protrude through your vagina. Rectocele can happen when the thin layer of muscles separating your rectum from your vagina becomes weak. Stool may stay in your rectum because the rectocele makes it harder to push stool out. More research is needed to be sure rectocele increases the risk of bowel control problems.

Inactivity. If you are inactive, especially if you spend many hours a day sitting or lying down, you may be keeping a large amount of stool in your rectum. Liquid stool can then leak around the more solid stool. Frail, older adults are most likely to develop constipation-related bowel control problems for this reason.

What do I tell my doctor about my bowel control problem?

You may be embarrassed to talk about your bowel control problem, but your doctor will not be shocked or surprised. The more details and examples you can give about your problem, the better your doctor will be able to help you. You should be prepared to tell your doctor

- when your bowel control problem started

310

- whether you leak liquid or solid stool

- if you have hemorrhoids that bulge through your anus when you lift things or at other times and if the hemorrhoids pull back in by themselves or have to be pushed in with a finger

- if the problem is worse after eating or if any specific foods seem to make the problem worse

- if you aren't able to control passing gas

Your doctor will probably also ask you questions like these:

- How often do you have a bowel control problem?

- Do you leak a little bit of stool or do you lose complete control of your bowel?

- Do you feel a strong urge to have a bowel movement or do you lose control without warning?

- Is your bowel control worse when you have diarrhea or constipation?

- How is your bowel control problem affecting your daily life?

You may want to keep a stool diary for several weeks before visiting your doctor so you can answer these questions. A stool diary is a chart for recording daily bowel movement details.

How is the cause of a bowel control problem diagnosed?

To diagnose what is causing your bowel control problem, your doctor will take your medical history, including asking the questions listed in "What do I tell my doctor about my bowel control problem?" Your doctor may refer you to a specialist who will perform a physical exam and may suggest one or more of the following tests:

- anal manometry

- anal ultrasound

- magnetic resonance imaging (MRI)

- defecography

- flexible sigmoidoscopy or colonoscopy

- anal electromyography (EMG)

Anal manometry. Anal manometry uses pressure sensors and a balloon that can be inflated in your rectum to check how sensitive your rectum is and how well it works. Anal manometry also checks the tightness of the muscles around your anus. To prepare for this test, you should use an enema and not eat anything 2 hours before the test. An enema involves flushing water or a laxative into your anus using a special squirt bottle. A laxative is medicine that loosens stool and increases bowel movements. For this test, a thin tube with a balloon on its tip and pressure sensors below the balloon is put into your anus. Once the balloon reaches the rectum and the pressure sensors are in the anus, the tube is slowly pulled out to measure muscle tone and contractions. No sedative is needed for this test, which takes about 30 minutes.

Anal ultrasound. Ultrasound uses a tool, called a transducer, that bounces safe, painless sound waves off your organs to create an image of their structure. An anal ultrasound is specific to the anus and rectum. The procedure is performed in a doctor's office, outpatient center, or hospital by a specially trained technician, and the images are interpreted by a radiologist—a doctor who specializes in medical imaging. A sedative is not needed. The images can show the structure of your anal sphincter muscles.

Magnetic Resonance Imaging (MRI) MRI machines use radio waves and magnets to produce detailed pictures of your internal organs and soft tissues without using X-rays. The procedure is performed in an outpatient center or hospital by a specially trained technician, and the images are interpreted by a radiologist. A sedative is not needed, though you may be given medicine to help you relax if you have a fear of confined spaces. An MRI may include the injection of special dye, called contrast medium. With most MRI machines, you lie on a table that slides into a tunnel-shaped device that may be open ended or closed at one end; some newer machines are designed to allow you to lie in a more open space. MRIs can show problems with your anal sphincter muscles. MRIs can provide more information than anal ultrasound, especially about the external anal sphincter.

Defecography. This X-ray of the area around your anus and rectum shows whether you have problems with

- pushing stool out of your body
- the functioning of your anus and rectum
- squeezing and relaxing your rectal muscles

The test can also show changes in the structure of your anus or rectum. To prepare for the test, you perform two enemas. You can't eat anything for 2 hours before the test. During the test, the doctor fills your rectum with a soft paste that shows up on X-rays and feels like stool. You sit on a toilet inside an X-ray machine. The doctor will ask you to first pull in and squeeze your sphincter muscles to prevent leakage and then to strain as if you're having a bowel movement. The radiologist studies the X-rays to look for problems with your rectum, anus, and pelvic floor muscles.

Flexible sigmoidoscopy or colonoscopy. These tests are similar, but a colonoscopy is used to view your rectum and entire colon, while a flexible sigmoidoscopy is used to view just your rectum and lower colon. These tests are performed at a hospital or outpatient center by a gastroenterologist—a doctor who specializes in digestive diseases. For both tests, a doctor will give you written bowel prep instructions to follow at home. You may be asked to follow a clear liquid diet for 1 to 3 days before either test. The night before the test, you may need to take a laxative. One or more enemas may be needed the night before and about 2 hours before the test.

In most cases, you will be given a light sedative, and possibly pain medicine, to help you relax during a flexible sigmoidoscopy. A sedative is used for colonoscopy. For either test, you will lie on a table while the doctor inserts a flexible tube into your anus. A small camera on the tube sends a video image of your bowel lining to a computer screen. The test can show problems in your lower gastrointestinal (GI) tract that may be causing your bowel control problem. The doctor may also perform a biopsy, a procedure that involves taking a piece of tissue from the bowel lining for examination with a microscope. You won't feel the biopsy. A pathologist—a doctor who specializes in diagnosing diseases—examines the tissue in a lab to confirm the diagnosis.

You may have cramping or bloating during the first hour after these tests. You're not allowed to drive for 24 hours after a colonoscopy or flexible sigmoidoscopy to allow the sedative time to wear off. Before the test, you should make plans for a ride home. You should recover fully by the next day and be able to go back to your normal diet.

Anal EMG. Anal EMG checks the health of your pelvic floor muscles and the nerves that control your muscles. The doctor inserts a very thin needle wire through your skin into your muscle. The wire on the needle picks up the electrical activity given off by the muscles. The electrical activity is shown as images on a screen or sounds through a speaker. Another type of anal EMG uses stainless steel plates attached to the sides of a plastic plug instead of a needle. The plug is put in your anus to measure the electrical activity of your external anal sphincter and other pelvic floor muscles. The test can show if there is damage to the nerves that control the external sphincter or pelvic floor muscles by measuring the average electrical activity when you

- relax quietly
- squeeze to prevent a bowel movement
- strain to have a bowel movement

How are bowel control problems treated?

Treatment for bowel control problems may include one or more of the following:

- eating, diet, and nutrition
- medicines
- bowel training
- pelvic floor exercises and biofeedback
- surgery
- electrical stimulation

Eating, Diet, and Nutrition

Changes in your diet that may improve your bowel control problem include

Eating the right amount of fiber. Fiber can help with diarrhea and constipation. Fiber is found in fruits, vegetables, whole grains, and beans. Fiber supplements sold in a pharmacy or health food store are another common source of fiber to treat bowel control problems. The Academy of Nutrition and Dietetics recommends getting 20 to 35 grams of fiber a day for adults and "age plus five" grams for children. A 7-year-old child, for example, should get "7 +5," or 12, grams of fiber a day. Fiber should be added to your diet slowly to avoid bloating.

Getting plenty to drink. Drinking eight 8-ounce glasses of liquid a day may help prevent constipation. Water is a good choice. You should avoid drinks with caffeine, alcohol, milk, or carbonation if they give you diarrhea.

Medicines

If diarrhea is causing your bowel control problem, medicine may help. Your doctor may suggest using bulk laxatives to help you make more solid stools that are easier to control. Your doctor may also suggest antidiarrheal medicines that slow down your bowels and help control the problem.

Bowel Training

Training yourself to have bowel movements at certain times during the day—such as after meals—may help. Developing a regular pattern may take a while, so don't give up if it doesn't work right away.

Pelvic Floor Exercises and Biofeedback

Exercises that strengthen your pelvic floor muscles can help with bowel control. To do pelvic floor exercises, you squeeze and relax these muscles 50 to 100 times a day. The trick is finding the right muscles to squeeze. Your doctor can help make sure you're doing the exercises the right way. Biofeedback therapy may also help you learn to do the exercises correctly. Biofeedback therapy is painless and uses a machine to let you know when you are squeezing the right muscles. You practice what you learn at home. Success with pelvic floor exercises depends on what is causing your bowel control problem, how severe the problem is, and your motivation and ability to follow your doctor's recommendations.

Surgery

Depending on the reason for your bowel control problem or how severe it is, your doctor may recommend surgery. Surgery options include

- Sphincteroplasty, which involves sewing back together the separated ends of a sphincter muscle torn by childbirth or another injury and is the most common type of surgery for bowel control problems

- Artificial anal sphincter, which is a procedure to place an inflatable cuff around your anus and implant a small pump beneath your skin to inflate or deflate the cuff

- Nonabsorbable bulking agent, which is injected into the wall of your anus to bulk up the tissue around your anus, making the opening of your anus narrower so your sphincters are able to close better

- Bowel diversion, which is an operation that reroutes the normal movement of stool out of the body when part of the bowel is removed; colostomy or ileostomy are the types of bowel diversion used to treat bowel control problems

Electrical Stimulation

Electrical stimulation involves placing wires in the sacral nerves to your anus and rectum and constantly stimulating the nerves with electrical pulses. Electrical stimulation is also called sacral nerve stimulation or neuromodulation. The sacral nerves connect to the part of your spine in the hip area. A battery-operated stimulator is placed under your skin. Based on your response, the doctor can adjust the amount of stimulation so it works best for you. You can turn the stimulator on or off at any time.

How do I cope with my bowel control problem?

There are steps you can take to manage your bowel control problem. Try these everyday tips:

- Carry a bag with cleanup supplies and a change of clothes with you when leaving the house.

- Find public restrooms before you need one.

- Use the toilet before leaving home.

- Wear disposable underwear or absorbent pads inserted in your underwear.

- If you lose bowel control often, use a fecal deodorant—a pill that you chew or swallow to reduce the smell of stool and gas. These pills are available without a prescription. Your doctor can help you choose which type is best for you.

You should also be aware that eating causes contractions in your large intestine that push stool towards your rectum. The rectum also contracts for 30 to 60 minutes after eating. Both of these events make it more likely that you will pass gas and have a bowel movement soon after eating. This activity may increase if you are anxious. You might want to avoid eating in restaurants or at social events, or you may want to take antidiarrheal medicines before eating in these situations.

What should I do about anal discomfort?

The skin around your anus is delicate and sensitive. Constipation and diarrhea or contact between skin and stool can cause pain or itching. Here are some things you can do to relieve discomfort:

Wash with water. Gently wash the anal area with water, but not soap, after a bowel movement. Soap can dry out and irritate your skin, and so can rubbing with dry toilet paper. Alcohol-free wipes are a better choice.

Air dry. Let the area air dry after washing. If you don't have time, gently pat yourself dry with a clean cloth.

Use a moisture-barrier cream. Use a cream that contains ingredients such as dimethicone—a type of silicone—that form a barrier between your skin and stool. Clean and dry the area before you apply the cream. Ask your doctor what kind of cream to use.

Try nonmedicated powders. Plain talcum powder or cornstarch may help relieve pain or itching.

Use wicking pads or disposable underwear. If you use pads or disposable underwear worn in close contact with your skin, make sure they have a wicking layer. The wicking layer protects your skin by pulling moisture away from your skin and into the pad.

Wear clothes and underwear that allow air to flow. Tight clothes and plastic or rubber underwear that block air can make skin problems worse. Clothes and underwear that allow air to flow help skin stay dry.

Change soiled underwear as soon as you can.

317

Chapter 33

Pressure Sores / Ulcers: What They Are and How to Prevent Them

Pressure ulcers—also known as bed sores, pressure sores, or decubitus ulcers—are wounds caused by constant pressure on the skin. They usually develop on body parts such as the elbow, heel, hip, shoulder, back, and back of the head.

People with disabilities who are bedridden or use a wheelchair are at risk for developing pressure sores.

Uninterrupted pressure exerted on the skin, soft tissue, muscle, and bone can lead to the development of localized ischemia, tissue inflammation, shearing, anoxia, and necrosis. Pressure ulcers affect up to three million adults in the United States. Areas of the body prone to the development of pressure ulcers are depicted in Figure 33.1. Estimates of the incidence of pressure ulcers vary according to the setting, with ranges of 0.4 to 38.0 percent in acute care hospitals, 2.2 to 23.9 percent in long-term nursing facilities, and 0 to 17.0 percent in home care settings. The prevalence of pressure ulcers in acute and

Text in this chapter is excerpted from "Related Conditions," Centers for Disease Control and Prevention (CDC), March 31, 2014; text from "Pressure Ulcer Treatment Strategies: Comparative Effectiveness," Agency for Healthcare Research and Quality's (AHRQ), May 8, 2013; and text from "Treating Wounds and Preventing Pressure Sores (Bed Sores)," Centers for Medicare & Medicaid Services (CMS), July 17, 2015.

long-term care settings was 9.2 to 11.1 percent between 1989 and 1995 and 14.7 to 15.5 percent between 1999 and 2005.

Pressure ulcer healing rates—which depend on comorbidities, clinical interventions, and ulcer severity—vary considerably. Ulcer severity is assessed using a variety of different staging or grading systems, but the National Pressure Ulcer Advisory Panel (NPUAP) staging system is the most commonly used. Comorbidities predisposing toward pressure ulcer development and affecting ulcer healing include those affecting patient mobility (e.g., spinal cord injury), wound environments (e.g., incontinence), and wound healing (e.g., diabetes and vascular disease). Delayed healing can add to the length of hospitalization and impede return to full functioning. Data on the costs of treatment vary, but some estimates range between $37,800 and $70,000 per ulcer, with total annual costs for pressure ulcers in the United States as high as $11 billion. Prevalence of pressure ulcers is used as an indicator of quality for long-term care facilities, and progression of pressure ulcers in hospitalized patients is often considered an avoidable complication representing failure of inpatient management.

Given the negative impact pressure ulcers have on health status and patient quality of life, as well as health care costs, treatments are needed that promote healing, shorten healing time, and minimize the risk of complications. Pressure ulcer treatment involves a variety of different approaches, including interventions to treat the conditions that give rise to pressure ulcers (support surfaces and nutritional support); interventions to protect and promote healing of the ulcer (wound dressings, topical applications, and various adjunctive therapies, including vacuum-assisted closure, ultrasound therapy, electrical stimulation, and hyperbaric oxygen therapy); and surgical repair of the ulcer. Most ulcers are treated using a combination of these approaches. Standards of care for pressure ulcer treatment are typically guided by clinical practice guidelines, such as those developed by NPUAP, but also are informed by patient-related factors such as comorbidities and nutritional status, local practice patterns, and the stage and features of the wound. An examination of the comparative effectiveness and

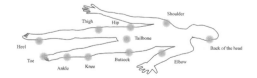

Figure 33.1. *Common pressure ulcer sites*

Table 33.1. Treating wounds and preventing pressure sores (bed sores)

Quality measures	What it is and why it's important
How often patients' wounds improved or healed after an operation	This shows how often the home health team helped patients' wounds improve or heal after an operation. Normal wound healing after an operation is an important marker of good care. One way to measure the quality of care that home health agencies give is to look at how well their patients' wounds heal after an operation. Patients whose wounds heal normally generally feel better and can get back to their daily activities sooner than those whose wounds don't heal normally. The home health team can assist with wound healing in several ways: • Change the wound dressing, depending on the doctor's orders, or teach the patient or caregiver to change the dressing • Teach the patient or caregiver about signs of wound healing • The types of foods that promote healing and restore normal functioning • Any drugs the doctor has ordered, like drugs used to relieve pain • Any signs of infection or other problems. If any signs of infection or other problems are present, the nurse should contact the doctor and ask if there are additional orders. • If the patient sees signs of infection or has concerns about the wound on a day when the nurse isn't scheduled to visit, the patient should be instructed to call the home health team to schedule a visit as soon as possible to look at the wound, or call the doctor. Some patients may not improve, or may get worse, even though the home health team provides good care.
How often the home health team checked patients for the risk of developing pressure sores (bed sores)	This shows how often the home health team checked to see if patients may be in danger of getting pressure sores (bed sores). This means the team may have checked the patient's skin, asked about nutrition, and asked whether patients have problems controlling their bowel or bladder. Some patients who get home health care are at greater risk of developing pressure sores (bed sores) because they're confined to bed, have problems moving around, don't eat a healthy diet, or have trouble controlling their bladder or bowels.

Table 33.1. Continued

Quality measures	What it is and why it's important
	By finding out if the patient is at risk for pressure sores (bed sores) as soon as care begins, the home health team can teach the patient or caregiver ways to avoid pressure sores, like: • Turning the patient often or encouraging them to move around • Eating and drinking healthy foods • Improving bladder or bowel control • Keeping the skin clean
How often the home health team included treatments to prevent pressure sores (bed sores) in the plan of care	This tells you how often the home health team, included ways to prevent pressure sores (bed sores) for patients at risk for developing them in the plan of care. Patients who get home health care can avoid getting pressure sores (bed sores) when the home health team takes steps to prevent them. The home health team can teach the patient or caregiver ways to avoid pressure sores, like: • Turning the patient often or encouraging them to move around • Eating and drinking healthy foods • Improving bladder or bowel control • Keeping the skin clean
How often the home health team took doctor-ordered action to prevent pressure sores (bed sores)	This shows how often the home health team got doctor's orders that included treatments to prevent pressure sores (bed sores) and provided those treatments to the patient. Patients who get home health care can avoid getting pressure sores (bed sores) when the home health team takes steps to prevent them. The home health team can teach the patient or caregiver ways to avoid pressure sores, like: • Turning the patient often or encouraging them to move around • Eating and drinking healthy foods • Improving bladder or bowel control • Keeping the skin clean

harms of different therapies and approaches to treating pressure ulcers is important to guide clinical practice.

Chapter 34

Managing Pain

Pain is commonly reported by people with many types of disabilities. For some, pain can affect functioning and activities of daily living. The length of time a person experiences pain can be classified as either long term (also called chronic) or short term.

Pain in its most benign form warns us that something isn't quite right, that we should take medicine or see a doctor. At its worst, however, pain robs us of our productivity, our well-being, and, for many of us suffering from extended illness, our very lives. Pain is a complex perception that differs enormously among individual patients, even those who appear to have identical injuries or illnesses.

The burden of pain in the United States is astounding. More than 100 million Americans have pain that persists for weeks to years. The financial toll of this epidemic cost $560 billion to $635 billion per year according to *Relieving Pain in America: A Blueprint for Transforming Prevention, Care, Education, and Research*, a recent report from an Institute of Medicine (IOM). Pain is ultimately a challenge for family, friends, and health care providers who must give support to the individual suffering from the physical as well as the emotional consequences of pain.

Text in this chapter is excerpted from "Related Conditions," Centers for Disease Control and Prevention (CDC), March 31, 2014; and text from "Pain: Hope Through Research," National Institute of Neurological Disorders and Stroke (NINDS), January 2014.

A Pain Primer: What Do We Know about Pain?

What is pain? The International Association for the Study of Pain (IASP) defines it as: *An unpleasant sensory and emotional experience associated with actual or potential tissue damage or described in terms of such damage.* The IASP definition means that pain is a subjective experience; one that cannot be objectively measured and depends on the person's self-report. As will be discussed later, there can be a wide variability in how a person experiences pain to a given stimulus or injury.

Pain can be classified as acute or chronic, and the two kinds differ greatly.

- **Acute pain**, for the most part, results from disease, inflammation, or injury to tissues. This type of pain generally comes on suddenly, for example, after trauma or surgery, and may be accompanied by anxiety or emotional distress. The cause of acute pain can usually be diagnosed and treated. The pain is self-limiting, which means it is confined to a given period of time and severity. It can become chronic.

- **Chronic pain** is now believed to be a chronic disease condition in the same manner as diabetes and asthma. Chronic pain can be made worse by environmental and psychological factors. By its nature, chronic pain persists over a long period of time and is resistant to many medical treatments. It can—and often does—cause severe problems. People with chronic pain often suffer from more than one painful condition. It is thought that there are common mechanisms that put some people at higher risk to develop multiple pain disorders. It is not known whether these disorders share a common cause.

We may experience pain as a prick, tingle, sting, burn, or ache. Normally, acute pain is a protective response to tissue damage resulting from injury, disease, overuse, or environmental stressors. To sense pain, specialized receptors (called nociceptors) which are found throughout the body, trigger a series of events in response to a noxious (painful) stimulus. The events begin with conversion of the stimulus to an electrical impulse that travels through nerves from the site of injury or disease process to the spinal cord. These signals are transmitted to a specialized part of the spinal cord called the dorsal horn, where they can be dampened or amplified before being relayed to the brain.

How is Pain Diagnosed?

There is no way to tell accurately how much pain a person has. Tools to measure pain intensity, to show pain through imaging technology, to locate pain precisely, and to assess the effect of pain on someone's life, offer some insight into how much pain a person has. They do not, however, provide objective measures of pain. Sometimes, as in the case of headaches, physicians find that the best aid to diagnosis is the person's own description of the type, duration, and location of pain. Defining pain as sharp or dull, constant or intermittent, burning or aching may give the best clues to the cause of pain. These descriptions are part of what is called the pain history, taken by the physician during the preliminary examination of a person with pain. Developing a test for assessing pain would be a very useful tool in diagnosing and treating pain.

Physicians, however, do have a number of approaches and technologies they use to find the cause of pain. Primarily these include:

- A **musculoskeletal** and **neurological examination** in which the physician tests movement, reflexes, sensation, balance, and coordination.

- **Laboratory tests** (e.g., blood, urine, cerebrospinal fluid) can help the physician diagnose infection, cancer, nutritional problems, endocrine abnormalities and other conditions that may cause pain.

- **Electrodiagnostic procedures** include **electromyography (EMG), nerve conduction studies, evoked potential (EP) studies**, and **quantitative sensory testing.** These procedures measure the electrical activity of muscles and nerves. They help physicians evaluate muscle symptoms that may result from a disease or an injury to the body's nerves or muscles. **EMG** tests muscle activity. It can help physicians tell which muscles or nerves are affected by weakness or pain. **Nerve conduction studies** are usually performed along with EMG. These studies record how nerves are functioning. **EP** studies measure electrical activity in the brain in response to sight, sound, or touch stimulation. **Quantitative sensory testing** can establish thresholds for sensory perception in individuals which can then be compared to normal values. These tests are used to detect abnormalities in sensory function and nerve disorders.

- Imaging, especially **magnetic resonance imaging** or **MRI**, provides physicians with pictures of the body's structures and tissues, such as the brain and spinal cord. MRI uses magnetic fields and radio waves to differentiate between healthy and diseased tissue.

- **X-rays** produce pictures of the body's structures, such as bones and joints.

How is Pain Treated?

The goal of pain management is to improve function, enabling individuals to work, attend school, and participate in day-to-day activities. People with pain and their physicians have a number of options for treatment; some are more effective than others. Sometimes, relaxation and the use of imagery as a distraction provide relief. These methods may be powerful and effective, according to those who advocate their use. Whatever the treatment regime, it is important to remember that, while not all pain is curable, all pain is **treatable.** The following treatments are among the most common.

Treatment varies depending on the duration and type of pain. For the most part, the medications listed below have been shown in clinical trials to relieve or prevent pain associated with a specific condition(s), but none have been proven fully effective in relieving all types of pain. A health care professional should be consulted to determine which medication is effective for a given pain condition and what to expect for pain relief and side effects. Evidence for the procedures listed below is variable in its quality. In some cases, evidence suggesting that some treatments are effective is anecdotal—or based on personal experience—and in other cases it is collected from well-designed clinical trials.

Acupuncture involves the application of needles to precise points on the body. It is part of a general category of healing called traditional Chinese medicine. The mechanism by which acupuncture provides pain relief remains controversial but is quite popular and may one day prove to be useful for a variety of conditions as it continues to be explored. Evidence of the effectiveness of acupuncture for pain relief is conflicting and clinical studies to investigate its benefits are ongoing.

Analgesic refers to the classes of drugs that includes most "painkillers". This includes classes of non-steroidal anti-inflammatory agents such as aspirin, ibuprofen, and naproxen as well as acetaminophen and opioids. The word analgesic is derived from ancient Greek and means to reduce or stop pain. Nonprescription or over-the-counter pain relievers (e.g., aspirin, ibuprofen, acetaminophen) are generally used for mild to moderate pain. Prescription opioid pain relievers, sold through a pharmacy under the direction of a physician, are used for moderate to severe pain.

Anticonvulsants are used to treat seizure disorders because they dampen abnormally fast electrical impulses. They also sometimes are prescribed to treat pain. Carbamazepine in particular is used to treat a number of painful conditions, including trigeminal neuralgia. Other antiepileptic drugs, including gabapentin and pregabalin, are also used to treat some forms of pain, including neuropathic pain. Some, such as valproic acid and topiramate, are helpful in preventing migraine headaches.

Antidepressants are sometimes used to treat chronic pain and, along with neuroleptics and lithium, belong to a category of drugs called psychotropic drugs.

Anxiolytics include medications in the class of benzodiazepines (which are used to decrease central nervous system activity). These drugs also act as muscle relaxants and are sometimes used for acute pain situations. Physicians usually try to treat the condition with analgesics before prescribing these drugs.

Capsaicin is a chemical found in chili peppers that is also a primary ingredient in prescription or over-the-counter pain-relieving creams available as a treatment for a number of pain conditions, such as shingles. This topical cream may be particularly good for deep pain. It works by reducing the amount of substance P found in nerve endings and interferes with the transmission of pain signals to the brain. Individuals can become desensitized to the compound, however, perhaps because of long-term capsaicin-induced damage to nerve tissue. Some individuals find the burning sensation they experience when using capsaicin cream to be intolerable, especially when they are already suffering from a painful condition, such as postherpetic neuralgia, which occurs in some people after a bout of shingles. Soon, however, better treatments that relieve pain by blocking vanilloid receptors (also called capsaicin receptors) may arrive in drugstores.

Chiropractic care may ease back pain, neck pain, headaches, and musculoskeletal conditions. It involves "hands-on" therapy designed to adjust the relationship between the body's structure (mainly the spine) and its functioning. Chiropractic spinal manipulation includes the adjustment and manipulation of the joints and adjacent tissues. Such care may also involve therapeutic and rehabilitative exercises. Numerous clinical trials have been done to assess the effectiveness of spinal manipulations. A review of these trials concludes that evidence of their benefit for acute and sub-acute low back pain is of low quality. For chronic back pain however, there is evidence for small to moderate treatment relief.

Cognitive-behavioral therapy is a well-established treatment for pain that involves helping the person improve coping skills, address negative thoughts and emotions that can amplify pain, and learn relaxation methods to help prepare for and cope with pain. It is used for chronic pain, postoperative pain, cancer pain, and the pain of childbirth. Many clinical studies provide evidence for the effectiveness of this form of treatment in pain management.

Counseling can give an individual suffering from pain much needed support, whether it comes from family, group, or individual counseling. Support groups can provide an important supplement to drug or surgical treatment. Psychological treatment can also help people learn about the physiological changes produced by pain.

Electrical stimulation, including transcutaneous electrical stimulation (TENS), implanted electric nerve stimulation, and deep brain or spinal cord stimulation, is the modern-day extension of age-old practices in which the nerves or muscles are subjected to a variety of stimuli, including heat or massage. The following techniques each require specialized equipment and personnel trained in the specific procedure being used:

- **TENS** uses tiny electrical pulses, delivered through the skin to nerve fibers, to cause changes in muscles, such as numbness or contractions. This in turn produces temporary pain relief. There is also evidence that TENS can activate subsets of peripheral nerve fibers that can block pain transmission at the spinal cord level, in much the same way that shaking your hand can reduce pain.

- **Peripheral nerve stimulation** uses electrodes placed surgically or percutaneously (through the skin using a needle) on a peripheral nerve. The individual is then able to deliver an electrical current as needed to the affected nerve, using a controllable electrical generator.

- **Spinal cord stimulation** uses electrodes surgically or percutaneously inserted within the epidural space of the spinal cord. The individual is able to deliver a pulse of electricity to the spinal cord using an implanted electrical pulse generator that resembles a cardiac pacemaker.

- **Deep brain stimulation** is considered a more extreme treatment and involves surgical stimulation of the brain, usually the thalamus or motor cortex. It is used to treat chronic pain in cases that do not respond to less invasive or conservative treatments.

Exercise also may be part of the pain treatment regime for some people with pain. Because there is a known link between many types of chronic pain and tense, weak muscles, exercise—even light to moderate exercise such as walking or swimming—can contribute to an overall sense of well-being by improving blood and oxygen flow to muscles. Just as we know that stress contributes to pain, we also know that exercise, sleep, and relaxation can all help reduce stress, thereby helping to alleviate pain. Exercise has been proven to help many people with low back pain. It is important, however, to work with a physician or physical therapist to create an appropriate routine.

Magnets are increasingly popular with athletes who are convinced of their effectiveness for the control of sports-related pain and other painful conditions. Usually worn as a collar or wristwatch, the use of magnets as a treatment dates back to the ancient Egyptians and Greeks. While it is often dismissed as quackery and pseudoscience by skeptics, proponents offer the theory that magnets may effect changes in cells or body chemistry, thus producing pain relief.

Marijuana or, by its Latin name, cannabis, continues to remain highly controversial as a pain killer. In the eyes of many individuals campaigning on its behalf, marijuana rightfully belongs with other pain remedies. Scientific studies are underway to test the safety and usefulness of cannabis for treating certain medical conditions. Currently, smoking marijuana is not recommended for the treatment of any disease or condition. In fact, federal law prohibits the use of cannabis. However, a number of states and the District of Columbia permit its use for certain medical problems.

Nerve blocks employ the use of drugs, chemical agents, or surgical techniques to interrupt the relay of pain messages between specific areas of the body and the brain. There are many different names for the procedure, depending on the technique or agent used. Types of surgical nerve blocks include neurectomy; spinal dorsal, cranial, and trigeminal rhizotomy; and sympathectomy, also called sympathetic blockade.

Nerve blocks may involve local anesthesia, regional anesthesia or analgesia, or surgery; dentists routinely use them for traditional dental procedures. Nerve blocks can also be used to prevent or even diagnose pain and may involve injection of local anesthetics to numb the nerve and/or steroids to reduce inflammation.

In the case of a local nerve block, any one of a number of local anesthetics may be used, such as lidocaine or bupivicaine. Peripheral nerve blocks involve targeting a nerve or group of nerves that innervate a part of the body. Nerve blocks may also take the form of what is commonly called an epidural, in which a drug is administered into the space between the spine's protective covering (the dura) and the spinal column. This procedure is most well known for its use during childbirth. However it is also used to treat acute or chronic leg or arm pain due to an irritated spinal nerve root.

Physical therapy and rehabilitation date back to the ancient practice of using physical techniques and methods, such as heat, cold, exercise, massage, and manipulation, in the treatment of certain conditions. These may be applied to increase function, control pain, and gain full recovery.

R.I.C.E.—Rest, Ice, Compression, and Elevation—are four components prescribed by many orthopedists, coaches, trainers, nurses, and other professionals for temporary muscle or joint injuries, such as sprains or strains. Ice is used to reduce the inflammation associated with painful and acute injuries. Ice or heat may be recommended to relieve subacute and chronic pain, allowing for reduced inflammation and increased mobility. While many common orthopedic problems can be controlled with these four simple steps, especially when combined with over-the-counter pain relievers, more serious conditions may require surgery or physical therapy, including exercise, joint movement or manipulation, and stimulation of muscles.

Surgery, although not always an option, may be required to relieve pain, especially pain caused by back problems or serious musculoskeletal injuries. Surgery may take the form of a nerve block or it may involve an operation to relieve pain from a ruptured disc. Surgical procedures for pain due to a vertebral disc pressing on a nerve root or spinal cord include **discectomy** or, when microsurgical techniques are used, microdiscectomy, in which the part of or the entire disc is removed; **laminectomy,** a procedure in which a surgeon opens up the arched portion of a vertebra thereby allowing the nerve root to exit more freely; and **spinal fusion,** a procedure where two or more vertebral segments are fused together. Although the operation can cause the spine to stiffen, resulting in lost flexibility, the procedure serves one critical purpose: protection of the spinal cord. Other operations for pain include **rhizotomy,** in which a nerve close to the spinal cord are burned or cut, and **cordotomy**, where bundles of nerves within the spinal cord are severed. Cordotomy is generally used only for the pain of terminal cancer that does not respond to other therapies. Another operation for pain is the **dorsal root entry zone operation,** or DREZ, in which spinal neurons corresponding to the individual's pain are destroyed surgically. **Microvascular decompression,** in which tiny blood vessels are surgically separated from surrounding nerves, is helpful for some individuals suffering from trigeminal neuralgia who are not responsive to drug treatment. Because surgery can result in scar tissue formation that may cause additional problems, people are well advised to seek a second opinion before proceeding.

Surgical procedures are not always successful. The related risks associated and other treatment options should be explored and considered. There is little measurable evidence to show which procedures work best for their particular indications.

Chapter 35

Coping with Depression and Anxiety

Mental Health and Depression

Mental health is how we think, feel, and act as we cope with life. People with disabilities report higher rates of stress and depression than people without disabilities. There are different ways to treat depression. Exercise can be effective for some people. Counseling or medication also might be needed.

What Is Depression?

Everyone occasionally feels blue or sad. But these feelings are usually short-lived and pass within a couple of days. When you have depression, it interferes with daily life and causes pain for both you and those who care about you. Depression is a common but serious illness.

Many people with a depressive illness never seek treatment. But the majority, even those with the most severe depression, can get better with treatment. Medications, psychotherapies, and other methods can effectively treat people with depression.

There are several forms of depressive disorders.

Text in this chapter is excerpted from "Related Conditions," Centers for Disease Control and Prevention (CDC), March 31, 2014; text from "Depression," National Institute of Mental Health (NIMH), 2013; and text from "Anxiety Disorders," National Institute of Mental Health (NIMH), May 2015.

Everyone occasionally feels blue or sad. But these feelings are usually short-lived and pass within a couple of days. When you have depression, it interferes with daily life and causes pain for both you and those who care about you. Depression is a common but serious illness.

Many people with a depressive illness never seek treatment. But the majority, even those with the most severe depression, can get better with treatment. Medications, psychotherapies, and other methods can effectively treat people with depression.

There are several forms of depressive disorders.

Major depression,—severe symptoms that interfere with your ability to work, sleep, study, eat, and enjoy life. An episode can occur only once in a person's lifetime, but more often, a person has several episodes.

Persistent depressive disorder—depressed mood that lasts for at least 2 years. A person diagnosed with persistent depressive disorder may have episodes of major depression along with periods of less severe symptoms, but symptoms must last for 2 years.

Some forms of depression are slightly different, or they may develop under unique circumstances. They include:

- **Psychotic depression**, which occurs when a person has severe depression plus some form of psychosis, such as having disturbing false beliefs or a break with reality (delusions), or hearing or seeing upsetting things that others cannot hear or see (hallucinations).

- **Postpartum depression**, which is much more serious than the "baby blues" that many women experience after giving birth, when hormonal and physical changes and the new responsibility of caring for a newborn can be overwhelming. It is estimated that 10 to 15 percent of women experience postpartum depression after giving birth.

- **Seasonal affective disorder (SAD)**, which is characterized by the onset of depression during the winter months, when there is less natural sunlight. The depression generally lifts during spring and summer. SAD may be effectively treated with light therapy, but nearly half of those with SAD do not get better with light therapy alone. Antidepressant medication and psychotherapy can reduce SAD symptoms, either alone or in combination with light therapy.

Bipolar disorder, also called manic-depressive illness, is not as common as major depression or persistent depressive disorder. Bipolar disorder is characterized by cycling mood changes—from extreme highs (e.g., mania) to extreme lows (e.g., depression).

Signs and Symptoms

"It was really hard to get out of bed in the morning. I just wanted to hide under the covers and not talk to anyone. I didn't feel much like eating and I lost a lot of weight. Nothing seemed fun anymore. I was tired all the time, and I wasn't sleeping well at night. But I knew I had to keep going because I've got kids and a job. It just felt so impossible, like nothing was going to change or get better."

People with depressive illnesses do not all experience the same symptoms. The severity, frequency, and duration of symptoms vary depending on the individual and his or her particular illness.

Signs and symptoms include:

- Persistent sad, anxious, or "empty" feelings

- Feelings of hopelessness or pessimism

- Feelings of guilt, worthlessness, or helplessness

- Irritability, restlessness

- Loss of interest in activities or hobbies once pleasurable, including sex

- Fatigue and decreased energy

- Difficulty concentrating, remembering details, and making decisions

- Insomnia, early-morning wakefulness, or excessive sleeping

- Overeating, or appetite loss

- Thoughts of suicide, suicide attempts

- Aches or pains, headaches, cramps, or digestive problems that do not ease even with treatment.

Diagnosis

Depression, even the most severe cases, can be effectively treated. The earlier that treatment can begin, the more effective it is.

335

The first step to getting appropriate treatment is to visit a doctor or mental health specialist. Certain medications, and some medical conditions such as viruses or a thyroid disorder, can cause the same symptoms as depression. A doctor can rule out these possibilities by doing a physical exam, interview, and lab tests. If the doctor can find no medical condition that may be causing the depression, the next step is a psychological evaluation.

The doctor may refer you to a mental health professional, who should discuss with you any family history of depression or other mental disorder, and get a complete history of your symptoms. You should discuss when your symptoms started, how long they have lasted, how severe they are, and whether they have occurred before and if so, how they were treated. The mental health professional may also ask if you are using alcohol or drugs, and if you are thinking about death or suicide.

Other illnesses may come on before depression, cause it, or be a consequence of it. But depression and other illnesses interact differently in different people. In any case, co-occurring illnesses need to be diagnosed and treated.

Anxiety disorders, such as post-traumatic stress disorder (PTSD), obsessive-compulsive disorder, panic disorder, social phobia, and generalized anxiety disorder, often accompany depression. PTSD can occur after a person experiences a terrifying event or ordeal, such as a violent assault, a natural disaster, an accident, terrorism or military combat. People experiencing PTSD are especially prone to having co-existing depression.

Alcohol and other substance abuse or dependence may also co-exist with depression. Research shows that mood disorders and substance abuse commonly occur together.

Depression also may occur with other serious medical illnesses such as heart disease, stroke, cancer, HIV/AIDS, diabetes, and Parkinson's disease. People who have depression along with another medical illness tend to have more severe symptoms of both depression and the medical illness, more difficulty adapting to their medical condition, and more medical costs than those who do not have co-existing depression. Treating the depression can also help improve the outcome of treating the co-occurring illness.

Treatments

Once diagnosed, a person with depression can be treated in several ways. The most common treatments are medication and psychotherapy.

How can I help myself if I am depressed?

If you have depression, you may feel exhausted, helpless, and hopeless. It may be extremely difficult to take any action to help yourself. But as you begin to recognize your depression and begin treatment, you will start to feel better.

To Help Yourself

- Do not wait too long to get evaluated or treated. There is research showing the longer one waits, the greater the impairment can be down the road. Try to see a professional as soon as possible.

- Try to be active and exercise. Go to a movie, a ballgame, or another event or activity that you once enjoyed.

- Set realistic goals for yourself.

- Break up large tasks into small ones, set some priorities and do what you can as you can.

- Try to spend time with other people and confide in a trusted friend or relative. Try not to isolate yourself, and let others help you.

- Expect your mood to improve gradually, not immediately. Do not expect to suddenly "snap out of" your depression. Often during treatment for depression, sleep and appetite will begin to improve before your depressed mood lifts.

- Postpone important decisions, such as getting married or divorced or changing jobs, until you feel better. Discuss decisions with others who know you well and have a more objective view of your situation.

- Remember that positive thinking will replace negative thoughts as your depression responds to treatment.

- Continue to educate yourself about depression.

Chapter 36

Health Insurance Concerns

Chapter Contents

Section 36.1

Current Healthcare Options for People with Disabilities

Text in this section is excerpted from "Coverage Options for People
with Disabilities," Centers for Medicare & Medicaid Services (CMS),
October 11, 2014; and text from "Health Insurance Marketplace,"
Centers for Medicare & Medicaid Services (CMS), July 20, 2013.

Health Insurance Marketplace (Marketplace)

A resource where individuals, families, and small businesses can:
learn about their health coverage options; compare health insurance
plans based on costs, benefits, and other important features; choose
a plan; and enroll in coverage. The Health Insurance Marketplace
(Marketplace) also provides information on programs that help people with low to moderate income and resources pay for coverage. This
includes ways to save on the monthly premiums and out-of-pocket
costs of coverage available through the Marketplace, and information
about other programs, including Medicaid and the Children's Health
Insurance Program (CHIP). The Marketplace encourages competition
among private health plans, and is accessible through websites, call
centers, and in-person assistance. In some states, the Marketplace is
run by the state. In others it is run by the federal government.

Coverage options for people with disabilities

If you have a disability, you have a number of options for health
coverage.

If you currently have Medicaid or Medicare, you're considered
covered under the health care law and don't need a Marketplace
plan.

If you don't have health coverage, you can fill out a Marketplace
application to find out if you qualify for savings on a private health
plan or for coverage through Medicaid.

Social Security Disability Insurance (SSDI) and Medicare coverage

If you get Social Security Disability Income (SSDI), you probably have Medicare or are in a 24-month waiting period before it starts. You have options in either case.

If you get Social Security Disability Income (SSDI) and have Medicare

- You're considered covered under the health care law and don't have to pay the penalty that people without coverage must pay.

- You can't enroll in a Marketplace plan to replace or supplement your Medicare coverage.

- **One exception**: If you enrolled in a Marketplace plan **before** getting Medicare, you can keep your Marketplace plan as supplemental insurance when you enroll in Medicare. But if you do this, you'll lose any premium tax credits and other savings for your Marketplace plan.

- Learn about other Medicare supplement options.

If you get SSDI benefits and are in a 24-month waiting period before getting Medicare

- You may be able to get Medicaid coverage while you wait. You can apply 2 ways:

- Fill out a Marketplace application. Answer "yes" when asked if you have a disability. We'll forward your application to your state Medicaid agency.

- Apply directly to your state Medicaid agency. Select your state from the menu on this Medicaid page for contact information.

- If you're eligible for Medicaid, your Medicaid eligibility may continue even after you enroll in Medicare.

- If you're turned down for Medicaid, you may be able to enroll in a private health plan through the Marketplace while waiting for your Medicare coverage to start. You may qualify for lower costs on Marketplace coverage based on your income and household size.

When asked about your income on your Marketplace application, be sure to include your SSDI income.

Supplemental Security Income (SSI) Disability and Medicaid coverage

If you have Supplemental Security Income (SSI) Disability, you may get Medicaid coverage automatically or you may have to apply.

If you get SSI Disability and have Medicaid

You're considered covered under the health care law. You don't need to get a Marketplace plan. You won't have to pay the penalty that people without coverage must pay.

If you get SSI Disability and don't have Medicaid

You can apply for Medicaid coverage. But whether you need to apply depends on your state

- In many states, SSI recipients automatically qualify for Medicaid and don't have to fill out a Medicaid application.

- In other states, your SSI guarantees you Medicaid eligibility, but you have to sign up for it.

- In a few states, SSI doesn't guarantee Medicaid eligibility. But most people who get SSI are still eligible.

- If you have SSI Disability and don't have Medicaid, you can apply for Medicaid coverage 2 ways:

- Select your state from the menu on this Medicaid page for contact information.

- Fill out a Marketplace application.

- Answer "yes" when asked if you have a disability, and we'll send your application to your state Medicaid office.

Note: When filling out your Marketplace application, don't include SSI Disability payments when estimating your income.

Some states have expanded their Medicaid programs to cover more people. Even if you get SSI but aren't automatically eligible for Medicaid, it's a good idea to apply. This is true even if you've been turned down for Medicaid in the past.

If you get a positive SSDI disability decision

If you get a positive disability decision, you may have to wait 24 months before Medicare coverage starts. See your health coverage options for the period while you're waiting for Medicare to start.

If you get a negative disability decision

If you get a negative disability decision, you can fill out a Marketplace application to apply for coverage. You'll find out if you qualify for a private health plan with premium tax credits and lower costs based on your household size and income. When you apply, you'll also find out if you qualify for Medicaid coverage.

- When you fill out your Marketplace application, answer "yes" when asked if you have a disability. We'll forward your application to your state Medicaid agency. If you qualify, they'll help you enroll.

- If you don't qualify for Medicaid, you may qualify for savings on a Marketplace health plan.

- You can also apply for Medicaid coverage directly through your state agency. Select your state from the menu on this Medicaid page for contact information.

No disability benefits, no health coverage

If you have a disability, don't qualify for disability benefits, and need health coverage, you have options in the Health Insurance Marketplace.

Applying for coverage through the Marketplace

When you fill out a Marketplace health coverage application, you'll find out if you qualify for a private health plan with premium tax credits and other savings based on your income. You'll also find out if you qualify for Medicaid coverage.

When you fill out your application, you may be asked if you:

- Have a physical disability or mental health condition that limits your ability to work, attend school, or take care of your daily needs

- Get help with daily living activities through personal assistance, a medical facility, or nursing home

> **Important:** Insurers offering coverage through the Marketplace can't deny coverage or charge you more based on your answers to these disability questions. Private insurance plans in the Marketplace and all Medicaid programs cover all pre-existing health conditions from the first day your coverage takes effect.

You can also apply for Medicaid coverage directly to your state agency. Select your state from the menu on this Medicaid page for contact information.

If you don't qualify for Medicaid based on your disability

If you don't qualify for Medicaid based on your disability, you have two more options for health coverage through the Marketplace:

1. You may qualify for Medicaid based only on your income. Some states have expanded their Medicaid programs to cover all adults who make less than a certain income level. Find out if your state is expanding Medicaid and what this means for you.

2. You may qualify to enroll in a health plan through the Health Insurance Marketplace with premium tax credits and other savings that make coverage more affordable. This will depend on your household size and income.

The fee for not having coverage

Under the health care law, most people must have health coverage, pay a fee, or get an exemption from the fee. This applies regardless of disability status.

If you don't have coverage through Medicare, Medicaid, another public program, a job, the Marketplace, or another source, you may have to pay the fee. Learn what kinds of insurance count as coverage under the health care law.

Some people can get an exemption from the fee based on low income, hardship, or other factors. Learn about exemptions from the fee.

The Marketplace application and disabilities

When you fill out an application for Marketplace coverage, you'll be asked several questions about disabilities. Information to help you answer the questions is below.

If you have a disability, mental health condition, or personal assistance needs, you may be eligible for Medicaid or for help paying for coverage.

Conditions that are considered disabilities

If you have one or more of these conditions, you're considered disabled:

- You're blind, deaf, or hard of hearing.

- You get Social Security Disability Insurance (SSDI) or Supplemental Security Insurance (SSI).

- You have a physical, cognitive, intellectual, or mental health condition, which causes one or more of these:

- Difficulty doing errands like visiting a doctor's office or shopping.

- Serious difficulty concentrating, remembering, or making decisions.

- Difficulty walking or climbing stairs.

Disabilities and children

For a child, these conditions are considered disabilities:

- They have limited ability to do the things most children of the same age can do.

- They need or use more health care than is usual for most children of the same age.

- They get special education services or services under a Section 504 plan.

What happens if you indicate you're disabled

If you indicate you have a disability on your Marketplace application, we'll send it to your state Medical Assistance (Medicaid) office to see if you qualify for Medicaid based on your disability. If we send your application to your state Medicaid office, they may contact you for more information on your disability. If you don't qualify for Medicaid based on your disability, you may still be eligible based on your income or you may qualify for a tax credit.

You should still indicate that you're disabled even if you're not sure if your state will consider you eligible for Medicaid based on your disability. This will help make sure you get the most help available. Your state will determine if you qualify for Medicaid.

If you say you're disabled, but your state determines you either don't qualify for Medicaid based on your income or determines that you don't have a qualifying disability, you can still buy health coverage through the Marketplace. Plans can't deny you coverage or charge you more because of your disability.

If you need help with activities of daily living

Activities of daily living include seeing, hearing, walking, eating, sleeping, standing, lifting, bending, breathing, learning, reading, communicating, thinking, and working.

If you have a cognitive or mental health condition, you may need help with these activities of daily living through coaching or instruction.

If a person only needs help because he or she is too young to be able to do these activities without help, don't indicate that they need help with daily activities on your application.

Section 36.2

Medicare and Nonelderly People with Disabilities

Text in this section is excerpted from "Medicare and You," Centers for Medicare and Medicaid Services, September 2015; and text from "Signing up for Medicare: special conditions," Centers for Medicare and Medicaid Services, March 2, 2015.

Medicare

Medicare is health insurance for people 65 or older, people under 65 with certain disabilities, and people of any age with End-Stage Renal Disease (ESRD) (permanent kidney failure requiring dialysis or a kidney transplant).

What are the different parts of Medicare?

Medicare Part A (Hospital Insurance) helps cover:

- Inpatient care in hospitals
- Skilled nursing facility care
- Hospice care
- Home health care

Medicare Part B (Medical Insurance) helps cover:

- Services from doctors and other health care providers
- Outpatient care
- Home health care
- Durable medical equipment
- Some preventive services

Medicare Part C (Medicare Advantage):

- Includes all benefits and services covered under Part A and Part B

347

- Usually includes Medicare prescription drug coverage (Part D) as part of the plan

- Run by Medicare-approved private insurance companies

- May include extra benefits and services for an extra cost

Medicare Part D (Medicare prescription drug coverage):

- Helps cover the cost of prescription drugs

- Run by Medicare-approved private insurance companies

- May help lower your prescription drug costs and help protect against higher costs in the future

What are Medicare Supplement Insurance (Medigap) Policies?

Original Medicare pays for many, but not all, health care services and supplies. Medicare Supplement Insurance policies, sold by private companies, can help pay some of the health care costs that Original Medicare doesn't cover, like copayments, coinsurance, and deductibles. Medicare Supplement Insurance policies are also called Medigap policies.

Some Medigap policies also offer coverage for services that Original Medicare doesn't cover, like medical care when you travel outside the U.S. If you have Original Medicare and you buy a Medigap policy, Medicare will pay its share of the Medicare-approved amount for covered health care costs. Then, your Medigap policy pays its share. You have to pay the premiums for a Medigap policy.

Medigap policies are standardized

Every Medigap policy must follow federal and state laws designed to protect you, and they must be clearly identified as "Medicare Supplement Insurance." Insurance companies can sell you only a "standardized" policy identified in most states by letters A through D, F through G, and K through N. All policies offer the same basic benefits, but some offer additional benefits so you can choose which one meets your needs. In Massachusetts, Minnesota, and Wisconsin, Medigap policies are standardized in a different way.

How do I compare Medigap policies?

Different insurance companies may charge different premiums for the same exact policy. As you shop for a policy, be sure you're comparing the same policy (for example, compare Plan A from one company with Plan A from another company).

In some states, you may be able to buy a type of Medigap policy called Medicare SELECT (a policy that requires you to use specific hospitals and, in some cases, specific doctors or other health care providers to get full coverage). If you buy a Medicare SELECT policy, you have the right to change your mind within 12 months and switch to a standard Medigap policy.

What else should I know about Medicare Supplement Insurance (Medigap)?

Important facts

- You must have Part A and Part B.

- You pay the private insurance company a monthly premium for your Medigap policy in addition to your monthly Part B premium that you pay to Medicare. Contact the company to find out how to pay your premium.

- A Medigap policy only covers one person. Spouses must buy separate policies.

- You can't have prescription drug coverage in both your Medigap policy and a Medicare drug plan.

- It's important to compare Medigap policies since the costs can vary and may go up as you get older. Some states limit Medigap premium costs.

When to buy

- The best time to buy a Medigap policy is during your Medigap Open Enrollment Period. This 6-month period begins on the first day of the month in which you're 65 or older **and** enrolled in Part B. (Some states have additional Open Enrollment Periods.) After this enrollment period, you may not be able to buy a Medigap policy. If you're able to buy one, it may cost more.

- If you delay enrolling in Part B because you have group health coverage based on your (or your spouse's) current employment, your Medigap Open Enrollment Period won't start until you sign up for Part B.

- Federal law generally doesn't require insurance companies to sell Medigap policies to people under 65. If you're under 65, you might not be able to buy the Medigap policy you want, or any Medigap policy, until you turn 65. However, some states require Medigap insurance companies to sell Medigap policies to people under 65.

FAQs

I'm under 65 and have Medicare because of a disability

I'm under 65 and have a disability. How do I enroll in Part A and B?

If you're under 65 and have a disability, you're automatically enrolled in Part A and Part B after you get Social Security or Railroad Retirement benefits for 24 months. Your Medicare card will be mailed to you about 3 months before your 25th month of disability benefits. If you don't want Part B, follow the instructions that come with the card.

I'm under 65 and have ALS (Amyotrophic Lateral Sclerosis, also called Lou Gehrig's disease). When can I get Medicare?

If you're under 65 and have ALS, you get your Medicare benefits the first month you get disability benefits from Social Security or the Railroad Retirement Board. For more information about disability benefits, contact Social Security or the Railroad Retirement Board.

I have a disability and Part A only. Can I get Part B when I turn 65?

If you're still getting disability benefits when you turn 65, you won't have to apply for Part B. Medicare will enroll you in Part B automatically. Your Medicare card will be mailed to you about 3 months before your 65th birthday. If you don't want Part B, follow the instructions that come with the card.

If you're not getting disability benefits and Medicare when you turn 65, contact Social Security to sign up for Medicare.

I'm under 65, have a disability, get disability benefits, and am covered under my spouse's (or family member's) group health plan coverage. How can I enroll in Part A only?

You should get the "Initial Enrollment Package" that includes your Medicare card about 3 months before your 65th birthday. If you don't want Part B, follow the instructions that come with the card. If you're covered under your working spouse's (or family member's) employer large group health plan (the employer has at least 100 employees), you may want to delay enrolling in Part B.

350

A family member includes domestic (or life) partner, as long as you have large group health plan coverage through your partner's current employer.

I'm under 65 and have a disability. I'd like to go back to work. Can I keep my Medicare coverage?

Yes. You can keep your Medicare coverage for as long as you're medically disabled. If you return to work, you won't have to pay your Part A premium for the first 8 ½ years. After that, you'll have to pay the Part A premium.

If you can't afford the Part A premium, you may be able to get help from your state. You may be eligible for the Medicare Savings Program called Qualified Disabled and Working Individuals Program (QDWI).

I'm 61 and have Part A due to a disability. I also have group health insurance through my current employer. When can I enroll in Part B?

If you have a disability, have Part A, and have current employer or union group health coverage, you can sign up for Part B during the Special Enrollment Period.

This period is available if you waited to enroll in Part B because you, your spouse, or family member are working and have group health coverage (or large group health plan coverage if you're covered by a family member) through an employer or union based on this current employment.

My spouse has a disability and has been getting Supplemental Security Income (SSI). Can my spouse get Medicare to supplement the Medicaid coverage they have now?

Getting Supplemental Security Income (SSI) doesn't make you eligible for Medicare. SSI provides a monthly cash benefit and health insurance coverage under Medicaid.

Your spouse may qualify for Medicare the same way as if they didn't have SSI. Your spouse may qualify for Medicare when they turn 65 or have been receiving disability benefits for 24 months.

When I first became eligible because of a disability, I didn't take Part B because I was covered under my spouse/family member's group health plan. They're retiring and I want to enroll in Part B. Will I have to pay more because I delayed my enrollment?

It depends. Generally, if you didn't sign up for Part B when you were first eligible because your spouse was working and you had group health plan coverage based on their work, you can sign up for Part B, without penalty, during the Special Enrollment Period.

I'm under 65, and I or my spouse is still working

My spouse has never worked. If they turn 65 before I do, can they get Medicare at 65? Or, do they have to wait until I turn 65 and have Medicare?

If you're at least 62 and have worked at least 10 years in Medicare-covered employment, your spouse can get Part A and Part B at 65.

If you've worked at least 10 years in Medicare-covered employment but aren't yet 62 when your spouse turns 65, they won't be eligible for premium-free Part A until your 62nd birthday. In this case, your spouse should still apply for Part B at 65, so they can avoid paying a higher Part B premium.

However, if you're still working and your spouse is covered under your group health plan, they could delay their Part B enrollment without paying higher premiums.

Next month, I'll be 65. I've only worked for a few years and my spouse is 60. Can I enroll in Medicare?

Yes, you can enroll in Medicare. But if you've worked less than 10 years in Medicare-covered employment, you'll have to pay a monthly premium for Part A. If you choose Part B, you'll also have to pay the Part B premium.

Enroll in Part A and Part B or find out how much your Part A premium will be.

Does a spouse, age 62, get Medicare when their husband/wife aged 65 does?

Generally, no. You can't get Medicare until you're 65. However, you may qualify for Medicare coverage if you're less than 65 if you have a disability or End-Stage Renal Disease (ESRD).

Section 36.3

Medicaid and Children's Health Insurance Program

Text in this section are excerpted from "Children's Health Insurance Program (CHIP)," Centers for Medicare & Medicaid Services, October 8, 2014.

Overview

The Children's Health Insurance Program (CHIP) provides health coverage to eligible children, through both Medicaid and separate CHIP programs. CHIP is administered by states, according to federal requirements. The program is funded jointly by states and the federal government.

Benefits

The Children's Health Insurance Program (CHIP) provides comprehensive benefits to children. Since states have flexibility to design their own program within federal guidelines, benefits vary by state and by the type of CHIP program.

Medicaid Expansion Benefits

Medicaid Expansion CHIP programs provide the standard Medicaid benefit package, including Early and Periodic Screening, Diagnostic, and Treatment (EPSDT) services, which includes all medically necessary services like mental health and dental services.

Separate CHIP Benefits Options

States can choose to provide benchmark coverage, benchmark-equivalent coverage, or Secretary-approved coverage:

Benchmark coverage based on one of the following:

- The standard Blue Cross/Blue Shield preferred provider option service benefit plan offered to federal employees

- State employee's coverage plan

- HMO plan that has the largest commercial, non-Medicaid enrollment within the state

Benchmark-Equivalent coverage must be actuarially equivalent and include:

- Inpatient and outpatient hospital services
- Physician's services
- Surgical and medical services
- Laboratory and X-ray services
- Well-baby and well-child care, including immunizations

Secretary-approved coverage: Any other health coverage deemed appropriate and acceptable by the Secretary of the U.S. Department of Health and Human Services.

Separate CHIP Dental Benefits

States that provide CHIP coverage to children through a Medicaid expansion program are required to provide the EPSDT benefit. Dental coverage in separate CHIP programs is required to include coverage for dental services "necessary to prevent disease and promote oral health, restore oral structures to health and function, and treat emergency conditions."

States with a separate CHIP program may choose from two options for providing dental coverage: a package of dental benefits that meets the CHIP requirements, or a benchmark dental benefit package. The benchmark dental package must be substantially equal to the (1) the most popular federal employee dental plan for dependents, (2) the most popular plan selected for dependants in the state's employee dental plan, or (3) dental coverage offered through the most popular commercial insurer in the state.

Vaccines

Coverage for age-appropriate immunizations is required in CHIP. States with a separate CHIP program (including the separate portion of a combination program) must purchase vaccines to be administered to enrolled children using only CHIP federal and state matching funds. Vaccines for federally vaccine-eligible children (through the Vaccines For Children program) should not be used by children enrolled in separate CHIP programs, and funds available under section 317 of the Public Health Service Act are designated for the purchase of vaccines for the uninsured and may not be used to purchase vaccines for children who have separate CHIP coverage.

States have two options for purchasing vaccines for children enrolled in separate CHIP programs: (1) purchase vaccines using the

CDC contract and distribution mechanism, or (2) purchase vaccines through the private sector.

The Centers for Medicare and Medicaid Services has worked with the Centers for Disease Control and Prevention (CDC) on issuing joint guidance for all states with a separate CHIP program on purchasing and claiming for vaccines administered to separate CHIP children. The guidance letter explains that, for states that purchase vaccines through the CDC, states are required to pay for vaccines at the time they are ordered. States claim federal financial participation against the CHIP allotment based on the purchase invoices rather than individual provider claims. The letter further explains that states will use a reconciliation process to ensure that future vaccine orders are adjusted based on the outstanding credit for unused vaccines from the previous order.

Eligibility

The Children's Health Insurance Program (CHIP) serves uninsured children up to age 19 in families with incomes too high to qualify them for Medicaid. States have broad discretion in setting their income eligibility standards, and eligibility varies across states.

Income Eligibility

46 States and the District of Columbia cover children up to or above 200% of the Federal Poverty Level (FPL) ($44,700 for a family of four in 2011), and 24 of these states offer coverage to children in families with income at 250% of the FPL or higher. States may get the CHIP enhanced match for coverage up to 300% of the FPL ($67,050 for a family of four in 2011), which is higher than the Medicaid federal funding matching rate.

States that expand coverage above 300% of the FPL get the Medicaid matching rate. States have the option to provide continuous eligibility to children who remain eligible for CHIP.

New Medicaid and CHIP Coverage Options

Lawfully Residing Children and Pregnant Women

Many states have elected the option under CHIPRA to restore Medicaid and/or CHIP coverage to children and pregnant women who are lawfully residing in the United States.

Pregnant Women

CHIPRA created an explicit eligibility category for pregnant women to receive coverage through CHIP in certain circumstances.

Some states have also chosen to provide prenatal care for pregnant women through the CHIP program through other available vehicles.

Children of Public Employees

The Affordable Care Act of 2010 provides states the option to extend CHIP eligibility to state employees' children. Before enactment of the Affordable Care Act children of public employees were not eligible for CHIP, regardless of their income.

Chapter 37

Dealing with Hospitalization

A trip to the hospital with a person who has memory loss or dementia can be stressful for both of you.

Here, you will find: steps you can take now to make hospital visits less traumatic; tips on making your relative or care partner more comfortable once you arrive at the hospital; and suggestions on how to work with hospital staff and doctors.

Hospital Emergencies: What You Can Do Now

Planning ahead is key to making an unexpected or planned trip to the hospital easier for you and your care partner. Here is what you should do now:

- **Think about and discuss hospitalization** before it happens and as the disease and associated memory loss progress.

- **Hospitalization is a choice.** Talk about when hospice may be a better and more appropriate alternative.

- **Register your relative for a MedicAlert® + Alzheimer's Association Safe Return® bracelet** through your local Alzheimer's Association chapter. People who are lost may be taken

---

Text in this chapter is excerpted from "Hospitalization Happens: A Guide to Hospital Visits for Individuals with Memory Loss," National Institute on Aging (NIA), January 2013.

to an emergency room. This bracelet will speed up the process of reconnecting you with your care partner.

- **Know who you can depend on.** You need a family member or trusted friend to stay with your care partner when he or she is admitted to the emergency room or hospital. Arrange to have at least two dependable family members, neighbors, or friends you can call on to go with you or meet you at the hospital at a moment's notice so that one person can take care of the paperwork and the other can stay with your care partner.

Pack an Emergency Bag with the Following:

Personal Information Sheet

Create a document that includes the following information about your care partner:

- Preferred name and language (some people may revert to native languages in late-stage Alzheimer's disease)
- Contact information for doctors, key family members, clergy and helpful friends (also program into cell phone, if applicable)
- Illness or medical conditions
- All current medicines and dosage instructions; update whenever there is a change
- Any medicines that have ever caused a bad reaction
- Any allergies to medicines or foods; special diets
- Need for glasses, dentures or hearing aids
- Degree of impairment and amount of assistance needed for activities
- Family information, living situation, major life events
- Work, leisure and spiritual history
- Daily schedule and patterns, self-care preferences
- Favorite foods, music, and things your care partner likes to touch and see
- Behaviors of concern; how your relative communicates needs and expresses emotions

Paperwork

Include copies of important documents such as:

- Insurance cards (include policy numbers and pre-authorization phone numbers)
- Medicaid and/or Medicare cards
- Durable Power of Attorney, Health Care Power of Attorney, Living Will and/or an original DNR (do not resuscitate) order

Supplies for the Care Partner

- A change of clothing, toiletries, and personal medications
- Extra adult briefs, if usually worn. These may not be available in the emergency room, if needed
- Moist hand wipes such as Wet Ones; plastic bags for soiled clothing and/or adult briefs
- Reassuring or comforting objects
- An iPod, MP3 or CD player; earphones or speakers

Supplies for the Caregiver

- A change of clothing, toiletries and personal medications
- Pain medicine such as Advil, Tylenol or aspirin. A trip to the emergency room may take longer than you think. Stress can lead to a headache or other symptoms.
- A pad of paper and pen to write down information and directions given to you by hospital staff. Keep a log of your care partner's symptoms and problems. You may be asked the same questions by many people. Show them what you have written instead of repeating your answers.
- A sealed snack such as a pack of crackers and a bottle of water or juice for you and your care partner. You may have to wait for quite a while.
- A small amount of cash.
- A note on the outside of the emergency bag to remind you to take your cell phone and charger with you.

By taking these steps in advance, you can reduce the stress and confusion that often accompany a hospital visit, particularly if the visit is an unplanned trip to the emergency room.

At the Emergency Room

A trip to the emergency room may fatigue or even frighten your care partner. There are some important things to remember:

- **Be patient.** It could be a long wait if the reason for your visit is not life-threatening.

- Recognize that results from lab tests take time.

- Offer physical and emotional comfort and verbal reassurance to your relative. Stay calm and positive. How you are feeling will get absorbed by others.

- Realize that just because you do not see staff at work does not mean they are not working.

- Be aware that emergency room staff often have limited training in Alzheimer's disease and related dementias, so try to help them better understand your care partner.

- Encourage hospital staff to see your relative as an individual and not just another patient with dementia who is confused and disoriented from the disease.

- Do not assume your care partner will be admitted to the hospital.

Do not leave the emergency room to go home without a follow-up plan. If you are sent home, make sure you have all instructions for follow-up care.

Chapter 38

Choosing a Long-Term Care Setting

What is Long-Term Care?

Long-term care is a **range of services and supports** you may need to meet your personal care needs. Most long-term care is not medical care, but rather assistance with the basic personal tasks of everyday life, sometimes called **Activities of Daily Living (ADLs)**, such as:

- Bathing

- Dressing

- Using the toilet

- Transferring (to or from bed or chair)

- Caring for incontinence

- Eating

Other common long-term care services and supports **are assistance with everyday tasks**, sometimes called **Instrumental Activities of Daily Living (IADLs)** including:

- Housework

Text in this chapter is excerpted from "What is Long-Term Care?" U.S. Department of Health and Human Services (HHS), April 10, 2013.

- Managing money
- Taking medication
- Preparing and cleaning up after meals
- Shopping for groceries or clothes
- Using the telephone or other communication devices
- Caring for pets
- Responding to emergency alerts such as fire alarms

Who Needs Care?

70% of people turning age 65 can expect to use some form of long-term care during their lives. There are a number of factors that affect the possibility that you will need care:

Age

- The older you are, the more likely you will need long-term care

Gender

- Women outlive men by about five years on average, so they are more likely to live at home alone when they are older

Disability

- Having an accident or chronic illness that causes a disability is another reason for needing long-term care
- Between ages 40 and 50, on average, eight percent of people have a disability that could require long-term care services
- 69 percent of people age 90 or more have a disability

Health Status

- Chronic conditions such as diabetes and high blood pressure make you more likely to need care
- Your family history such as whether your parents or grandparents had chronic conditions, may increase your likelihood
- Poor diet and exercise habits increase your chances of needing long-term care

Living Arrangements

- If you live alone, you're more likely to need paid care than if you're married, or single, and living with a partner

How Much Care Will You Need?

The duration and level of long-term care will **vary from person to person** and often change over time. Here are some statistics (all are "on average") you should consider:

- Someone turning age 65 today has almost a 70% chance of needing some type of long-term care services and supports in their remaining years

- **Women need care longer** (3.7 years) than men (2.2 years)

- **One-third of today's 65 year-olds** may never need long-term care support, but 20 percent will need it for longer than 5 years

The table below shows that, overall, more people use long-term care services at home (and for longer) than in facilities.

Table 38.1. Distribution and duration of long-term care services

Type of care	Average number of years people use this type of care	Percent of people who use this type of care (%)
Any Services	3 years	69
At Home		
Unpaid care only	1 year	59
Paid care	Less than 1 year	42
Any care at home	2 years	65
In Facilities		
Nursing facilities	1 year	35
Assisted living	Less than 1 year	13
Any care in facilities	1 year	37

Who Will Provide Your Care?

Long-term care services and support typically come from:

- An **unpaid caregiver** who may be a family member or friend

- A nurse, home health or home care aide, and/or therapist who comes to the home

- Adult day services in the area

- A **variety** of long-term care facilities

A caregiver can be your family member, partner, friend or neighbor who helps care for you while you live at home. About **80 percent of**

care at home is provided by unpaid caregivers and may include an array of emotional, financial, nursing, social, homemaking, and other services. On average, caregivers spend **20 hours a week** giving care. More than half (58 percent) have intensive caregiving responsibilities that may include assisting with a personal care activity, such as bathing or feeding.

Information on caregivers show that:

- About 65.7 million people in the United States **(one in four adults)** were unpaid family caregivers to an adult or child in 2009

- About **two-thirds are women**

- Fourteen percent who care for older adults are themselves **age 65 or more**

- Most people can live at home for many years with help from unpaid family and friends, and from other paid community support

Where Can You Receive Care?

Most long-term care is provided at home. Other kinds of long-term care services and supports are provided by community service organizations and in long-term care facilities.

Examples of **home care services** include:

- An unpaid caregiver who may be a family member or friend

- A nurse, home health or home care aide, and/or therapist who comes to the home

Community support services include:

- Adult day care service centers

- Transportation services

- Home care agencies that provide services on a daily basis or as needed

Often these services supplement the care you receive at home or provide time off for your family caregivers.

Outside the home, a variety of **facility-based programs** offer more options:

- **Nursing homes** provide the most comprehensive range of services, including nursing care and 24-hour supervision

- Other facility-based choices **include assisted living, board and care homes, and continuing care retirement communities.** With these providers, the level of choice over who delivers your care varies by the type of facility. You may not get to choose who will deliver services, and you may have limited say in when they arrive.

Participant Directed Services are a way to provide services that lets you control what services you receive, who provides them, and how and when those services are delivered. They provide you with information and assistance to choose and plan for the services and supports that work best for you including:

- Who you want to provide your services (can include family and friends)

- Whether you want to use a home care service agency

In **facility-based services** you generally don't have the option to hire someone independently, but you should have choices about:

- Which staff members provide your care

- The schedule you keep

- The meals you eat

In home and community-based settings, you should have the ability to participate or **direct the development** of a service plan, provide feedback on services and activities, and request changes as needed.

Chapter 39

Family Support Services

Chapter Contents

Section 39.1

Understanding Respite Care

Text in this section is excerpted from "Respite Care," U.S.
Department of Veterans Affairs (VA), July 7, 2015.

What is Respite Care?

Respite Care is a service that pays for a person to come to a Veteran's home or for a Veteran to go to a program while their family caregiver takes a break. While a Veteran gets Respite Care, the family caregiver can run errands or go out of town for a few days without worrying about leaving the Veteran alone at home.

Respite Care can be helpful to Veterans of all ages, and their caregiver. Veterans can receive Respite Care in an inpatient, outpatient or home setting.

The program is for Veterans who need skilled services, case management and help with activities of daily living. Examples include help with bathing, dressing, fixing meals or taking medicines. This program is also for Veterans who are isolated or their caregiver is experiencing burden. Respite Care can be used in combination with other Home and Community Based Services.

Respite Care can help lower the stress the Veterans and their family caregiver may feel when managing a Veteran's long-term care needs at home.

Am I eligible for Respite Care?

Since **Respite Care** is part of the VHA Standard Medical Benefits Package, all enrolled Veterans are eligible **IF they meet the clinical need for the service and it is available.**

A copay for Respite Care may be charged based on your VA service-connected disability status and financial information. Contact your VA social worker/case manager to complete the Application for Extended Care Benefits (VA Form 10-10EC) to learn the amount of your copay.

What services can I get?

You may be able to get Respite Care in a number of ways:

- A paid Home Health Aide could come to your home

- You could attend an Adult Day Health Care center

- You could go to a Community Living Center (VA Nursing Home) or a VA medical center for a short inpatient stay

Depending on the Respite Care services in your area, you can choose which options are best for you and your family caregiver. For example: If your caregiver has lots of errands to run or appointments, you could have a Home Health Aide come to your home while your caregiver is out of the house. If your caregiver needs time at your home alone, you could attend an Adult Day Health Care center for the day. Or, if your caregiver is out of town for a few days, you could stay at a Community Living Center (VA Nursing Home) during the time they are away.

No matter which option you use, trained staff will help you with your care needs.

Respite Care services may be available up to 30 days each calendar year. These 30 days may be used in different ways. For example:

- You might stay in a Community Living Center (VA Nursing Home) for 1 visit of 30 days, or have 10 short stays of 3 days each during the year.

- You might have a Home Health Aide come to your home to stay with you for up to 6 hours in a row, day or night. Each visit (even if it is less than the 6-hour maximum) counts as 1 day of Respite Care.

You may also be able to divide your 30 days among the 3 different types of Respite Care.

How do I decide if this is right for me?

You can use a Shared Decision Making Worksheet to help you figure out what long-term care services or settings may best meet your needs now or in the future.

There's also a Caregiver Self-Assessment. It can help your caregiver identify their own needs and decide how much support they can offer to you. Having this information from your caregiver, along with the involvement of your care team and social worker, will help you reach good long-term care decisions.

Your physician or other primary care provider can answer questions about your medical needs. Some important questions to talk about with your social worker and family include:

- How much assistance do I need for my activities of daily living (e.g., bathing and getting dressed)?

- What are my caregiver's needs?

- What type of Respite Care does my family caregiver prefer?

- What mix of Respite Care options will work best?

- What is the best way to use the 30 days per year?

If Respite Care seems right for you, your VA social worker can help you locate VA Respite Care services and assist with making arrangements.

Section 39.2

Adult Day Care

Text in this section is excerpted from "Adult Day Care," Eldercare Locator, October 15, 2015.

Adult Day Care Centers are designed to provide care and companionship for older adults who need assistance or supervision during the day. Programs offer relief to family members and caregivers, allowing them to go to work, handle personal business, or just relax while knowing their relative is well cared for and safe.

The goals of the programs are to delay or prevent institutionalization by providing alternative care, to enhance self-esteem, and to encourage socialization. There are two types of adult day care: adult social day care and adult day health care. Adult social day care provides social activities, meals, recreation, and some health-related services. Adult day health care offers intensive health, therapeutic, and social services for individuals with serious medical conditions and those at risk of requiring nursing home care.

Older adults generally participate on a scheduled basis. Services may include:

- Counseling
- Education
- Evening care
- Exercise
- Health screening
- Meals
- Medical care

- Physical therapy
- Recreation
- Respite care
- Socialization
- Supervision
- Transportation
- Medication management

Center Operations

Centers are usually open during normal business hours and may stand alone or be located in senior centers, nursing facilities, places of faith, hospitals, or schools. The staff may monitor medication, serve hot meals and snacks, perform physical or occupational therapy, and arrange social activities. They may also help to arrange transportation to and from the center.

Case Study

The following is an example of someone who needs adult day care services, both for his well-being and that of his family caregivers.

Paul is 69 years old and recently experienced a stroke. He needs some care and supervision, so he lives with his son, David, and daughter-in-law, Kira. Because they both work, David and Kira need help to care for Paul during the day. They found a solution by having Kira take Paul to the local adult day care center in the morning, and having David pick him up after work. The center monitors Paul's medication and offers him lunch, some physical therapy, and a chance to socialize with other seniors.

Finding a Center

Not all states license and regulate adult day care centers. There may be a great deal of difference between individual centers; therefore, it is important to learn more about each center near you. If possible, visit the centers closest to you, and talk with the staff and other families that use the centers to determine whether the facilities meet your needs. You may also want to find out if your state has an adult day care association.

Paying for Services

Costs vary and can range from $25 to over $100 per day, depending on the services offered, type of reimbursement, and geographic region. While an adult day care center is not usually covered by Medicare insurance, some financial assistance may be available through a federal or state program (e.g., Medicaid, Older Americans Act, Veterans Health Administration).

Local Programs

To find out more about centers where you live, contact your local aging information and assistance provider or Area Agency on Aging (AAA). For help connecting to these agencies, contact the Eldercare Locator at 1-800-677-1116 or www.eldercare.gov.

The National Adult Day Services Association is a good source for general information about adult day care centers, programs, and associations. Call 1-877-745-1440 or visit www.nadsa.org.

Section 39.3

A Guide for Caregivers of People with Disabilities

Text in this section is excerpted from "Family Caregivers," Centers for Disease Control and Prevention (CDC), April 2, 2014.

Family Caregivers

If you are a family member who cares for someone with a disability, whether a child or an adult, combining personal, caregiving, and everyday needs can be challenging. This site has information for

372

family caregivers such as yourself to help you and those you care for stay safe and healthy.

Caregiving Tips for Families of People with Disabilities

These general caregiving tips provide families with information on how to stay healthy and positive. Keep in mind that these tips can be used to address many family issues. Information, support, advocacy, empowerment, care, and balance can be the foundation for a healthy family and are appropriate no matter what the challenge.

Be Informed

- Gather information about your family member's condition, and discuss issues with others involved in the care of your family member. Being informed will help you make more knowledgeable health decisions and improve your understanding about any challenges your family might face.

- Notice how others care for the person with special needs. Be aware of signs of mental or physical abuse.

Get Support

- Family members and friends can provide support in a variety of ways and oftentimes want to help. Determine if there are big or small things they can do to assist you and your family.

- Join a local or online support group. A support group can give you the chance to share information and connect with people who are going through similar experiences. A support group may help combat the isolation and fear you may experience as a caregiver.

- Don't limit your involvement to support groups and associations that focus on a particular need or disability. There are also local and national groups that provide services, recreation, and information for people with disabilities.

- Friends, family, health care providers, support groups, community services, and counselors are just a few of the people available to help you and your family.

Be an Advocate

- Be an advocate for your family member with a disability. Caregivers who are effective advocates may be more successful at getting better service.

- Ask questions. For example, if your family member with a disability uses a wheelchair and you want to plan a beach vacation, find out if the beaches are accessible via a car, ramp, portable walkway mat, or other equipment.

- Inform other caregivers of any special conditions or circumstances. For example, if your family member with a disability has a latex allergy, remind dental or medical staff each time you visit them.

- Document the medical history of your family member with a disability, and keep this information current.

- Make sure your employer understands your circumstances and limitations. Discuss your ability to travel or to work weekends or evenings. Arrange for flexible scheduling when needed.

- Become familiar with the Americans with Disabilities Act, the Family Medical Leave Act, and other state and national provisions. Know how and when to apply them to your situation.

Be Empowering

- Focus on what you and your family member with a disability can do.

- Find appropriate milestones and celebrate them.

- If someone asks you questions about the family member with a disability, let him or her answer when possible. Doing so may help empower the individual to engage with others.

- When appropriate, teach your family member with a disability to be as independent and self-assured as possible. Always keep health and safety issues in mind.

Take Care of Yourself

- Take care of yourself. Caring for a family member with a disability can wear out even the strongest caregiver. Stay healthy for yourself and those you care for.

- Work hard to maintain your personal interests, hobbies, and friendships. Don't let caregiving consume your entire life. This is not healthy for you or those you care for. Balance is key.

- Allow yourself not to be the perfect caregiver. Set reasonable expectations to lower stress and make you a more effective caregiver.

- Delegate some caregiving tasks to other reliable people.

- Take a break. Short breaks, like an evening walk or relaxing bath, are essential. Long breaks are nurturing. Arrange a retreat with friends or get away with a significant other when appropriate.

- Don't ignore signs of illness: if you get sick, see a health care provider. Pay attention to your mental and emotional health as well. Remember, taking good care of yourself can help the person you care for as well. Exercising and eating healthy also are important.

Keep Balance in the Family

- Family members with a disability may require extra care and attention. Take time for all family members, taking into account the needs of each individual. For example, it's important for parents of a child with a disability to also spend time with each other and with any other children they might have.

- Consider respite care. "Respite" refers to short-term, temporary care provided to people with disabilities so that their families can take a break from the daily routine of caregiving.

Disabilities: Healthy Living

People with or without disabilities can stay healthy by learning about and living healthy lifestyles.

Emergency and Disaster Preparedness

It is important that people with disabilities and their caregivers make plans to protect themselves in the event of an emergency or disaster. Emergencies and disasters can strike quickly and without warning and can force people to leave their home or be confined in their home. For the millions of Americans who have disabilities, emergencies such as acts of terrorism and disasters such as fires and floods present a real challenge.

Part Five

Special Education and Support Services for Children with Disabilities

Chapter 40

Laws about Educating Children with Disabilities

Chapter Contents

Section 40.1

Individuals with Disabilities Education Act (IDEA)

Text in this section is excerpted from "Individuals with Disabilities
Education Act (IDEA)," Disability.gov, May 20, 2014.

Two of the main laws that help fund special education and protect
the rights of students with disabilities are the Individuals with Disabilities Education Act (IDEA) and Section 504 of the Rehabilitation Act
(often just called "Section 504."). The IDEA was originally passed in
1975 to make sure that children with disabilities have the opportunity
to receive a free, appropriate public education, just like other children.
IDEA requires that special education and related services be made
available to every eligible child with a disability. Section 504, on the
other hand, is a civil rights law that protects children with disabilities
from discrimination.

Every year, millions of children receive services under the IDEA.
This law governs how states and public agencies provide early intervention, and special education and related services to more than 6.5
million eligible infants, toddlers, children and youth with disabilities.
Infants and toddlers with disabilities and their families receive early
intervention services under IDEA Part C. Children and youth (ages
3–21) receive special education and related services under IDEA Part
B. A couple of good places to help parents better understand this
law are the Center for Parent Information and Resources and the
National Center on Learning Disabilities' "An Overview of IDEA
Parent Guide."

The services that IDEA requires can be very important in helping
children and youth with disabilities develop, learn and succeed in
school. Under the law, states are responsible for meeting the needs of
eligible children with disabilities. To find out if a child is eligible for
services, he or she must first be evaluated. This evaluation is free and
can determine if a child has a disability, as defined by IDEA, and what
special education and related services he or she may need.

Special education is instruction that is specially designed to meet the specific needs of a child with a disability. Since each child is unique, it's difficult to give an overall example of special education. Special education can be for things like travel training or vocational education, and it can take place in the classroom, in a home, in a hospital or institution, among other places. This is why you might also hear that "special education is not a place." Where it is provided depends on the child's unique needs as decided by the group of individuals (which includes the parents) that makes the placement decision. Some students with disabilities may need accommodations and other related services to help them benefit from special education. These related services may include speech-language pathology and audiology services; interpreting services; psychological services; physical and occupational therapy; therapeutic recreation; and early identification and assessment of disabilities in children. Read "Knowing Your Child's Rights" for an overview of what the IDEA requires regarding special education and related services.

Under the IDEA, special education instruction must be provided to students with disabilities in what is known as the "least restrictive environment," or LRE. IDEA's LRE provisions ensure that children with disabilities are educated with children who do not have disabilities, to the maximum extent appropriate. LRE requirements apply to students in public or private institutions or other care facilities.

There are several local organizations that help parents of children with disabilities better understand how the IDEA can help as their kids advance through the school system. Every state has at least one Parent Training and Information Center (PTI). PTIs provide parents with important information about special education so they can participate effectively in meeting the educational needs of their children. If your child is struggling with learning, visit the website of the National Center for Learning Disabilities. The Center website has a section of resources specifically for parents that includes a "Parent Guide to the IDEA." The Learning Disabilities Association of America (LDA) also has special education resources for parents. Find a LDA chapter near you. Finally, your state's department of education is an important point of entry for getting information about all the programs and services required under IDEA, and how you can help your child get the most out of their education.

Section 40.2

No Child Left Behind Act

Text in this section is excerpted from "What is ESEA?" U.S.
Department of Education (ED), April 8, 2015.

What is ESEA?

Fifty years ago, U.S. President Lyndon B. Johnson signed the Elementary and Secondary Education Act (ESEA) of 1965. The law represented a major new commitment by the federal government to "quality and equality" in educating our young people.

When President Johnson sent the bill to Congress, he urged that the country, "declare a national goal of full educational opportunity."

The purpose of ESEA was to provide additional resources for vulnerable students. ESEA offered new grants to districts serving low-income students, federal grants for textbooks and library books, created special education centers, and created scholarships for low-income college students. The law also provided federal grants to state educational agencies to improve the quality of elementary and secondary education.

In the 35 years following ESEA, the federal government increased the amount of resources dedicated to education. However, education remains a local issue. The federal government remained committed to ensuring that disadvantaged students had additional resources, however, because as a nation we were falling short of meeting the law's original goal of full educational opportunity.

No Child Left Behind

In 2001, with strong bipartisan support, Congress passed the No Child Left Behind Act (NCLB) to reauthorize ESEA, and President George W. Bush signed the law in January 2002.

NCLB put in place important new measures to expose achievement gaps, and started an important national dialogue on how to close them. By promoting accountability for the achievement of all students, the law has played an important role in protecting the civil rights of at-risk students.

However, while NCLB has played an important role in closing achievement gaps and requiring transparency, it also has significant flaws. It created incentives for states to lower their standards; emphasized punishing failure over rewarding success; focused on absolute scores, rather than recognizing growth and progress; and prescribed a pass-fail, one-size-fits-all series of interventions for schools that miss their state-established goals.

Teachers, parents, school district leaders, and state and federal elected officials from both parties have recognized that NCLB needs to be fixed. Congress was due to reauthorize the law in 2007, but has yet to do so.

Flexibility under NCLB

In 2012, after six years without reauthorization, and with strong state and local consensus that many of NCLB's outdated requirements were preventing progress, the Obama Administration began offering flexibility to states from some of the law's most onerous provisions. To receive flexibility, states demonstrated that they had adopted and had plans to implement college and career-ready standards and assessments, put in place school accountability systems that focused on the lowest-performing schools and schools with the largest achievement gaps, and ensured that districts were implementing teacher and principal evaluation and support systems.

The flexibility required states to continue to be transparent about their achievement gaps, but provided schools and districts greater flexibility in the actions they take to address those gaps.

Section 40.3

Section 504 of the Rehabilitation Act

This section includes excerpts from "Accessibility Help," U.S.
Social Security Administration (SSA), June 7, 2014; and text
from "Protecting Students With Disabilities," U.S. Department of
Education (ED), October 16, 2015.

Section 504 is a federal law designed to protect the rights of individuals with disabilities in programs and activities that receive federal financial assistance from the U.S. Department of Education (ED). Section 504 provides: "No otherwise qualified individual with a disability in the United States . . . shall, solely by reason of her or his disability, be excluded from the participation in, be denied the benefits of, or be subjected to discrimination under any program or activity receiving Federal financial assistance . . . ."

Students Protected under Section 504

Section 504 covers qualified students with disabilities who attend schools receiving federal financial assistance. To be protected under Section 504, a student must be determined to: (1) have a physical or mental impairment that substantially limits one or more major life activities; or (2) have a record of such an impairment; or (3) be regarded as having such an impairment. Section 504 requires that school districts provide a free appropriate public education (FAPE) to qualified students in their jurisdictions who have a physical or mental impairment that substantially limits one or more major life activities.

Evaluation

At the elementary and secondary school level, determining whether a child is a qualified disabled student under Section 504 begins with the evaluation process. Section 504 requires the use of evaluation procedures that ensure that children are not misclassified, unnecessarily labeled as having a disability, or incorrectly placed, based on inappropriate selection, administration, or interpretation of evaluation materials.

Procedural Safeguards

Public elementary and secondary schools must employ procedural safeguards regarding the identification, evaluation, or educational placement of persons who, because of disability, need or are believed to need special instruction or related services.

Chapter 41

Evaluating Children for Disability

Early Screening is Vital to Children and Their Families

How a child plays, learns, speaks, moves, and behaves all offer important clues about a child's development. A delay in any of these developmental milestones could be a sign of developmental challenges, according to the Centers for Disease Control and Prevention (CDC). Early intervention services, like those services that help a child learn to speak, walk, or interact with others, can really make a difference and enhance a child's learning and development. Unfortunately, too many young children do not have access to the early screening that can help detect developmental delays.

Additionally, the CDC states that an estimated one in every 68 children in the United States has been identified as having an autism spectrum disorder (ASD). ASD is a developmental disability that can cause significant social, communication, and behavioral challenges. Unfortunately, most children identified with ASD were not diagnosed until after age four, even though children can be diagnosed as early as age two or younger.

This chapter includes excerpts from "Early Screening is Vital to Children and Their Families," U.S. Department of Education (ED), April 17, 2014; and text from "Developmental Monitoring and Screening," Centers for Disease Control and Prevention (CDC), August 24, 2015.

While it is imperative that all young children have access to screening and appropriate services, research highlights the need to ensure developmental screening in low-income, racially diverse urban populations, where the risk of delay is greater and access to services can be more difficult. Studies found that by 24 months of age, black children were almost five times less likely than white children to receive early intervention services, and that a lack of receipt of services appeared more consistently among black children who qualified based on developmental delay alone compared to children with a diagnosed condition. The research suggests that children of color are disproportionately underrepresented in early intervention services and less likely than white children to be diagnosed with developmental delays.

Statistics such as these can help us raise the awareness about the importance of early screening. The American Academy of Pediatrics recommends that children receive developmental screenings with a standardized developmental screening tool at 9, 18, and either 24 or 30 months of age. Children who are screened and identified as having, or at risk for, a developmental delay can be referred to their local early intervention service program (if they are under 3 years of age), or their local public school (if they are 3 years of age or older), for additional evaluation to determine whether they are eligible for IDEA Part C or Part B 619 services. Further, screening young children early may help families to better access other federal and State-funded early learning and development services, such as home visiting, Early Head Start, Head Start, preschool, and child care.

Early screening and identification are critically important steps towards giving young children with disabilities a strong start in life.

Developmental Monitoring and Screening

Developmental Monitoring

Your child's growth and development are kept track of through a partnership between you and your health professional. At each well-child visit the doctor looks for developmental delays or problems and talks with you about any concerns you might have. This is called developmental monitoring (or surveillance). Any problems noticed during developmental monitoring should be followed-up with developmental screening.

Children with special health care needs should have developmental monitoring and screening just like those without special needs. Monitoring healthy development means paying attention not only to symptoms related to the child's condition, but also to the child's physical, mental, social, and emotional well-being.

Developmental Screening

Well-child visits allow doctors and nurses to have regular contact with children to keep track of?or monitor? your child's health and development through periodic developmental screening. Developmental screening is a short test to tell if a child is learning basic skills when he or she should, or if there are delays. Developmental screening can also be done by other professionals in health care, community, or school settings.

The doctor might ask you some questions or talk and play with the child during an examination to see how he or she plays, learns, speaks, behaves, and moves. A delay in any of these areas could be a sign of a problem.

The American Academy of Pediatrics recommends that all children be screened for developmental delays and disabilities during regular well-child doctor visits at:

- 9 months
- 18 months
- 24 or 30 months

Additional screening might be needed if a child is at high risk for developmental problems due to preterm birth, low birthweight, or other reasons.

If your child's doctor does not routinely check your child with this type of developmental screening test, you can ask that it be done.

Why It's Important

Many children with developmental delays are not being identified as early as possible. As a result, these children must wait to get the help they need to do well in social and educational settings (for example, in school).

In the United States, about 13% of children 3 to 17 years of age have a developmental or behavioral disability such as autism, intellectual disability (also known as mental retardation), and attention-deficit/hyperactivity disorder. In addition, many children have delays in language or other areas that can affect school readiness. However, many children with developmental disabilities are not identified before age

389

10, by which time significant delays already might have occurred and opportunities for treatment might have been missed.

Early Intervention Services

Research shows that early intervention treatment services can greatly improve a child's development. Early intervention services help children from birth through 3 years of age (36 months) learn important skills. Services include therapy to help the child talk, walk, and interact with others.

The Individuals with Disabilities Education Act (IDEA) says that children younger than 3 years of age (36 months) who are at risk of having developmental delays, might be eligible for early intervention treatment services even if the child has not received a formal diagnosis. These services are provided through an early intervention system in each state.

In addition, treatment for particular symptoms, such as speech therapy for language delays, often does not require a formal diagnosis. Although early intervention is extremely important, intervention at any age can be helpful.

Chapter 42

Individualized Education Programs (IEPs)

When a child has been determined eligible for special education, school systems are required to develop an Individualized Education Program (IEP) in collaboration with the parents to articulate the details of the child's educational program and commit the resources necessary to complete the program.

The process for developing an IEP

The writing of your child's IEP is one aspect of the special education process under the Individuals with Disabilities Education Act (IDEA). The procedures for identifying a student as having a disability, needing special education, and, therefore, requiring an IEP, include:

- **Identification as possibly needing special education services**. The IDEA requires states to identify, locate, and evaluate all children with disabilities in the state who need special education and related services. In addition to proactive state efforts, a school professional may request an evaluation for your child. Parents can contact a child's teacher or other school professional to ask for an evaluation.

Text in this chapter is excerpted from "Individualized Education Program," Military OneSource, September 22, 2015.

- **Evaluation**. The evaluation must assess your child in all areas related to the suspected disability. The evaluation results will be used to decide your child's eligibility for special education and related services and to make decisions about an appropriate educational program for your child. If you disagree with the evaluation, you have the right to take your child for an Independent Educational Evaluation (IEE) and you can ask that the school system pay for this IEE.

- **Eligibility determination.** After the evaluation, the parents will meet with a group of qualified professionals to look over your child's evaluation results. Together, you decide if your child is a "child with a disability," as defined by IDEA. If your child is found to be a "child with a disability," he or she is eligible for special education and related services. Within thirty calendar days after your child is determined eligible, the IEP team must meet to write an IEP for your child.

- **IEP meeting**. The school system schedules and conducts the IEP meeting. The IEP team will gather to talk about your child's needs and write the IEP. Parents and their child (when appropriate) are part of the team. Before the school system can provide special education and related services to your child for the first time, you must give consent. The child begins to receive services as soon as possible after the meeting. If you do not agree with the IEP and placement, you may discuss your concerns with other members of the IEP team and try to work out an agreement. If there is still disagreement, you can ask for mediation, or the school may offer mediation. You can file a complaint with the state education agency and can request a due process hearing, at which time mediation must be available.

- **Special education services provided**. The school ensures that your child's IEP is being carried out as it was written. Parents are given a copy of the IEP. Each of your child's teachers and service providers has access to the IEP and knows his or her specific responsibilities for carrying out the IEP. This includes the accommodations, modifications, and supports that must be provided to the child, in keeping with the IEP.

- **Progress is measured and reported.** Your child's progress toward the annual goals is measured, as stated in the IEP. You are regularly informed of your child's progress and whether that progress is enough for the child to achieve the goals by the end of the year. These progress reports must be given to you at least as often as parents are informed of any nondisabled children's progress.

- **Review of the IEP.** Your child's IEP is reviewed by the IEP team at least once a year, or more often if you or the school ask for a review.

- **Reevaluation.** At least every three years, your child must be reevaluated. This evaluation is often called a triennial review. This reevaluation determines whether your child continues to be a "child with a disability," as defined by IDEA, and what your child's educational needs are.

Contents of an IEP

The IEP is the focal point of each student's special education program. It articulates the details of the program as agreed upon by both parents and school personnel and commits the resources necessary to complete the program. It also serves as a management tool for school systems to ensure appropriate education and related services. School systems, parents, and individual students all have a stake in having a well-written, comprehensive, and accurate IEP that is revised at least annually to reflect a student's most current needs and progress. All DoD schools use a standardized form for the IEP, but individual state agencies have their own formats for documenting the required components of the IEP. By law, the IEP must include certain information about your child and the educational program designed to meet his or her unique needs. This includes the following:

- **Special educational and related services**. The IEP must list the specific educational and related services the student will receive including the extent to which the child will or will not participate in the regular education program. This includes supplementary aids and services needed, as well as modifications to the program or supports for school personnel – such as training or professional development – that will be provided to assist your child.

- **Time and duration of services**. The IEP lists the time and duration of services including dates for the beginning and ending of each service, where the related services will be provided, and how often services will be provided.

393

- **Goals**. The IEP lists annual goals and specific objectives for reaching those goals. The goals are broken down into short-term objectives or benchmarks. Goals may be academic, address social or behavioral needs, relate to physical needs, or address other educational needs. The goals must be measurable—meaning that it must be possible to determine if the student has achieved the goals.

- **Evaluation methods**. The IEP contains criteria, methods, and timelines for evaluating achievement of short-term objectives contained in the program. The IEP must also state what modifications are needed for your child to participate in any required state and district-wide achievement tests. If a test is not appropriate for your child, the IEP must state why the test is not appropriate and how your child will be tested instead.

- **Current performance**. The IEP must state how your child is currently doing in school. Typically, this is collected from classroom tests and assignments, individual tests given to decide eligibility for services or during reevaluation, and observations made by parents, teachers, related service providers, and other school staff.

- **Participation with nondisabled children**. The IEP must explain the extent (if any) to which your child will not participate with nondisabled children in the regular class and other school activities. Your child's IEP must be delivered in the least restrictive environment that is able to accommodate your child's needs without jeopardizing the educational needs of other students. In other words, children should only be removed from the regular classroom when the nature and severity of their disability makes it necessary to do so. The school's intent to educate students with disabilities in the regular classroom to the greatest degree possible is also called "inclusion."

- **Transition services**. Once your child is sixteen, the IEP must address the courses he or she needs to take to reach his or her post-school goals. A statement of transition services needs must also be included in each of the child's subsequent IEPs. Once your child is sixteen, the IEP must state what transition services are needed to help your child prepare for leaving school.

- **Age of majority**. Beginning at least one year before the child reaches the age of majority (usually the age of eighteen), the IEP must include a statement that your child has been told of any rights that will transfer to him or her at the age of majority.

Chapter 43

Scholarships and Financial Aid Available to Students with Disabilities

In addition to scholarships available to the general public, minorities and people pursuing a particular field of study, there are many scholarships specifically for students with disabilities. Below are some examples:

- Council for Exceptional Children (CEC) Scholarships recognize outstanding student members and CEC student chapter advisors who make significant contributions to CEC and exceptional children (fall deadline).

- The disABLEDperson.com Scholarship Competition asks students to write an essay for the chance to win a $1,000 scholarship (spring deadline).

- Each year, Incight provides up to 100 scholarships to help students with disabilities pay for college, vocational school or Masters or Doctoral programs. Applicants must be residents of

Text in this chapter is excerpted from "Are There Any Scholarships Specifically for Students with Disabilities?" Disability.gov, March 2, 2014; and text from "Students With Intellectual Disabilities," U.S. Department of Education (ED), July 1, 2015.

Oregon, Washington or California, although they don't have to attend a college or university in those states (spring deadline).

- Newcombe Scholarships for Students with Disabilities are grants paid directly to colleges or universities to help students with disabilities who demonstrate financial need.

- The American Association of Health & Disability (AAHD) Scholarship Program is for students who are full-time undergraduates (freshman or greater status) or part-time or full-time graduate students. You must provide documentation of a disability. (Applicants who have not yet graduated from high school will not be considered.)

- The Ability Center of Greater Toledo Scholarship is for Greater Toledo, OH area residents with disabilities (spring deadline).

- The Business Plan Scholarship for Students with Disabilities is a $1,000 scholarship open to undergraduate or graduate students with disabilities who've written a business plan for a class, competition or to start a business. Submit a 500 to 1,000 word essay on what you learned from writing a business plan to mprosser@fitsmallbusiness.com (spring and winter deadlines).

For Students Who Are Blind

- American Foundation for the Blind awards scholarships from $500 to $3,500 to students who are blind or visually impaired (spring deadline).

- The American Council of the Blind awards scholarships to students who are legally blind. A 3.3 cumulative point average is usually required (spring deadline).

- The Association of Blind Citizens runs the Assistive Technology Fund, which covers 50 percent of the retail price of adaptive services or software for individuals who are legally blind (summer and winter deadlines).

- Christian Record Services for the Blind offers partial scholarships to young people who are legally blind to obtain a college education (spring deadline).

- Learning Ally's Mary P. Oenslager Scholastic Achievement Awards are given to Learning Ally members who are blind or visually impaired and have received or will be receiving their bachelor's, master's or doctoral degree. The top three winners each receive a $6,000 scholarship and a chance to participate in a celebration in Washington, DC (spring deadline).

- The Lighthouse Guild scholarship program offers scholarships of up to $10,000 to help high school students who are legally blind pay for college (spring deadline).

- The National Federation of the Blind Scholarship Program offers many scholarships from $3,000 to $12,000 to college students who are blind, in recognition of their achievements (spring deadline).

- The United States Association of Blind Athletes (USABA) Copeland Scholarship is awarded to USABA members who are legally blind and enrolled at a two-year or four-year college, university or technical school as a full-time student (fall deadline).

For Students Who Are Deaf or Hard-of-Hearing

- The Alexander Graham Bell Scholarship Program offers scholarships for students who have moderately severe to profound hearing loss and are getting a bachelor's, master's or doctoral degree (spring deadline).

- Cochlear Americas has two scholarship programs—the Graeme Clark Scholarship, which is open to people who have the Nucleus® Cochlear Implant, and the Anders Tjellstrom Scholarship, which is open to people who have the Baha® System (fall deadline).

- The Gallaudet University Alumni Association provides financial assistance to graduates of Gallaudet University and other accredited colleges and universities who are deaf and are getting their graduate degree at colleges and universities not specifically for deaf or hard of hearing people (spring deadline).

- The Sertoma Hard of Hearing or Deaf Scholarship helps undergraduate students with clinically significant bilateral hearing loss pay for college (spring deadline).

For Students with Learning Disabilities

- LD Resources Foundation Awards help college students with learning disabilities pay for testing and in some cases award specific types of assistive technologies, such as Dragon Naturally Speaking (fall deadline).

- National Center for Learning Disabilities (NCLD) Scholarships are offered to high school seniors with documented learning disabilities who are getting a higher education (winter deadline). NCLD also offers a list of scholarships for students with learning disabilities or attention deficit hyperactivity disorder (ADHD).

- Learning Ally offers the Marion Huber Learning Through Listening Awards for outstanding students with print or learning disabilities. The top three winners each receive a $6,000 scholarship and a chance to participate in a celebration in Washington, DC (spring deadline).

- P. Buckley Moss Foundation Scholarships and Awards offer financial assistance to high school seniors with learning disabilities who are getting a higher education or are planning a career in the visual arts (spring deadline).

- RiSE Scholarships Foundation, Inc. offers scholarships for students who learn differently (winter deadline).

- The Western Illinois University Chad Stovall Memorial Scholarship is a $500 scholarship for Western Illinois University students who have Tourette Syndrome, obsessive-compulsive disorder (OCD), or attention deficit disorder (spring deadline).

- The Learning Disabilities Association of Iowa offers scholarships of $1,000 each to high school seniors planning to enroll in college or vocational programs (spring deadline).

For Students with Physical Disabilities

- The ChairScholars Foundation Scholarship Program gives high school seniors and college students up to $20,000 to help them attend a college or university (spring deadline).

- The Marianjoy Scholarship Program awards scholarships to students with physical disabilities or neuromuscular disorders who are residents of Cook, Will, Kane, DuPage, McHenry, Lake, DeKalb, or Kendall Counties in IL (spring deadline).

- The National Amputation Foundation Scholarship offers $500 to full-time college students who have a major limb amputation and will be attending an accredited university (summer deadline).

- The 1800Wheelchair.com Scholarship is an essay competition that awards $500 to high school seniors and college students with or without a disability (spring deadline).

- The Paralyzed Veterans of America Scholarship Program awards scholarships to PVA members, spouses of PVA members or an unmarried child (under 24 years of age) who is a dependent.

For Students with Other Disabilities

- The Cystic Fibrosis Scholarship Foundation awards scholarships to students based on financial need, academic achievement and leadership (spring deadline).

- The Dr. Angela E. Grant Memorial Scholarship Fund gives awards to students affected by cancer. You must be a cancer survivor who is actively pursuing or planning to pursue a college education, or be an applicant with an immediate family member who has been diagnosed with cancer (spring deadline).

- The Little People of America Scholarship Program awards scholarships to students with and without disabilities. Priority is given to applicants who have a medically diagnosed form of dwarfism (spring deadline).

- The Elizabeth Nash Foundation awards scholarships from $1,000 to $2,500 to help people with cystic fibrosis pursue under-graduate and graduate degrees (spring deadline).

- Google Lime Scholarship Program awards $10,000 scholarships to undergraduate, graduate or Ph.D. computer science students with a disability currently enrolled at a university.

- Ruby's Rainbow grants scholarships to adults with Down syndrome seeking post-secondary education, enrichment or vocational classes.

- The Lilly Reintegration Scholarship is for people diagnosed with bipolar disorder, schizophrenia, schizophreniform or schizoaffective disorder or major depressive disorder.

- The Microsoft DisAbility Scholarship is awarded to high school seniors who plan on successfully completing a vocational or academic college program and have a financial need. The amount of this non-renewable scholarship is $5,000.

- The Diabetes Scholars Foundation program is available to incoming freshmen seeking a higher education at an accredited four-year university, college, technical or trade school. This scholarship recognizes students who are actively involved in the diabetes community and who have high academic performance (spring deadline).

- The Eric Marder Scholarship Program awards scholarships to undergraduate students living with primary immunodeficiency diseases who plan on completing their post-secondary education (spring deadline).

- The National Multiple Sclerosis (MS) Society Scholarship Program offers scholarships to high school seniors with MS, or who have a parent with MS, and will be attending an accredited post-secondary school for the first time).

- Hemophilia Foundation of America Scholarships awards ten scholarships of $1,500 each to promising students with bleeding disorders (spring deadline).

- The Able Flight Training Scholarship Program offers flight and career training scholarships for people with disabilities who want to learn how to fly or train for a career in aviation.

- The Hydrocephalus Association's Scholarship Program provides $1,000 scholarships to promising young adults with hydrocephalus (spring deadline).

- The UCB Family Epilepsy Scholarship Program offers educational scholarships to people living with epilepsy, family members and caregivers who demonstrate academic and personal achievement (spring deadline).

- Organization for Autism Research Scholarship Program people with an autism diagnosis (DSM-IV or later criteria) pursuing full-time, post-secondary, undergraduate education or vocational-technical training.

- Through the Looking Glass offers scholarships for students who have at least one parent with a disability. To qualify, you must be a high school senior planning to attend college or technical school, or currently in college or technical school.

Students with intellectual disabilities may be able to get certain types of federal student aid

If you have an intellectual disability, you may receive funding from the Federal Pell Grant, Federal Supplemental Educational Opportunity Grant, and Federal Work-Study programs if you

- are enrolled or accepted for enrollment in a comprehensive transition and postsecondary (CTP) program for students with intellectual disabilities at an institution of higher education (a college or career school) that participates in the **federal student aid programs**;

- are maintaining **satisfactory academic progress**; and

- meet the basic federal student aid eligibility requirements, except that you are not required to have a high school diploma or GED and are not required to be pursuing a degree or certificate.

A CTP program for students with intellectual disabilities means a degree, certificate, or nondegree program that

- is offered by a college or career school and approved by the U.S. Department of Education;

- is designed to support students with intellectual disabilities who want to continue academic, career, and independent living instruction to prepare for gainful employment;

- offers academic advising and a structured curriculum; and

- requires students with intellectual disabilities to participate, for at least half of the program, in

  - regular enrollment in credit-bearing courses with nondisabled students,

  - auditing or participating (with nondisabled students) in courses for which the student does not receive regular academic credit,

  - enrollment in noncredit-bearing, nondegree courses with nondisabled students, or

  - internships or work-based training with nondisabled individuals.

401

The following states have schools that offer CTP programs:

- California
- Delaware
- Florida
- Georgia
- Illinois
- Kentucky
- Minnesota
- Missouri
- New Jersey
- New York
- North Carolina
- Ohio
- Pennsylvania
- South Carolina
- Tennessee
- Virginia

Part Six

Legal, Employment, and Financial Support for People with Disabilities

Chapter 44

A Guide to Disability Rights Laws

This chapter examines federal disability rights laws and provides an overview of their applicability to the parenting rights of Americans with disabilities. Specifically, the chapter examines the protections afforded by the Rehabilitation Act of 1973 and the Americans with Disabilities Act (ADA) of 1990 and their application to the efforts of people with disabilities to create and maintain families.

Federal Disability Rights Laws: An Overview

The landmark ADA and its predecessor, the Rehabilitation Act of 1973, established comprehensive national mandates prohibiting discrimination on the basis of disability. Collectively, these two laws prohibit public and private entities from discriminating against people with disabilities and ensure equal opportunity to participate in and benefit from a wide range of services and programs.

Under federal law, a person is defined as having a disability if he or she (a) has a physical or mental impairment that substantially limits one or more major life activities; (b) has a record of such impairment; or (c) is regarded as having such impairment. Pursuant to the 2008

Text in this chapter is excerpted from "Chapter 3: Disability Law Framework," National Council on Disability (NCD), September 27, 2012.

ADA amendments, major life activities include but are not limited to seeing, walking, and learning, as well as the operation of major bodily functions, such as the reproductive system. The amendments clarify that the ADA covers people with episodic conditions, such as epilepsy. Today, a person is protected under the ADA if he or she has a disability that substantially limits a life activity when the condition is in an active state, even if the condition is not evident or does not limit a life activity at all times. Furthermore, public entities and places of public accommodation may not discriminate against an "individual or entity because of the known disability of an individual with whom the individual or entity is known to have a relationship or association."

Rehabilitation Act of 1973

The first federal civil rights law protecting people with disabilities was the Rehabilitation Act of 1973. The intent of the Rehabilitation Act is to "Empower individuals with disabilities to maximize employment, economic self-sufficiency, independence and inclusion and integration into society through. . . .the guarantee of equal opportunity."

The most well-known provision of the Rehabilitation Act is Section 504, which states,

"No otherwise qualified individual with a disability . . . Shall, solely by reason of her or his disability, be excluded from the participation in, be denied the benefits of, or be subjected to discrimination under any program or activity receiving Federal financial assistance. . . ."

Section 504 prohibits discrimination against people with disabilities by programs conducted by federal agencies as well as any program or activity that receives federal financial assistance. Section 504 applies to nearly all public schools, public and private colleges, human services programs (including the child welfare system and adoption agencies), and public housing agencies. Notably, Section 504 applies to all health care entities and providers that receive federal monies, including through Medicaid, Medicare, or federal block grants.

The Rehabilitation Act includes other significant provisions as well. Section 501 requires affirmative action and nondiscrimination in employment by federal agencies.

Section 503 requires affirmative action and prohibits employment discrimination by federal government contractors and subcontractors with contracts of more than $10,000. Section 508 requires that all electronic and information technology developed, maintained, procured, or used by the federal government must be accessible to people with disabilities, including employees.

Americans with Disabilities Act

On July 26, 1990, U.S. President George W. Bush signed into law the Americans with Disabilities Act, which extended the protections and prohibitions of the Rehabilitation Act to private conduct, with the goal of reducing the social discrimination and stigma experienced by people with disabilities. In passing the ADA, Congress recognized that "historically, society tended to isolate and segregate individuals with disabilities, and, despite some improvements, such forms of discrimination against individuals with disabilities continue to be a serious and pervasive social problem." In furtherance of the objective of eliminating discrimination, Congress stated that "the Nation's proper goals regarding individuals with disabilities are to assure equality of opportunity, full participation, independent living, and economic self-sufficiency for such individuals." In light of the ADA's intended "clear and comprehensive national mandate for the elimination of discrimination," the ADA ensures the rights of people with disabilities to create and maintain families in a variety of ways. Indeed, before the passage of the ADA, Congress gathered an unprecedented amount of testimony concerning discrimination against people with disabilities, including stories of people with disabilities who had lost custody of their children and people with disabilities who were denied the opportunity to adopt children.

The ADA is divided into five titles that cover the various protections afforded by the law:

- Title I covers employment.

- Title II Part A covers public entities: state and local government.

- Title II Part B covers public transportation provided by public entities.

- Title III covers private entities: public accommodations, commercial facilities, examinations and courses related to licensing or certification, and transportation provided to the public by private entities.

- Title IV covers telecommunications.

- Title V contains miscellaneous provisions.

Titles II and III are most relevant here because they govern access to public entities run by state and local governments, and places of public accommodation, respectively.

Title II of the Americans with Disabilities Act

Title II of the ADA prohibits discrimination by public entities run or funded by state and local governments. It mandates, "No qualified individual with a disability shall, by reason of such disability, be excluded from participation in or be denied the benefits of the services, programs, or activities of a public entity, or be subjected to discrimination by any such entity." The ADA defines public entity to include "any department, agency, special purpose district, or other instrumentality of a State or States or local government." Examples of covered programs and entities include state courts, state legislatures, town meetings, police and fire departments, and state and local offices and programs. Entities that receive federal financial assistance from DOJ, including state judicial systems, are also prohibited from discriminating on the basis of disability under Section 504 of the Rehabilitation Act Further, the Supreme Court has held that providing people with disabilities access to courts is a mandate of Title II. According to the Court, "Unequal treatment of disabled persons in the administration of judicial services has a long history," which the ADA seeks to redress. Title II (and Section 504) are thus crucial, because they mandate access for people with disabilities to the child welfare system, family law courts, and public adoption agencies.

Title II requires the following of public entities:

- Public entities must provide people with disabilities an equal opportunity to participate in programs, services or activities. To implement this mandate, public entities must make reasonable modifications in policies, practices, or procedures unless such modifications would fundamentally alter the nature of the service, program or activity.

- Public entities shall administer services, programs, and activities in the most integrated setting appropriate to the needs of qualified individuals with disabilities;

- Public entities shall not impose or apply eligibility criteria that screen out or tend to screen out any individual with a disability from fully and equally enjoying any service, program, or activity, unless such criteria can be shown to be necessary for the provision of the service, program, or activity being offered;

- Public entities must furnish auxiliary aids and services when necessary to ensure effective communication, unless an undue burden or fundamental alteration would result;

- Public entities may provide benefits, services, or advantages, beyond those required by the regulation, to people with disabilities;

- Public entities may not place surcharges on individuals with disabilities to cover the costs of measures to ensure nondiscriminatory treatment, such as making necessary modifications required to provide program accessibility or providing qualified interpreters;

- Public entities may not deny the benefits of programs, activities, and services to individuals with disabilities because entities' facilities are inaccessible. A public entity's services, programs or activities, when viewed in their entirety, must be readily accessible to, and usable by, people with disabilities.

Title II also requires newly constructed or altered facilities to comply with the ADA's 2010 Standards for Accessible Design (2010 Standards), if the start date for construction is on or after March 15, 2012. If elements in existing facilities already comply with corresponding elements in the 1991 Standards or the Uniform Federal Accessibility Standards (UFAS) and are not being altered, Title II entities are not required to make changes to those elements to bring them into compliance with the 2010 Standards. Under the "program accessibility" standard, public entities are not necessarily required to make each of their existing facilities accessible if other methods are effective in achieving compliance with the regulations. Instead, a public entity's services, programs, or activities, when viewed in their entirety, must be readily accessible to, and usable by, people with disabilities.

Examples of alternative methods to ensure accessibility include relocating a service to an accessible floor or facility, or providing the service at home. There are limits to the program accessibility requirement; public entities are not required to take any action that they can demonstrate would result in an "undue financial and administrative burden" or that would "fundamentally alter" the nature of the program, activity, or service. However, they must take other necessary action to ensure that people with disabilities receive the benefits or services provided by the public entity. Moreover, public entities may impose legitimate safety requirements necessary for the safe operation of services, programs, or activities. However, the public entity must ensure that its safety requirements are based on actual risks, not on mere speculation, stereotypes, or generalizations about people with disabilities. Similarly, public entities are not required to permit a person to participate in or benefit from its services, programs, or activities if that person poses a direct threat to the health or safety of others. In determining whether a person poses a direct threat, a public entity must make an individualized assessment, based on reasonable judgment that relies on current medical knowledge or on the best available objective evidence, to ascertain the nature, duration, and severity of the risk; the probability that the potential injury will actually occur; and whether reasonable modifications of policies, practices, or procedures or the provision of auxiliary aids or services will mitigate the risk.

Title III of the Americans with Disabilities Act

Title III of the Americans with Disabilities Act (ADA) prohibits any public accommodation from discriminating against people with disabilities by denying them access to the full and equal enjoyment of goods, services, or facilities. Public accommodations include all areas open to the public, including restaurants, stores, banks, pharmacies, legal offices, doctors' offices, and hospitals. Pursuant to Title III, "private entities are considered public accommodations if the operations of such entities affect commerce and fall within one of the 12 categories set out in the statute." Title III is relevant here because it unquestionably governs access to private adoptions, as it precisely includes "adoption agency" in the definition of public accommodations. Similarly, assisted reproductive technology providers must comply with Title III because they provide services in a health care provider's office or hospital, which are included in the definition of public accommodations.

The purpose of Title III is to ensure that no person with a disability is denied goods or services offered to the public because of their disability. Under Title III,

- A public accommodation shall not impose or apply eligibility criteria that screen out or tend to screen out an individual with a disability from fully and equally enjoying any goods, services, facilities, privileges, advantages, or accommodations, unless such criteria can be shown to be necessary for the provision of such goods, services, etc.

- A public accommodation shall make reasonable modifications in policies, practices, or procedures when such modifications are necessary to ensure that people with disabilities have access to the goods, services, facilities, privileges, advantages, or accommodations, unless the public accommodation can demonstrate that making the modifications would fundamentally alter the nature of such goods, services, etc.

- A public accommodation shall take those steps that may be necessary to ensure that no individual with a disability is excluded, denied services, segregated or otherwise treated differently because of the absence of auxiliary aids and services, unless the public accommodation can demonstrate that taking those steps would result in a fundamental alteration or undue burden.

Public accommodations must also provide physical access for people with disabilities. Generally, new construction and alterations must comply with the 2010 Standards if the start date for construction is on or after March 15, 2012. A public accommodation must remove architectural barriers where such removal is readily achievable; that is, easily accomplished without much difficulty or expense. On or after March 15, 2012, elements in a facility that do not comply with the 1991 Standards requirements for those elements (e.g., where an existing restaurant has never undertaken readily achievable barrier removal) must be modified using the 2010 Standards to the extent readily achievable. The standards include revisions to the 1991 Standards as well as supplemental requirements for which there are no technical or scoping requirements in the 1991 Standards (such as swimming pools, play areas, marinas, and golf facilities). Public accommodations must comply with the 2010 Standards' supplemental requirements in existing facilities to the extent readily achievable.

Public accommodations may deny a person the opportunity to participate in or benefit from the goods, services, facilities, privileges, advantages, and accommodations if the person poses a direct threat to the health or safety of others. In determining whether a person poses a direct threat, a public accommodation must make an individualized assessment based on reasonable judgment that relies on current medical knowledge or on the best available objective evidence to ascertain the nature, duration, and severity of the risk; the probability that the potential injury will actually occur; and whether reasonable modifications of policies, practices, or procedures or the provision of auxiliary aids or services will mitigate the risk. Moreover, public accommodations may impose legitimate safety requirements that are necessary for safe operation. Safety requirements must be based on actual risks and not on mere speculation, stereotypes, or generalizations about people with disabilities.

Ensuring Accessibility for the Whole Family

Despite the laudable requirements of the Rehabilitation Act and the ADA, parents with disabilities and their families continue to experience significant accessibility barriers. These barriers not only impede the abilities of these parents to fulfill their parenting responsibilities but also affect the entire family.

For example, parents with disabilities regularly experience accessibility barriers at their children's schools and daycare centers. In October 2006, TLG convened 55 representatives from the Bay Area to initiate the Bay Area Parents with Disabilities and Deaf Parents Task Force. According to TLG:

"Bay Area Task Force participants reiterated a frequent complaint of parents with disabilities nationally: they are excluded from active participation in their children's school life. Typically, because the majority of children of disabled parents are not disabled, center and/ or school administrators and teachers are unaware of or insensitive to the needs of parents with diverse disabilities. This can be owing to a number of factors: the physical inaccessibility of the center and/or school (e.g., inaccessible sites for a parent-teacher meeting or other school activities that other parents attend); inaccessible communication modes (e.g., no interpreters for deaf parents or inaccessible media for parents who are blind); assumptions about parents helping their children with homework if the materials are not in accessible formats. Further, because of a lack of education or familiarity with diverse disabilities, center and/or school officials may make inaccurate or negative assumptions about the capabilities of parents with disabilities."

The task force cited the following specific accessibility problems parents with disabilities encounter:

- Parents with disabilities do not know what their rights are with regard to their children's centers and schools.

- Centers or school systems do not know what their legal obligations are with regard to parents with disabilities.

- Center or school administrators and teachers often do not know if any of their children's parents have disabilities or are deaf.

- Communication from center or school personnel—in person, by phone, or by written communication—may be inaccessible or inappropriate (e.g., no interpreters, inaccessible formats for written materials, linguistically difficult information for parents with intellectual disabilities).

- Information from the centers or schools is often not sent in a timely manner (e.g., a parent may need several days' notice to arrange transportation or get materials in braille).

- Even centers or schools that have classrooms/programs for children with disabilities may not consider the perspectives or needs of adults with disabilities or the fact that they can be parents.

- If there are multiple children in the family or if the child changes centers or schools, navigating different schools or different school districts can be challenging.

- Although most centers or schools include curricula on diverse ethnicities and languages, few address disabilities unless the focus is on children with disabilities.

- Deaf parents particularly noted that teachers inappropriately use their hearing children to interpret conversations between teachers and parents. Other parents with disabilities described center or school personnel who are visibly uncomfortable, paternalistic, or insensitive when talking with them.

Conclusion

The proper application of federal disability rights laws for parents with disabilities is crucial to achieving and promoting the purposes and goals of the Rehabilitation Act and the ADA: namely, the full participation of people with disabilities in society and protection against discrimination that would limit such participation. Until these laws are properly applied and enforced, people with disabilities will continue to face barriers to exercising their fundamental right to create and maintain families.

Chapter 45

Housing and Safety Issues for People with Disabilities

Chapter Contents

Section 45.1

Housing for People with Disabilities

Text in this section is excerpted from "Disability.gov's Guide to
Housing," Disability.gov, December 22, 2013.

Where Can I Get Help Finding a Place to Live?

The Department of Housing and Urban Development (HUD), as
well as many housing organizations in your state, can help you with
your search for an affordable, accessible home. Below are a few search
tools and organizations that can help you get started.

- HUD's Low Rent Apartment Search can help you find low-rent
  apartments near you. You can search by city, town or zip code
  to find apartments of any size that are accessible to people with
  disabilities or senior citizens. You can also contact the HUD
  office in your state or a HUD Approved Housing Counseling
  Agency for help finding a place to live. These offices provide
  advice on buying a home, programs that can help you pay your
  rent and answer other housing-related questions you may have.
  For more information call HUD at 1-800-569-4287.

- Use HUD's Resource Locator mobile application (app) on your
  smartphone or electronic tablet to find available HUD housing in your area, including affordable housing for people with
  disabilities and seniors. Download the app in Apple iTunes or
  Google Play Marketplace to get connected to public housing
  authorities, property management companies and building
  managers.

- Socialserve.com has information about affordable and accessible housing in most states. You can search for housing based
  on where you want to live, how much you can afford to pay, and
  accessibility features such as wheelchair ramps, accessible parking, widened doorways and low kitchen counters for wheelchair
  users. Socialserve.com can be reached toll-free at 1-877-428-8844
  and in Spanish at 1-877-428-8844.

- State Housing Finance Agencies (HFA) help meet the affordable housing needs of the residents in their states, including people with disabilities and low-income families. Many of these offices also have online tools you can use to search for an affordable apartment or house.

- The U.S. Department of Agriculture (USDA) provides funding for rural multi-family apartment complexes for seniors and families throughout the country. For more information, call USDA's Office of Rural Development at 1-800-670-6553 or contact your state office.

- The National Low Income Housing Coalition (NLIHC) works with state housing and homelessness advocacy organizations to make sure that people with low incomes have affordable, safe housing. Many of these state and local organizations can help you with your search for affordable housing.

- Habitat for Humanity volunteers build and repair safe, affordable houses throughout the world. For more information, read "How to Apply for a Habitat for Humanity House."

Are There Any Programs That Can Help Me Pay My Rent?

- Housing Choice Vouchers (formerly called "Section 8" vouchers) help very low-income families, the elderly and people with disabilities pay for decent, safe housing. Housing may include single-family homes, townhouses and apartments, and is not limited to just units in subsidized housing projects. The individual who is approved for a housing voucher is responsible for finding a housing unit where the owner agrees to rent under the program. To apply, contact your local Public Housing Agency or HUD office. Be aware that the demand for this type of housing assistance is high, so there are often waiting lists of individuals in need of subsidized housing.

- HUD's Public Housing Program provides housing for eligible low-income families, the elderly and persons with disabilities. Public housing comes in all sizes and types, from single family houses to high-rise apartments. For more information or to apply, contact your local Public Housing Agency.

- State Housing Finance Agencies provide information about rental assistance programs in each state, as well as resources to help you buy a home, learn about your housing rights and find accessible housing for people with disabilities.

- HUD's Housing Counseling Program works through organizations in cities and towns across the country to help people with their housing needs. Counselors can help you search for affordable housing and learn about rental assistance programs. They can also provide advice and referrals on foreclosure and credit issues.

- HUD's Housing Opportunities for Persons with AIDS Program (HOPWA) is the only federal program dedicated to address the housing needs of persons living with HIV/AIDS and their families. HOPWA works through local nonprofit organizations and housing agencies to provide housing and support to individuals and families. HOPWA programs provide short- and long-term rental assistance, run community residences and provide supportive housing facilities.

- In addition, some Community Action Agencies, and organizations such as Catholic Charities and Lutheran Services in America, provide housing and rental assistance.

Where Can I Get Help Paying for Home Repairs or Modifications to Make My Home Accessible?

Home modifications may involve converting or adapting your environment so you can live independently. Examples of home modifications include replacing regular door handles with ones that open by using a push button; adding handrails on both sides of a staircase and outside steps; installing ramps for so you can come and go from your home by wheelchair or scooter; building a walk-in shower; and lowering kitchen counters. These types of home modifications enable people with disabilities and older adults to "age in place" and live independently. An occupational or physical therapist may be able to suggest other ways to adapt your home for safety and accessibility.

Here are a few resources and organizations that will help you get information about making your home accessible:

- The Rebuilding Together program helps people with disabilities adapt their homes so they can stay independent. Rebuilding Together's Veterans Housing Initiative focuses on home modification and repair services for retired and active service members so they can live independently and safely in their own homes.

Contact a Rebuilding Together Affiliate near you for more information.

- The National Resource Center on Supportive Housing and Home Modification promotes aging in place for seniors and people who are aging with a disability. The Center gives families and individuals the knowledge they need to plan for their housing, health and supportive service needs. Check your state's listings for agencies and organizations near you that can help with home modifications.

- Your local Independent Living Center (ILC) may be able to make some suggestions about how to pay for home modifications such as adding a wheelchair ramp or widening the doorway to your bathroom. ILCs also provide advocacy and support services for people with disabilities, including assistance with housing, health care and independent living skills.

- Easy Access Housing for Easier Living is a brochure from Easter Seals that has tips on how to adapt your home to accommodate a person with a disability. Your local Easter Seals chapter can provide you with information about possible financing options to pay for modifications to make your home accessible.

- Your local Aging and Disability Resource Center (ADRC) may be able to refer you to an organization or company that provides home modifications services. ADRCs offer information on long-term supports and services for older adults and people with disabilities.

- The Department of Veterans Affairs (VA) makes grants available to service members and veterans with certain permanent and total service-connected disabilities to help them buy or build an adapted home, or modify an existing home to accommodate a disability. The two grant programs are the Specially Adapted Housing (SAH) grant and the Special Housing Adaptation (SHA) grant. You can apply online or call VA toll free at 1-800-827-1000 to have a claim form mailed to you.

- According to Eldercare.gov, many minor home modifications and repairs cost between $150 and $2,000. Some home remodeling contractors offer reduced rates and charge sliding-scale fees based on a person's income and ability to pay. Some Area Agencies on Aging (AAA) have home modification programs or can refer you to other organizations that can help pay for home repairs and modifications.

- The USDA's Single Family Housing Repair program provides loans to very low-income homeowners to repair, improve or modernize their homes and grants to elderly very low-income homeowners to remove health and safety hazards. Contact your USDA state office for more information about this program.

- Some state housing finance agencies have loan programs that help people with disabilities (or who have a family member living in the household with disabilities) who are buying a home that needs accessibility modifications. Many states have home modification programs that are part of their state Assistive Technology programs. These programs provide low-interest loans to buy assistive technology or to help pay for home modifications and adaptations to make your home safe and accessible.

- The National Spinal Cord Injury Association has a fact sheet on home modifications that includes information about resources that can help people with spinal cord injuries pay for home modifications. The American Occupational Therapy Association has more information on this subject.

Where Can I Get Information about Assisted Living Facilities?

According to the Assisted Living Federation of America (ALFA), assisted living is a long-term care option that combines housing, support services and health care. Assisted living is usually for individuals who need assistance with everyday activities such as cooking, taking medications, or help with bathing, getting dressed and transportation. Some assisted living residents may have memory disorders such as Alzheimer's, or may need help related to mobility, incontinence or other challenges.

Here are some search tools and organizations that can help you find assisted living facilities near you:

- Your Area Agency on Aging (AAA) can refer you to assisted living facilities in your state, as well as information about other long-term care services and supports and information for caregivers.

- Every state has a Department of Aging (your state's agency may be called something slightly different) that protects the rights and quality of life of older persons. These agencies can provide you with information about programs for seniors relating to housing, health education and in-home services. Many of these state offices have lists of certified assisted living communities, as well as information on how to pay for the monthly cost of assisted living.

- The Eldercare Locator connects you to services for older adults and their families. You can also call 1-800-677-1116 for information about assisted living facilities and other long-term care options in your state.

- A Guide for Making Housing Decisions – Housing Options for Older Adults provides information on housing options for older adults, including types of assisted living facilities, home modifications and legal and financial issues involved in long-term care.

- Long-term care ombudsmen are advocates for residents of nursing homes, board and care homes and assisted living facilities. They are trained to resolve problems and can assist you with complaints. Ombudsmen also provide information about how to find a facility and how to get quality care.

Section 45.2

Understanding the Fair Housing Amendments Act

Text in this section is excerpted from "Joint Statement Of The Department Of Housing And Urban Development And The Department Of Justice Reasonable Accommodations Under The Fair Housing Act," U.S.Department of Justice, August 6, 2015.

Introduction

The Department of Justice ("DOJ") and the Department of Housing and Urban Development ("HUD") are jointly responsible for enforcing the federal Fair Housing Act (the "Act"), which prohibits discrimination in housing on the basis of race, color, religion, sex, national origin, familial status, and disability. One type of disability discrimination prohibited by the Act is the refusal to make reasonable accommodations in rules, policies, practices, or services when such accommodations may be necessary to afford a person with a disability the equal opportunity to use and enjoy a dwelling. HUD and DOJ frequently respond to complaints alleging that housing providers have violated the Act by refusing reasonable accommodations to persons with disabilities. This Statement provides technical assistance regarding the rights and obligations of persons with disabilities and housing providers under the Act relating to reasonable accommodations.

Questions and Answers

What types of discrimination against persons with disabilities does the Act prohibit?

The Act prohibits housing providers from discriminating against applicants or residents because of their disability or the disability of anyone associated with them and from treating persons with disabilities less favorably than others because of their disability. The Act also makes it unlawful for any person to refuse "to make reasonable accommodations in rules, policies, practices, or services, when such accommodations may be necessary to afford ... person(s) [with disabilities] equal opportunity to use and enjoy a dwelling."

The Act also prohibits housing providers from refusing residency to persons with disabilities, or placing conditions on their residency, because those persons may require reasonable accommodations. In addition, in certain circumstances, the Act requires that housing providers allow residents to make reasonable structural modifications to units and public/common areas in a dwelling when those modifications may be necessary for a person with a disability to have full enjoyment of a dwelling. With certain limited exceptions, the Act applies to privately and publicly owned housing, including housing subsidized by the federal government or rented through the use of Section 8 voucher assistance.

Who must comply with the Fair Housing Act's reasonable accommodation requirements?

Any person or entity engaging in prohibited conduct – i.e., refusing to make reasonable accommodations in rules, policies, practices, or services, when such accommodations may be necessary to afford a person with a disability an equal opportunity to use and enjoy a dwelling – may be held liable unless they fall within an exception to the Act's coverage. Courts have applied the Act to individuals, corporations, associations and others involved in the provision of housing and residential lending, including property owners, housing managers, homeowners and condominium associations, lenders, real estate agents, and brokerage services. Courts have also applied the Act to state and local governments, most often in the context of exclusionary zoning or other land-use decisions.

Who qualifies as a person with a disability under the Act?

The Act defines a person with a disability to include individuals with a physical or mental impairment that substantially limits one or more major life activities; individuals who are regarded as having such an impairment; and individuals with a record of such an impairment.

The term "physical or mental impairment" includes, but is not limited to, such diseases and conditions as orthopedic, visual, speech and hearing impairments, cerebral palsy, autism, epilepsy, muscular dystrophy, multiple sclerosis, cancer, heart disease, diabetes, Human Immunodeficiency Virus infection, mental retardation, emotional illness, drug addiction (other than addiction caused by current, illegal use of a controlled substance) and alcoholism.

The term "substantially limits" suggests that the limitation is "significant" or "to a large degree."

The term "major life activity" means those activities that are of central importance to daily life, such as seeing, hearing, walking, breathing, performing manual tasks, caring for one's self, learning, and speaking. This list of major life activities is not exhaustive.

Does the Act protect juvenile offenders, sex offenders, persons who illegally use controlled substances, and persons with disabilities who pose a significant danger to others?

No, juvenile offenders and sex offenders, by virtue of that status, are not persons with disabilities protected by the Act. Similarly, while the Act does protect persons who are recovering from substance abuse, it does not protect persons who are currently engaging in the current illegal use of controlled substances.

Additionally, the Act does not protect an individual with a disability whose tenancy would constitute a "direct threat" to the health or safety of other individuals or result in substantial physical damage to the property of others unless the threat can be eliminated or significantly reduced by reasonable accommodation.

How can a housing provider determine if an individual poses a direct threat?

The Act does not allow for exclusion of individuals based upon fear, speculation, or stereotype about a particular disability or persons with disabilities in general. A determination that an individual poses a direct threat must rely on an individualized assessment that is based on reliable objective evidence (e.g., current conduct, or a recent history of overt acts). The assessment must consider: the nature, duration, and severity of the risk of injury; the probability that injury will actually occur; and whether there are any reasonable accommodations that will eliminate the direct threat.

Consequently, in evaluating a recent history of overt acts, a provider must take into account whether the individual has received intervening treatment or medication that has eliminated the direct threat (i.e., a significant risk of substantial harm). In such a situation, the provider may request that the individual document how the circumstances have changed so that he no longer poses a direct threat. A provider may also obtain satisfactory assurances that the individual will not pose a direct threat during the tenancy. The housing provider must have reliable, objective evidence that a person with a disability poses a direct threat before excluding him from housing on that basis.

What is a "reasonable accommodation" for purposes of the Act?

A "reasonable accommodation" is a change, exception, or adjustment to a rule, policy, practice, or service that may be necessary for a person with a disability to have an equal opportunity to use and enjoy a dwelling, including public and common use spaces. Since rules, policies, practices, and services may have a different effect on persons with disabilities than on other persons, treating persons with disabilities exactly the same as others will sometimes deny them an equal opportunity to use and enjoy a dwelling. The Act makes it unlawful to refuse to make reasonable accommodations to rules, policies, practices, or services when such accommodations may be necessary to afford persons with disabilities an equal opportunity to use and enjoy a dwelling.

To show that a requested accommodation may be necessary, there must be an identifiable relationship, or nexus, between the requested accommodation and the individual's disability.

Are there any instances when a provider can deny a request for a reasonable accommodation without violating the Act?

Yes. A housing provider can deny a request for a reasonable accommodation if the request was not made by or on behalf of a person with a disability or if there is no disability-related need for the accommodation. In addition, a request for a reasonable accommodation may be denied if providing the accommodation is not reasonable - i.e., if it would impose an undue financial and administrative burden on the housing provider or it would fundamentally alter the nature of the provider's operations. The determination of undue financial and administrative burden must be made on a case-by-case basis involving various factors, such as the cost of the requested accommodation, the financial resources of the provider, the benefits that the accommodation would provide to the requester, and the availability of alternative accommodations that would effectively meet the requester's disability-related needs.

When a housing provider refuses a requested accommodation because it is not reasonable, the provider should discuss with the requester whether there is an alternative accommodation that would effectively address the requester's disability-related needs without a fundamental alteration to the provider's operations and without imposing an undue financial and administrative burden. If an alternative accommodation would effectively meet the requester's disability-related needs and is reasonable, the provider must grant it. An interactive process in which the housing provider and the requester discuss the requester's disability-related need for the requested accommodation and possible alternative accommodations is helpful to all concerned because it often results in an effective accommodation for the requester that does not pose an undue financial and administrative burden for the provider.

There may be instances where a provider believes that, while the accommodation requested by an individual is reasonable, there is an alternative accommodation that would be equally effective in meeting the individual's disability-related needs. In such a circumstance, the provider should discuss with the individual if she is willing to accept the alternative accommodation. However, providers should be aware that persons with disabilities typically have the most accurate knowledge about the functional limitations posed by their disability, and an individual is not obligated to accept an alternative accommodation suggested by the provider if she believes it will not meet her needs and her preferred accommodation is reasonable.

What is a "fundamental alteration"?

A "fundamental alteration" is a modification that alters the essential nature of a provider's operations.

What happens if providing a requested accommodation involves some costs on the part of the housing provider?

Courts have ruled that the Act may require a housing provider to grant a reasonable accommodation that involves costs, so long as the reasonable accommodation does not pose an undue financial and administrative burden and the requested accommodation does not constitute a fundamental alteration of the provider's operations. The financial resources of the provider, the cost of the reasonable accommodation, the benefits to the requester of the requested accommodation, and the availability of other, less expensive alternative accommodations that would effectively meet the applicant or resident's disability-related needs must be considered in determining whether a requested accommodation poses an undue financial and administrative burden.

What happens if no agreement can be reached through the interactive process?

A failure to reach an agreement on an accommodation request is in effect a decision by the provider not to grant the requested accommodation. If the individual who was denied an accommodation files a Fair Housing Act complaint to challenge that decision, then the agency or court receiving the complaint will review the evidence in light of applicable law and decide if the housing provider violated that law.

May a housing provider charge an extra fee or require an additional deposit from applicants or residents with disabilities as a condition of granting a reasonable accommodation?

No. Housing providers may not require persons with disabilities to pay extra fees or deposits as a condition of receiving a reasonable accommodation.

When and how should an individual request an accommodation?

Under the Act, a resident or an applicant for housing makes a reasonable accommodation request whenever she makes clear to the housing provider that she is requesting an exception, change, or adjustment to a rule, policy, practice, or service because of her disability. She should explain what type of accommodation she is requesting and, if the need for the accommodation is not readily apparent or not known to the provider, explain the relationship between the requested accommodation and her disability.

An applicant or resident is not entitled to receive a reasonable accommodation unless she requests one. However, the Fair Housing Act does not require that a request be made in a particular manner or at a particular time. A person with a disability need not personally make the reasonable accommodation request; the request can be made by a family member or someone else who is acting on her behalf. An individual making a reasonable accommodation request does not need to mention the Act or use the words "reasonable accommodation."

However, the requester must make the request in a manner that a reasonable person would understand to be a request for an exception, change, or adjustment to a rule, policy, practice, or service because of a disability.

Although a reasonable accommodation request can be made orally or in writing, it is usually helpful for both the resident and the housing provider if the request is made in writing. This will help prevent misunderstandings regarding what is being requested, or whether the request was made. To facilitate the processing and consideration of the request, residents or prospective residents may wish to check with a housing provider in advance to determine if the provider has a preference regarding the manner in which the request is made. However, housing providers must give appropriate consideration to reasonable accommodation requests even if the requester makes the request orally or does not use the provider's preferred forms or procedures for making such requests.

Must a housing provider adopt formal procedures for processing requests for a reasonable accommodation?

No. The Act does not require that a housing provider adopt any formal procedures for reasonable accommodation requests. However, having formal procedures may aid individuals with disabilities in making requests for reasonable accommodations and may aid housing providers in assessing those requests so that there are no misunderstandings as to the nature of the request, and, in the event of later disputes, provide records to show that the requests received proper consideration.

A provider may not refuse a request, however, because the individual making the request did not follow any formal procedures that the provider has adopted. If a provider adopts formal procedures for processing reasonable accommodation requests, the provider should ensure that the procedures, including any forms used, do not seek information that is not necessary to evaluate if a reasonable accommodation may be needed to afford a person with a disability equal opportunity to use and enjoy a dwelling.

Is a housing provider obligated to provide a reasonable accommodation to a resident or applicant if an accommodation has not been requested?

No. A housing provider is only obligated to provide a reasonable accommodation to a resident or applicant if a request for the accommodation has been made. A provider has notice that a reasonable accommodation request has been made if a person, her family member, or someone acting on her behalf requests a change, exception, or adjustment to a rule, policy, practice, or service because of a disability, even if the words "reasonable accommodation" are not used as part of the request.

What if a housing provider fails to act promptly on a reasonable accommodation request?

A provider has an obligation to provide prompt responses to reasonable accommodation requests. An undue delay in responding to a reasonable accommodation request may be deemed to be a failure to provide a reasonable accommodation.

What inquiries, if any, may a housing provider make of current or potential residents regarding the existence of a disability when they have not asked for an accommodation?

Under the Fair Housing Act, it is usually unlawful for a housing provider to ask if an applicant for a dwelling has a disability or if a person intending to reside in a dwelling or anyone associated with an applicant or resident has a disability, or ask about the nature or severity of such persons' disabilities. Housing providers may, however, make the following inquiries, provided these inquiries are made of all applicants, including those with and without disabilities:

- An inquiry into an applicant's ability to meet the requirements of tenancy;

- An inquiry to determine if an applicant is a current illegal abuser or addict of a controlled substance;

- An inquiry to determine if an applicant qualifies for a dwelling legally available only to persons with a disability or to persons with a particular type of disability; and

- An inquiry to determine if an applicant qualifies for housing that is legally available on a priority

What kinds of information, if any, may a housing provider request from a person with an obvious or known disability who is requesting a reasonable accommodation?

A provider is entitled to obtain information that is necessary to evaluate if a requested reasonable accommodation may be necessary because of a disability. If a person's disability is obvious, or otherwise known to the provider, and if the need for the requested accommodation is also readily apparent or known, then the provider may not request any additional information about the requester's disability or the disability-related need for the accommodation.

If the requester's disability is known or readily apparent to the provider, but the need for the accommodation is not readily apparent or known, the provider may request only information that is necessary to evaluate the disability-related need for the accommodation.

If a disability is not obvious, what kinds of information may a housing provider request from the person with a disability in support of a requested accommodation?

A housing provider may not ordinarily inquire as to the nature and severity of an individual's disability. However, in response to a request for a reasonable accommodation, a housing provider may request reliable disability-related information that is necessary to verify that the person meets the Act's definition of disability (i.e., has a physical or mental impairment that substantially limits one or more major life activities), describes the needed accommodation, and shows the relationship between the person's disability and the need for the requested accommodation. Depending on the individual's circumstances, information verifying that the person meets the Act's definition of disability can usually be provided by the individual himself or herself (e.g., proof that an individual under 65 years of age receives Supplemental Security Income or Social Security Disability Insurance benefits or a credible statement by the individual). A doctor or other medical professional, a peer support group, a non-medical service agency, or a reliable third party who is in a position to know about the individual's disability may also provide verification of a disability. In most cases, an individual's medical records or detailed information about the nature of a person's disability is not necessary for this inquiry.

Once a housing provider has established that a person meets the Act's definition of disability, the provider's request for documentation should seek only the information that is necessary to evaluate if the reasonable accommodation is needed because of a disability. Such information must be kept confidential and must not be shared with other persons unless they need the information to make or assess a decision to grant or deny a reasonable accommodation request or unless disclosure is required by law (e.g., a court-issued subpoena requiring disclosure).

If a person believes she has been unlawfully denied a reasonable accommodation, what should that person do if she wishes to challenge that denial under the Act?

When a person with a disability believes that she has been subjected to a discriminatory housing practice, including a provider's wrongful denial of a request for reasonable accommodation, she may file a complaint with HUD within one year after the alleged denial or may file a lawsuit in federal district court within two years of the alleged denial. If a complaint is filed with HUD, HUD will investigate the complaint at no cost to the person with a disability.

- There are several ways that a person may file a complaint with HUD:

- By placing a toll-free call to 1-800-669-9777 or TTY 1-800-927-9275;

- By completing the "on-line" complaint form available on the HUD Website: www.hud.gov

Section 45.3

Resources for Homeless Disabled People

Text in this section is excerpted from "Disability.gov's Guide to
Housing," Disability.gov, December 22, 2013.

Where Can I Find Information about Programs for People Who Are Homeless?

- HUD's Local Homelessness Assistance website can connect you
  to many organizations in your state that help people who are
  homeless. Just click on your state and then "Find Homeless
  Resources" under "I Want to." Your local housing counseling
  agency can also refer you to programs and organizations that
  serve people who are homeless.

- The Substance Abuse and Mental Health Services Administration's (SAMHSA) Homelessness Resource Center provides information on local housing contacts, including housing and social
  services agencies that offer permanent and temporary housing,
  emergency shelters and alcohol and drug treatment programs.

- The Department of Housing and Urban Development – VA Supportive Housing (HUD-VASH) Program helps homeless veterans
  and their families find permanent housing. If you need housing
  assistance, call the National Call Center for Homeless Veterans
  at 1-877-424-3838 to be connected with a trained counselor at
  any time.

- The Homelessness Resource Exchange provides information and
  resources for government agencies, homeless service providers
  and individuals and families who are homeless. The site also has
  a section on Resources for Homeless Youth.

- The National Coalition for the Homeless has a Directory of
  Homeless Assistance Organizations that includes contact information for programs in every state that serve people who are
  homeless. Many of the organizations listed also offer health
  care.

- The National Coalition for Homeless Veterans has a list of organizations that provide services to homeless Veterans in every state. Check their list of organizations to contact if you need immediate help.

Section 45.4

Disaster Preparedness for People with Disabilities and Special Needs

Text in this section is excerpted from "Individuals With Disabilities And Others With Access And Functional Needs," Ready.gov, October 7, 2015.

Individuals with Disabilities and Others with Access and Functional Needs

How to Make a Plan and Create a Support Network

How might a disaster affect me? What are my personal needs during a disaster? By evaluating your own individual needs and making an emergency plan that fits those needs, you and your loved ones can be better prepared.

Here are three easy steps to start your emergency communication plan:

1. **Collect information**. Create a paper copy of the contact information including phone, email, and social media info for your family, friends, caregivers, neighbors and other important people/offices, such as medical facilities, doctors, schools, workplace contacts or service providers.

   - Add information for connecting through relay services on a landline phone, mobile device and computer, if you are Deaf, hard of hearing, or have a speech disability and use traditional relay services or video relay service (VRS)

2. **Share your emergency plans** with the trusted people in your support network – tell them:

   • Where your emergency supplies are kept

   • What you need and how to contact you if the power goes out

   • If you will call, email or text agreed upon friends or relatives if you're unable to contact each other directly

   • What medical devices or assistive technology devices that you need to have with you if there is an evacuation order from local officials

   • Your plans to remain independent if you require oxygen or mechanical ventilation

3. **Practice your plan with your support network**, just like you would a fire drill.

   • Discuss your needs and/or the needs of a family member; learn about their assistance or services. Advocate including people with disabilities and others with access and functional needs into emergency planning in your community.

   • Talk with your employer about your emergency plan, and find out how your employer includes the needs of people with disabilities and others with access and functional needs.

   • Contact your city, county, or state office of emergency management, local fire and police department, disability organizations, such as the local Independent Living Center, or community groups.

Check your Emergency Supply Kit

• Stock a basic disaster supply kit. Plan for sheltering at home, at work and on the road.

• Inventory what you use every day to maintain your health, safety and independence. Identify essential items you and your family will need to survive for three to five days or longer, if emergency responders or other people cannot get to you following an emergency or disaster and if you have needs that are not easily accommodated, even when you aren't on your own.

• As you go about your usual routines, carry a pad for several days and jot down anything that might be difficult for you to manage without in an emergency, and then begin to brainstorm solutions that might work for you.

- **Stock your kit with essential items** which may include medical supplies, assistive devices, food for your specific dietary needs, prescription medicines, diabetic supplies, hearing aid batteries, phone charger and back up battery land line phone (and TTY if you use this technology), manual wheelchair, extra seat cushion, egg crate padding and other medical equipment and mobility devices you may need to maintain your health, safety and independence, and supplies for your service animal.

- **Plan for the specific needs of children with disabilities and people who may have difficulty in unfamiliar or chaotic environments.** This may include handheld electronic devices loaded with movies and games (including spare chargers or batteries), sheets and twine or a small pop up tent to decrease visual stimulation in a busy room or to provide instant privacy, headphones to decrease auditory distractions, and comfort snacks and toys that meet needs for stimulation.

Make a Medical Plan: Including Medications and Medical Supplies

Even if you do not use a computer, put important information onto a flash drive or mobile device for easy transport in the event of an evacuation. Have your medical professionals update it every time they make changes in your treatment or care.

- Maintain a list of phone numbers for your doctors, pharmacy, service providers and medical facilities.

- Ask your local pharmacy or doctor to provide a list of your prescription medicine and medically prescribed devices.

- Make hard copies and maintain electronic versions, including a portable thumb drive containing:

- Medical prescriptions

- Doctors' orders for Durable Medical Equipment, Consumable Medical Supplies and assistive devices that you use. Include the style and serial numbers of the support devices you use and where you purchased them.

- Medical insurance cards, Medicare or Medicaid card, a list of your allergies, and your health history.

- The U.S. Department of Health and Human Services online tool helps people locate and access their electronic health records from a variety of sources.

- If you own a medical alert tag or bracelet, wear it. Keep medical alert tags or bracelets or written descriptions of your disability and support needs, in case you are unable to describe the situation in an emergency.

- If possible, stock extra over the counter and prescription medicine, oxygen, insulin, catheters, feeding tubes, cannulas, tubing, trach tubes, wipes, pads, undergarments, ostomy supplies, leg bags, adhesive and other medical supplies you use.

- If you have allergies or chemical or environmental sensitivities, be sure to include cleaning, filtering and personal items that you may be able to use to decrease the impact of irritants as much as possible.

- If you work with a medical provider or organization to receive life sustaining medical treatment such as dialysis, oxygen, or cancer treatment, work with the provider in advance of an emergency to identify alternative locations where you could continue to receive treatment if you are unable to go to your regular medical provider.

- If you receive in-home assistance or personal assistance services and meals on wheels, work with your provider agency in advance of an emergency and develop a backup plan for continued care.

- Ask how you can continue to receive services from providers such as disability, mental and behavioral health and social service providers, or medical and life alert services.

Plan for Possible Evacuation

- During an emergency, be ready to explain to first responders and emergency officials that you need to evacuate and choose to go to a shelter with your family, service animal, caregiver, personal assistant, and your assistive technology devices and supplies. You may want to have laminated instructions in print or pictograms if you may find it difficult to describe your needs and preferences or to be understood.

- Plan ahead for accessible transportation that you may need for evacuation or getting to a medical clinic. Work with local services, public transportation or paratransit to identify your local or private accessible transportation options.

- Be sure all of your assistive devices are clearly labeled with your name and contact information using methods that are resistant to water and other kinds of damage.

- If you cannot evacuate with your wheelchair, take your cushion.

Note: People should only be referred to a medical shelter when they have acute health care needs and would typically be admitted to a hospital. Work with your community emergency planners to plan for meeting the health, safety and independence needs of disaster survivors with disabilities in general shelters with their family and neighbors.

Make a Power Outage Plan

- Plan alternative ways to charge your mobile devices, and communication and assistive technology devices before disaster strikes.

- Plan how you will address your dependence on electricity. Tell your power company if you use oxygen- or mechanical ventilation. Be very clear about what you can expect from them in a power outage.

- Before disaster strikes, you may register with your power company. They may alert you when power will be restored in an unplanned outage and before a planned outage. This is particularly important if you use oxygen or mechanical ventilation.

- If you cannot be without power, plan for how you will obtain power backup. If possible, have backup battery, generator, solar or alternate electrical resources. Explore newer solutions, and also consider foot pumps and other simple tools that might suffice when nothing else works.

- Charge devices that will maintain power to your equipment during electric outages.

- Purchase extra batteries for power wheelchairs or other battery-operated medical or assistive technology devices. Keep the **batteries trickle charged at all times**. Find out if you can charge your wheelchair or devices from a car or using rechargeable marine batteries. Make sure you assemble what you'll need in advance.

- Backup chargers for a cell phone could include a hand-crank USB cell phone emergency charger, a solar charger, or a battery pack. Some weather radios have a built in hand crank charger.

- Backup chargers for a laptop or tablet could include a 12V USB adapter that plugs into a car, an inverter, or a battery jump pack with an USB port.

- Receive important information on a cell phone or smart phone. Sign up for emergency emails and text messages on your cell phone from your local government alert system.

- Plan how you are going to receive emergency information if you are unable to use a television, radio or computer. This may include having an adaptive weather alert system to alert you in the event of severe weather.

- Plan for medications that require refrigeration.

Deaf or Hard of Hearing

- Extra batteries and a spare charger for hearing aids, cochlear implant and/or personal assistive listening device. Keep records of where you got your hearing aids and exact types of batteries.

- Consider how to receive emergency information if you are unable to use a TV, radio or computer, such as social media or through your mobile device.

- Use a NOAA Weather Radio for Deaf and Hard of Hearing that has an adaptive weather alert system.

- Many new cell phones and smart phones have an alerting capability that includes specific sounds and vibrations that can be set to signal users of an emergency. Download the FEMA app to receive safety tips and weather alerts from the National Weather Service for up to five locations across the nation, maps of open shelters and disaster recovery centers, information in Spanish and to apply for assistance.

- Keep a TTY or other analog-based amplified or captioned phone as part of your emergency supply kit.

Blind or Low Vision

- Keep Braille/text communication cards, if used, for 2-way communication.

437

- Mark emergency supplies with Braille labels or large print. Keep a list of your emergency supplies on a portable flash drive, or make an audio file that is kept in a safe place where you can access it.

- Keep a Braille, or Deaf-Blind communications device as part of your emergency supply kit.

- If you use assistive technology devices, such as white canes, CCTV, text-to-speech software, keep information about model numbers and where you purchased the equipment, etc.

Speech Disability

- If you use an augmentative communications device or other assistive technologies, plan how you will evacuate with the devices or how you will replace equipment if lost or destroyed. Keep Model information, where the equipment came from (Medicaid, Medicare, private insurance, etc.).

- Plan how you will communicate with others if your equipment is not working, including laminated cards with phrases and/or pictograms.

Mobility Disability

- If you use a power wheelchair, if possible, have a lightweight manual chair available as a backup. Know the size and weight of your wheelchair in addition to whether or not it is collapsible, in case it has to be transported.

- Purchase an extra battery for a power wheelchair or other battery-operated medical or assistive technology devices. If you are unable to purchase an extra battery, find out what agencies, organizations, or local charitable groups can help you with the purchase. Keep extra batteries on a trickle charger at all times.

- Consider keeping a patch kit or can of sealant for flat tires and/ or extra inner tube if wheelchair or scooter is not puncture proof.

- Keep an extra mobility device such as a cane or walker, if you use one.

- If you use a seat cushion to protect your skin or maintain your balance, and you must evacuate without your wheelchair, take your cushion with you.

Service Animals

- Make plans in advance for your service animal's health and safety whether you both stay at home, or throughout evacuation.

- Stock food, water, portable, water dish, potty pads and bags, and medications. Have identification, licenses, leash, harness and a favorite toy for your service animal.

- Consider paw protection. You may be evacuating over sharp objects such as debris and broken glass.

- If you go to a public shelter, by law all service dogs and miniature horses (but no other animals) are allowed inside and must be allowed to remain with you in all areas of the shelter. You do not need to show any proof but you may be asked to answer two questions that service animal owners are taught to anticipate. Some shelters will accommodate other service animals. Know what to expect before you need sheltering.

- Plan for someone else to take care of your service animal if you are not able to following a disaster.

Behavior Support

- Plan for children with disabilities and people, who may have difficulty in unfamiliar or chaotic environments.

- This may include handheld electronic devices loaded with movies and games (and spare chargers), sheets and twine or a small pop up tent to decrease visual stimulation in a busy room or to provide instant privacy, headphones to decrease auditory distractions, and comfort snacks and toys that meet needs for stimulation.

Chapter 46

Disabilities and the Workplace

Best Practices for Recruiting Candidates with Disabilities

People with disabilities are a growing and highly qualified candidate pool. They work in all levels of employment in public sector agencies, private companies, small businesses, and nonprofit organizations, and across all industries. For examples of successful employees with disabilities, view the U.S. Department of Labor's Office of Disability Employment Policy's *"Policies in Practice"* webpage and the *"Campaign for Disability Employment"* website.

What steps can businesses take to ensure people with disabilities are included in a company's overall recruitment efforts?

In *"Business Strategies that Work: A Framework for Disability Inclusion,"* the U.S. Department of Labor's Office of Disability Employment Policy outlines practical strategies to ensure that a company's recruitment efforts are successful. Strategies for success include:

* Establishing internal policies that prioritize hiring people with disabilities;

Text in this chapter is excerpted from "Recruiting, Hiring, Retaining, and Promoting People With Disabilities," WhiteHouse.gov, February 3, 2015.

- Ensuring that the hiring of people with disabilities is part of a company's overall hiring plan;

- Conducting targeted outreach to attract qualified candidates with disabilities;

- Developing community linkages;

- Retaining and reviewing applications from applicants with disabilities when future openings occur; and

- Ensuring fully accessible online job applications and electronic and social media recruitment materials.

Below are specific steps employers may wish to implement:

Conduct Targeted Outreach: Successful recruitment efforts can be built through collaboration with community-based partners that have connections to qualified candidates. These partners include nonprofit organizations, national and local disability organizations, and federally funded state and local employment programs for people with disabilities such as:

- Vocational Rehabilitation: Vocational rehabilitation state agencies facilitate a wide range of services for youth and adults with disabilities that help prepare them with skills to meet the workplace needs of business. The Council of State Administrators of Vocational Rehabilitation has created a National Employment Team (The NET) that offers businesses a single point of contact to connect with qualified applicants, resources, and support services in their local area.

- Employment Networks: Employment Networks are public or private organizations that are authorized by the Social Security Administrations Ticket to Work Program to provide free employment support services to Social Security disability beneficiaries ages 18 to 64.

- Vocational Rehabilitation and Employment (VR&E): The Vocational Rehabilitation and Employment program, administered by the Department of Veterans Affairs, assists Veterans with service-connected disabilities and an employment handicap and service members who are in the process of transitioning from the military to civilian employment in preparing for, finding, and retaining suitable employment.

- American Job Centers: The American Job Centers, funded by the Department of Labor's Employment and Training Administration, provide free employment assistance services to job seekers. Local American Job Centers can help businesses with drafting job postings, recruiting candidates, and developing retention and training programs.

- Centers for Independent Living (CILs): The Centers for Independent Living are federally funded consumer-controlled nonprofit, nonresidential organizations. The CILs' mission is to empower people with disabilities by providing information and referral services, independent living skills training, peer counseling, and transition services, and by developing additional services based on community needs. A growing number of CILs are Employment Networks and offer additional services such as job interview practice and other pre-employment services to people with disabilities.

In addition, the *"Disability and Veterans Community Resources Directory,"* created by the Department of Labor's Office of Federal Contract Compliance Programs, provides a searchable, non-exhaustive list of organizations that deliver employment services for people with disabilities and Veterans.

1. **Form Community Linkages or Partnerships**: Community linkages are on-going relationships that facilitate an employer's ability to diversify its workforce.

2. **Post Job Announcements in Targeted Spaces:** Posting vacancies on job boards designed for people with disabilities, in disability-related publications, and with disability organizations will increase the diversity of the applicant pool. Examples of national job boards for people with disabilities include:

   - Workforce Recruitment Program

   - The Talent Acquisition Portal

3. **Start an Internship Program.** Internship programs specifically for people with disabilities are an effective and cost efficient recruitment strategy. According to a Research Brief on Disability Recruitment and Hiring, businesses that have internship programs for people with disabilities were 4.5 times more likely to hire a person with a disability than businesses without such a program.

What are some strategies to recruit young people with disabilities?

Hiring young people with disabilities is no different than hiring young people without disabilities. A number of federal, state, and private initiatives focus on ensuring that young people with disabilities can enter and succeed in the workforce.

To build a talent pipeline of young people with disabilities, businesses should consider:

Starting an internship program that targets youth with disabilities.

- The Workforce Recruitment Program, a recruitment and referral program, co- sponsored by the U. S. Department of Labor's Office of Disability Employment Policy, and the U. S. Department of Defense, connects federal sector, private, and nonprofit employers nationwide with highly motivated, qualified, and pre-screened postsecondary students and recent graduates with disabilities who are ready to prove their abilities in summer or permanent jobs.

1. Developing registered apprenticeship programs for young people that target youth with disabilities.

2. Conducting outreach to high school transition initiatives, college and university disability student services offices, and community colleges that have programs designed for students with disabilities.

What are some strategies to recruit Veterans with disabilities?

A number of public and private sector initiatives are designed to help employers recruit and hire Veterans with disabilities. The Veterans Hiring Guide is a comprehensive toolkit designed to help employers start a recruitment program for Veterans.

- The Veterans Employment Center (VEC): The VEC connects transitioning service members, Veterans, and their families to meaningful career opportunities. The VEC provides employers with access to a database of verified career profiles that can be searched by keyword and/or geographic location as well as by special criteria, including disability.

- The U.S. Department of Labor's Veterans Employment and Training Service (VETS) program provides a number of services for employers looking to hire Veterans.

What are some best practices employers can implement to provide equal access to employment opportunities for applicants with disabilities?

To ensure a level playing field for applicants with disabilities, employers should:

1. Ensure that job announcements posted on job boards and social/professional networking sites are in formats that are accessible to jobseekers with disabilities.

2. Indicate on job announcements that qualified individuals with disabilities are encouraged to apply and that reasonable accommodations will be provided.

3. Ensure online application systems, including online pre-employment tests, are accessible to candidates with disabilities.

4. Confirm that interview locations are physically accessible.

5. Inform all applicants ahead of time what the interview process may include and provide them with the opportunity to request a reasonable accommodation, if needed.

6. Be prepared to provide reasonable accommodations for applications, interviews, pre- employment tests, and other aspects of the hiring process when needed, including assigning staff to arrange and approve requested accommodations in a timely fashion.

What can an interviewer ask about a person's disability during the hiring process? What questions may not be asked?

In general, the ADA does not allow an employer to ask any questions about disability or to conduct any medical examinations until after the employer makes a conditional job offer to the applicant. Although employers may not ask disability-related questions or require medical examinations at the pre-offer stage, they may do a wide variety of things to evaluate whether an applicant is qualified for the job, including the following:

- Employers may ask about an applicant's ability to perform specific job functions or tasks.

- Employers may request that an applicant describe or demonstrate how they would perform job tasks or achieve job outcomes.

- Employers may ask about an applicant's qualifications and skills, such as the applicant's education, work history, and required certifications and licenses.

The ADA does, however, provide an exception to the general rule prohibiting disability-related questions in the interview process. Under the ADA, an employer may invite applicants to voluntarily self-identify as individuals with disabilities for affirmative action purposes.

If a business is a **federal contractor** subject to the written affirmative action program (AAP) requirements of Section 503, it has an obligation to invite applicants to voluntarily self-identify as an individual with a disability, using a specific Government form designed for this purpose. Applicant responses to the form should be provided only to Human Resources offices, and not shared with interviewing, testing, or hiring officials.

Best Practices On Respecting, Retaining, and Promoting Employees with Disabilities

Most businesses are well aware that high employee turnover rates have a detrimental impact on a business's bottom line. On the other hand, a workplace culture that embraces diversity and fosters inclusion boosts employee productivity and generates revenue. Thus, it is smart for businesses to develop and implement retention strategies as part of their overall disability employment initiative.

What can employers do to develop retention programs for employees with disabilities?

It is not difficult to implement retention programs for employees with disabilities. In fact, many existing employee programs can be tweaked to focus on the needs of employees with disabilities. Examples of employment practices that can be modified or implemented to increase retention rates of employees with disabilities include:

- Orientation and On-Boarding Programs
- Career Development Programs (including on the job training)
- Mentoring Programs
- Employee Resource Groups

What are tailored on-boarding programs?

Employee on-boarding programs are designed to ensure that new employees have the tools and resources necessary to succeed in their new workplace. Typical on-boarding programs acclimate new employees to the workplace culture and educate them on relevant policies and procedures. The objective of on-boarding that is tailored to new employees with disabilities is the same, but includes disability specific information such as reasonable accommodation procedures and orientation materials that are in accessible formats.

According to a study by the Society for Human Resource Management, the long-term benefits of effective employee on-boarding programs include improved employee retention rates and increased productivity. In addition, structured on-boarding programs have been shown to ease the transition of Veterans with disabilities into the civilian workforce.

How can employers provide employees with disabilities equal access to career development programs?

Career development programs—such as conferences, trainings, tuition assistance, and rotational assignments—are proven employee retention strategies. Below are some best practices to ensure employees with disabilities have equal access to such programs:

- Hold supervisors accountable for implementing management practices that support diversity;

- Ensure all online professional development classes and materials are fully accessible;

- Reserve a portion of employee training funds to provide disability related accommodations for training opportunities;

- Offer specialized leadership programs for employees with disabilities similar to existing leadership programs for other traditionally underrepresented groups;

- Ensure workplace events are accessible to employees with disabilities.

How can disability awareness and etiquette training help employee retention?

Disability awareness training is a cost effective way to address unconscious bias, increase workplace inclusivity, and attract prospective candidates who are people with disabilities.

Educating all staff on disability etiquette builds a corporate culture that embraces diversity

447

How can workplace mentoring programs and employee resource groups improve employment outcomes?

Workplace mentoring programs and employee resource groups are tools businesses can use to address the needs of their increasingly diverse workforce. Both tools help increase recruitment and retention, improve organizational culture, and provide guidance to employees and managers about disability issues.

How can return to work programs be more inclusive of employees with disabilities?

Return to Work (RTW) programs are designed to return an injured, disabled, or temporarily impaired worker to the workplace as soon as medically feasible. Such programs can help businesses boost employee morale, save organizational resources, reduce workers compensation costs and retain top talent.

The anticipated result of an RTW program is the progressive return of the injured or recuperating employee to full duty. RTW programs are historically associated with returning employees from occupational injuries, but many companies are now integrating RTW programs for non- occupational injuries and health issues into their overall disability management strategy.

Many individuals with disabilities who wish to return to work after a period of leave may need reasonable accommodations in order to do their jobs. As a result, an RTW program will generally include temporary or permanent accommodations such as modified schedules, modified job duties, modified methods for completing job duties, or reassignment to an alternate position.

How can workplace flexibility programs help employers retain employees with disabilities?

Increasingly, businesses are implementing workplace flexibility programs in an effort to remain competitive. Flexible work arrangements include a wide variety of solutions including flexible start and end times, compressed work weeks, shift swaps, and telework programs.

Best Practices for Providing Reasonable Accommodations

What is a reasonable accommodation?

A reasonable accommodation is any change in the work environment or in the way things are usually done that enables an individual with a disability to enjoy equal employment opportunities. Reasonable accommodations include:

1. Changes to the job application process;

2. Changes to the work environment or the way the job is done; and

3. Changes to enable the employee to enjoy equal access to the benefits and privileges of the job.

Where can employers find resources on appropriate accommodations for specific disabilities or work settings?

Employers should begin by asking the employee or applicant with a disability about the type(s) of accommodations he or she needs. The accommodation may be a change or modification that can easily be provided.

On average, how much will it cost to provide a reasonable accommodation?

Generally, employers have found that it may cost little to nothing to accommodate most employees with a disability. Studies by the Job Accommodation Network have found:

- Approximately 56% of accommodations have no associated costs;

- Approximately 37% of accommodations have a onetime cost of $500 or less;

- Approximately 4% of accommodations result in ongoing expenses on an annual basis.

There are also a number of tax benefits available to help employers offset the costs related to accommodations. Employers who hire Veterans with disabilities might be entitled to additional tax credits, salary subsidies, and salary reimbursement.

What are some common reasonable accommodation requests?

Some common accommodation requests include requests for:

- **Adjusting or modifying tests and training materials**—such as providing materials in alternate formats (e.g., Braille or large print or reading instructions out loud to a person with a vision or cognitive impairment).

- **Allowing the use of a job coach**—permitting a job coach paid by a public or private social service agency to accompany an employee at a job site in order to assist the employee in learning and accurately carrying out job duties.

- **Modifying or acquiring equipment or devices**—such as raising the height of a desk to accommodate an employee who uses a wheelchair, purchasing amplified stethoscopes for use by nurses and physicians with hearing impairments, or providing assistive technology, such as computer screen readers, for employees with vision impairments.

- **Modifying policies or workplace rules**—such as allowing an employee with diabetes to eat at her desk or allowing a retail store cashier with a back impairment to use a stool.

- **Modifying work schedules**—such as adjusting arrival or departure times, providing periodic breaks, or altering the times when certain job tasks are performed.

- **Providing qualified readers or interpreters**—such as a reader to read written materials to an employee with a vision impairment or a sign language interpreter for a person who is deaf.

- **Job restructuring**—making changes to when and/or how a task is performed, or shifting responsibility to other employees for minor tasks that an employee is unable to perform because of a disability.

- **Leave**—allowing an employee to use accrued paid leave, and providing additional unpaid leave once an employee has exhausted all available leave, for disability related reasons such as receiving or recovering from treatment or when a condition flares up."

- **Reassignment to a vacant position**—moving a current employee to an existing vacant position for which he or she is qualified when the employee can no longer perform his or her current job because of a disability.

- **Telework**—allowing an employee to work from home or a remote location

Chapter 47

Social Security Disability Benefits

Disability Benefits

Disability is something most people don't like to think about. But the chances that you'll become disabled probably are greater than you realize. Studies show that a 20-year-old worker has a 1-in-4 chance of becoming disabled before reaching full retirement age.

This chapter provides basic information on Social Security disability benefits and isn't meant to answer all questions. For specific information about your situation, you should speak with a Social Security representative.

Disability benefits are paid through two programs: the Social Security disability insurance (SSDI) program and the Supplemental Security Income (SSI) program.

Who can get Social Security disability benefits?

Social Security pays benefits to people who can't work because they have a medical condition that's expected to last at least one year or result in death. Federal law requires this very strict definition of disability. While some programs give money to people with partial disability or short-term disability, Social Security does not.

Text in this chapter is excerpted from "Disability Benefits," Social Security Administration (SSA), May 2015.

Certain family members of disabled workers can also receive money from Social Security.

How do I meet the earnings requirement for disability benefits?

In general, to get disability benefits, you must meet two different earnings tests:

1. A recent work test, based on your age at the time you became disabled; and

2. A duration of work test to show that you worked long enough under Social Security.

Certain blind workers have to meet only the duration of work test.

The following table shows the rules for how much work you need for the recent work test, based on your age when your disability began. The rules in this table are based on the **calendar quarter** in which you turned or will turn a certain age.

The calendar quarters are

First Quarter: January 1 through March 31

Second Quarter: April 1 through June 30

Third Quarter: July 1 through September 30

Fourth Quarter: October 1 through December 31

Table 59.1. Rules for work

Rules for work needed for the recent work test	
If you become disabled...	Then, you generally need:
In or before the quarter you turn age 24	1.5 years of work during the three-year period ending with the quarter your disability began.
In the quarter after you turn age 24 but before the quarter you turn age 31	Work during half the time for the period beginning with the quarter after you turned 21 and ending with the quarter you became disabled. Example: If you become disabled in the quarter you turned age 27, then you would need three years of work out of the six-year period ending with the quarter you became disabled.
In the quarter you turn age 31 or later	Work during five years out of the 10-year period ending with the quarter your disability began.

The following table shows examples of how much work you need to meet the duration of work test if you become disabled at various selected ages. For the duration of work test, your work doesn't have to fall within a certain period of time.

NOTE: *This table doesn't cover all situations.*

Table 59.2. Examples of work

Examples of work needed for the duration of work test	
If you become disabled...	**Then, you generally need:**
Before age 28	1.5 years of work
Age 30	2 years
Age 34	3 years
Age 38	4 years
Age 42	5 years
Age 44	5.5 years
Age 46	6 years
Age 48	6.5 years
Age 50	7 years
Age 52	7.5 years
Age 54	8 years
Age 56	8.5 years
Age 58	9 years
Age 60	9.5 years

How do I apply for disability benefits?

There are two ways that you can apply for disability benefits. You can

Apply online at **www.socialsecurity.gov**; or

Call the toll-free number, **1-800-772-1213**, to make an appointment to file a disability claim at your local Social Security office or to set up an appointment for someone to take your claim over the telephone. The disability claims interview lasts about one hour. If you're deaf or hard of hearing, you may call the toll-free TTY number, **1-800-325-0778**, between 7 a.m. and 7 p.m. on business days. If you schedule an appointment, a Disability Starter Kit will be sent to help you get ready for your disability claims interview. The Disability Starter Kit also is available online at **www.socialsecurity.gov/disability.**

You have the right to representation by an attorney or other qualified person of your choice when you do business with Social Security.

When should I apply and what information do I need?

You should apply for disability benefits as soon as you become disabled. **Processing an application for disability benefits can take three to five months.** To apply for disability benefits, you'll need to complete an application for Social Security benefits. You can apply online at **www.socialsecurity.gov**. Your application may be processed faster if you provide the below information as well:

- Your Social Security number;

- Your birth or baptismal certificate;

- Names, addresses and phone numbers of the doctors, caseworkers, hospitals and clinics that took care of you, and dates of your visits;

- Names and dosage of all the medicine you take;

- Medical records from your doctors, therapists, hospitals, clinics, and caseworkers that you already have in your possession;

- Laboratory and test results;

- A summary of where you worked and the kind of work you did; and

- A copy of your most recent W-2 Form (Wage and Tax Statement) or, if you're self-employed, your federal tax returns for the past year.

In addition to the basic application for disability benefits, you'll also need to fill out other forms. One form collects information about your medical condition and how it affects your ability to work. Other forms give doctors, hospitals and other health care professionals who have treated you, permission to send the information about your medical condition.

Chapter 48

Tax Benefits and Credits for People with Disabilities

Tax Benefits for Disabled Taxpayers

Taxpayers with disabilities and parents of children with disabilities may qualify for a number of IRS tax credits and benefits. Listed below are seven tax credits and other benefits which are available if you or someone else listed on your federal tax return is disabled.

1. **Standard Deduction.** Taxpayers who are legally blind may be entitled to a higher standard deduction on their tax return.

2. **Gross Income.** Certain disability-related payments, Veterans Administration disability benefits, and Supplemental Security Income are excluded from gross income.

3. **Impairment-Related Work Expenses.** Employees who have a physical or mental disability limiting their employment may be able to claim business expenses in connection with their workplace. The expenses must be necessary for the taxpayer to work.

4. **Credit for the Elderly or Disabled.** This credit is generally available to certain taxpayers who are 65 and older as well as

This chapter includes excerpts from "Tax Benefits for Disabled Taxpayers," Internal Revenue Service (IRS), November 4, 2013; and text from "Tax Highlights for Persons with Disabilities," Internal Revenue Service (IRS), December 20, 2014.

to certain disabled taxpayers who are younger than 65 and are retired on permanent and total disability.

5. **Medical Expenses.** If you itemize your deductions using Form 1040, Schedule A, you may be able to deduct medical expenses.

6. **Earned Income Tax Credit.** EITC is available to disabled taxpayers as well as to the parents of a child with a disability. If you retired on disability, taxable benefits you receive under your employer's disability retirement plan are considered earned income until you reach minimum retirement age. The EITC is a tax credit that not only reduces a taxpayer's tax liability but may also result in a refund. Many working individuals with a disability who have no qualifying children, but are older than 25 and younger than 65 do—in fact—qualify for EITC. Additionally, if the taxpayer's child is disabled, the age limitation for the EITC is waived. The EITC has no effect on certain public benefits. Any refund you receive because of the EITC will not be considered income when determining whether you are eligible for benefit programs such as Supplemental Security Income and Medicaid.

7. **Child or Dependent Care Credit.** Taxpayers who pay someone to care for their dependent or spouse so they can work or look for work may be entitled to claim this credit. There is no age limit if the taxpayer's spouse or dependent is unable to care for themselves.

Tax Highlights for Persons with Disabilities

This heading concerns people with disabilities and those who care for them. It includes highlights about:

- Income,

- Itemized deductions,

- Tax credits,

- Household employers, and

- Business tax incentives.

You will find most of the information you need to complete your tax return in its instructions.

Income

All income is taxable unless it is specifically excluded by law. The following discussions highlight some taxable and nontaxable income items.

Dependent Care Benefits

Dependent care benefits include:

- Amounts your employer paid directly to you or your care provider for the care of your qualifying person(s) while you worked,

- The fair market value of care in a daycare facility provided or sponsored by your employer, and

- Pre-tax contributions you made under a dependent care flexible spending arrangement.

Exclusion or deduction. If your employer provides dependent care benefits under a qualified plan, you may be able to exclude these benefits from your income. Your employer can tell you whether your benefit plan qualifies. To claim the exclusion, you must complete Part III of Form 2441, Child and Dependent Care Expenses. You cannot use Form 1040EZ.

If you are self-employed and receive benefits from a qualified dependent care benefit plan, you are treated as both employer and employee. Therefore, you would not get an exclusion from wages. Instead, you would get a deduction on one of the following Form 1040 schedules: Schedule C, line 14; Schedule E, line 19 or 28; or Schedule F, line 15. To claim the deduction, you must use Form 2441.

The amount you can exclude or deduct is limited to the smallest of:

1. The total amount of dependent care benefits you received during the year,

2. The total amount of qualified expenses you incurred during the year,

3. Your earned income,

4. Your spouse's earned income, or

5. $5,000 ($2,500 if married filing separately).

Disability Pensions

If you retired on disability, you must include in income any disability pension you receive under a plan that is paid for by your employer.

You must report your taxable disability payments as wages on line 7 of Form 1040 or Form 1040A until you reach minimum retirement age. Minimum retirement age generally is the age at which you can first receive a pension or annuity if you are not disabled.

> **TIP:** You may be entitled to a tax credit if you were permanently and totally disabled when you retired.

Beginning on the day after you reach minimum retirement age, payments you receive are taxable as a pension or annuity. Report the payments on Form 1040, lines 16a and 16b, or on Form 1040A, lines 12a and 12b. See Publication 575, Pension and Annuity Income.

Terrorist attacks. Do not include in your income disability payments you receive for injuries incurred as a direct result of terrorist attacks directed against the United States (or its allies), whether outside or within the United States. However, you must include in your income any amounts that you received that you would have received in retirement had you not become disabled as a result of a terrorist attack.

> **TIP:** Contact the company or agency making these payments if it incorrectly reports your payments as taxable income to the IRS on Form 1099-R, Distributions From Pensions, Annuities, Retirement or Profit-Sharing Plans, IRAs, Insurance Contracts, etc., to request that it re-issue the form to report some or all of these payments as nontaxable income on Form W-2, box 12 (under code J), or Form 1099-R, box 1, but not in box 2a. If income taxes are being incorrectly withheld from these payments, you may also submit Form W-4P, Withholding Certificate for Pension or Annuity Payments, to the company or agency to stop the withholding of income taxes from the payments.

Disability payments you receive for injuries not incurred as a direct result of a terrorist attack, or for illnesses or diseases not resulting from an injury incurred as a direct result of a terrorist attack, cannot be excluded from your income under this provision, but may be excludable for other reasons as described in this publication.

Retirement and profit-sharing plans. If you receive payments from a retirement or profit-sharing plan that does not provide for disability retirement, do not treat the payments as a disability pension. The payments must be reported as a pension or annuity.

Accrued leave payment. If you retire on disability, any lump-sum payment you receive for accrued annual leave is a salary payment. The payment is not a disability payment. Include it in your income in the tax year you receive it.

Military and Government Disability Pensions

Generally, you must report disability pensions as income, but do not include certain military and government disability pensions.

VA disability benefits. Do not include disability benefits you receive from the Department of Veterans Affairs (VA) in your gross income. If you are a military retiree and do not receive your disability benefits from the VA,

Do not include in your income any veterans' benefits paid under any law, regulation, or administrative practice administered by the VA. These include:

- Education, training, and subsistence allowances;

- Disability compensation and pension payments for disabilities paid to veterans or their families;

- Grants for homes designed for wheelchair living;

- Grants for motor vehicles for veterans who lost their sight or the use of their limbs;

- Veterans' insurance proceeds and dividends paid to veterans or their beneficiaries, including the proceeds of a veteran's endowment policy paid before death;

- Interest on insurance dividends left on deposit with the VA;

- Benefits under a dependent-care assistance program;

- The death gratuity paid to a survivor of a member of the Armed Forces who died after September 10, 2001; or

- Payments made under the VA's compensated work therapy program.

Other Payments

You may receive other payments that are related to your disability. The following payments are not taxable.

- Benefit payments from a public welfare fund, such as payments due to blindness.

- Workers' compensation for an occupational sickness or injury if paid under a workers' compensation act or similar law.

- Compensatory (but not punitive) damages for physical injury or physical sickness.

- Disability benefits under a "no-fault" car insurance policy for loss of income or earning capacity as a result of injuries.

- Compensation for permanent loss or loss of use of a part or function of your body, or for your permanent disfigurement.

Long-Term Care Insurance

Long-term care insurance contracts generally are treated as accident and health insurance contracts. Amounts you receive from them (other than policyholder dividends or premium refunds) generally are excludable from income as amounts received for personal injury or sickness.

Accelerated Death Benefits

You can exclude from income accelerated death benefits you receive on the life of an insured individual if certain requirements are met. Accelerated death benefits are amounts received under a life insurance contract before the death of the insured. These benefits also include amounts received on the sale or assignment of the contract to a viatical settlement provider. This exclusion applies only if the insured was a terminally ill individual or a chronically ill individual.

Itemized Deductions

If you file Form 1040, to lower your taxable income you generally can claim the standard deduction or itemize your deductions, such as medical expenses, using Schedule A (Form 1040). For impairment-related work expenses, use the appropriate business form (1040 Schedules: C, C-EZ, E, and F; Form 2106, Employee Business Expenses; or Form 2106-EZ, Unreimbursed Employee Business Expenses).

Medical Expenses

When figuring your deduction for medical expenses, you can generally include medical and dental expenses you pay for yourself, your spouse, and your dependents.

Medical expenses are the cost of diagnosis, cure, mitigation, treatment, or prevention of disease and the costs for treatments affecting any part or function of the body. They include the costs of equipment, supplies, diagnostic devices, and transportation for needed medical care and payments for medical insurance.

You can deduct only the amount of your medical and dental expenses that is more than 10% (7.5% if you or your spouse were born before January 2, 1949) of your adjusted gross income shown on Form 1040, line 38.

The following list highlights some of the medical expenses you can include in figuring your medical expense deduction.

- Artificial limbs, contact lenses, eyeglasses, and hearing aids.

- The part of the cost of Braille books and magazines that is more than the price of regular printed editions.

- Cost and repair of special telephone equipment for hearing-impaired persons.

- Cost and maintenance of a wheelchair or a three-wheel motor vehicle commercially known as an "autoette."

- Cost and care of a guide dog or other animal aiding a person with a physical disability.

- Costs for a school that furnishes special education if a principal reason for using the school is its resources for relieving a mental or physical disability. This includes the cost of teaching Braille and lip reading and the cost of remedial language training to correct a condition caused by a birth defect.

- Premiums for qualified long-term care insurance, up to certain amounts.

- Improvements to a home that do not increase its value if the main purpose is medical care. An example is constructing entrance or exit ramps.

> **TIP:** Improvements that increase a home's value, if the main purpose is medical care, may be partly included as a medical expense.

Impairment-Related Work Expenses

If you are disabled, you can take a business deduction for expenses that are necessary for you to be able to work. If you take a business deduction for these impairment-related work expenses, they are not subject to the 10% (7.5% if you or your spouse is age 65 or older) limit that applies to medical expenses.

You are disabled if you have:

- A physical or mental disability (for example, blindness or deafness) that functionally limits your being employed; or

- A physical or mental impairment (including, but not limited to, a sight or hearing impairment) that substantially limits one or more of your major life activities, such as performing manual tasks, walking, speaking, breathing, learning, or working.

Impairment-related expenses defined. Impairment-related expenses are those ordinary and necessary business expenses that are:

- Necessary for you to do your work satisfactorily;

- For goods and services not required or used, other than incidentally, in your personal activities; and

- Not specifically covered under other income tax laws.

Tax Credits

This heading highlights three tax credits which may lower your tax due and may be refundable.

Child and Dependent Care Credit

If you pay someone to care for your dependent under age 13 or your spouse or dependent who is not able to care for themselves, you may be able to get a credit of up to 35% of your expenses. To qualify, you must pay these expenses so you can work or look for work. The care must be provided for:

1. Your qualifying child who is your dependent and who was under age 13 when the care was provided;

2. Your spouse who was not physically or mentally able to care for themselves and lived with you for more than half the year; or

3. A person who was not physically or mentally able to care for themselves, lived with you for more than half the year, and either:

    *   Was your dependent, or

    *   Would have been your dependent except that:

4. He or she received gross income of $3,950 or more,

    *   He or she filed a joint return, or

    *   You, or your spouse if filing jointly, could be claimed as a dependent on someone else's 2014 return.

You can claim the credit on Form 1040 or 1040A. You cannot claim the credit on Form 1040EZ or Form 1040NR-EZ. You figure the credit on Form 2441.

Credit for the Elderly or the Disabled

You may be able to claim this credit if you are a U.S. citizen or a resident alien and either of the following apply.

*   You were 65 or older at the end of 2014.

*   You were under 65 at the end of 2014, and retired on permanent or total disability.

You can claim the credit on Form 1040 or 1040A. You figure the credit on Schedule R, Credit for the Elderly or the Disabled.

Chapter 49

Preparing for the Future: End-of-Life Planning

Chapter Contents

Section 49.1

Frequently Asked Questions about End-of-Life Care

This section includes excerpts from "End of Life, Frequently Asked Questions," NIHSeniorHealth, March 2014.

What is end-of-life care?

End-of-life care is the broad term used to describe the special support and attention given during the period leading up to death, when the goals of care focus on comfort and quality of life. It may include hospice care and palliative care.

Where is end-of-life care provided?

End-of-life care can be provided in many places, including at home, in hospice care centers, in nursing homes, and in hospitals/critical care units.

What are some tips to help a dying person get relief from pain?

Here are some tips to help a dying person get effective pain relief.

- Help the dying person describe the pain in as much detail as possible, including where it is, what it feels like, how long it lasts, when it started, what makes it better, and what makes it worse.

- Help the dying person keep a record to track the pain. You may want to use a number from 0 to 10 to describe the pain, with 10 being the worst pain the dying person can imagine and 0 being no pain at all.

- When the dying person cannot communicate her or his pain or other symptoms, watch for and record other cues such as grimacing or agitation, which may signal the person needs symptom relief.

What pain medications are typically used near the end-of-life?

Pain medications typically used near the end of life include opiates such as morphine, hydrocodone, and oxycodone, which are used to treat serious pain that is not relieved by drugs such as acetaminophen (also known as Tylenol®) or ibuprofen (also known as Advil® or Motrin®). Tylenol® or Advil® are often given along with morphine or other opiates to treat the underlying causes of a patient's pain, such as inflammation.

What kinds of physical discomfort might a dying person face?

Signs and symptoms of physical discomfort in a dying person may include

- pain
- breathing problems
- digestive problems
- skin problems
- feeling too hot or cold

- fatigue
- distress
- dementia
- delirium

If a dying person has dementia, how could that affect his or her behavior?

A person with moderate to severe dementia may not be able to think well enough to do normal activities, such as getting dressed or eating. The person may lose the ability to solve problems or control emotions. The personality may change and the person may eventually become nonresponsive.

If a dying person has delirium, how could that affect his or her behavior?

Delirium is a confused mental state that causes changes in awareness and behavior and may come and go during the day. A person with delirium may also have problems with

- attention
- thinking and memory

- hallucinations, either hearing or seeing people or things that are not there

- emotion

- judgment

- muscle control

- sleeping and waking

A person near the end of life may experience delirium. It is common in the last 24–48 hours of life due to organ failure.

What mental or emotional issues might a dying person face?

Mental or emotional issues faced by a dying person might include depression, anxiety, or fear. Encouraging the person to talk about feelings, either with a close friend, family member, or counselor, could be helpful. Some counselors specialize in talking about end-of-life issues. If the depression or anxiety is severe, medicine might provide relief.

What are some ways to address a dying person's mental and emotional distress?

Here are some ways to address a dying person's mental and emotional distress.

- **Be there.** Don't avoid spending time with someone who is dying.

- **Offer reassurance**. If the dying person is worried about who will take care of things, be present with them and listen to his or her concerns.

- **Make physical contact**. Simple acts like holding hands, a touch, or a gentle massage can help a dying person feel connected to those he or she loves.

- **Respect visiting preferences**. Schedule visits in accordance with the dying person's preferences. Some people enjoy being surrounded by many visitors at once, creating a party-like atmosphere. Others may prefer quiet moments with just one or two people at a time.

- **Consider using music**. Experts suggest that when death is very near, music at low volume and soft lighting are soothing. Music can help improve mood, lessen pain, and relax a dying person. Music may also evoke memories those present can share.

- **Reduce noise**. Keep distracting noises like televisions and radios to a minimum, unless the dying person requests them.

What are tips on communicating with a dying person?

When you come into a dying person's room, identify yourself and let the person know you've come to see him or her. Always talk to, not about, the person who is dying.

Ask someone to write down what is said at this time -- both by and to the dying person. In time, these words might serve as a comfort to family and friends. People who are looking for ways to help may welcome the chance to aid the family by writing down what is said.

There may come a time when a dying person who has been confused suddenly seems clear-minded. Take advantage of these moments, understanding that they may be only temporary and are not necessarily a sign that he or she is getting better.

What is palliative care?

Palliative care is comprehensive treatment of the discomfort, symptoms, and stress of serious illness, whatever the diagnosis. It works with a patient's main treatment and can be given along with all other medical care. The main goal of palliative care is to improve quality of life. It focuses not just on a patient's physical and medical needs, but also his or her emotional, social, and spiritual concerns. It also provides support to the patient's family.

Palliative care is not just for people who might die soon. It is a resource for anyone with a long-term chronic disease such as heart failure, chronic obstructive pulmonary disease (COPD), cystic fibrosis, HIV/AIDS, and Parkinson's disease. Palliative care can be provided in any setting, including hospitals, nursing homes, outpatient palliative care clinics, other specialized clinics, or at home. All Veterans Health Administration hospitals now have a palliative care program.

The organized services available through palliative care can also be helpful to any older person having a lot of general discomfort and disability late in life. Palliative care can also help patients, family members, and health care providers talk through treatment and care decisions.

What is hospice care?

Hospice care provides comprehensive comfort care to the dying person as well as support to his or her family. Attempts to cure the person's illness are stopped. Candidates for hospice care are people with a serious illness who a health care provider thinks has less than 6 months to live. The goal of hospice is to relieve symptoms and make a dying person as comfortable as possible, maintaining that person's quality of life and dignity.

Hospice care does not provide 24-hour, around-the-clock nursing care, so many patients are cared for by family members, hired caregivers, or nursing home staff in between visits from hospice care providers. Hospice care can be provided in the home, at an assisted living facility or nursing home, or in a hospital.

Some people think a health care provider's suggestion to consider hospice means death is very near, but that is not always the case. Sometimes people do not start hospice care soon enough to take full advantage of the help it offers.

What end-of-life services can be provided at home?

End-of-life services for at-home care include a variety of services. The dying person's health care provider will arrange for new services, adjust treatments, and order medicines as needed. If the patient is coming home from a hospital, a hospital discharge planner may help you plan how best to provide palliative care in the home.

Arranging for special equipment, such as a hospital bed, and hiring a home health aide can also help make caring for a dying person at home easier and more comfortable.

Personal and home health aides—also called homemakers, caregivers, companions, and personal attendants—help with activities of daily living such as bathing, dressing, and feeding, and making sure a dying person is safe. They can also provide housekeeping services such as doing laundry, changing bed linens, food shopping, and cooking.

What type of care is provided at a nursing home?

Nursing homes, also called skilled nursing facilities, provide a wide range of health and personal care services. These services typically include nursing care, 24-hour supervision, three meals a day, and assistance with everyday activities. Rehabilitation services such as physical, occupational, and speech therapy are also available.

What type of care is provided at an in-patient hospice center?

In general, hospice is not tied to a specific place, but can be provided in the home, at an assisted living facility or nursing home, or in a hospital.

There are also in-patient hospice centers, which typically admit only patients with difficult-to-manage symptoms who are actively dying.

The average stay in an in-patient hospice center is typically just a few days. If a patient improves, he or she is usually discharged to home hospice or a long-term care facility such as a nursing home.

What type of care is provided in a hospital intensive care unit (ICU)?

In a hospital intensive care unit (ICU), specially trained staff (often called intensivists) can do everything medically possible to keep someone alive. Patients in an ICU usually require technology to support life. They are attached to monitors to measure their heart rate, breathing, blood pressure, and other vital signs. They often have various pumps and machines to deliver fluids, food, oxygen, and medicines. They require constant care by skilled nurses, doctors, therapists, and other clinicians.

ICU technologies are intended to maintain life while the body heals. However, it is important to know that being in the ICU may only prolong the dying process.

What are advance directives and who should have them?

Advance directives are instructions that let others know the type of care you want if you are seriously ill or dying. They typically include a living will, a health care proxy, a Do Not Resuscitate (DNR) order, and/or Physician Orders for Life-Sustaining Treatment (POLST).

A health care power of attorney is a document that names the person who will make medical decisions for you if you cannot make them yourself.

A living will records your wishes for medical treatment near the end of life. It spells out what life-sustaining treatment you do or do not want if you are terminally ill, permanently unconscious, or in the final stage of a fatal illness.

A Do-Not-Resuscitate (DNR) order tells health care providers not to perform cardiopulmonary resuscitation (CPR) or other life-support procedures if your heart stops or if you stop breathing. A DNR order is signed by a health care provider and put in your medical chart. Hospitals and long-term care facilities have DNR forms that a staff member can help you fill out. You do not have to have a DNR order.

A document similar to the DNR is the Physician Orders for Life-Sustaining Treatment (POLST) form. Created specifically for patients with serious, advanced illness, a POLST form provides standing, actionable medical orders concerning end-of-life care. Patients can create a POLST by discussing their treatment options with a health care professional, who then signs the form. Research shows patients using a POLST form are more likely to have their end-of-life care wishes honored.

What resources do people use to pay for end-of-life care?

To pay for end-of-life care, people rely on a variety of payment sources including personal funds, government health insurance programs such as Medicare and Medicaid, and private financing options such as long-term care insurance.

How are costs for nursing home care covered?

Because nursing homes cost so much—thousands of dollars a month—most people who live in them for more than six months cannot pay the entire bill on their own. Instead, they "spend down" their resources until they qualify for Medicaid. There are rules for spending down resources. Nursing home care generally costs more than home-based care unless you need extensive services at home.

How are costs for palliative care covered?

Two government health insurance programs, Medicare and Medicaid, help pay for palliative care. Standard Medicare Part B and, depending on the state, Medicaid cover certain palliative treatments and medications, as well as visits from palliative care specialists and social workers.

If you are eligible for Medicare or Medicaid, the palliative care provider (the organization offering you the services) will bill Medicare or Medicaid for services provided. (Not all states participate, or participate fully, in Medicaid.)

How are costs for hospice care covered?

Medicare covers many different hospice services, including nursing care, medical equipment, and social work services, and pays nearly all of their costs. Eligible patients are those who have been certified by a doctor and hospice medical director to have six months or less to live.

The Medicaid Hospice Benefit is identical to Medicare's benefit in states where it is offered. Some states impose limitations on the length of time coverage is offered or who is considered eligible, however, so it is important to check with your state's Department of Health or Agency on Aging. Some private health insurance plans also cover hospice care.

What are common health care questions that may come up as a patient nears the end of life?

These are common health care questions that may come up as a patient nears the end of life.

* Should life support be used?

* What if the patient's heart stops beating?

* What if breathing or feeding tubes are suggested?

* Should the patient be sedated?

* Should antibiotics be used?

* What if the patient has a pacemaker?

* Does the medical staff know the patient's wishes?

* Will refusing treatment cause the family legal trouble?

* What if a health care provider disagrees with family members?

* What if a health care provider is unfamiliar with the family's views about dying?

What is respite care and how can it help caregivers?

Respite care temporarily relieves people of the responsibility of caring for a person who is dying. A person can receive respite care in a variety of settings, including homes, adult day centers and nursing homes. Respite care providers can ease the day-to-day demands of caregiving by assisting with bathing, giving medicines, housecleaning, and other tasks. Respite care allows you to have a break while knowing that the dying person is being well cared for.

What community-based services can caregivers turn to for help?

Community-based services are designed to promote the health, well-being, and independence of older adults. These services can also supplement the supportive activities of family caregivers. Such services often offer companionship visits, help around the house, meal programs, caregiver respite, adult day care services, and transportation.

How can caregivers enlist the help of friends and family?

Family and friends often want to help caregivers, but they may be uncertain of what kind of help is needed. Be prepared to ask for help with specific tasks, such as grocery shopping, sitting with the dying person while you rest, bringing over a meal, doing the laundry or babysitting.

Consider the interests of family and friends—if someone you know enjoys reading, ask him or her to read aloud to your loved one. Someone who enjoys cooking may be happy to prepare an extra serving for you.

What are some common signs that death is near?

Common signs that death is near include

- shortness of breath (known as dyspnea)

- depression

- anxiety

- tiredness and sleepiness

- mental confusion

- constipation or incontinence

- nausea

- refusal to eat or drink

- parts of the body (hands, arms, feet, legs) becoming cool to the touch and/or darker or blue-colored

Each of these signs, taken alone, does not mean someone is dying. But when many are experienced by someone with a serious illness or declining health, it suggests a person is nearing the end of life.

What should you do right after someone dies?

Immediately following death, nothing has to be done. Take the time you need to grieve. Some people want to stay in the room with the body, while others prefer to leave. How long you stay depends on where death happens and if you wish to observe any special customs based on your religious, cultural, or ethnic background.

If you choose to leave the room, you may want to have someone make sure the body is lying flat before the joints become stiff and cannot be moved. Known as rigor mortis, this stiffness sets in during the first hours after death.

You may have several people you wish to notify, who might want to come see the body before it is moved. Some people ask a member of the community or a spiritual counselor to come as well.

How is a death certified?

As soon as possible, the death must be "pronounced" by someone in authority, like the health care provider in a hospital or nursing home or a hospice nurse. This person fills out the forms certifying the cause, time, and place of death. If death happens at home without hospice, talk to the health care provider, local medical examiner (coroner), local health department, or funeral home representative to find out how to proceed.

Pronouncing the death makes it possible for an official death certificate to be prepared. A death certificate is a legal form necessary for many reasons, such as filing a life insurance claim and settling financial and property issues.

What are some common signs of grief?

Common signs of grief include feeling sad, lost, and alone. You may experience grief as a mental, physical, social, and/or emotional reaction.

- **Mental reactions** can include having trouble concentrating and making decisions.

- **Physical reactions** can include sleeping problems, changes in appetite, physical problems, or illness.

- **Social reactions** can include avoiding the people, places, and activities you enjoyed with the person you lost.

- **Emotional reactions** can include cycling repeatedly through feelings of numbness, disbelief, anger, and despair. You may cry more easily. It's common to have rollercoaster emotions for a while.

It's a good idea to wait for a while before making big decisions like moving or changing jobs when you are grieving.

What resources are available to help with grief?

There are many resources to help people cope with grief. They include support from family and friends, hospice providers, and bereavement support groups. Short-term talk therapy with a counselor (individual or group) and visits with a representative of your religious community may also help you move through the grieving process and come to terms with your loss.

Section 49.2

Wills, Advance Directives, and Other Documents Associated with End-of-Life Planning

This section includes excerpts from "Advance Care Planning," National Institute on aging (NIA), August 12, 2015; text from "Getting Your Affairs in Order," National Institute on aging (NIA), January 22, 2015; and text from "Legal and Financial Planning for People with Alzheimer's Disease Fact Sheet," National Institute on aging (NIA), January 22, 2015.

Advance Care Planning

Advance care planning is not just about old age. At any age, a medical crisis could leave someone too ill to make his or her own healthcare decisions. Even if you are not sick now, making healthcare plans for the future is an important step toward making sure you get the medical care you would want, even when doctors and family members are making the decisions for you.

More than one out of four older Americans face questions about medical treatment near the end of life but are not capable of making those decisions. This tip sheet will discuss some questions you can think about now and describe ways to share your wishes with others. Write them down or at least talk about them with someone who would make the decisions for you. Knowing how you would decide might take some of the burden off family and friends.

What Is Advance Care Planning?

Advance care planning involves learning about the types of decisions that might need to be made, considering those decisions ahead of time, and then letting others know about your preferences, often by putting them into an *advance directive*. An advance directive is a legal document that goes into effect **only** if you are incapacitated and unable to speak for yourself. This could be the result of disease or severe injury—no matter how old you are. It helps others know what type of medical care you want. It also allows you to express your values and desires related to end-of-life care. You might think of an advance directive as a living document—one that you can adjust as your situation changes because of new information or a change in your health.

Medical Research and Advance Care Planning

Medical research plays an important role in the health of Americans of all ages. Because of advances in medicine and in public health, Americans are living longer and staying healthier as they grow older. The National Institute on Aging (NIA) supports much of the research around the country that looks at how people age and how to improve their health in their later years. NIA is part of the National Institutes of Health (NIH), the nation's medical research agency.

Some NIA-supported research focuses on advance care planning, including examining why people might complete advance directives and the effect of these directives on end-of-life care. In one study, for example, scientists funded by NIA found that advance directives can make a difference and that people who document their preferences in this way are more likely to get the care they prefer at the end of life than people who do not.

Decisions That Could Come Up Near Death

Sometimes when doctors believe a cure is no longer possible and you are dying, decisions must be made about the use of emergency treatments to keep you alive. Doctors can use several artificial or mechanical ways to try to do this. Decisions that might come up at this time relate to:

- CPR (cardiopulmonary resuscitation)
- ventilator use

- artificial nutrition (tube feeding) or artificial hydration (intravenous fluids)

- comfort care

CPR. CPR (cardiopulmonary resuscitation) might restore your heartbeat if your heart stops or is in a life-threatening abnormal rhythm. The heart of a young, otherwise healthy person might resume beating normally after CPR. An otherwise healthy older person, whose heart is beating erratically or not beating at all, might also be helped by CPR. CPR is less likely to work for an older person who is ill, can't be successfully treated, and is already close to death. It involves repeatedly pushing on the chest with force, while putting air into the lungs. This force has to be quite strong, and sometimes ribs are broken or a lung collapses. Electric shocks known as defibrillation and medicines might also be used as part of the process.

Ventilator use. Ventilators are machines that help you breathe. A tube connected to the ventilator is put through the throat into the trachea (windpipe) so the machine can force air into the lungs. Putting the tube down the throat is called intubation. Because the tube is uncomfortable, medicines are used to keep you sedated (unconscious) while on a ventilator. If you can't breathe on your own after a few days, a doctor may perform a tracheotomy or "trach" (rhymes with "make"). During this bedside surgery, the tube is inserted directly into the trachea through a hole in the neck. For long-term help with breathing, a trach is more comfortable, and sedation is not needed. People using such a breathing tube aren't able to speak without special help because exhaled air goes out of the trach rather than past their vocal cords.

Artificial nutrition or artificial hydration. A feeding tube and/or intravenous (IV) liquids are sometimes used to provide nutrition when a person is not able to eat or drink. These measures can be helpful if you are recovering from an illness. However, if you are near death, these could actually make you more uncomfortable. For example, IV liquids, which are given through a plastic tube put into a vein, can increase the burden on failing kidneys. Or if the body is shutting down near death, it is not able to digest food properly, even when provided through a feeding tube. At first, the feeding tube is threaded through the nose down to the stomach. In time, if tube feeding is still needed, the tube is surgically inserted into the stomach.

Comfort care. Comfort care is anything that can be done to soothe you and relieve suffering while staying in line with your wishes. Comfort care includes managing shortness of breath; offering ice chips for dry mouth; limiting medical testing; providing spiritual and emotional counseling; and giving medication for pain, anxiety, nausea, or constipation. Often this is done through hospice, which may be offered in the home, in a hospice facility, in a skilled nursing facility, or in a hospital. With hospice, a team of healthcare providers works together to provide the best possible quality of life in a patient's final days, weeks, or months. After death, the hospice team continues to offer support to the family. Learn more about providing comfort at the end of life.

Getting Started

Start by thinking about what kind of treatment you do or do not want in a medical emergency. It might help to talk with your doctor about how your present health conditions might influence your health in the future. For example, what decisions would you or your family face if your high blood pressure leads to a stroke?

If you don't have any medical issues now, your family medical history might be a clue to thinking about the future. Talk to your doctor about decisions that might come up if you develop health problems similar to those of other family members.

In considering treatment decisions, your personal values are key. Is your main desire to have the most days of life, or to have the most life in your days? What if an illness leaves you paralyzed or in a permanent coma and you need to be on a ventilator? Would you want that?

What makes life meaningful to you? You might want doctors to try CPR if your heart stops or to try using a ventilator for a short time if you've had trouble breathing, if that means that, in the future, you could be well enough to spend time with your family. Even if the emergency leaves you simply able to spend your days listening to books on tape or gazing out the window watching the birds and squirrels compete for seeds in the bird feeder, you might be content with that.

But, there are many other scenarios. Here are a few. What would you decide?

- If a stroke leaves you paralyzed and then your heart stops, would you want CPR? What if you were also mentally impaired by a stroke—does your decision change?

- What if you develop dementia, don't recognize family and friends, and, in time, cannot feed yourself? Would you want a feeding tube used to give you nutrition?

- What if you are permanently unconscious and then develop pneumonia? Would you want antibiotics and a ventilator used?

For some people, staying alive as long as medically possible is the most important thing. An advance directive can help make sure that happens.

Your decisions about how to handle any of these situations could be different at age 40 than at age 85. Or they could be different if you have an incurable condition as opposed to being generally healthy. An advance directive allows you to provide instructions for these types of situations and then to change the instructions as you get older or if your viewpoint changes.

Do you or a family member have Alzheimer's disease?

Many people are unprepared to deal with the legal and financial consequences of a serious illness such as Alzheimer's disease. Advance planning can help people with Alzheimer's and their families clarify their wishes and make well-informed decisions about health care and financial arrangements.

Making Your Wishes Known

There are two elements in an advance directive—a living will and a durable power of attorney for health care. There are also other documents that can supplement your advance directive or stand alone. You can choose which documents to create, depending on how you want decisions to be made. These documents include:

- living will

- durable power of attorney for health care

- other documents discussing DNR (do not resuscitate) orders, organ and tissue donation, dialysis, and blood transfusions

Living will. A living will is a written document that helps you tell doctors how you want to be treated if you are dying or permanently unconscious and cannot make decisions about emergency treatment. In a living will, you can say which of the procedures described above you would want, which ones you wouldn't want, and under which conditions each of your choices applies.

Durable power of attorney for health care. A durable power of attorney for health care is a legal document naming a healthcare proxy, someone to make medical decisions for you at times when you might not be able to do so. Your proxy, also known as a surrogate or agent, should be familiar with your values and wishes. This means that he or she will be able to decide as you would when treatment decisions need to be made. A proxy can be chosen in addition to or instead of a living will. Having a healthcare proxy helps you plan for situations that cannot be foreseen, like a serious auto accident.

A durable power of attorney for health care enables you to be more specific about your medical treatment than a living will.

Some people are reluctant to put specific health decisions in writing. For them, naming a healthcare agent might be a good approach, especially if there is someone they feel comfortable talking with about their values and preferences.

Other advance care planning documents. You might also want to prepare separate documents to express your wishes about a single medical issue or something not already covered in your advance directive. A living will usually covers only the specific life-sustaining treatments discussed earlier. You might want to give your healthcare proxy specific instructions about other issues, such as blood transfusion or kidney dialysis. This is especially important if your doctor suggests that, given your health condition, such treatments might be needed in the future.

Two medical issues that might arise at the end of life are DNR orders and organ and tissue donation.

A DNR (do not resuscitate) order tells medical staff in a hospital or nursing facility that you do not want them to try to return your heart to a normal rhythm if it stops or is beating unevenly. Even though a living will might say CPR is not wanted, it is helpful to have a DNR order as part of your medical file if you go to a hospital. Posting a DNR next to your bed might avoid confusion in an emergency situation. Without a DNR order, medical staff will make every effort to restore the normal rhythm of your heart. A non-hospital DNR will alert emergency medical personnel to your wishes regarding CPR and other measures to restore your heartbeat if you are not in the hospital. A similar document that is less familiar is called a DNI (do not intubate) order. A DNI tells medical staff in a hospital or nursing facility that you do not want to be put on a breathing machine.

Organ and tissue donation allows organs or body parts from a generally healthy person who has died to be transplanted into people who need them. Commonly, the heart, lungs, pancreas, kidneys, corneas, liver, and skin are donated. There is no age limit for organ and tissue donation. You can carry a donation card in your wallet. Some states allow you to add this decision to your driver's license. Some people also include organ donation in their advance care planning documents. At the time of death, family may be asked about organ donation. If those close to you, especially your proxy, know how you feel about organ donation, they will be ready to respond.

What about Pacemakers and ICDs?

Some people have pacemakers to help their hearts beat regularly. If you have one and are near death, it may not necessarily keep you alive. But, you might have an ICD (implantable cardioverter-defibrillator) placed under your skin to shock your heart back into regular beatings if the rhythm becomes irregular. If other life-sustaining measures are not used, the ICD may also be turned off. You need to state in your advance directive what you want done if the doctor suggests it is time to turn it off.

Selecting Your Healthcare Proxy

If you decide to choose a proxy, think about people you know who share your views and values about life and medical decisions. Your proxy might be a family member, a friend, your lawyer, or someone with whom you worship. It's a good idea to also name an alternate proxy. It is especially important to have a detailed living will if you choose not to name a proxy.

You can decide how much authority your proxy has over your medical care—whether he or she is entitled to make a wide range of decisions or only a few specific ones. Try not to include guidelines that make it impossible for the proxy to fulfill his or her duties. For example, it's probably not unusual for someone to say in conversation, "I don't want to go to a nursing home," but think carefully about whether you want a restriction like that in your advance directive. Sometimes, for financial or medical reasons, that may be the best choice for you.

Of course, check with those you choose as your healthcare proxy and alternate before you name them officially. Make sure they are comfortable with this responsibility.

Making It Official

Once you have talked with your doctor and have an idea of the types of decisions that could come up in the future and whom you would like as a proxy, if you want one at all, the next step is to fill out the legal forms detailing your wishes. A lawyer can help but is not required. If you decide to use a lawyer, don't depend on him or her to help you understand different medical treatments. That's why you should start the planning process by talking with your doctor.

Many states have their own advance directive forms. Your local Area Agency on Aging can help you locate the right forms.

Some states want your advance directive to be witnessed; some want your signature notarized. A notary is a person licensed by the state to witness signatures. You might find a notary at your bank, post office, or local library, or call your insurance agent. Some notaries charge a fee.

Some people spend a lot of time in more than one state—for example, visiting children and grandchildren. If that's your situation also, you might consider preparing an advance directive using forms for each state—and keep a copy in each place, too.

Future Directions

A number of states are developing or starting to use an advance care planning form known as POLST (Physician Orders for Life-Sustaining Treatment) or MOLST (Medical Orders for Life-Sustaining Treatment). These forms serve in addition to your advance directive. They make it possible for you to provide more detailed guidance about your medical care preferences. Your doctor will talk with you and/or your family for guidance, but the form is filled out by the doctor or, sometimes, a nurse practitioner or physician's assistant. Once signed by your doctor, this form has the force of any other medical order. These forms are often printed on brightly colored paper so they are easily found in a medical or hospital file. Check with your state department of health to find out if this form is available where you live.

After You Set Up Your Advance Directive

There are key people who should be told that you have an advance directive. Give copies to your healthcare proxy and alternate proxy. Give your doctor a copy for your medical records. Tell key family members and friends where you keep a copy. If you have to go to the hospital, give staff there a copy to include in your records. Because you might change your advance directive in the future, it's a good idea to keep track of who receives a copy.

Review your advance care planning decisions from time to time—for example, every 10 years, if not more often. You might want to revise your preferences for care if your situation or your health changes. Or, you might want to make adjustments if you receive a serious diagnosis; if you get married, separated, or divorced; if your spouse dies; or if something happens to your proxy or alternate. If your preferences change, you will want to make sure your doctor, proxy, and family know about them.

Still Not Sure?

What happens if you have no advance directive or have made no plans and you become unable to speak for yourself? In such cases, the state where you live will assign someone to make medical decisions on your behalf. This will probably be your spouse, your parents if they are available, or your children if they are adults. If you have no family members, the state will choose someone to represent your best interests.

Always remember, an advance directive is only used if you are in danger of dying and need certain emergency or special measures to keep you alive but are not able to make those decisions on your own. An advance directive allows you to continue to make your wishes about medical treatment known.

Plan for the Future

Steps for Getting Your Affairs in Order

- **Put your important papers and copies of legal documents in one place.** You could set up a file, put everything in a desk or dresser drawer, or just list the information and location of papers in a notebook. If your papers are in a bank safe deposit box, keep copies in a file at home. Check each year to see if there's anything new to add.

- **Tell a trusted family member or friend where you put all your important papers.** You don't need to tell this friend or family member about your personal affairs, but someone should know where you keep your papers in case of an emergency. If you don't have a relative or friend you trust, ask a lawyer to help.
- **Give consent in advance for your doctor or lawyer to talk with your caregiver as needed.** There may be questions about your care, a bill, or a health insurance claim. Without your consent, your caregiver may not be able to get needed information. You can give your okay in advance to Medicare, a credit card company, your bank, or your doctor. You may need to sign and return a form.

Legal Documents

There are many different types of legal documents that can help you plan how your affairs will be handled in the future. Many of these documents have names that sound alike, so make sure you are getting the documents you want. Also, State laws do vary, so find out about the rules, requirements, and forms used in your State.

- **Wills** and **trusts** let you name the person you want your money and property to go to after you die.

- **Advance directives** let you make arrangements for your care if you become sick. There are two ways to do this:

- A **living will** gives you a say in your health care if you are too sick to make your wishes known. In a living will, you can state what kind of care you do or don't want. This can make it easier for family members to make tough healthcare decisions for you.

- A **durable power of attorney for health care** lets you name the person you want to make medical decisions for you if you can't make them yourself. Make sure the person you name is willing to make those decisions for you.

For legal matters, there are two ways to give someone you trust the power to act in your place:

- A **general power of attorney** lets you give someone else the authority to act on your behalf, but this power will end if you are unable to make your own decisions.

- A **"durable" power of attorney** allows you to name someone to act on your behalf for any legal task, but it stays in place if you become unable to make your own decisions.

What Exactly Is an "Important Paper"?

The answer to this question may be different for every family. The following lists can help you decide what is important for you. Remember, this is a starting place. You may have other information to add. For example, if you have a pet, you will want to include the name and address of your vet.

Please remember to include complete information about the following:

Personal records

- Full legal name

- Social Security number

- Legal residence

- Date and place of birth

- Names and addresses of spouse and children

- Location of birth and death certificates and certificates of marriage, divorce, citizenship, and adoption

- Employers and dates of employment

- Education and military records

- Names and phone numbers of religious contacts

- Memberships in groups and awards received

- Names and phone numbers of close friends, relatives, and lawyer or financial advisor

- Names and phone numbers of doctors

- Medications taken regularly

- Location of living will and other legal documents

Financial records

- Sources of income and assets (pension from your employer, IRAs, 401(k)s, interest, etc.)

- Social Security and Medicare information

- Insurance information (life, health, long-term care, home, car) with policy numbers and agents' names and phone numbers

- Names of your banks and account numbers (checking, savings, credit union)

- Investment income (stocks, bonds, property) and stockbrokers' names and phone numbers

- Copy of most recent income tax return

- Location of most up-to-date will with an original signature

- Liabilities, including property tax—what is owed, to whom, when payments are due

- Mortgages and debts—how and when paid

- Location of original deed of trust for home and car title and registration

- Credit and debit card names and numbers

- Location of safe deposit box and key

Resources

You may want to talk with a lawyer about setting up a general power of attorney, durable power of attorney, joint account, trust, or advance directive. Be sure to ask about the fees before you make an appointment.

You should be able to find a directory of local lawyers at your library, or you can contact your local bar association for lawyers in your area. An informed family member may be able to help you manage some of these issues.

Legal and Financial Planning for People with Alzheimer's Disease

Many people are unprepared to deal with the legal and financial consequences of a serious illness such as Alzheimer's disease. Legal

487

and medical experts encourage people recently diagnosed with a serious illness—particularly one that is expected to cause declining mental and physical health—to examine and update their financial and health care arrangements as soon as possible. Basic legal and financial instruments, such as a will, a living trust, and advance directives, are available to ensure that the person's late-stage or end-of-life health care and financial decisions are carried out.

A complication of diseases such as Alzheimer's is that the person may lack or gradually lose the ability to think clearly. This change affects his or her ability to participate meaningfully in decision making and makes early legal and financial planning even more important. Although difficult questions often arise, advance planning can help people with Alzheimer's and their families clarify their wishes and make well-informed decisions about health care and financial arrangements.

When possible, advance planning should take place soon after a diagnosis of early-stage Alzheimer's disease while the person can participate in discussions. People with early-stage disease are often capable of understanding many aspects and consequences of legal decision making. However, legal and medical experts say that many forms of planning can help the person and his or her family even if the person is diagnosed with later-stage Alzheimer's.

There are good reasons to retain the services of a lawyer when preparing advance planning documents. For example, a lawyer can help interpret different State laws and suggest ways to ensure that the person's and family's wishes are carried out. It's important to understand that laws vary by State, and changes in situation—for instance, a divorce, relocation, or death in the family—can influence how documents are prepared and maintained.

Legal, Financial, and Health Care Planning Documents

When families begin the legal planning process, there are a number of strategies and legal documents they need to discuss. Depending on the family situation and the applicable State laws, some or all of the following terms and documents may be introduced by the lawyer hired to assist in this process. Broadly speaking, these documents can be divided into two groups:

- documents that communicate the health care wishes of someone who may no longer be able to make health care decisions

- documents that communicate the financial management and estate plan wishes of someone who may no longer be able to make financial decisions

Advance Directives for Health Care

Advance directives for health care are documents that communicate the health care wishes of a person with Alzheimer's disease. These decisions are then carried out after the person no longer can make decisions. In most cases, these documents must be prepared while the person is legally able to execute them.

A **Living Will** records a person's wishes for medical treatment near the end of life. It may do the following:

- specify the extent of life-sustaining treatment and major health care the person wants

- help a terminal patient die with dignity

- protect the physician or hospital from liability for carrying out the patient's instructions

- specify how much discretion the person gives to his or her proxy (discussed below) about end-of-life decisions

A **Durable Power of Attorney for Health Care** designates a person, sometimes called an agent or proxy, to make health care decisions when the person with Alzheimer's disease no longer can do so. Depending on State laws and the person's preferences, the proxy might be authorized to:

- refuse or agree to treatments

- change health care providers

- remove the person from an institution

- decide about making organ donations

- decide about starting or continuing life support (if not specified in a living will)

- decide whether the person with Alzheimer's will end life at home or in a facility

- have access to medical records

A **Do Not Resuscitate (DNR) Order** instructs health care professionals not to perform cardiopulmonary resuscitation if a person's heart stops or if he or she stops breathing. A DNR order is signed by a doctor and put in a person's medical chart.

Advance Directives for Financial and Estate Management

Advance directives for financial and estate management must be created while the person with Alzheimer's still can make these decisions (sometimes referred to as "having legal capacity" to make decisions). These directives may include some or all of the following:

A **Will** indicates how a person's assets and estate will be distributed upon death. It also can specify:

- arrangements for care of minors
- gifts
- trusts to manage the estate
- funeral and/or burial arrangements

Medical and legal experts say that the newly diagnosed person with Alzheimer's and his or her family should move quickly to make or update a will and secure the estate.

A **Durable Power of Attorney for Finances** names someone to make financial decisions when the person with Alzheimer's disease no longer can. It can help people with the disease and their families avoid court actions that may take away control of financial affairs.

A **Living Trust** provides instructions about the person's estate and appoints someone, called the trustee, to hold title to property and funds for the beneficiaries. The trustee follows these instructions after the person no longer can manage his or her affairs.

The person with Alzheimer's disease also can name the trustee as the health care proxy through the durable power of attorney for health care.

A living trust can:

- include a wide range of property
- provide a detailed plan for property disposition
- avoid the expense and delay of probate (in which the courts establish the validity of a will)
- state how property should be distributed when the last beneficiary dies and whether the trust should continue to benefit others

Who Can Help?

Health Care Providers—Health care providers cannot act as legal or financial advisors, but they can encourage planning discussions between patients and their families. Qualified clinicians can also guide patients, families, the care team, attorneys, and judges regarding the patient's ability to make decisions.

Elder Law Attorneys (ELAs)—An ELA helps older people and families:

- interpret State laws

- plan how their wishes will be carried out

- understand their financial options

- learn how to preserve financial assets while caring for a loved one

The National Academy of Elder Law Attorneys and the American Bar Association can help families find qualified ELAs.

Geriatric Care Managers—Geriatric care managers (GCMs) are trained social workers or nurses who can help people with Alzheimer's disease and their families:

- discuss difficult topics and complex issues

- address emotional concerns

- make short- and long-term plans

- evaluate in-home care needs

- select care personnel

- coordinate medical services

- evaluate other living arrangements

- provide caregiver stress relief

Other Advance Planning Advice

Start discussions early. The rate of decline differs for each person with Alzheimer's disease, and his or her ability to be involved in planning will decline over time. People in the early stages of the disease may be able to understand the issues, but they may also be defensive or emotionally unable to deal with difficult questions. Remember that

491

not all people are diagnosed at an early stage. Decision making already may be difficult when Alzheimer's disease is diagnosed.

Review plans over time. Changes in personal situations—such as a divorce, relocation, or death in the family—and in State laws can affect how legal documents are prepared and maintained. Review plans regularly, and update documents as needed.

Reduce anxiety about funeral and burial arrangements. Advance planning for the funeral and burial can provide a sense of peace and reduce anxiety for both the person with Alzheimer's and the family.

Resources for Low-Income Families

Families who cannot afford a lawyer still can do advance planning. Samples of basic health planning documents can be downloaded from State government websites. Area Agency on Aging officials may provide legal advice or help. Other possible sources of legal assistance and referral include State legal aid offices, the State bar association, local nonprofit agencies, foundations, and social service agencies.

Summary

Facing Alzheimer's disease can be emotionally wrenching for all concerned. A legal expert and members of the health care team can help the person and family address end-of-life issues. Advance health care and financial planning can help people diagnosed with Alzheimer's and their families confront tough questions about future treatment, caregiving, and legal arrangements.

Table 49.1. Overview of Medical Documents

Medical Document	How It Is Used
Living Will	Describes and instructs how the person wants end-of-life health care managed
Durable Power of Attorney for Health Care	Gives a designated person the authority to make health care decisions on behalf of the person with Alzheimer's disease
Do Not Resuscitate (DNR) Form	Instructs health care professionals not to perform CPR in case of stopped heart or stopped breathing

Table 49.2. Overview of Legal/Financial Document Documents

Legal/Financial Document	How It Is Used
Will	Indicates how a person's assets and estate will be distributed among beneficiaries after his/her death
Durable Power of Attorney for Finances	Gives a designated person the authority to make legal/financial decisions on behalf of the person with Alzheimer's disease
Living Trust	Gives a designated person (trustee) the authority to hold and distribute property and funds for the person with Alzheimer's disease

Part Seven

Additional Help and Information

Chapter 50

Glossary of Terms Related to Disabilities

access: An individual's ability to obtain appropriate health care services. Barriers to access can be financial, geographic, organizational, and sociological. Efforts to improve access often focus on providing/improving health coverage.

accessibility: Removal of barriers that would hinder a person with a disability from entering, functioning, and working within a facility. Required restructuring of the facility cannot cause undue hardship for the employer.

activities of daily living (ADLs): Basic personal activities that include bathing, eating, dressing, mobility, transferring from bed to chair, and using the toilet. ADLs are used to measure how dependent a person may be on requiring assistance in performing any or all of these activities.

acute care: Recovery is the primary goal of acute care. Physician, nurse, or other skilled professional services are typically required and usually provided in a doctor's office or hospital. Acute care is usually short term.

adult day care: A daytime community-based program for functionally impaired adults that provides a variety of health, social, and related support services in a protective setting.

adult day services: Services provided during the day at a community-based center. Programs address the individual needs of functionally

---

This glossary contains terms excerpted from documents produced by several sources deemed reliable.

or cognitively impaired adults. These structured, comprehensive programs provide social and support services in a protective setting during any part of a day, but not 24-hour care. Many adult day service programs include health-related services.

Alzheimer's disease: Progressive, degenerative form of dementia that causes severe intellectual deterioration. First symptoms are impaired memory, followed by impaired thought and speech, and finally complete helplessness.

amblyopia: Amblyopia is the medical term used when the vision of one eye is reduced because it fails to work properly with the brain. The eye itself looks normal, but for various reasons the brain favors the other eye. This condition is also sometimes called lazy eye.

analgesics: Medications designed to relieve pain. Pure analgesics do not have an effect on inflammation.

arthritis: Disease involving inflammation of a joint or joints in the body.

assistive devices: Refer to any device that helps a person with hearing loss or a voice, speech, or language disorder to communicate. These terms often refer to devices that help a person to hear and understand what is being said more clearly or to express thoughts more easily. With the development of digital and wireless technologies, more and more devices are becoming available to help people with hearing, voice, speech, and language disorders communicate more meaningfully and participate more fully in their daily lives.

audiologists: Assess and treat persons with hearing and related disorders. May fit hearing aids and provide auditory training. May perform research related to hearing problems.

biopsy: A procedure in which tissue or other material is removed from the body and studied for signs of disease.

birth defect: Conditions that cause structural changes in one or more parts of the body; are present at birth; and have an adverse effect on health, development, or functional ability.

bronchiectasis: Is a condition in which damage to the airways causes them to widen and become flabby and scarred. The airways are tubes that carry air in and out of your lungs.

cardiomyopathy: Refers to diseases of the heart muscle. In cardiomyopathy, the heart muscle becomes enlarged, thick, or rigid. In rare cases, the muscle tissue in the heart is replaced with scar tissue.

caregiver: Person who provides support and assistance with various activities to a family member, friend, or neighbor. May provide emotional or financial support, as well as hands-on help with different tasks. Caregiving may also be done from long distance.

carrier: An individual who doesn't have a disease but has one normal gene and one gene for a genetic disorder and is therefore capable of passing this disease to her or his children.

cartilage: A tough, elastic tissue that covers the ends of the bones where they meet to form joints. In rheumatoid arthritis, the inflamed synovium invades and destroys joint cartilage.

cerebral: Relating to the two hemispheres of the human brain.

chromosomes: Genetic structures that contains DNA.

cochlear implant: A cochlear implant is an implanted electronic hearing device, designed to produce useful hearing sensations to a person with severe to profound nerve deafness by electrically stimulating nerves inside the inner ear.

cognitive impairment: Deterioration or loss of intellectual capacity that requires continual supervision to protect the person or others, as measured by clinical evidence and standardized tests that reliably measure impairment in the area of (1) short- or long-term memory, (2) orientation as to person, place and time, or (3) deductive or abstract reasoning. Such loss in intellectual capacity can result from Alzheimer disease or similar forms of dementia.

complementary and alternative medicine (CAM): Refers to products and practices that are not currently part of "mainstream" medicine. Technically, complementary medicine is used along with standard medical care, and alternative medicine is used in place of standard care. The term "integrative medicine" has also been used in recent years to refer to care that blends both mainstream and alternative practices.

cyclothymic disorder (cyclothymia): A mild form of bipolar disorder. People with cyclothymia have episodes of hypomania as well as mild depression for at least two years. However, the symptoms do not meet the diagnostic requirements for any other type of bipolar disorder.

developmental delay: Behind schedule in reaching the milestones of early childhood development.

developmental disability: A disability that originates before age 18, can be expected to continue indefinitely, and constitutes a substantial handicap to the disabled's ability to function normally.

diabetic retinopathy: Diabetic retinopathy is a complication of diabetes and a leading cause of blindness. It occurs when diabetes damages the tiny blood vessels inside the retina in the back of the eye.

disability: The limitation of normal physical, mental, social activity of an individual. There are varying types (functional, occupational, learning), degrees (partial, total), and durations (temporary, permanent) of disability.

electromyography: A recording and study of the electrical properties of skeletal muscle.

epilepsy: Called a seizure disorder. A person is diagnosed with epilepsy when they have had two or more seizures.

glaucoma: Glaucoma is a group of diseases that can damage the eye's optic nerve and result in vision loss and blindness.

group home: Also called adult care home or board and care home. Residence that offers housing and personal care services for 3 to 16 residents. Services (such as meals, supervision, and transportation) are usually provided by the owner or manager. May be single family home.

Hirschsprung disease: Is a disease of the large intestine that causes severe constipation or intestinal obstruction.

home health care: Includes a wide range of health-related services such as assistance with medications, wound care, intravenous (IV) therapy, and help with basic needs such as bathing, dressing, mobility, etc., which are delivered at a person's home.

impairment: Any loss or abnormality of psychological, physiological, or anatomical function.

individualized education program (IEP): A written statement of the educational program designed to meet a child's individual needs. Every child who receives special education services must have an IEP.

independent living facility: A facility (house, apartment, etc.) in which a child/youth is permitted to live or reside independently without a paid caretaker.

inflammation: A reaction of body tissues to injury or disease, typically marked by five signs: swelling, redness, heat, pain, and loss of function.

learning disability: A disorder in one or more of the basic psychological processes involved in understanding or in using language, spoken or written, which may manifest itself in an imperfect ability to listen, think, speak, read, write, spell, or to do mathematical calculation. The term includes such conditions as perceptual handicaps, brain injury, and minimal brain dysfunction.

long-term care: Range of medical and/or social services designed to help people who have disabilities or chronic care needs. Services may be short- or long-term and may be provided in a person's home, in the community, or in residential facilities (e.g., nursing homes or assisted living facilities).

lupus: A chronic inflammatory condition in which the immune system attacks the skin, joints, heart, lungs, blood, kidneys and brain. Also called systemic lupus erythematosus.

neuron: Also known as a nerve cell; the structural and functional unit of the nervous system. A neuron consists of a cell body and its processes: an axon and one or more dendrites.

newborn screening: Newborn screening identifies conditions that can affect a child's long-term health or survival. Early detection, diagnosis, and intervention can prevent death or disability and enable children to reach their full potential.

nursing home: Facility licensed by the state to offer residents personal care as well as skilled nursing care on a 24-hour-a-day basis. Provides nursing care, personal care, room and board, supervision, medication, therapies, and rehabilitation. Rooms are often shared, and communal dining is common.

occupational therapist: A health professional who teaches ways to protect joints, minimize pain, perform activities of daily living, and conserve energy.

occupational therapy: Designed to help patients improve their independence with activities of daily living through rehabilitation, exercises, and the use of assistive devices. May be covered in part by Medicare.

oppositional defiant disorder (ODD): Oppositional Defiant Disorder is one of the most common disorders occurring with ADHD. ODD usually starts before age eight, but no later than early adolescence.

osteoporosis: Is a disease in which the bones become weak and are more likely to break. People with osteoporosis most often break bones in the hip, spine, and wrist.

otolaryngologist: An otolaryngologist is a physician specializing in ear, nose, and throat disorders who can determine the cause of hearing loss as well as possible treatment options.

palsy: Paralysis, or the lack of control over voluntary movement.

pancreatitis: Is inflammation of the pancreas. Pancreatitis can be acute or chronic. Either form is serious and can lead to complications. In severe cases, bleeding, infection, and permanent tissue damage may occur.

paralysis: The inability to control movement of a part of the body.

paraplegia: A condition involving paralysis of the legs.

physical therapy: Designed to restore/improve movement and strength in people whose mobility has been impaired by injury and disease. May include exercise, massage, water therapy, and assistive devices. May be covered in part by Medicare.

pneumothorax: Air or gas can build up in the pleural space. When this happens, it's called a pneumothorax. A lung disease or acute lung injury can cause a pneumothorax. Some lung procedures also can cause a pneumothorax. Examples include lung surgery, drainage of fluid with a needle, bronchoscopy, and mechanical ventilation.

presbycusis: One form of hearing loss, presbycusis, comes on gradually as a person ages. Presbycusis can occur because of changes in the inner ear, auditory nerve, middle ear, or outer ear.

rehabilitation: The combined and coordinated use of medical, social, educational, and vocational measures for training or retaining individuals disabled by disease or injury to the highest possible level of functional ability. Several different types of rehabilitation are distinguished—vocational, social, psychological, medical, and educational.

respite care: Service in which trained professionals or volunteers come into the home to provide short-term care (from a few hours to a few days) for a disabled person to allow caregivers some time away from their caregiving role.

response to intervention (RTI) strategies: Are tools that enable educators to target instructional interventions to children's areas of specific need as soon as those needs become apparent.

rubella (also known as German measles): A viral infection that can damage the nervous system of an unborn baby if a mother contracts the disease during pregnancy.

sacral: Refers to the part of the spine in the hip area.

special education: A type of education some children with disabilities receive. Special education may include specially designed instruction in classrooms, at home, or in private or public institutions, and may be accompanied by related services such as speech therapy, occupational and physical therapy, psychological counseling, and medical diagnostic services necessary to the child's education.

speech-language pathologists (sometimes called speech therapists): Assess, diagnose, treat, and help to prevent communication and swallowing disorders in patients. Speech, language, and swallowing disorders result from a variety of causes, such as a stroke, brain injury, hearing loss, developmental delay, a cleft palate, cerebral palsy, or emotional problems.

support groups: Groups of people who share a common bond (e.g., caregivers) who come together on a regular basis to share problems and experiences. May be sponsored by social service agencies, senior centers, religious organizations, as well as organizations such as the Alzheimer's Association.

tinnitus: Tinnitus is commonly described as a ringing in the ears, but it also can sound like roaring, clicking, hissing, or buzzing. It may be soft or loud, high pitched or low pitched. You might hear it in either one or both ears.

traumatic brain injury (TBI): A form of acquired brain injury, occurs when a sudden trauma causes damage to the brain. TBI can result when the head suddenly and violently hits an object, or when an object pierces the skull and enters brain tissue.

X-ray: A procedure in which low-level radiation is passed through the body to produce a picture called a radiograph. X-rays of joints affected by rheumatoid arthritis are used to determine the degree of joint destruction.

yoga: Yoga is a mind and body practice with origins in ancient Indian philosophy. The various styles of yoga typically combine physical postures, breathing techniques, and meditation or relaxation.

Chapter 51

Directory of Organizations That Help People with Disabilities

Government Agencies That Provide Information about Disabilities

Administration on Aging (AOA)
One Massachusetts Ave., N.W.
Washington, DC 20001
Phone: 202-619-0724
Fax: 202-357-3555
Website:www.aoa.gov
E-mail: aoainfo@aoa.hhs.gov

Agency for Healthcare Research and Quality (AHRQ)
Office of Communications and Knowledge Transfer
540 Gaither Rd., Ste. 2000
Rockville, MD 20850
Phone: 301-427-1104
Website: www.ahrq.gov

Centers for Disease Control and Prevention (CDC)
1600 Clifton Rd.
Atlanta, GA 30333
Toll-Free: 800-CDC-INFO (232-4636)
Toll-Free TTY: 888-232-6348
Phone: 404-639-3311
Website: www.cdc.gov
E-mail: cdcinfo@cdc.gov

Resources in this chapter were compiled from several sources deemed reliable; all contact information was verified and updated in October 2015. The information under the heading "Americans with Disabilities Act National Network Centers" is excerpted from "Disability and Rehabilitation Research and Related Projects," U.S. Department of Education (ED), April 20, 2015.

Disability.gov
Website: www.disability.gov

Eldercare Locator
Toll-Free: 800-677-1116
Website: www.eldercare.gov
E-mail: eldercarelocator@n4a.org

Federal Communications Commission (FCC)
445 12th St., S.W.
Washington, DC 20554
Toll-Free: 888-225-5322
Toll-Free TTY: 888-835-5322
Toll-Free Fax: 866-418-0232
Website: www.fcc.gov
E-mail: fccinfo@fcc.gov

Healthfinder®
National Health Information Center
P.O. Box 1133
Washington, DC 20013-1133
Toll-Free: 800-336-4797
Fax: 301-984-4256
Website: www.healthfinder.gov
E-mail: healthfinder@nhic.org

Library of Congress (LOC)
101 Independence Ave., SE
Washington, DC 20540
Phone: 202-707-5000
Website: www.loc.gov

National Cancer Institute (NCI)
NCI Office of Communications and Education, Public Inquiries Office
6116 Executive Blvd., Ste. 300
Bethesda, MD 20892-8322
Toll-Free: 800-4-CANCER (422-6237)
Toll-Free TTY: 800-332-8615
Website: www.cancer.gov
E-mail: cancergovstaff@mail.nih.gov

National Center for Health Statistics (NCHS)
3311 Toledo Rd.
Hyattsville, MD 20782
Toll-Free: 800-232-4636
Website: www.cdc.gov/nchs
E-mail: cdcinfo@cdc.gov

National Council on Disability (NCD)
1331 F St., N.W., Ste. 850
Washington, DC 20004
Phone: 202-272-2004
TTY: 202-272-2074
Fax: 202-272-2022
Website: www.ncd.gov
E-mail: ncd@ncd.gov

National Heart, Lung and Blood Institute (NHLBI)
NHLBI Health Information Center
P.O. Box 30105
Bethesda, MD 20824-0105
Phone: 301-592-8573
TTY: 240-629-3255
Fax: 240-629-3246
Website: www.nhlbi.nih.gov
E-mail: nhlbiinfo@nhlbi.nih.gov

National Institute of Arthritis and Musculoskeletal and Skin Diseases (NIAMS)
Information Clearinghouse, National Institutes of Health
1 AMS Cir.
Bethesda, MD 20892-3675
Toll-Free: 877-22-NIAMS (226-4267)
Phone: 301-495-4484
TTY: 301-565-2966
Fax: 301-718-6366
Website: www.niams.nih.gov
E-mail: NIAMSInfo@mail.nih.gov

National Institute of Child Health and Human Development (NICHD)
P.O. Box 3006
Rockville, MD 20847
Toll-Free: 800-370-2943
Toll-Free TTY: 888-320-6942
Toll-Free Fax: 866-760-5947
Website: www.nichd.nih.gov
E-mail: NICHDInformation ResourceCenter@mail.nih.gov

National Institute of Dental and Craniofacial Research (NIDCR)
National Institutes of Health
Bethesda, MD 20892-2190
Toll-Free: 866-232-4528
Phone: 301-496-4261
Fax: 301-480-4098
Website: www.nidcr.nih.gov
E-mail: nidcrinfo@mail.nih.gov

National Institute of Mental Health (NIMH)
Science Writing, Press, and Dissemination Branch
6001 Executive Blvd.
Rm. 8184, MSC 9663
Bethesda, MD 20892-9663
Toll-Free: 866-615-6464
Toll-Free TTY: 866-415-8051
Phone: 301-443-4513
TTY: 301-443-8431
Fax: 301-443-4279
Website: www.nimh.nih.gov
E-mail: nimhinfo@nih.gov

National Institute of Neurological Disorders and Stroke (NINDS)
NIH Neurological Institute
P.O. Box 5801
Bethesda, MD 20824
Toll-Free: 800-352-9424
Phone: 301-496-5751
TTY: 301-468-5981
Website: www.ninds.nih.gov
E-mail: braininfo@ninds.nih.gov

National Institute on Aging (NIA)
Bldg. 31, Rm. 5C27, 31 Center Dr.
MSC 2292
Bethesda, MD 20892
Toll-Free TTY: 800-222-4225
Phone: 301-496-1752
Fax: 301-496-1072
Website: www.nia.nih.gov

National Institute on Deafness and Other Communication Disorders (NIDCD)
National Institutes of Health
31 Center Dr.
MSC 2320
Bethesda, MD 20892-2320
Toll-Free: 800-241-1044
Toll-Free TTY: 800-241-1055
Phone: 301-496-7243
Fax: 301-402-0018
Website: www.nidcd.nih.gov
E-mail: nidcdinfo@nidcd.nih.gov

National Institute on Disability and Rehabilitation Research (NIDRR)
U.S. Department of Education
400 Maryland Ave., S.W.
Mailstop PCP-6038
Washington, DC 20202
Phone: 202-245-7640 (Voice and TTY)
Fax: 202-245-7323 or 202-245-7643
Website: www.ed.gov/about/offices/list/osers/nidrr

National Technical Information Service (NTIS)
5301 Shawnee Rd.
Alexandria, VA 22312
Toll-Free: 800-553-NTIS (553-6847)
Phone: 703-605-6000
Website: www.ntis.gov
E-mail: info@ntis.gov

National Women's Health Information Center (NWHIC)
Office on Women's Health
200 Independence Ave., S.W.
Rm. 712E
Washington, DC 20201
Toll-Free: 800-994-9662
Toll-Free TDD: 888-220-5446
Phone: 202-690-7650
Fax: 202-205-2631
Website: www.womenshealth.gov

Office of Disability Employment Policy (ODEP)
U.S. Department of Labor
200 Constitution Ave., N.W.
Washington, DC 20210
Toll-Free: 866-4-USA-DOL (487-2365)
Toll-Free TTY: 877-889-5627
Website: www.dol.gov/odep

U.S. Department of Education (ED)
400 Maryland Ave., S.W.
Washington, DC 20202
Toll-Free: 800-USA-LEARN (872-5327)
Toll-Free TTY: 800-437-0833
Website: www2.ed.gov

U.S. Department of Justice
Civil Rights Division, Disability
Rights Section–NYA
950 Pennsylvania Ave., N.W.
Washington, DC 20530
Toll-Free: 800-514-0301
Toll-Free TTY: 800-514-0383
Fax: 202-307-1197
Website: www.ada.gov

U.S. Department of Veterans Affairs (VA)
810 Vermont Ave., N.W.
Washington, DC 20420
Toll-Free: 800-827-1000
Website: www.va.gov

U.S. Equal Employment Opportunity Commission (EEOC)
131 M St., N.E.
Washington, DC 20507
Toll-Free: 800-669-4000
Toll-Free TTY: 800-669-6820
Phone: 202-663-4900
Website: www.eeoc.gov
E-mail: info@eeoc.gov

U.S. Food and Drug Administration (FDA)
10903 New Hampshire Ave.
Silver Spring, MD 20993
Toll-Free: 888-INFO-FDA
(463-6332)
Website: www.fda.gov

U.S. Government Printing Office (GPO)
732 North Capitol St., N.W.
Washington, DC 20401-0001
Toll-Free: 866-512-1800
Phone: 202-512-1800
Fax: 202-512-2104
Website: www.gpo.gov
E-mail: ContactCenter@gpo.gov

U.S. National Library of Medicine (NLM)
8600 Rockville Pike
Bethesda, MD 20894
Toll-Free: 888-FIND-NLM
(346-3656)
Toll-Free TDD: 800-735-2258
Phone: 301-594-5983
Fax: 301-402-1384
Website: www.nlm.nih.gov
E-mail: custserv@nlm.nih.gov

U.S. Social Security Administration (SSA)
Office of Public Inquiries,
Windsor Park Bldg.
6401 Security Blvd.
Baltimore, MD 21235
Toll-Free: 800-772-1213
Toll-Free TTY: 800-325-0778
Website: www.ssa.gov

Private Agencies That Provide Information about Disabilities

AARP
601 E St., N.W.
Washington DC 20049
Toll-Free: 888-OUR-AARP
(687-2277)
Toll-Free TTY: 877-434-7598
Website: www.aarp.org
E-mail: member@aarp.org

AbilityJobs
ABILITY Mail Center
P.O. Box 10878
Costa Mesa, CA 92627
Website: www.abilityjobs.com

Alzheimer's Association
225 North Michigan Ave.
Fl. 17
Chicago, IL 60601-7633
Toll-Free: 800-272-3900
Toll-Free Fax: 866-699-1246
Phone: 312-335-8700
TDD: 312-335-5886
Website: www.alz.org
E-mail: info@alz.org

Alzheimer's Foundation of America
322 Eighth Ave.
7th Fl.
New York, NY 10001
Toll-Free: 866-232-8484
Fax: 646-638-1546
Website: www.alzfdn.org
E-mail: info@alzfdn.org

American Academy of Family Physicians
P.O. Box 11210
Shawnee Mission, KS
66207-1210
Toll-Free: 800-274-2237
Phone: 913-906-6000
Fax: 913-906-6075
Website: www.aafp.org
E-mail: contactcenter@aafp.org

American Academy of Physical Medicine and Rehabilitation
9700 West Bryn Mawr Ave.
Ste. 200
Rosemont, IL 60018-5701
Phone: 847-737-6000
Fax: 847-737-6001
Website: www.aapmr.org
E-mail: info@aapmr.org

American Council of the Blind
2200 Wilson Blvd., Ste. 650
Arlington, VA 22201
Toll-Free: 800-424-8666
Phone: 202-467-5081
Fax: 703-465-5085
Website: www.acb.org
E-mail: info@acb.org

American Foundation for the Blind
2 Penn Plaza, Ste. 1102
New York, NY 10121
Toll-Free: 800-AFB-LINE
(232-5463)
Toll-Free Fax: 888-545-8331
Phone: 212-502-7600
Website: www.afb.org
E-mail: afbinfo@afb.net

American Geriatrics Society Foundation for Health in Aging
40 Fulton St., 18th Fl.
New York, NY 10118
Toll-Free: 800-563-4916
Phone: 212-755-6810
Website: www.healthinaging.org

American Heart Association National Center
7272 Greenville Ave.
Dallas, TX 75231
Toll-Free: 800-AHA-USA-1
(242-8721)
Website: www.heart.org

American Medical Association
515 North State St.
Chicago, IL 60654
Toll-Free: 800-621-8335
Website: www.ama-assn.org

American Parkinson Disease Association
135 Parkinson Ave.
Staten Island, NY 10305
Toll-Free: 800-223-2732
Phone: 718-981-8001
Fax: 718-981-4399
Website: www.apdaparkinson.org
E-mail: apda@apdaparkinson.org

American Printing House for the Blind
1839 Frankfort Ave.
P.O. Box 6085
Louisville, KY 40206-0085
Toll-Free: 800-223-1839
Phone: 502-895-2405
Fax: 502-899-2284
Website: www.aph.org
E-mail: info@aph.org

American Psychological Association
750 First St., N.E.
Washington, DC 20002-4242
Toll-Free: 800-374-2721
Phone: 202-336-5500
TDD/TTY: 202-336-6123
Website: www.apa.org

American Society on Aging
71 Stevenson St., Ste. 1450
San Francisco, CA 94105-2938
Toll-Free: 800-537-9728
Phone: 415-974-9600
Fax: 415-974-0300
Website: www.asaging.org
E-mail: info@asaging.org

American Speech-Language-Hearing Association
2200 Research Blvd.
Rockville, MD 20850-3289
Toll-Free: 800-638-8255
Phone: 301-296-5700
TTY: 301-296-5650
Fax: 301-296-8580
Website: www.asha.org
E-mail: actioncenter@asha.org

511

Amputee Coalition of America
900 East Hill Ave., Ste. 205
Knoxville, TN 37915-2566
Toll-Free: 888-AMP-KNOW
(888-267-5669)
Phone: 865-524-8772
TTY: 865-525-4512
Fax: 865-525-7917
Website: www.amputee-coalition.org

Amyotrophic Lateral Sclerosis Association
1275 K St., N.W., Ste. 1050
Washington, DC 20005
Toll-Free: 800-782-4747
Phone: 202-407-8580
Fax: 202-289-6801
Website: www.alsa.org
E-mail: alsinfo@alsa-national.org

The Arc
1660 L St., N.W., Ste. 301
Washington, DC 20036
Toll-Free: 800-433-5255
Phone: 202-534-3700
Fax: 202-534-3731
Website: www.thearc.org
E-mail: info@thearc.org

Arthritis Foundation
P.O. Box 7669
Atlanta, GA 30357-0669
Toll-Free: 800-283-7800
Website: www.arthritis.org

Assisted Living Federation of America
1650 King St., Ste. 602
Alexandria, VA 22314
Phone: 703-894-1805
Website: www.alfa.org
E-mail: info@ALFA.org

Associated Services for the Blind and Visually Impaired
919 Walnut St.
Philadelphia, PA 19107
Phone: 215-627-0600
Fax: 215-922-0692
Website: www.asb.org
E-mail: asbinfo@asb.org

Association of University Centers on Disabilities
1010 Wayne Ave., Ste. 920
Silver Spring, MD 20910
Phone: 301-588-8252
Fax: 301-588-2842
Website: www.aucd.org
E-mail: aucdinfo@aucd.org

Autism Society
4340 East-West Hwy, Ste. 350
Bethesda, MD 20814
Phone: 301-657-0881
Toll-Free: 800-3AUTISM (328-8476)
Website: www.autism-society.org

Birth Defect Research for Children, Inc.
976 Lake Baldwin Lan, Ste. 104
Orlando, FL 32814
Phone: 407-895-0802
Website: www.birthdefects.org
E-mail: staff@birthdefects.org

Brain Injury Association of America
1608 Spring Hill Rd., Ste. 110
Vienna, VA 22182
Toll-Free: 800-444-6443
Phone: 703-761-0750
Fax: 703-761-0755
Website: www.biausa.org
E-mail: braininjuryinfo@biausa.org

Brain Trauma Foundation
1 Broadway
6th Fl.
New York, NY 10017
Phone: 212-772-0608
Fax: 212-772-0357
Website: www.braintrauma.org

Cleveland Clinic
9500 Euclid Ave.
Cleveland, OH 44195
Toll-Free: 800-223-2273
TTY: 216-444-0261
Website: my.clevelandclinic.org

Cystic Fibrosis Foundation
6931 Arlington Rd.
2nd Fl.
Bethesda, MD 20814
Toll-Free: 800-FIGHT CF
(344-4823)
Phone: 301-951-4422
Fax: 301-951-6378
Website: www.cff.org
E-mail: info@cff.org

Easter Seals
233 South Wacker Dr., Ste. 2400
Chicago, IL 60606
Toll-Free: 800-221-6827
Phone: 312-726-6200
Fax: 312-726-1494
Website: www.easterseals.com

Family Caregiver Alliance
180 Montgomery St., Ste. 900
San Francisco, CA 94104
Toll-Free: 800-445-8106
Phone: 415-434-3388
Website: www.caregiver.org
E-mail: info@caregiver.org

Goodwill Industries
15810 Indianola Dr.
Rockville, MD 20855
Toll-Free: 800-741-0186
Website: www.goodwill.org
E-mail: contactus@goodwill.org

Job Accommodation Network
Toll-Free: 800-526-7234
Toll-Free TTY: 877-781-9403
Website: www.askjan.org
E-mail: jan@askjan.org

March of Dimes
1275 Mamaroneck Ave.
White Plains, NY 10605
Phone: 914-997-4488
Website: www.marchofdimes.
com

National Adult Day Services Association
1421 East Broad St., Ste. 425
Fuquay Varina, NC 27526
Toll-Free: 877-745-1440
Fax: 919-825-3945
Website: www.nadsa.org
E-mail: NADSAnews@gmail.com

National Alliance for Caregiving
4720 Montgomery Lane
2nd Fl.
Bethesda, MD 20814
Website: www.caregiving.org
E-mail: info@caregiving.com

National Association of the Deaf
8630 Fenton St., Ste. 820
Silver Spring, MD 20910
Phone: 301-587-1788
TTY: 301-587-1789
Fax: 301-587-1791
Website: www.nad.org

National Center for Learning Disabilities
381 Park Ave. S., Ste. 1401
New York, NY 10016
Toll-Free: 888-575-7373
Phone: 212-545-7510
Fax: 212-545-9665
Website: www.ncld.org

National Center of Physical Activity and Disability
1640 West Roosevelt Rd.
Chicago, IL 60608-6904
Toll-Free: 800-900-8086
Fax: 312-355-4058
Website: www.ncpad.org
E-mail: ncpad@uic.edu

National Consortium on Deaf-Blindness
345 North Monmouth Ave.
Monmouth, OR 97361
Toll-Free: 800-438-9376
Toll-Free TTY: 800-854-7013
Fax: 503-838-8150
Website: www.nationaldb.org
E-mail: info@nationaldb.org

National Down Syndrome Society
666 Broadway
8th Fl.
New York, NY 10012
Toll-Free: 800-221-4602
Fax: 212-979-2873
Website: www.ndss.org
E-mail: info@ndss.org

National Federation of the Blind
200 East Wells St.
Baltimore, MD 21230
Phone: 410-659-9314
Fax: 410-685-5653
Website: www.nfb.org
E-mail: pmaurer@nfb.org

National Hospice and Palliative Care Organization / National Hospice Foundation
1731 King St., Ste. 100
Alexandria, VA 22314
Toll-Free: 800-658-8898
Phone: 703-837-1500
Fax: 703-837-1233
Website: www.nhpco.org
E-mail: nhpco_info@nhpco.org

National Multiple Sclerosis Society
733 Third Ave.
3rd Fl.
New York, NY 10017
Toll-Free: 800-344-4867
Website: www. nationalmssociety.org

National Organization for Rare Disorders
55 Kenosia Ave.
P.O. Box 1968
Danbury, CT 06813-1968
Toll-Free: 800-999-6673
Phone: 203-744-0100
TDD: 203-797-9590
Fax: 203-798-2291
Website: www.rarediseases.org
E-mail: orphan@rarediseases.org

National Parkinson Foundation, Inc.
1501 N.W. 9th Ave., Bob Hope Rd.
Miami, FL 33136-1494
Toll-Free: 800-4PD-Info (473-4636) (Helpline)
Toll-Free: 800-327-4545 (National Headquarters)
Phone: 305-243-6666
Fax: 305-243-6073
Website: www.parkinson.org
E-mail: contact@parkinson.org

National Rehabilitation Information Center
8201 Corporate Dr., Ste. 600
Landover, MD 20785
Toll-Free: 800-346-2742
Phone: 301-459-5900
TTY: 301-459-5984
Fax: 301-459-4263
Website: www.naric.com
E-mail: naricinfo@heitechservices.com

National Respite Network and Resource Center
Website: www.archrespite.org

National Spinal Cord Injury Association
75-20 Astoria Blvd., Ste. 120
Jackson Heights, NY 11370
Toll-Free: 800-962-9629
Phone: 718-512-0010
Fax: 866-387-2196
Website: www.spinalcord.org
E-mail: info@spinalcord.org

National Stroke Association
9707 East Easter Lane, Ste. B
Centennial, CO 80112-3747
Toll-Free: 800-787-6537
Phone: 303-649-9299
Fax: 303-649-1328
Website: www.stroke.org
E-mail: info@stroke.org

Nemours Foundation Center for Children's Health Media
1600 Rockland Rd.
Wilmington, DE 19803
Phone: 302-651-4000
Website: www.kidshealth.org
E-mail: info@kidshealth.org

Parkinson's Disease Foundation
1359 Broadway, Ste. 1509
New York, NY 10018
Toll-Free: 800-457-6676
Phone: 212-923-4700
Fax: 212-923-4778
Website: www.pdf.org
E-mail: info@pdf.org

PsychCentral
55 Pleasant St., Ste. 207
Newburyport, MA 01950
Phone: 978-992-0008
Website: www.psychcentral.com
E-mail: talkback@psychcentral.
com

Rehabilitation Institute of Chicago
345 East Superior St.
Chicago, IL 60611
Toll-Free: 800-354-REHAB
(354-7342)
Phone: 312-238-1000
Website: www.ric.org

Spina Bifida Association
4590 MacArthur Blvd., N.W.
Ste. 250
Washington, DC 20007
Toll-Free: 800-621-3141
Phone: 202-944-3285
Fax: 202-944-3295
Website: www.
spinabifidaassociation.org
E-mail: sbaa@sbaa.org

United Cerebral Palsy
1660 L St., N.W., Ste. 700
Washington, DC 20036
Toll-Free: 800-872-5827
Phone: 202-776-0406
Fax: 202-776-0414
Website: www.ucp.org

United Spinal Association
75-20 Astoria Blvd., Ste. 120
Jackson Heights, NY 11370
Toll-Free: 800-404-2898
Phone: 718-803-3782
Fax: 718-803-0414
Website: www.unitedspinal.org
E-mail: info@unitedspinal.org

Very Special Arts
818 Connecticut Ave., N.W.
Ste. 600
Washington, DC 20006
Toll-Free: 800-933-8721
Phone: 202-628-2800
TDD: 202-737-0645
Fax: 202-429-0868
Website: www.vsarts.org

Visiting Nurses Associations of America
900 19th St., N.W.
Ste. 200
Washington, DC 20006
Phone: 202-384-1420
Fax: 202-384-1444
Website: www.vnaa.org
E-mail: vnaa@vnaa.org

Web Accessibility Initiative
MIT/CSAIL, Bldg. 32-G530, 32
Vassar St.
Bronx, NY 10471
Phone: 617-253-2613
Website: www.w3.org/WAI
E-mail: site-comments@w3.org

Americans with Disabilities Act National Network Centers

The Americans with Disabilities Act (ADA) prohibits discrimination against people with disabilities in employment, transportation, public accommodation, communications, and governmental activities. The ADA National Network offers training, technical assistance, information dissemination, and capacity building services on the Americans with Disabilities Act (ADA). The ADA National Network consists of 10 regional ADA National Network Centers located across the United States. The ADA National Network is not an enforcement or regulatory agency, but a helpful resource supporting the ADA's mission to "make it possible for everyone with a disability to live a life of freedom and equality."

New England ADA Center
Serves Region 1 (Connecticut, Maine, Massachusetts, New Hampshire, Rhode Island, and Vermont), Institute for Human Centered Design
180-200 Portland St.
First Fl.
Cambridge, MA 02139
Phone: 617-695-0085
Fax: 617-482-8099
Website: www. NewEnglandADA.org

Northeast ADA Center
Serves Region 2 (New Jersey, New York, Puerto Rico, and the U.S. Virgin Islands), Cornell University
201 Dolgen Hall
Boston, MA 02114
Phone: 607-225-6686
Fax: 607-255-2763
Website: www.dbtacnortheast. org

Mid-Atlantic ADA Center
Serves Region 3 (Delaware, District of Columbia, Maryland, Pennsylvania, Virginia, and West Virginia), TransCen, Inc.,
451 Hungerford Dr.
Ste. 700
Ithaca, NY 14853-3901
Phone: 301-217-0124
Fax: 301-217-0754
Website: www.adainfo.org

Great Lakes ADA Center
Serves Region 5 (Illinois, Indiana, Michigan, Minnesota, Ohio, and Wisconsin), University of Illinois/Chicago Department on Disability and Human Development
1640 West Roosevelt Rd.
Rm. 405
Rockville, MD 20850
Phone: 312-413-1407
Fax: 312-413-1856
Website: www.adagreatlakes.org

Southwest ADA Center

Serves Region 6 (Arkansas,
Louisiana, New Mexico,
Oklahoma, and Texas),
Independent Living Research
Utilization
2323 South Shepherd Blvd.
Ste. 1000
Chicago, IL 60608
Phone: 713-520-0232
Fax: 713-520-5785
Website: www.dlrp.org

Rocky Mountain ADA Center

Serves Region 8 (Colorado,
Montana, North Dakota, South
Dakota, Utah, and Wyoming),
Meeting the Challenge, Inc.
3630 Sinton Rd.
Ste. 103
Houston, TX 77019
Phone: 719-444-0268
Fax: 719-444-0269
Website: www.adainformation.
org

Pacific ADA Center

Serves Region 9 (Arizona,
California, Hawaii, Nevada, and
the Pacific Basin)
555 12th St.
Ste. 1030
Colorado Springs, CO 80907
Phone: 510-285-5600
Fax: 510-285-5614
Website: www.adapacific.org

Chapter 52

Directory of Organizations for Athletes with Disabilities

Organizations That Provide Information on Multiple Sports

Adaptive Sports Center
Toll-Free: 866-349-2296
Phone: 970-349-5075
Website: www.adaptivesports.org
E-mail: info@adaptivesports.org

Disabled Sports USA
Phone: 301-217-0960
Website: disabledsportsusa.org
E-mail: programs@dsusa.org

National Sports Center for the Disabled (NSCD)
Phone: 970-726-1540 or 303-316-1540
Website: www.nscd.org
E-mail: info@nscd.org

Partners for Access to the Woods (PAW)
Phone: 970-887-3435
Website: www.outdoors4all.org
E-mail: Partners4all@earthlink.net

Special Olympics
Toll-Free: 800-700-8585
Phone: 202-628-3630
Website: www.specialolympics.org
E-mail: info@specialolympics.org

SPLORE (Special Populations Learning Outdoor Recreation and Education)
Phone: 801-484-4128
Website: www.splore.org
E-mail: info@splore.org

Resources in this chapter were compiled from several sources deemed reliable; all contact information was verified and updated in October 2015.

*United States Association of
Blind Athletes (USABA)*
Phone: 719-630-0422
Website: www.usaba.org

*United States Paralympic
Team*
Phone: 719-866-2030
Website: www.usparalympics.
org
E-mail: paralympicinfo@usoc.org

*USA Deaf Sports Federation
(USADSF)*
Phone: 605-367-5760
TTY: 605-367-5761
Website: www.usdeafsports.org
E-mail: homeoffice@
usdeafsports.org

*Wheelchair & Ambulatory
Sports, USA*
Phone: 732-266-2634
Website: www.wsusa.org

Wilderness Inquiry
Toll-Free: 800-728-0719
Phone: 612-676-9400
TTY: 612-676-9475
Website: www.
wildernessinquiry.org
E-mail: info@wildernessinquiry.
org

World T.E.A.M. Sports
Phone: 855-987-8326
Website: www.worldteamsports.
org
E-mail: info@worldteamsports.
org

Organizations for Blind and Deaf Athletes

*American Blind Bowling
Association (ABBA)*
Website: www.abba1951.org
E-mail: president@abba1951.org

*American Blind Skiing
Foundation (ABSF)*
Website: www.absf.org
E-mail: absf@absf.org

*National Softball
Association for the Deaf*
Website: www.nsad.org
E-mail: commissioner@nsad.org

*Skating Athletes Bold at
Heart (SABAH)*
Phone: 716-362-9600
Website: www.sabahinc.org
E-mail: sabah@sabahinc.org

Ski for Light, Inc.
Phone: 612-827-3232
Website: www.sfl.org
E-mail: info@sfl.org

*United States Association of
Blind Athletes (USABA)*
Phone: 719-630-0422
Website: www.usaba.org

*United States Blind Golf
Association (USBGA)*
Website: www.blindgolf.com
E-mail: mjpopp@bellsouth.net

United States Deaf Cycling Association (USDCA)
Website: www.usdeafcycling.org

United States Deaf Ski and Snowboard Association (USDSSA)
Website: www.usdssa.org
E-mail: president@usdssa.org

United States Flag Football for the Deaf (USFFD)
Website: www.usffd.org

USA Deaf Soccer Association
Website: www.usdeafsoccer.com

USA Deaf Sports Federation (USADSF)
Phone: 605-367-5760
TTY: 605-367-5761
Website: www.usdeafsports.org
E-mail: homeoffice@usdeafsports.org

USA Deaf Track and Field
Website: www.usadtf.org
E-mail: info@usadtf.org

Organizations That Provide Information on Specific Sports

Access to Sailing
Website: www.accesstosailing.org

Achilles International
Phone: 212-354-0300
Website: www.achillesinternational.org
E-mail: info@achillesinternational.org

American Amputee Hockey Association (AAHA)
Phone: 781-297-1393
Website: www.amputeehockey.org.prod.sportngin.com

American Amputee Soccer Association
Website: www.ampsoccer.org

American Wheelchair Bowling Association (AWBA)
Website: www.awba.org
E-mail: info@awba.org

Dancing Wheels
Toll-Free: 800-901-8485
Phone: 440-266-1732
Website: www.gggreg.com/DW/pages/dancingwheels.htm
E-mail: gggregagy@aol.com

Fishing Has No Boundaries, Inc.
Toll-Free: 800-243-3462
Phone: 715-634-3185
Website: www.fhnbinc.org

Freedom's Wings International (FWI)
Toll-Free: 800-382-1197
Website: www.freedomswings.org
E-mail: rrfucci@earthlink.net

International Wheelchair Aviators
Phone: 817-229-4634
Website: www.wheelchairaviators.org
E-mail: wheelchairaviators@yahoo.com

International Wheelchair Basketball Federation (IWBF)
Website: www.iwbf.org

National Alliance for Accessible Golf
Phone: 703-299-4296
Website: www.accessgolf.org
E-mail: info@accessgolf.org

National Amputee Golf Association (NAGA)
Toll-Free: 800-633-6242
Website: www.nagagolf.org
E-mail: info@nagagolf.org

National Shooting Sports Foundation (NSSF)
Phone: 203-426-1320
Website: www.nssf.org
E-mail: info@nssf.org

National Wheelchair Basketball Association (NWBA)
Phone: 719-266-4082
Website: www.nwba.org

National Wheelchair Poolplayers Association (NWPA)
Website: www.nwpainc.org

Professional Association of Therapeutic Horsemanship (PATH) International
Toll-Free: 800-369-RIDE (369-7433)
Phone: 303-452-1212
Website: www.pathintl.org
E-mail: pathintl@pathintl.org

Physically Challenged Bowhunters of America, Inc. (PCBA)
Toll-Free: 855-247-7222
Website: www.pcba-inc.org

United Foundation for Disabled Archers (UFFDA)
Phone: 320-634-3660
Website: www.uffdaclub.com
E-mail: info@uffdaclub.com

United States Electric Wheelchair Hockey Association (U.S.EWHA)
Phone: 763-535-4736
Website: www.powerhockey.com
E-mail: info@powerhockey.com

United States Rowing
Toll-Free: 800-314-4ROW (314-4769)
Website: www.usrowing.org
E-mail: members@usrowing.org

United States Tennis Wheelchair
Website: www.usta.com

USA Swimming
Phone: 719-866-4578
Website: www.usa-swimming.org

USA Water Ski
Phone: 863-324-4341
Website: www.usawaterski.org
E-mail: usawaterski@usawaterski.org

Chapter 53

How Can I Get Help Finding and Paying for Assistive Technology?

Finding the right Assistive Technology (AT) to meet your needs doesn't have to be difficult. However, there is also the matter of paying for it once you determine what AT works for you. Fortunately, AT doesn't necessarily have to be expensive, and if your needs include some higher priced items, there are several local and national sources that may be able to help you pay for them.

Disability.gov's "Finding & Paying for Assistive Technology" section is a good place to start to find AT or adaptive devices, and resources to pay for them (select your state from the "Locations" menu on the left side of the page to find resources in your area). Disability.gov's "Paying for Prescription Drugs or Medical Equipment" section has additional information. Check out the resources below for more information.

Funding Sources:

State and Local Funding Sources:

Your state's Assistive Technology Financial Loan Program or Alternative Finance Program can help you find low-interest loans

---

The text in this chapter is excerpted from "How Can I Get Help Finding & Paying for Assistive Technology?" Disability.gov, June 23, 2014.

or other ways to pay for AT. Read "Applying for AT Loans" to learn more.

Your state's Vocational Rehabilitation Agency can help pay for AT if you need it for work-related or career training purposes.

Your local Independent Living Center (ILC) may be able to help you pay for AT devices or equipment, or refer you to programs that can.

Your local Easter Seals or United Cerebral Palsy (UCP) chapter may be able to provide assistance finding or paying for AT, or refer you to another organization that can.

Reuse and recycling of AT helps people with disabilities who need AT devices or adaptive equipment find them for free or reduced cost. It also keeps used AT devices out of landfills. The Pass It On Center website has a map of locations throughout the U.S. where you can find recycled AT for free or reduced cost, as well as a list of AT Exchange Networks.

Government Programs:

Medicare or Medicaid: Medicare may pay for AT or adaptive devices under certain circumstances. Call 1-800-MEDICARE (1-800-633-4227) for more information. You may also be able to pay for AT through a waiver from your state's Medicaid program. Contract your state's Medicaid office to learn more.

Social Security Administration (SSA): SSA's Supplemental Security Income (SSI) program offers the Plan to Achieve Self-Support (PASS) program, which helps people with disabilities pay for items or services related to employment goals. If you are a PASS participant and need AT in order to perform work-related tasks, SSA may be able to help you pay for it. For more information about PASS, call the Social Security Administration at 1-800-772-1213 between 7 a.m. and 7 p.m. Monday – Friday.

U.S. Department of Veterans Affairs (VA): VA Automobile and Special Adaptive Equipment Grants help pay for Veterans with certain service-connected disabilities to buy or adapt a vehicle to meet their needs, or pay for other adaptive equipment or AT. You can apply for the grant by completing VA Form 21-4502, and submitting it to your local VA Regional Benefits Office. Call 1-800-827-1000 for more information.

Funding Guides:

AbleData's guide "What Are Your Options to Pay for Assistive Devices?" has information on how to find the right AT for your needs and lists of state organizations and agencies that can help you pay for assistive devices.

The Assistive Technology Industry Association (ATIA) has a Funding Resources Guide with information on federal, state and local AT funding sources. It includes information on insurance options for paying for AT, AT scholarships and special education funding for AT.

The article "Funding Assistive Technology and Accommodations" has information on how to pay for AT, especially when it is related to employment. It includes ways employers can pay for assistive technology, as well as how to get funding from public sources and private foundations.

The Family Center on Technology and Disability has a "Family Information Guide to AT," which includes sections on finding the right type of AT for your child and tips on paying for AT. This guide is also available in Spanish.

"Getting a 'Yes' from Your Insurance Company" explains how to work with your insurance company to pay for AT. The Illinois AT program website also has a list of national organizations that can help pay for AT. It includes disability-specific organizations, such as the Association of Blind Citizens, which has an Assistive Technology Fund that will pay 50 percent of the price of adaptive devices or software for people who qualify.

United Cerebral Palsy's (UCP)'s AT funding tips include steps to take to find funding for AT and adaptive equipment.

The National Assistive Technology Project has a series of guides about programs and agencies that can help people with disabilities pay for AT, including state vocational rehabilitation agencies, public schools, and programs for transition-age youth with disabilities.

The Early Childhood Technical Assistance Center has a guide to AT funding sources that includes information about AT provisions under the Individuals with Disabilities Education Act (IDEA), Medicaid, and other programs that can help pay for AT.

The National Multiple Sclerosis (MS) Society guide "Assistance for Adaptive Equipment" includes information on paying for AT devices and medical equipment. It includes a section on paying for ramps and buying recycled or used equipment. Contact your local MS Society chapter to learn about adaptive equipment or AT funding in your state.

The Alexander Graham Bell Association for the Deaf and Hard of Hearing offers a list of organizations that provide help paying for hearing aids and other assistive technology for people with hearing disabilities.

Websites:

Organizations that offer financial assistance for Assistive Technologies

AbleData
Website: www.abledata.com

Alexander Graham Bell Association for the Deaf and Hard of Hearing
Website: www.agbell.org

Assistive Technology Industry Association
Website: www.atia.org

Center on Technology and Disability
Website: ctdinstitute.org

Early Childhood Technical Assistance Center
Website: ectacenter.org

Easter Seals Inc.
Website: www.easterseals.com

Illinois Assistive Technology Program
Website: www.iltech.org

National Multiple Sclerosis Society
Website: www.nationalmssociety.org

United Cerebral Palsy
Website: ucp.org/resources/assistive-technology/funding-tips

RESNA Catalyst Project
Website: www.resnaprojects.org

Organizations that offer Assistive Technology Software

Ai Squared
Website: www.aisquared.com

Clarix
Website: www.getwinzoom.com

Dolphin Computer Access Ltd.
Website: www.yourdolphin.com

Freedom Scientific, Inc.
Website: www.freedomscientific.com

Issist
Website: issist1.com

NV Access
Website: www.nvaccess.org

Serotek Corp.
Website: www.screenreader.net

Window-Eyes
Website: www.gwmicro.com

Index

Index

Page numbers followed by 'n' indicate a footnote. Page numbers in italics indicate a table or illustration.

535

537

H

544

National Stroke Association, contact
515
National Technical Information
Service (NTIS), contact 508
National Wheelchair Basketball
Association (NWBA), contact 522
National Wheelchair Poolplayers
Association (NWPA), website
address 522
National Women's Health
Information Center (NWHIC),
contact 508
NCI *see* National Cancer Institute
NCLD *see* National Center for
Learning Disabilities
needs assessment, assistive
technology 216
Nemours Foundation Center for
Children's Health Media, contact
515
nerve conduction study (NCS),
diagnosis 190
neural tube defects, described 89
neuron, defined 501
neurostimulation, rehabilitation
engineering 218
New England ADA Center, contact
517
newborn screening, defined 501
NHLBI *see* National Heart, Lung, and
Blood Institute
NHTSA *see* National Highway Traffic
Safety Administration
NIA *see* National Institute on Aging
NIAMS *see* National Institute of
Arthritis and Musculoskeletal and
Skin Diseases
NIDCD *see* National Institute on
Deafness and Other Communication
Disorders
NIDCR *see* National Institute of
Dental and Craniofacial Research
"NIH-commissioned report highlights
disability among older population"
(NIA) 29n
NIHSeniorHealth
publication
end-of-life care 466n

NIMH *see* National Institute of
Mental Health
"Ninds Aphasia Information Page"
(NINDS) 138n
NINDS *see* National Institute of
Neurological Disorders and Stroke
"NLS Factsheets" (LOC) 247n
NOFAS *see* National Organization on
Fetal Alcohol Syndrome
No Child Left Behind Act, overview
382–3
Northeast ADA Center, contact 517
NPUAP *see* National Pressure Ulcer
Advisory Panel
nursing facilities
center operations 371
nursing home 470
nursing homes
community support services 364
defined 501
palliative care 469
NV Access, website address 529
nystagmus, multiple sclerosis 199

O

obesity
depicted *288*
dietary changes 87
health consequences 289
healthy weight 49
statistics 287
"Obesity and Disability" (CDC) 286n
obsessive-compulsive disorder (OCD),
described 177
occulta, described 90
occupational therapist, defined 501
"Occupational Therapists" (BLS) 274n
occupational therapy
defined 501
described 60
rehabilitation 256
OCD *see* obsessive-compulsive disorder
OCR *see* optical character recognition
ODD *see* oppositional defiant disorder
ODEP *see* Office of Disability
Employment Policy Employment
Policy